Ohr Nissan Talmud Center, Inc.

Spreading *Torah* Throughout the World!

With the strong support of world-renowned *Torah* leaders, **Ohr Nissan Talmud Center, Inc.** has been devoted to training educators and scholars in the finest tradition of *Sefaradi* Jewry for more than twenty-five years.

In the words of Rabbi Aharon Feldman שליט״א, dean of Ner Israel Rabbinical College, "Virtually every institution which provides for the spiritual needs of Iranian Jewry in the United States is staffed by former members of **Ohr Nissan Talmud Center, Inc.**"

Ohr Nissan Talmud Center, Inc. provides scholarships to more than thirty highly dedicated *Torah* scholars who study full-time with the goal of gaining the knowledge necessary to strengthen and perpetuate the *Sefaradi* heritage.

We appreciate your generous support. Please help us continue our vital work by sending in your tax-deductible contribution today.

Ohr Nissan Talmud Center, Inc.
400 Mount Wilson Lane
Baltimore, MD 21208
(410) 340-4496

ראשית חכמה יראת ה'

REACHING FOR
THE HEAVENS

סודות האמונה

Rabbi Yehuda Cahn

Copyright 2021 by:

Rabbi Yehuda Cahn
2509 Shelleydale Drive
Baltimore, MD 21209

Published and distributed by:

OHR NISSAN TALMUD CENTER, INC.

400 Mount Wilson Lane
Baltimore, MD 21208

(410) 340-4496

ISBN: 978-1-7343708-0-5

Cover design by Elka Aviva Cahn

Cover photography by Aryeh Nirenberg featuring his brother, Shaya, at Bass Harbor, Maine and recalling the verse:

> "Raise your eyes above and observe! Who created all of these?"
>
> — Isaiah 40:26

For more photos of the wonders of *Hashem's* Creation, follow Aryeh at art_only@instagram.com.

Printed in the United States of America by
Sefer Press 732-606-2589

Table of Contents

THE RELATIONSHIP BETWEEN THE SPIRITUAL AND THE PHYSICAL

Acknowledgments

I would like to thank my principal teacher, Rabbi Moshe Heinemann שליט״א, for his steadfast support and guidance over many years.

The *Mishnah* that whoever seeks more advice gains more understanding.[1] In addition to consulting many sources, I have been able to gain valuable insights from the many people who read and commented on the manuscript for this book.

I would like to thank my wife, Rebbetzin Geoula Cahn, Rabbi Yoel Feldman ז״ל, Rabbi Emmanuel Terenyo, Rabbi Yaakov Zabludowski, Yehoshua Solomon, Aryeh Nirenberg, and Yosef Khaver, all of whom read the manuscript in Hebrew or English and pointed out instances where clarifications were advisable. In addition, Mrs. Moriah Stern, and Mrs. Meirav Netzach-Maggeni edited the Hebrew edition. I greatly appreciate their efforts.

I want to thank my son, Yisroel C. Cahn, for directing my attention to the Monty Hall problem and explaining it.

I also wish to recognize my long-time friend, Rabbi Reuben Khaver, the founder and director of **Ohr Nissan Talmud Center**, for his tireless efforts in support of publication of this book.

— Yehuda Cahn

---

[1] *Pirkei Avoth* 2:7 מַרְבֶּה עֵצָה מַרְבֶּה תְבוּנָה

ORTHODOX
UNION תורה ומצוות
Enhancing Jewish Life

ELEVEN BROADWAY | NEW YORK, NY 10004-1303

RABBI DR. TZVI HERSH WEINREB
Executive Vice President, Emeritus
212.613.8264 tel
212.613.0635 fax
execthw@ou.org email

November 5, 2013

Rabbi Cahn begins his excellent new book by forcefully demonstrating that the contemporary observant Jew must be familiar with Jewish philosophy. The powerful ideological challenges which we inevitably confront in the general culture cannot be met without a thorough knowledge of the ways in which our tradition meets those challenges.

Regretfully, many observant Jews, including some with extensive Jewish educations, are insufficiently familiar with the philosophical aspects of our tradition. Such subjects are typically not part of the *yeshiva* curriculum, and students avoid studying the relevant sources independently because they find them daunting.

Rabbi Cahn's new book addresses this problem. He uses clear and cogent language without compromising the sophisticated and often highly nuanced nature of the subject. He provides the reader with an advanced treatise on the tenets of our faith, but avoids overwhelming him with technical language and unessential complexity.

The reader can restrict himself to the text, ignoring the footnotes, and thus gain the basic familiarity required to address the ideological challenges which he faces. Or, he can use the footnotes to guide him as he delves deeper into the profundities of genuine Jewish philosophy.

Many Jewish individuals have become conditioned to think of philosophy as something very esoteric and uninteresting. With Rabbi Cahn's book they are in for a surprise. By reading it they will discover the fascinations of authentic Jewish philosophy. Rabbi Cahn proves that Jewish philosophy can be both illuminating and engaging.

Congratulations to Rabbi Cahn for addressing a very pressing need in our community, and additional congratulations on a job well done.

Rabbi Dr. Tzvi Hersh Weinreb
Executive Vice President, Emeritus
Orthodox Union

KOSHER
CERTIFICATION
SERVICE

Endorsement of Rabbi Shlomo Moshe Amar שליט״א, Chief Rabbi Emeritus of the State of Israel, and current Chief Rabbi of Jerusalem:

Shlomo Moshe Amar
Rishon Lezion Chief Rabbi Of Jerusalem

שלמה משה עמאר
הראשון לציון הרב הראשי לירושלים

בעהי״ת ש׳, באחד בשבת שבעה ושרים יום בטבת התשע״ה.

אגרת ברכה

ראה ראיתי האי ספרא טבא, דאתי ממערבא, איש דגול מרבבה, המחבר ממרחק בא, והביא עמו ספרו הנחמד, על אמונת ה׳ ובטחונו נעמד, וקרא שמו "סודות האמונה" שעמל עליו וחיברו הרב החשוב ומפואר במדות טובות, נעימות גם חשובות מיסודי התורה חצובות, זה שמו הטוב מהר״ר יהודה קאהן שליט״א, והביא עמו המלצות ועדויות מרבנים חשובים ומפורסמים בארה״ב המעידים בגודלם, על הרב המחבר שליט״א, וכן גם על החיבור הנ״ל.

ומן המעט שהספקתי להציץ לפי דוחק הזמן והשעה, ראיתי שבונה יסודותיו על הנחות לקוחות מפנימיות התורה, ובודאי שיהיו תוצאות טובות, והשפעות חשובות על המעיינים, בסוגיות ובעניינים, ויה״ר שיזכה להשלים מלאכתו מלאכת הקדש בשובה ונחת, בבריאות איתנה ונהורא מעלייא וחיים עד העולם.

באה״ר

ב.א. צמאל
שלמה משה עמאר

הראשון לציון

הרב הראשי לירושלים

Endorsement of Grand Rabbi Avraham Shalom Yisachar Dov Lipschitz Halberstam שליט״א, the Stropkover Rebbe:

Letter from Rabbi Moshe Heinemann שליט״א authorizing the author to teach *Torah* to the public:

RABBI MOSHE HEINEMANN
6109 Gist Avenue
Baltimore, MD 21215
Tel. (410) 358-9828
Fax. (410) 358-9838

משה היינעמאן
אב״ד ק״ק אגודת ישראל
באלטימאר
טל. 764-7778 (410)
פקס 764-8878 (410)

בס״ד

באתי בשורות אלו להשמיע בשער בת רבים מעלת האברך היקר והחשוב הרב ר' יהודה בן חברהם למשפחת קאן שליט״א שלמד תורה כמה שנים בישיבת נר ישראל בבאלטימאר וחיבר כמה ספרים ומהם פירוש על אגדת הירושלמי בסדר זרעים ב״ח אשר מצא חן בעיני. הוא עוסק בגמילת חסדים ובצרכי ציבור ומני מכירו מראשית לאיש ישר ירא שמים ובעל מדות טובות אשר יש לו הרבה ידיעות בגמרא ובפוסקים.

האברך הנ״ל איוקלע לאתרין ותוך משא ומתן של תידה ימים נוכחתי לדעת שהוא בן תורה היודע לישא וליתן במלחמתה של תורה ולאפוקי שמעתתא אליבא דהלכתא.

תאיתי על קנקנו באיזהו מקומן של שוע יו'ד בהלכות מליחה בשר בחלב ותערובות והשיב כהן לדק ולאו לדק בהבנה ישרה קולע אל המטרה וכו'ח יתעריא, ותשובותיו על מקומם בא בשלו'.

לכן אמינא איש לו רשות להקרא רב בישראל יורה יורה כדת ותורה, היות שמובטחני בו שלא יפסוק שום הוראה כל'תי עיון בספרי הפוסקים. וגם רשאי לקבל משרת רבנות בכל עדה המתנהגת על פי חוקי תורתנו הקדושה ומנהגי ישראל קדושים המסורים לנו מדור דור. אשרי העדה אשר תבחר בו להיות להם לראש ולתפארת וינהלם על מבועי התורה והמצוה.

ועל זאת באתי עה״ח בשלישי בשבת לסדר הדינו השמים ודברה ותשמע האר־ץ אמרי פי שבה ועשרים יום לחדש אלול יום שנבדלו בו המים לשנים, שנת חמשת אלפים ושבע מאות וששים ושש לבריאת עולם.

יעשה בהח״ר ברוך גדליה למשפחת היינעמען החונף מתא באלטימאר.

In Memory of
Nissim Elalouf ז״ל
Aviva Elalouf ז״ל
Beloved Parents and Grandparents

לעילוי נשמות

נסים בן יצחק ז״ל
נפטר ז׳ אדר תשל״ה

אביבה בת שלמה ז״ל
נפטרה כ״ב תשרי תשס״ח

תהיינה נשמותיהם צרורות בצרור החיים

In Memory of
Brothers, Sister, Uncles and Aunt

לעילוי נשמות

רפאל בן נסים
נפטר י"ב שבט תשכ"ו

שלמה בן נסים
נפטר כ"ה סיון תש"ע

יצחק בן נסים
נפטר כ"ה חשון תשע"ח

עליזה בת יוסף
נפטרה י"א כסלו תשנ"ז

רינה בת נסים
נפטרה א' באב תשע"ב

תהיינה נשמותיהם צרורות בצרור החיים

In Memory of
Yaakov Elalouf ז״ל
Beloved Father, Grandfather,
Brother and Uncle

לעילוי נשמת

יעקב בן נסים ז״ל
נפטר י״ח תמוז תשע״ז

תהא נשמתו צרור בצרור החיים

In Memory of

Shirley Ellison Cahn ז״ל

Beloved Mother,

Sister, Grandmother &

Great-Grandmother

February 5, 1926 – September 22, 2018

לעילוי נשמת

שרה ריבה ב״ר אברהם יהודה ז״ל

נפטרה י״ג תשרי ה״תשע״ט

תהא נשמתה צרורה בצרור החיים

In Memory of
Joseph Ellison ז״ל
Beloved Father,
Grandfather, Brother,
Uncle & Great-Uncle

November 9, 1928 - December 15, 2020

לעילוי נשמת

יוסף ב״ר אברהם יהודה ז״ל

נפטר כ״ט כסלו ה׳׳תשפ״א

תהא **נ**שמתו **צ**רור **ב**צרור **ה**חיים

In Loving Memory of

Stewart Pensak ז״ל

אשר זעליג בן צבי ז״ל

May his soul be bound in the bond of life
תהא נשמתו צרור בצרור החיים

לעילוי נשמות

אפרים בן דוד
Efraim Blum
24 Adar 5761

פרידה בת יחיאל
Frieda Blum
23 Elul 5762

דוד בן אפרים
David Blum
24 Tishrei 5779

דניאל בן אפרים
Danny Blum
2 Tammuz 5770

תהיינה נשמותיהם צרורות בצרור החיים

In Memory of

Rebbetzin Dr. Aviva Weisbord ז״ל
אביבה בת מוה״ר שמואל יעקב

and the other members
of the Jewish community
who departed this world
during the COVID-19 pandemic

תהי נשמתם צרורה בצרור החיים

Ohr Nissan Talmud Center, Inc.

לעילוי נשמת

שפטעל מאיר בן נפתלי הלוי

לזכר עולם יהיה צדיק

In Memory of our Beloved President

Rabbi Sheftel Meir Neuberger ז"ל

This dedication is made in memory of our beloved president who worked tirelessly and was a beacon of guidance and support to our Kollel and its projects.

The publication of the first volume of this sefer brought great simcha and nachas to Rabbi Neuberger, and it is therefore truly providential that this volume went to print on the day of his passing.

May the study of this sefer bring nachas and merit to the neshama of this great leader, may his children continue in his ways, and may the Kollel continue to enlighten and serve Klal Yisroel.

תהי נשמתו צרורה בצרור החיים

Ohr Nissan Talmud Center, Inc.

May the merit of this Sefer bring a speedy recovery to all those afflicted by COVID-19, and may Hashem remove this illness from Klal Yisrael and all humanity.

Ohr Nissan Talmud Center, Inc.

Introduction: Reaching for the Heavens

❧ Humanity Has Infinite Value

Some self-proclaimed "rationalists" argue that the universe is so vast that it makes no sense to suppose that it was all created for humankind. As they express it, "Would a wise person use billions of dollars of highly advanced equipment solely for the purpose of producing a single tiny steel pin?"[1]

This question reflects a misunderstanding about the nature of God. Since He is infinite, from His perspective the vastness of the entire universe and the minute dimensions of a subatomic particle are identical. Accordingly, the fact that the

---

[1] *Malbim* mentions this question in his commentary to Psalms 8:1, ויאמר המליץ,
"הזה פועל חכם שיכין כלים משקלם עשרת אלפים ככר כסף כדי לעשות מחט ברזל אחד?"

universe is large and complex is no reason to say that He did not create it all for human beings.

Furthermore, whereas human beings must expend time, effort, and money to produce things, *Hashem* created the universe effortlessly. Accordingly, although people weigh the results of their exertions against what those exertions yield, *Hashem's* calculations are different.

Finally, the comparison between creating human beings and creating pins is incorrect. Since human beings have souls and free will, they are infinitely more valuable than anything else in the universe. A wise person would indeed use billions of dollars of highly advanced equipment to achieve a priceless result. That is why scientists use expensive equipment to study subatomic particles which are far smaller than steel pins — they hope to discover priceless information.

১৩৪ The Priceless Result

What was the priceless result *Hashem* sought when He created human beings?

A popular story tells about a young boy playing on a sandy beach. Pretending to be a fierce pirate holding a sword, he took a stick and stabbed at the air. As he continued to play, a large ship sailed into view. Seeing it, the boy dropped the stick and began jumping up and down, waving his hands.

After a short time, an elderly man came along.

"What kind of game is this?" asked the old man.

"I'm trying to signal the crew on that ship," explained the boy breathlessly. "I want them to blow their horn."

The old man laughed. "I doubt they can see you, but even if they do, the ship's crew isn't going to blow the horn for you."

No sooner had he finished speaking than the ship's horn sounded loudly. The astonished gentleman squinted his eyes and made out a group of sailors gathered on the deck waving.

"What in the world!?!" exclaimed the old man.

"You see," explained the boy, "the captain of that ship is my father!"

Just as much as the little boy in the story wanted his father to recognize him, his father wanted to do so. It is this type of relationship that *Hashem* wants with humanity, and He considers it priceless.[2]

Although we believe in *Hashem* and His *Torah*, it is impossible for any created being to fully understand the Creator. That does not mean that we should not try, however, because when we reach for the Heavens, our Father reaches out to us.

---

[2] Heard from Rabbi Yissocher Frand שליט״א, a *Rosh Yeshivah* at *Ner Yisroel*, Baltimore.

THE LIMITS OF
HUMAN INTELLECT

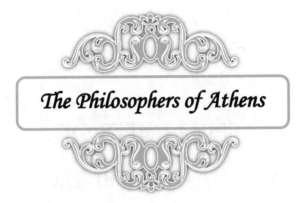

The Philosophers of Athens

∞ Rabbi Yehoshua ben Chananya Encounters the Elders of Athens

The *Gemara* relates the following mysterious tale:

A [Roman] Caesar asked Rabbi Yehoshua ben Chananya, "How long does it take for a snake to become pregnant and give birth?"

"Seven years," he answered.

"But," [countered the Caesar], "the elders of Athens [conducted an experiment in which they] mated them, and [the female] gave birth after three."

"[That female] had already been pregnant for four years."[3]

..."But," objected the Caesar, "[the elders of Athens] are renowned for their wisdom."

"We are smarter than they are."

"If you are so clever, go defeat them [in intellectual battle] and bring them to me."

"How many are there?" [inquired the rabbi].

"Sixty men."

"Make me a ship which has sixty compartments, and [install] in each compartment sixty elegant chairs."

[The Caesar] made it for him. When [Rabbi Yehoshua] arrived [in Athens], he entered a butcher shop [where] he found the butcher skinning an animal.

"Is your head for sale?" inquired [the rabbi].

"Yes," replied [the butcher].

"For how much?"

"For half a *Zuz*."

He gave [the money] to him [and demanded the head off the butcher's shoulders].

"I meant the head of the animal," explained [the butcher].

---

[3] There are no known species of snakes with gestation periods as long as three or seven years. It therefore appears that Rabbi Yehoshua and the Caesar were conversing in a kind of code which the *Mishnah* calls "Greek argumentation" (*Sotah* 9:14). Rabbi Ovadiah of Bartenura comments that, "This refers to hints and riddles that the Greeks possessed, and they were not understood except by those familiar with them" (והם רמזים וחידות שהיו ליוונים, ולא היו מכירים בהם אלא הרגילים בהם).

The *Gemara* indeed records how Rabbi Yehoshua communicated in the Caesar's court through coded gestures (B.T. *Chagigah* 5B רַבִּי יְהוֹשֻׁעַ בֶּן חֲנַנְיָה הֲוָה קָאֵי בֵּי קֵיסָר. אַחְוִי לֵיהּ הַהוּא אֶפִּיקוֹרְסָא – עַמָּא דְּאַהְדְּרִינְהוּ מָרֵיהּ לְאַפֵּיהּ מִינֵּיהּ. אַחְוִי לֵיהּ – יָדוֹ נְטוּיָה עָלֵינוּ.).

In the alternative, perhaps Rabbi Yehoshua and the Caesar were referring to a species of snake or reptile which is now extinct.

"If you want me to leave you alone, show me the entrance to the academy of the Athenian elders."

"I am afraid to do so because they kill whoever discloses it."

"Carry a bundle of reeds, and when you reach it, set them down as if you are taking a break. [I will then know where it is, and you will not get into any trouble]."

[Rabbi Yehoshua ben Chananya] went [into the academy] and discovered guards [posted] inside and guards [posted] outside. [Unknown to the guards, the elders had sprinkled dust or flour in the entranceway] so that if they saw a footprint entering [the academy], they killed the outer guards [for permitting an unauthorized person to enter], and [if they saw a footprint] leading outside, they killed the inner guards [for permitting someone to leave]. [Rabbi Yehoshua ben Chananya] put on one of his sandals backwards [and stepped on the doorsill so that one footprint pointed inside and the other pointed outside. The guards threw him out, but when the elders discovered] the reversed footprint [leading outside], they killed the inside guards. [When they discovered] the opposite footprint, they killed all the [remaining] guards, [and Rabbi Yehoshua ben Chananya entered].

When [the rabbi] came inside, he found the younger men seated above and the older ones seated below. [The rabbi] said [to himself], "If I greet the [younger men first], these [older ones] will kill me, for they will figure that, 'We are older, and they are mere babes.'" [On the other hand, greeting the elders first would also prove fatal because the younger men would argue that their seating position showed that they ranked higher than the older men, and they would have an excuse to kill him.]

[Rabbi Yehoshua ben Chananya therefore] said, "Greetings to you all."

"What is your business here?" [they demanded].

"I am a Jewish sage, and I want to learn wisdom from you."

"If so, let us test you."

"Very well. If you outwit me, you can do whatever you want with me, but if I outwit you, then dine with me inside my ship."

They [agreed and] asked him, "If a man courts a woman, but [her family] rejects him [because they consider him to be of inferior social rank], does it make sense for him to pursue a woman of even higher social standing?"

[The rabbi] took a peg and tried to insert it into [a row of stones] at the base [of a wall, but the stones were too tight, and] it did not fit. [When he stuck it] into the upper ones, it fit. He then explained, "This man also will fit in with the one for whom he is destined." [If God intended him to marry a woman of higher social rank, then he will indeed be accepted.]

[The elders raised another question.] "If a person lends money and [cannot recover it from the borrower without] seizing collateral held by a third party,[4] would it be fitting to go back and lend again [to the same undependable borrower]?[5]

[Rabbi Yehoshua ben Chananya] responded: "Suppose a man goes to a wood where he chops down a load [of sticks] but finds himself unable [to position them onto his shoulders. Realizing that he will need help from a passerby to load them onto his shoulders,] he cuts more and places [another bundle]

---

[4] Although the borrower sold land which was collateral for the loan to a third party, the lender's lien remained unaffected, so the lender instituted legal proceedings and seized the land from the third party.

[5] This translation follows the view of the *Maharsha* and the *Maharal*. *Rashi*, however, understands the text as referring to a lender making a loan to a different borrower (*Rashi*, sub verba *"Mai Chazei"* (מאי חזי) לאחריני ולא נתייסר מן הראשון).

onto [the first one] until someone happens along who can lift them onto his shoulders.

[The elders] said to him, "Tell us a fictitious story."

He replied, "There was a certain mule which gave birth [after mating with another mule], and around the neck [of its offspring] was a note on which it was written that its father's household was worth a hundred thousand *Zuz*."[6]

"Can a mule bear young!?!" they exclaimed.

"This is just one of those fictitious stories."

[They asked him], "If salt spoils, with what does one salt it [to preserve it]?"

"With the afterbirth of a female mule."

"Does a female mule have an afterbirth!?!"

"Does salt spoil?"

"Build us a house in midair," [they demanded].

[Rabbi Yehoshua ben Chananya] uttered a [Divine] Name and suspended himself between heaven and earth. "Send me up bricks and mortar!" he said.

"Where is the center of the world?" they asked.

He raised his finger and said, "Here."

"Who says so?" they demanded.

"Bring measuring ropes and measure it."

"We have a wellspring in the field. Bring it to town!"

"Twine together ropes out of bran, and I will bring it."

"We have a broken millstone," continued the elders.

"Sew it back together [for us]!"

---

[6] The original text reads "דְּמַסִּיק בְּבֵי אַבָּא מֵאָה אַלְפָּא זוּזֵי" which is translated here in accordance with *Baba Kama* 10:1 where the term "מְסִיקִין" refers to government officials who assessed property values in order to impose taxes. Alternatively, this phrase means that the note was a debt instrument which held the mule's father's household liable for 100,000 *Zuz*.

[Rabbi Yehoshua ben Chananya put a piece of the millstone in front of them][7] and said, "Wind threads from this, and I'll [use them to] sew it."

["Is it possible to wind threads from a millstone?"

"Is it possible to sew a millstone together?"][8]

…They brought him two eggs and queried, "Which comes from a black hen, and which comes from a white hen?"

He brought them two cheeses and asked them, "Which comes from a black goat and which from a white goat?"

…[Having defeated the elders in intellectual battle, Rabbi Yehoshua ben Chananya] brought them [to his ship]. Each one observed sixty elegant chairs [in his compartment and] said [to himself], "All of the [other] colleagues must be coming here."

[Rabbi Yehoshua ben Chananya then] told the captain, "Set sail!"

As they left, [the rabbi] took [some] dirt from their [native Athenian] soil.

When they arrived at the "place of swallowing," [where water had the peculiar trait of absorbing other water, the rabbi] filled a container with it.

[When they arrived in Rome,] he stood them before the Caesar, who observed that they behaved submissively, so he said, "These [men] cannot be them!"

[Rabbi Yehoshua ben Chananya] took some of the dirt [from their homeland], threw it on them, and they became arrogant towards the Caesar,[9] [so] the Caesar told him, "Do whatever you please with them."

---

[7] This bracketed phrase is not found in the Romm Vilna text of the Babylonian *Talmud* but appears in the *Ein Yaakov* edition.

[8] This bracketed section is not found in the Romm Vilna text of the Babylonian *Talmud* but appears in the *Ein Yaakov* edition.

[9] They felt timid and out of place until reminded of their homeland.

He brought the water he had taken from the "place of swallowing," put it into a [different] container, and told them, "Fill [this container with water], and you can go your way."

They filled it, [but] each [quantity of water they poured] was absorbed [by the water from the "place of swallowing"]. They [continued trying] to fill it until their shoulders became dislocated, and they became weary and perished.[10]

This story may be understood as follows:

๛ Science and Philosophy Versus Torah

Loyal Jews accept the supreme authority of the *Torah's* wisdom and reject anything that conflicts with it. By contrast, other nations insist that scientific inquiry is paramount and that *Torah* concepts must be abandoned whenever they contradict the results of scientific investigation.

Scientific research consists of three key elements: (a) observation, (b) experimentation, and (c) extrapolation or interpolation from the data so obtained. This means that the conclusions scientists reach based on current information often change when they develop better methods of observation or more carefully constructed experiments. In addition, the reasoning scientists use to reach their conclusions is subject to challenge.

As an example, the *Ben Ish Chai* cites a verse in the Book of Job which states that air has weight.[11] For many years, philosophers and scientists mocked this idea because human beings are surrounded by air but do not feel it weighing down on them.

---

[10] B.T. *Bechoroth* 8B-9A. See Appendix A for the Hebrew text.

[11] Job 28:25 לַעֲשׂוֹת לָרוּחַ מִשְׁקָל וּמַיִם תִּכֵּן בְּמִדָּה

Only much later did scientists develop instruments sensitive enough to detect that air has weight.[12]

৪০৪০ An Ancient Challenge

The idea of using scientific experimentation to refute the *Torah* is very ancient. *Hashem* commanded Adam and Chavah not to eat from the fruit of the Tree of Knowledge, but when Chavah repeated this to the serpent, she added that touching it was also forbidden. The serpent decided to disprove her claims by conducting an experiment. He pushed Chavah against the tree and when nothing happened, he convinced Chavah that just as touching the tree was safe, so eating its fruits would prove safe.[13]

In the above passage of the *Gemara*, the Caesar asked Rabbi Yehoshua ben Chananya about the gestation period of a certain species of snake. When the rabbi's answer conflicted with that shown by experimentation, the Caesar insisted that results obtained through experimentation are superior to *Torah* wisdom. The rabbi confidently asserted that the experiment must be flawed if its results contradicted the *Torah*.[14]

---

[12] *Benayahu ben Yehoyada* on *Baba Bathra* 84A יען כי כל דברייהם בנויים על פי השערת השכל ועושים מדה ומשקל לכל מקומות ולכל דברים אשר לא ראו בעיניהם על פי ההשערה, והגם דהשערה זו מביאים לה הוכחות וראיות ממידות ושיעורים אשר ימודו וישערו בכלים מכלים שונים, בדברים אשר רואים אותם בעיניהם, עם כל זה יש פתחון פה לדבר ולומר לא ראי זה כראי זה, ושמא זה כך וכך נמצא בו, וכך וכך ישתנה טבעו... ואפשר כי יבואו ימים אשר חכמי הטבע והתכונה עצמם יוסיפו חכמה יותר, או יפלא להם בחוש דברים אשר עדיין לא נגלו, ואז מחמת זה הם עצמן יבואו לסתור כל ראיות אלו שיש ביד חכמי הטבע והתכונה, אשר על פיהם גוזרין ושופטין בדברים אשר סוברין עתה... וכבר נודע בענייני כובד האויר ומשקל הרוח אשר היו הפילוסופים כולם מכחישים דבר זה ומשחקים על האומר שיש לאויר כובד ומשקל לרוח ופערו פיהם לבלי חוק על הכתוב באיוב בזה... וראשית הוכחתם הייתה ממה שחלל העולם מלא אויר ואין האדם מרגיש בכובדו. ואחר כך הם והם עמד השטן בהם והלעיגו על המכחישים והכריחו על פיהם שיש לאויר כובד ומשקל אחר שעשו כלי שבהם מגרשים ומריקים האויר מן הכלי ושקלו אותו קודם הרקתו ואחר הרקתו ומצאו שיש לאויר כובד ומשקל.

[13] *Breishith Rabbah* 19:3 כך אמר הקב"ה: "כִּי בְיוֹם אֲכָלְךָ מִמֶּנּוּ וְגוֹ'" (בראשית ב:יז). והיא לא אמרה כן אלא: "אמר א-להים לא תאכלו ממנו ולא תגעו בו". כיון שראאה אותה עוברת לפני העץ נטלה ודחפה עליו. אמר לה: "הא לא מיתת! כמה דלא מיתת במקרביה כן לא מיתת במיכליה".

[14] B.T. *Bechoroth* 8A explains how the sages knew that some snakes remain pregnant for seven years. God told the serpent, "Cursed are you more than all

The reader should note that the rabbi did not reject the use of scientific experimentation. He simply pointed out that if it conflicted with the *Torah*, it must be flawed, just as the primordial serpent's experiment was flawed. *Hashem* had never forbidden touching the Tree of Knowledge, only eating its fruits. The fact that it was safe to touch the tree proved nothing about what would happen if Adam and Chavah ate its fruit.

The *Gemara* then proceeds to point out some other flaws inherent in the scientific method.

ೞೞ Defining Terms

What customers ordinarily mean when they ask a butcher, "How much does your head cost?" is the price of the animal's head, not the butcher's. By insisting on the absurd idea that he meant the butcher's head, Rabbi Yehoshua ben Chananya pointed out one reason why philosophical and scientific inquiry may prove faulty — the difficulty of defining terms precisely. This is true not only when philosophers try to define such amorphous ideas as beauty or justice, but also when scientists try to pin down definitions of physical phenomena.

For instance, for many years, scientists classified Pluto as a planet. In recent times, however, they reconsidered this issue

---

domesticated animals and more than the animals of the field" (Genesis 3:14). Cats are classified as "animals of the field" (חַיַּת הַשָּׂדֶה) and give birth after fifty-two days. Some large domesticated animals such as donkeys give birth after one solar year, which contains three hundred sixty-five days and is therefore about seven times as long. The verse implies that serpents are cursed with respect to large domesticated animals in the same ratio as those animals are cursed with respect to animals of the field. Since large domesticated animals remain pregnant for a year, serpents must remain pregnant for seven years.

אָמַר רַב יְהוּדָה אָמַר רַב וּמַטוּ בָּה מִשּׁוּם דְּרַבִּי יְהוֹשֻׁעַ בֶּן חֲנַנְיָא שֶׁנֶּאֱמַר, "אָרוּר אַתָּה מִכָּל הַבְּהֵמָה וּמִכֹּל חַיַּת הַשָּׂדֶה" (בראשית ג', י"ד). אִם מִבְּהֵמָה נִתְקַלְּלָה מֵחַיָּה לֹא כָּל שֶׁכֵּן ? אֶלָּא לוֹמַר לְךָ כְּשֵׁם שֶׁנִּתְקַלְּלָה הַבְּהֵמָה מֵחַיָּה מֶחָד לְשִׁבְעָה — וּמַאי נִיהוּ ? חֲמוֹר מֵחָתוּל — כָּךְ נִתְקַלֵּל הוּא מִבְּהֵמָה אֶחָד לְשֶׁבַע.

and declared that Pluto is not a regular planet but a "dwarf planet."[15]

On the surface, this may not seem like a serious problem, but consider the following argument:

> A terminal illness is an illness followed by death.
> Bob was nearsighted throughout his life and eventually died.
> Therefore, nearsightedness is a terminal illness.

This argument is defective because death not only follows a terminal illness but is also caused by it. This shows how an incomplete or imprecise definition can lead to a false conclusion.

ഇൽ The Difficulty of Making Accurate Observations

The elders of Athens camouflaged the entrance to their academy so that it matched its surroundings, and only those with special knowledge of its whereabouts could locate it. Others observing the same scene would never realize that it lay there.

The *Talmud* mentions this to point out how scientific observations are sometimes flawed.

The optical illusions below illustrate this point.

---

[15] This decision was made official by the International Astronomical Union in 2006.

When readers move their eyes around the above image at close range, their peripheral vision perceives flitting dark spots at the intersections of the gray lines even though the intersections are in fact white. This holds true even though the observer knows that no dark spots exist.[16]

In the next optical illusion, when looked at from a short distance, the gray circle on the right appears larger than the one on the left even though both circles are the same size.[17]

---

[16] This scintillating grid illusion, developed by E. and B. Lingelbach and M. Schrauf in 1994, is based on the work of German scientist Ludimar Hermann who reported a similar phenomenon around 1870.

[17] This optical illusion was discovered by German psychologist Hermann Ebbinghaus (1850-1909).

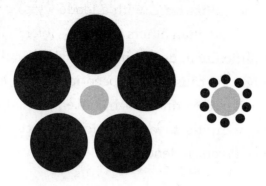

These optical illusions, and others like them, illustrate how careful people must be to make sure that their observations are accurate before using them to reach scientific conclusions. If even simple observations such as these can be misleading, certainly data obtained using complex equipment or techniques may prove deceptive.

ಙಬ I've Got You Coming and Going

Rabbi Yehoshua ben Chananya put on his sandals in opposite directions to trick the Athenian elders into thinking that someone had left the academy and that someone else had entered. This demonstrates another problem with scientific inquiry — how to interpret circumstantial evidence, especially when trying to determine causation. The elders assumed that the footprints they found were caused by people entering and leaving, but they really came from the rabbi standing on the doorsill.

A simple example will clarify this issue further. Suppose that research shows that teens who commit violent crimes have a history of watching twice as many violent videos as other teens. This might mean that such videos cause teens to behave violently or it might mean that teens with a tendency to commit violent acts are more likely than others to watch violent videos.

The difficulty in determining (a) whether all possible factors that might be causes have been identified, and (b) which phenomenon is a cause and which is an effect, highlights another reason why scientific theories which conflict with the *Torah* should not be given credence.

People Sometimes Accept an Opinion because of the Prestige of its Originator instead of its Merits

Rabbi Yehoshua ben Chananya's dilemma about which wisemen to greet first illustrates yet another problem with scientific methodology. On one hand, a young person taking a fresh look at a problem for the first time sometimes sees something that older and more experienced people have overlooked. On the other hand, the accumulated knowledge and experience with problem-solving which older people possess is a valid reason for deferring to their opinions.

This may explain why the elders of Athens adopted a peculiar seating arrangement. They were uncertain about who deserved more deference — the younger scholars or the older ones.

According to the *Torah*, however, neither viewpoint is correct. One should not accept a person's opinion just because of age or reputation. Instead, every opinion should be analyzed to determine whether it is consistent with Jewish tradition. If it is, then it is acceptable. If it is not, then it must be rejected. As Rabbi Yehudah Hanassi stated, "Do not look at the container, but rather at what it contains. There are new containers [i.e., young people,] full of old [wisdom], and old [containers, i.e., old people,] which do not even have anything new in them."[18]

Tifereth Yisrael explains that one who is sharp-witted should wait to speak until after hearing what one who is well-versed in tradition has to say because intellectual ingenuity does not take priority over reliable tradition.[19] A case in point happened when the greatest *Tannaim* argued about a certain *Halachic* issue but made their final decision according to a tradition known by two weavers who lived near a garbage dump. Their trade was not considered highly respectable nor was their residence, and they were not as bright as the scholars of the *Sanhedrin*. Nevertheless, the fact that they had a reliable tradition outweighed all other considerations.[20]

Aristotle and Albert Einstein were brilliant thinkers, but any of their opinions which contradict those of the *Torah* must be rejected.

৪৩৪৩ Tzaddikim Merit Divine Assistance

The Athenian elders asked Rabbi Yehoshua ben Chananya in so many words, "If a woman of low social rank rejects a suitor, how can he hope to marry a woman whose social position is higher?" By this they hinted that human knowledge must develop incrementally through scientific investigation.

---

[18] *Pirkei Avoth* 4:20 רַבִּי אוֹמֵר: אַל תִּסְתַּכֵּל בַּקַּנְקַן, אֶלָּא בַּמֶה שֶׁיֵּשׁ בּוֹ. יַשׁ קַנְקַן חָדָשׁ מָלֵא יָשָׁן, וְיָשָׁן שֶׁאֲפִלוּ חָדָשׁ אֵין בּוֹ.

[19] *Tifereth Yisrael* on *Pirkei Avoth* 5:7, note 44 (חָכָם אֵינוֹ מְדַבֵּר) בִּפְנֵי מִי שֶׁהוּא גָדוֹל מִמֶּנּוּ בְּחָכְמָה – רוצה לומר אף על פי שהוא חריף ומפולפל יותר, אפילו הכי מדיודע שאידך גדול יותר בחכמה, דהיינו שהוא בעל שמועות רבות, שותק עד שידבר הוא, כי אין חריצות השכל מכריע נגד הקבלה הנאמנה, ועדות ב' הגרדיים שהכריעו לכל חכמי ישראל במה שקבלו הם.

[20] *Tifereth Yisrael* on *Eduyoth* 1:3, note 23 מְשַׁעֵר הָאַשְׁפּוֹת שֶׁבִּירוּשָׁלַיִם – קמ"ל דאף שאומנתם הייתה בזוייה [כקידושין פ"ב, א'], וגם מקום מדורן היה היותר מבוזה בירושלים, אפילו הכי הכריעו כל חכמי ישראל בדבריהן, ללמדך שאין מסתכלין בקנקן אלא במה שיש בו.

People must first establish the truth of basic principles. Only then can they proceed to more advanced concepts.

The rabbi responded that *Hashem* grants special insight to prophets and *Tzaddikim*. A pin may not fit between stones at the bottom of a wall but may fit between those at the top. Those who rely on human intellect alone must exert great effort and even then, the pin may not fit — their conclusions may be wrong. Conversely, those who merit Divine assistance can achieve the greatest heights effortlessly — the pin fits easily among the stones at the top of the wall.

A *Midrash* which has a different version of the beginning of the above section of the *Gemara* illustrates this idea:

> A philosopher wanted to know how long it takes a [certain species of] serpent to give birth. When he found them mating, he took them and placed them inside a barrel. He gave them food until [the female] gave birth.
>
> When the [Jewish] elders visited Rome, [that same philosopher] consulted Rabban Gamliel and asked, "How long does it take for a serpent to give birth?"
>
> …[Rabban Gamliel did not know the answer, but Rabbi Yehoshua interpreted a verse from the *Torah* and told him it was seven years. When Rabban Gamliel told this to the philosopher, the philosopher] banged his head against the wall and said, "I went to all that trouble for seven years, and this one comes along and hands it to me on a single reed."[21]

---

[21] *Breishith Rabbah* 20:4 פילוסופוס אחד בקש לידע לכמה הנחש מוליד. כיון שראה אותם מתעסקין זה עם זה נטלן ונתנן בחבית והיה מספיק להם מזונות עד שילדו. כיון שעלו הזקנים לרומי שאלו את רבן גמליאל. אמר ליה: "לכמה הנחש מוליד?" ולא יכול להשיבו ונתכרכמו פניו. פגע בו רבי יהושע ופניו חולנית. אמר לו: "למה פניך חולנית?" אמר לו: "שאלה אחת נשאלתי ולא יכולתי להשיבו". אמר לו: "מה היא?" אמר: "לכמה נחש מוליד?" אמר לו: "לשבע שנים". אמר לו: "מנא לך?" אמר לו: "הכלב חיה טמאה ומוליד לחמשים יום ובהמה טמאה יולדת לי"ב חודש וכתיב, 'אָרוּר אַתָּה מִכָּל הַבְּהֵמָה וּמִכֹּל חַיַּת הַשָּׂדֶה'. (בראשית ג', י"ד). וכשם שהבהמה ארורה מן החיה שבעה כך נחש ארור מהבהמה שבעה". כמפני רמשא סלק ואמר ליה. התחיל מטיח ראשו לכותל. אמר: "כל מה שעמלתי שבע שנים בא זה והושיטו לי בקנה אחד!"

৪০৪০ Jews Trust Hashem Despite Difficulties and Setbacks

According to the scientific method, once a valid experiment which can be replicated proves a matter, it becomes a settled fact and no further research or experimentation is necessary. For example, repeated scientific experimentation shows that the speed of light in a vacuum is approximately 300,000 kilometers per second. This is an established fact, and there is no need to devise other experiments or do further research to prove it.

The elders of Athens argued that a similar principle applies when evaluating human behavior. A wise lender who has had a bad experience with a borrower would be foolhardy to advance another loan to the same person. Indeed, such an experience might well deter him from lending again to anyone at all.

Jews have endured severe suffering throughout the ages. Nevertheless, argued the Athenians, like a foolish lender who does not learn his lesson when an irresponsible borrower fails to repay a loan, Jews continue to trust *Hashem* and, in a manner of speaking, extend Him further credit, clinging to their belief in the *Torah* despite all they have endured.

Rabbi Yehoshua ben Chananya answered with a parable about a person who could not lift a bundle of sticks onto his shoulders. Rather than abandoning a seemingly foolish and useless enterprise, the woodcutter invested even more effort into chopping an additional load of wood, all the while anticipating that someone else would come along who could help him manage to load both bundles onto his shoulders.

The same applies to the Jewish people. Although the nation has suffered tremendously, it has also experienced many salvations and miracles. It is therefore reasonable to assume that no matter how bad things appear, *Hashem* will rescue His nation in the end. Those who redouble their efforts and persist in *Hashem's* service will be rewarded many times over, just as the fellow who chopped an additional bundle of wood while awaiting help gained the advantage of bringing home twice as much as he otherwise would have. As the sages state, "Your Employer can be counted upon to pay you the wages for your work."[22]

ഇൽ Can a Mule Bear Young from another Mule?

Even when scientific observation is accurate, interpreting the data correctly can be tricky. A good example of this was the discovery of Uranus and Neptune. People previously saw these heavenly bodies, but those who observed them assumed they were stars. It was not until 1781 when Sir William Herschel recorded his observations of Uranus that scientists realized that it was a planet. The same was true of Neptune, which was not correctly identified until 1846.

The Athenian scholars challenged Rabbi Yehoshua ben Chananya to tell them a fictious story — to explain why he thought that interpretation of scientific data might produce a false conclusion. The rabbi told them about a mule giving birth. The elders objected that such a thing is impossible, but the rabbi was pointing out the difficulty scientists would have if an animal possessing all the traits of a mule gave birth. Would it be a mule, or would it be something else?

This resembles the problem scientists had identifying heavenly bodies that resembled stars but moved differently. When scientists make new observations, they usually try to match them with theories and principles they already know. It

---

[22] *Pirkei Avoth* 2:14, 2:16, and 6:5 וְנֶאֱמָן הוּא בַּעַל מְלַאכְתְּךָ שֶׁיְשַׁלֶם לָךְ שְׂכַר פְּעֻלָתֶךְ

may take time and additional observations for them to realize that their initial conclusions were false.

⊗⊗ One Must Take Care When Applying Logic

The question about what to do when salt spoils refers to the *Torah* which is called a "covenant of salt."[23] The Greek elders wanted to know what one should do when the *Torah* "spoils," that is, when it appears to conflict with "reason."

Rabbi Yehoshua ben Chananya answered that it can be preserved with the afterbirth of a mule. A mule is the product of a horse and a donkey. When horses mate among themselves, they produce other horses which are also capable of reproducing. When donkeys mate among themselves, they produce other donkeys also capable of reproducing. Using only these facts, logic would dictate that the product of a horse and a donkey should also be capable of reproducing, but this is not the case. Mules cannot mate with one another to produce offspring. This shows that logic and reason do not always yield sound results. By contrast, the *Torah* comes from the Creator, and its tenets are always true. Salt does not spoil.

⊗⊗ The Torah's Wisdom Far Exceeds Human Wisdom

The Greeks challenged the concept of having faith in the truth of the *Torah* by asking how a person can build a house in midair. They meant that one must use logic to build knowledge from valid premises just as one builds a house from the ground up. This contradicts the Jewish approach of accepting the

---

[23] *Maharsha* on B.T. *Bechoroth* 8B מבואר כי הברית אשר לו יתברך עמנו הוא הברית לעולם כמו המלח שהיא הדבר המתקיים לעולם וכמו שכתוב, "בְּרִית מֶלַח עוֹלָם" (במדבר, י״ח, י״ט)

pronouncements of the *Torah* regardless of whether or not people understand them.

Rabbi Yehoshua ben Chananya uttered a Divine Name and suspended himself between the Earth and the Heavens. This means that he revealed some of the secrets of the universe to the philosophers, thereby demonstrating that by studying the *Torah* he had access to knowledge that cannot be obtained by natural means. The rabbi then turned the challenge back against the Athenian elders. He asked them to pass him bricks and mortar — to use human intellect to achieve the same result. Of course, they could not.

ಣಱ Asking the Right Question

One of philosophy's shortcomings is that philosophers sometimes fail to frame a question properly. When this happens, they can spend a great deal of time and effort trying to answer a question which is irrelevant or useless.

The Athenian elders posed a foolish question: Where does the center of the Earth's surface lie? Since the world is round, one may as well say that the center lies in any one place as in any other. Accordingly, Rabbi Yehoshua ben Chananya picked a place at random. When the elders challenged this, the rabbi told them to measure the result — an obviously impossible task.

If philosophers and scientists have difficulty formulating a valid question, perhaps their conclusions are not as reliable as they claim.

෴ Man is the Measure of All Things

The attitude of western civilization is that whether something is good or bad depends solely on whether people approve of it. This contrasts with the Jewish view that whether something is good or bad depends upon whether it conforms to God's will as expressed in the *Torah*.

This explains the modern approach to all moral questions. For instance, the *Torah* generally forbids suicide and those who believe in the *Torah* adhere to this position. By contrast, so-called progressive thinkers favor assisted suicide. Since, in their opinion, a person's comfort and enjoyment outweigh all other considerations, someone whose enjoyment of life is limited is fully justified in committing suicide.

The same outlook clarifies why modern "philosophers" see no problem with removing terminally ill patients from life-support equipment even when the *Halachah* forbids it. In their view, a person's "quality of life" — an ill-defined term — overrides all other considerations.

෴ There Is Nothing New under the Sun[24]

This way of thinking is not as novel as its proponents claim. Many ancient philosophers thought the same way, and the Athenian elders offered a reason in support of it.

The Greeks admitted the existence of a Supreme Being whom they called the First Cause.[25] As they saw matters, everything in Creation comes from a lengthy chain of causes and effects which eventually leads back to God. According to their

---

[24] Ecclesiates 1:9 מַה שֶּׁהָיָה הוּא שֶׁיִּהְיֶה וּמַה שֶּׁנַּעֲשָׂה הוּא שֶׁיֵּעָשֶׂה וְאֵין כָּל חָדָשׁ תַּחַת הַשָּׁמֶשׁ

[25] *Torath Ha'olah L'rama* 3:45 ואף דרך הפילוסופים כן הוא אשר צריכים להודות שהכל נתהווה מאת הסיבה הראשונה על ידי השתלשלות הסיבות

reasoning, however, God is too far removed from Creation to care about what anyone does.

It follows that the Greeks not only denied that God gave the *Torah* to Israel, but also held that such an event could never happen because God is unconcerned about the world and would have no reason to do such a thing.

A corollary of this approach is that people are free to do as they please without having to answer to God, and a correct moral philosophy is for them to follow whatever course of action gives them the most personal satisfaction.

This is what the Athenian elders meant when they said, "We have a wellspring in the wilderness. Bring it to town!" They admitted that God is the Source, or Wellspring, of all Creation. Nevertheless, He is distant and detached from it. Just as one cannot transport a wellspring from a field to a town, so too *Hashem* has nothing to do with the world, and people are free to conduct themselves as they please.

Rabbi Yehoshua ben Chananya replied that if the elders of Athens could fashion ropes from bran, he would bring the wellspring to town.[26] "Bran" (סֻבִּים) alludes to "reasons" (סִבּוֹת).[27] The rabbi meant that if these philosophers acknowledged the existence of God and that He is the First Cause, then they should also admit that He must have created the universe for a reason. Just as it makes no sense to try to fashion a rope out of bran because such a rope would be useless, it makes no sense to think

---

[26] *Rashi* on B.T. *Bechoroth* 8B מְפָאֲרֵי – עשו לי חבלים מסובין ואם אינכם עושין שאילתי, אף אני לא אעשה שאילתכם.

[27] The Aramaic text bears the same implication. פָּאֲרֵי, meaning "bran," derives from פרר, meaning "to break apart," an allusion to the way in which scientists break apart and analyze phenomena to find their causes.

that God created the universe through a chain of cause and effect for no reason.

The rabbi answered the Athenian elders according to their logic, as King Solomon advised, "[Sometimes one should] answer a fool according to his folly lest he seem wise in his own eyes."[28] According to the *Torah*, however, *Hashem's* relationship with the universe is not the same as the relationship between cause and effect people commonly observe where the two exist independently of one another. For example, when a potter fashions a ceramic piece, it exists independently of the potter so that if the potter leaves and forgets about it, the pottery remains unaffected. By contrast, *Hashem* permeates Creation and constantly keeps it in existence. If He would cease to will the existence of Creation, it would no longer exist. This means that no matter how distant *Hashem* appears to be from Creation, He is present in it.[29] He supervises every minute detail of Creation and is most definitely concerned about human affairs.

৵৽৵ Proving Hashem's Existence

Although most Greek philosophers believed in God, some were atheists.

The elders of Athens challenged Rabbi Yehoshua ben Chananya: "We have a broken millstone. Sew it back together for us!" By this they meant that a philosopher analyzes ideas by breaking them apart and refining them just as a millstone breaks apart wheat, separating the kernels from the bran. If a

---

[28] Proverbs 26:5 עֲנֵה כְסִיל כְּאִוַּלְתּוֹ פֶּן יִהְיֶה חָכָם בְּעֵינָיו

[29] *Likutei Amarim Tanya, Iggereth Hakodesh* 25 פרטית בהשגחה שכופרים כהפילוסופים ולא
ומדמין בדמיונם הכוזב את מעשה ה' עושה שמים וארץ למעשה אנוש ותחבולותיו, כי כאשר יצא לצורף כלי
שוב אין הכלי צריך ידי הצורף שאף שידיו מסולקות הימנו הוא קיים מעצמו. טח מראות עיניהם ההבדל הגדול
שבין מעשה אנוש ותחבולותיו שהוא יש מיש — רק שמשנה הצורה והתמונה — למעשה שמים וארץ שהוא יש
מאין.

philosopher himself is "broken" — if his analysis fails to convince him that God exists — how can one repair him? What proof can be offered to persuade him that God exists?

The rabbi explained that the limits of human intellect make it impossible to produce a logical proof of God's existence that will convince a stalwart non-believer because every logical proof requires faith that the axioms upon which it is founded are true. This means that people cannot develop faith in *Hashem* unless they possess a fundamental concept of faith to begin with, something not possible for people who are skeptical of everything — a common theme in ancient Greek philosophy. Some Greek philosophers even went to the extreme of questioning the reality of their own sense perceptions and claimed that people can have no certain knowledge of anything at all.[30] When dealing with such individuals, it is impossible to offer any satisfactory proof of God's existence.[31]

In addition, the rabbis state that Adam could see from one end of the world to the other,[32] implying that Adam and Chavah could clearly grasp the concept of infinity.[33] They could

---

[30] This was the view of Arcesilaus of Pitane, one of the leaders of Plato's academy, who was born around 318 B.C.E. He even took this view to its bizarre logical conclusion: One cannot know that nothing can be known with certainty because nothing at all is certain!

The impracticality of this view is obvious. If people cannot rely on their own sense perceptions, how can they successfully interact with their environment or with one another?

[31] *Likutei Halachoth, Orach Chaim, Hilchoth Shabbath* 6 וּבְוַדַּאי לְמִי שֶׁאֵין לוֹ אֱמוּנָה כְּלָל חַס וְשָׁלוֹם אֵין מוֹעִיל שׁוּם עֵצָה מֵאַחַר שֶׁאֵינוּ מַאֲמִין בְּהָעֵצָה עַצְמָהּ... וְזֶה בְּחִינַת, "אוֹדְךָ שִׁמְךָ כִּי עָשִׂיתָ פֶּלֶא עֵצוֹת מֵרָחֹק אֱמוּנָה אֹמֶן" (ישעיה כ"ה, א'). לְשׁוֹן כָּפוּל "אֱמוּנָה אֹמֶן" הַיְנוּ מִי שֶׁיֵּשׁ בּוֹ עֲדַיִן אֵיזֶה נְקוּדַּת הָאֱמוּנָה הוּא יָכוֹל לַחֲזֹר וּלְתַקֵּן וּלְהַעֲלוֹת הָאֱמוּנָה.

[32] B.T. *Chagigah* 12A דְּאָמַר רַבִּי אֶלְעָזָר: אוֹר שֶׁבָּרָא הַקָּדוֹשׁ בָּרוּךְ הוּא בַּיּוֹם רִאשׁוֹן, אָדָם צוֹפֶה בּוֹ מִסּוֹף הָעוֹלָם וְעַד סוֹפוֹ. כֵּיוָן שֶׁנִּסְתַּכֵּל הַקָּדוֹשׁ בָּרוּךְ הוּא בְּדוֹר הַמַּבּוּל וּבְדוֹר הַפַּלָּגָה וְרָאָה שֶׁמַּעֲשֵׂיהֶם מְקוּלְקָלִים, עָמַד וּגְנָזוֹ מֵהֶן... וּלְמִי גְּנָזוֹ ? לַצַּדִּיקִים לַעֲתִיד לָבֹא.

[33] See *Yitav Lev, Parashath Vayechi* (ויקרא רבה כ', ב'), "כִּי תַפּוּחַ עֲקֵבוֹ שֶׁל אָדָם הָיָה מַכְהֶה גַּלְגַּל חַמָּה" כְּלוֹמַר שֶׁהָיָה אָדָם הָרִאשׁוֹן כֻּלּוֹ שִׂכְלִי מִכַּף רַאשׁוֹ וְעַד רַגְלוֹ, וְהָיָה תַפּוּחַ עֲקֵבוֹ יוֹתֵר מַגְלְגַל חַמָּה. וְאַחַר

therefore accept certain axioms which permitted them to use logic to answer questions about *Hashem* which appear insoluble to us. As matters currently stand, however, human intellect is not capable of fully comprehending concepts such as infinity and accepting those concepts as axiomatic. Accordingly, we cannot fully grasp logical proof of God's existence. In the future, however, *Hashem* will restore human intellect to the level enjoyed by Adam and Chavah, and people will then be able to use reason to conclude that *Hashem* exists.

As mentioned above, a millstone symbolizes philosophical inquiry. The *Torah* also uses the metaphor of a "rock" as an expression of complete faith in *Hashem* even regarding matters which people cannot understand intellectually: "The Rock whose work is perfect, for all His ways are just; a faithful God without injustice. Righteous and upright is He."[34] Rabbi Yehoshua ben Chananya explained to the Athenian elders that the faith symbolized by the concept of a "rock," or millstone, can only be mended by strands of the "rock" itself. To convince atheistic skeptics, those skeptics must (a) have faith in the reliability of certain fundamental axioms; and (b) be able to appreciate certain concepts which the current state of human intellect is incapable of grasping. Since they are unwilling or unable to meet these prerequisites, their faith cannot be repaired. One cannot

---

החטא נעשה כתנות "עור"...בעי"ן (וזהר בראשית ל"ו, ב'), ואין בו השגה רק בלב ומוח בלבד. וזהו שנאמר, כי האדם הראשון יראה מה שתאוה לעיניים, על כן (אלקים) [ה'] יראה רק ללבב.

[34] Deuteronomy 32:4 הַצּוּר תָּמִים פָּעֳלוֹ כִּי כָל דְּרָכָיו מִשְׁפָּט אֵל אֱמוּנָה וְאֵין עָוֶל צַדִּיק וְיָשָׁר הוּא. When Rabbi Chanina ben Tradyon and his wife were condemned to death by the Romans, they used this verse to express faith in *Hashem's* judgment (B.T. *Avodah Zarah* 18A "בְּשָׁעָה שֶׁיָּצְאוּ שְׁלָשְׁתָּן הִצְדִּיקוּ הַצִּדּוּק עֲלֵיהֶם אֶת הַדִּין. הוּא אָמַר,"הַצּוּר תָּמִים פָּעֳלוֹ [וְגו'], (וְאִשְׁתּוֹ אָמְרָה, "אֵל אֱמוּנָה וְאֵין עָוֶל"). Whoever sees the site where the Temple was destroyed also recites this verse (*Mishnah B'rurah*, note 6 on *Shulchan Aruch, Orach Chaim* 561:2).

twist strands of a millstone into thread to mend a broken millstone.

৪৩৪৩ The Verifiability of Scientific Claims

After Rabbi Yehoshua ben Chananya pointed out the many drawbacks of favoring scientific observation and experimentation over *Torah* knowledge, the Athenian elders argued that at least scientific claims can be verified. If an experiment yields a certain result, then others can repeat the experiment, produce the same result, and thereby verify scientific findings. Moreover, as scientists refine their methods and equipment over time, their knowledge improves and becomes more complete.

This is what the Athenian elders meant by presenting two eggs and asking which came from a black hen and which from a white hen. One can discover which egg comes from which hen simply by waiting to see which egg produces a black chick and which produces a white chick. If one can then identify some distinguishing characteristic between the two eggs, he will know how to tell which comes from which type of hen in future cases. This is how science progresses.

Rabbi Yehoshua ben Chananya presented the elders with cheese from a black goat and cheese from a white goat and asked them to determine which was which. Unlike the case of the eggs, there is no way to figure out which cheese came from which goat by waiting to see what will happen.

There are limits to what science can accomplish, but no limits to the wisdom of the *Torah* which comes from the Creator Himself.[35]

---

[35] Modern scientific methods, such as DNA analysis, may permit scientists to determine which cheese comes from which type of goat, but Rabbi Yehoshua

✏️ Philosophers and Scientists Often Cannot Agree among Themselves

The *Gemara* records the following story:

> King Ptolemy gathered seventy-two [Jewish] elders and placed them inside seventy-two chambers without informing them why he did so. [The king] then visited each one and commanded, "Write out the *Torah* of your master Moshe [in Greek]."
>
> The Holy One, Blessed be He, put it into the heart of each one so that all their thoughts coincided, and they wrote, "God created in the beginning" [instead of "In the beginning God created" which might be misinterpreted to mean that something called "in the beginning" (בְּרֵאשִׁית) created God];[36] "I will make man in the image and resemblance" [instead of "We will make man in our image and resemblance" which might be misinterpreted to imply the existence of more than one God];[37] "[God] finished [Creation] on the sixth day and rested on the seventh day" [instead of "God finished His labor on the seventh day" (וַיְכַל אֱ-לֹהִים בַּיּוֹם הַשְּׁבִיעִי) which might be misinterpreted to mean that He performed acts of Creation on the seventh day as well.][38]

---

ben Chananya's point remains valid. There will always be questions which science cannot answer, as the Book of Job states, "He makes great [creations] which cannot be fathomed" (Job 9:10 עֹשֶׂה גְדֹלוֹת עַד אֵין חֵקֶר וְנִפְלָאוֹת עַד אֵין מִסְפָּר).

[36] In contrast to English syntax, the verb appears before the noun in this verse (בְּרֵאשִׁית בָּרָא אֱ-לֹהִים), a common feature of Hebrew grammar.

[37] The plural form is merely an honorable way of referring to God, just as (pardon the comparison) human monarchs refer to themselves in the plural.

[38] B.T. *Megillah* 9A דְּתַנְיָא: מַעֲשֶׂה בְּתַלְמַי הַמֶּלֶךְ שֶׁכִּנֵּס שִׁבְעִים וּשְׁנַיִם זְקֵנִים וְהִכְנִיסָן בְּשִׁבְעִים וּשְׁנַיִם בָּתִּים וְלֹא גִּלָּה לָהֶם עַל מַה כִּנְּסָן. וְנִכְנַס אֵצֶל כָּל אֶחָד וְאֶחָד וְאָמַר לָהֶם, "כִּתְבוּ לִי תּוֹרַת מֹשֶׁה רַבְּכֶם!" נָתַן הַקָּדוֹשׁ בָּרוּךְ הוּא בְּלֵב כָּל אֶחָד וְאֶחָד וְהִסְכִּימָה כּוּלָן לְדַעַת אַחַת וְכָתְבוּ לוֹ, "אֱ-לֹהִים בָּרָא בְּרֵאשִׁית" (בראשית א', א') "אֶעֱשֶׂה אָדָם בְּצֶלֶם וּבִדְמוּת" (בראשית א', כ"ו) "וַיְכַל בַּיּוֹם הַשִּׁשִּׁי וַיִּשְׁבּוֹת בַּיּוֹם הַשְּׁבִיעִי" (בראשית ב:ב)...

The seventy-two sages who translated the *Torah* all came up with the same translation because *Hashem* granted them a special gift of wisdom. Just as many different translations from one language to another are possible, many different interpretations of scientific data are possible.

Rabbi Yehoshua ben Chananya gave each of the sixty Athenian scholars a separate compartment on his ship to stress that each had an independent philosophical approach. When each one observed sixty seats in his compartment, each supposed that the others would soon arrive.

The meaning of this parable is that each philosopher smugly assumed that his approach to philosophical questions was so well grounded in reason that everyone else would surely arrive at the same conclusion he did. In fact, philosophers and scientists frequently disagree because the nature of the human intellect is such that each person interprets data according to his personality traits and life experiences.[39] By contrast, knowledge acquired from Divine revelation is absolutely certain.

ಜಜ The Dangers of Extrapolation

Rabbi Yehoshua ben Chananya highlighted another drawback of scientific inquiry by arranging for each of the Athenians to have his own compartment with sixty chairs. Each scholar assumed that because he had been escorted into a room with sixty chairs, his comrades would be joining him.

---

[39] *Maharal* on B.T. *Bechoroth* 8B דע כי סבי דבי אתונא היו חוקרים מדעתם ושכלם על החכמות. ומפני שאין שכל בני אדם שווה, כי יש שהוא מוכן להשיג דבר זה ויש שהוא מוכן להשיג דבר אחר, ולפיכך השגת השלימות אי אפשר שיהיה (עוד) ע״י אדם אחד פרטי.

This demonstrates another limitation of scientific reasoning — extrapolating from known facts — a procedure which does not always lead to correct conclusions.

A good illustration of this principle appears below.

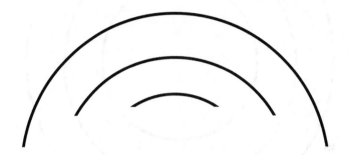

At first glance, the curvature of the bottom arc appears to be less than the curvature of the top one, but in reality, their curvatures are the same. To prove this, below are the three concentric circles from which these arcs were taken. The author did nothing more than simply block out parts of the circles.

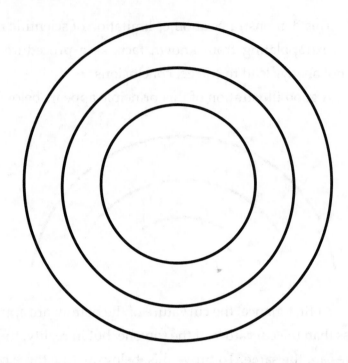

The explanation for this phenomenon is that when people observe the world around them, they do more than simply take in information with their eyes. Their brains also interpret what they see, comparing it to nearby objects. In the above example, people usually extrapolate the bottom arc incorrectly.[40] This shows how extrapolation does not always lead to a correct conclusion even when making what appears to be a simple observation.

ಬಿಬಿ Cultural Bias

When the Athenian elders arrived in Rome and stood before the Caesar, they were subdued and self-doubting until

---

[40] This illusion is sometimes called "Tolansky's curvature illusion" after the Anglo-Jewish physicist Samuel Tolansky (1907-1973), who first described it.

Rabbi Yehoshua ben Chananya threw some Athenian dirt on them.

With this, the authors of the *Talmud* point out how cultural preconceptions can cause people to misconstrue things.

As an example, the *Gemara* records how Rabbi Yossi used to say, "May my lot be among those who eat three meals on the Sabbath."[41] To modern ears this sounds strange because it is customary to eat breakfast, lunch, and supper every day. What is so special about doing on *Shabbath* what everyone does every day? In ancient times, however, people had only two set meals each day — one in the morning and one in the evening. Adding a third meal on *Shabbath* made it a special day.

Another example is the major outbreak of bubonic plague which occurred in Europe in the late 1600's. The Black Death, as it was called, destroyed almost one-third of the population. Many Europeans were biased against Jews, whom they considered to be "in league with the devil." As a result, they accused the Jews of poisoning their drinking water, and pogroms broke out in several communities. Not only did this harm innocent Jews, but it also diverted attention from the real cause of the plague — rats and the fleas they carry. This is a tragic example of how bias can misdirect and mislead people.

Whereas self-confidence has its importance, it is not the same as biased arrogance — the assumption that one's own point of view must always be correct because his culture is superior to all others. Outside Athens, the elders could be receptive to other points of view. They even behaved submissively. Once reminded of their origins, however, they reverted to their

---

[41] B.T. *Shabbath* 118B אָמַר רַבִּי יוֹסֵי: יְהֵא חֶלְקִי מֵאוֹכְלֵי שָׁלֹשׁ סְעוּדוֹת בְּשַׁבָּת

conceited assumption that their way of thinking was the only correct one.

This explains why the elders of Athens maintained their refusal to recognize the truth of the *Torah* even after Rabbi Yehoshua ben Chananya bested them in the disputations discussed above.

✽✽✽ Only those who Have Faith (אֱמוּנָה) Can Grasp the Torah Fully

God conveyed the teachings of the *Torah* in a mysterious fashion. Many ideas are hidden in seemingly simple stories and mundane statements. This is why heretics ask, "Did *Moshe* have nothing better to write than [statements such as], 'The sister of Lotan was Timna'?"[42]

The allegory of the water which absorbs other water alludes to this. Water symbolizes the *Torah*,[43] and the *Torah*, so to speak, absorbs itself. It is hidden in parables and terse statements which one cannot understand without the oral tradition passed down from *Moshe Rabbeinu*. In addition, one must spend many years of study and deep thought to fully grasp it. Even with all this, however, one must realize that the *Torah* is *Hashem's* wisdom. As such, one cannot gain a true understanding of it without Divine assistance. To merit this, one must have deep faith in *Hashem* and in the truth of the *Torah*.

No matter how wise the Greek philosophers may have been, they were idolaters who lacked this crucial element of faith. Even though the Athenian elders ultimately acknowledged

---

[42] B.T. *Sanhedrin* 99B זֶה מְנַשֶּׁה בֶּן חִזְקִיָּה שֶׁהָיָה יוֹשֵׁב וְדוֹרֵשׁ בְּהַגָּדוֹת שֶׁל דּוֹפִי. אָמַר: "וְכִי לֹא הָיָה לוֹ לְמֹשֶׁה לִכְתּוֹב אֶלָּא, 'וַאֲחוֹת לוֹטָן תִּמְנָע' (בראשית ל"ו, כ"ב)?"

[43] B.T. *Baba Kama* 17A וְאֵין מַיִם אֶלָּא תּוֹרָה

the greatness of the *Torah*, when they tried to study it, they wearied of the task and perished — they failed to discern its true meaning.

Gog and Magog: Rational Thought Gone Haywire

The commitment of the non-Jewish nations to "rational thought" and "science" will be carried to an extreme in the era of *Mashiach*.

The Prophet Ezekiel prophesied a future war involving "Gog of the Land of the Magogites,"[44] concerning which the *Talmud* contains the following cryptic passage:

---

[44] Ezekiel 38:2 בֶּן אָדָם שִׂים פָּנֶיךָ אֶל גּוֹג אֶרֶץ הַמָּגוֹג נְשִׂיא רֹאשׁ מֶשֶׁךְ וְתֻבָל וְהִנָּבֵא עָלָיו

Genesis 10:2 identifies Magog as a son of Japheth and a brother of Javan (בְּנֵי יֶפֶת גֹּמֶר וּמָגוֹג וּמָדַי וְיָוָן וְתֻבָל וּמֶשֶׁךְ וְתִירָס). The nation which descended from Magog was evidently named after him. Since Javan (יָוָן) was the ancestor of Greece, it is possible that the names Gog and Magog are related to the Greek "*agogos*" (αγωγός) meaning "leader." This is the source of the modern English "demagogue," which literally means "leader of people."

[In the end of days, the nations of the world will complain that it is unfair for God to reward Israel but not them. *Hashem* will answer that the other nations did not observe the laws of the *Torah*.]

...This is what the idolaters will contend before the Holy One, Blessed be He — "Master of the Universe, as for Israel which accepted [the *Torah*], when did they fulfill it?"

The Holy One, Blessed be He, will answer, "I testify concerning them that they fulfilled the entire *Torah*."

...They will plead before him, "Master of the Universe, give us a fresh start and we will do it."

The Holy One, Blessed be He, will respond, "Most foolish ones! One who exerts effort on the Sabbath eve will eat on the Sabbath. [As for] one who exerts no effort on the Sabbath eve, from what will he eat on the Sabbath? Nevertheless, I have an easy *Mitzvah*, and its name is '*Sukkah*.' Go and perform it!"

...for the Holy One, Blessed be He, does not treat His creatures tyrannically.

...Immediately each one [of the Gentiles] will take [the necessary materials] and go and make a *Sukkah* on top of his roof. The Holy One, Blessed be He, will focus the sun upon them as if it were the middle of the summer. Each will then kick down his *Sukkah* and leave...

[Will *Hashem* indeed] focus [the rays of the sun on them]? But you said that the Holy One, Blessed be He, does not treat His creatures tyrannically!?!

[This is a fair test] because for Israel, too, there are times when summer weather extends until *Sukkoth*, and they experience discomfort [sitting inside the *Sukkah*].

But did not Rava say: One who is uncomfortable is exempt from [staying inside the] *Sukkah*, [so the non-Jews will be justified in leaving]?

True, a person is exempt [from staying inside the *Suk-kah* when it is too hot], but should he kick it down? [This reaction shows that they are unworthy of enjoying the world to come.]

Immediately, the Holy One, Blessed be He, will mock them...

Rabbi Yitzchak said: There is no mockery before the Holy One, Blessed be He, except on that day.

Some say that Rabbi Yitzchak's statement refers to that which is learned...[that in the time of *Mashiach*, idolaters] will become self-made converts, [meaning people who have not undergone proper conversion but declare themselves to be Jewish and undertake the performance of some *Mitzvoth*]. They will place *Tefillin* on their heads and on their arms, *Tzitzioth* on their garments, and *Mezuzoth* on their doors. Once they see the war-party of Gog and Magog, they will inquire, "Why have you come?"

[Gog and his people will reply, "To fight] against *Hashem* and His anointed one."

...[Hearing this,] each one will cast off his *Mitzvah* and leave...and the Holy One, Blessed be He, will sit and mock them.

...[It is concerning this that] Rabbi Yitzchak said: There is no mockery before the Holy One, Blessed be He, except on that day.[45]

---

[45] B.T. *Avodah Zarah* 3A-3B. See Appendix B for the Hebrew text.

The statements of the sages concerning non-Jewish nations refer to those nations in general, but not necessarily to every member of those nations (*Derech Hashem* 2:4:5 ואך זה נשאר לכל איש ואיש מן העניפים בפרטיהם, שיתגייר בעצמו ויכנס בבחירתו תחת אילנו של אברהם אבינו). Every human being has free will and may become a *Tzaddik*.

It seems strange that the nations will reject *Hashem* even after He clearly manifests Himself in the future. Why will they kick down the *Sukkah*? What will possess Gog and his countrymen to fight against *Hashem*, and why will others who appear to recognize the truth of the *Torah* abandon Israel to join them?

Gog symbolizes the antithesis of absolute faith, namely, irrational atheism. He does not merely doubt that God exists. Instead, he is certain that God does not exist, and no evidence to the contrary can shake this belief.

What is the source of such radical atheism?

Most things which happen in the physical world follow predictable patterns commonly called "laws of nature." Jews believe that these laws are not immutable. Rather, God created them and, if He so desires, He can alter or discontinue them at any time.

Gog and his people believe the exact opposite. A miracle which contradicts the usual laws of nature is no proof of God's existence. Rather, it is simply a natural occurrence whose explanation has not yet been discovered. In their view, people are naturally curious to know why things happen as they do. When people do not know the scientific explanation for something, they claim that God caused it. Belief in God is nothing more than a superstition people use to explain phenomena for which they have no scientific explanation. Eventually, science will reveal the truth.

How do Jews know that Gog and Magog are wrong?

❧ The Fiftieth Level of Impurity

The sages teach that when the Jews were in Egypt, they descended to the forty-ninth level of impurity. Had they remained in Egypt any longer, they would have descended to the fiftieth level of impurity, and their redemption would have been impossible.[46]

What is the fiftieth level of impurity?

For everything in the realm of holiness, there is something which corresponds to it in the realm of impurity.[47]

There are fifty gates of understanding, but even *Moshe Rabbeinu* reached only the forty-ninth level, as the Psalms state, "You made him a bit less than God."[48]

When *Moshe Rabbeinu* asked to see *Hashem's* Glory, *Hashem* explained that He could not permit him to do so because "no man can see My face and live."[49] *Midrash Tanchuma* clarifies that this only applies now, "but in the future when I restore My Presence to Zion, I will be revealed in My glory before Israel, and they will behold Me and live forever, as it states, 'For eye to eye they will behold [the Divine Presence] when *Hashem* returns to Zion.'[50]"[51] The fiftieth level of understanding is a direct perception of the Divine Presence so clear and distinct that there can be no doubt or misconception about it.

---

[46] *Ohev Yisrael, Parashath Beshalach* בני ישראל בעת גלות מצרים נכנסו ונשקעו במ"ט שערי טומאה ע"י גילולי מצרים ותועבותיהם שהיה מקום תכלית הטומאה. ואילו ח"ו היו נכנסין לשער הנו"ן משארי הטומאה אזי אנו ובנינו ובני בנינו היינו משועבדים לפרעה במצרים.

[47] *Yismach Moshe, Parashath Kedoshim* p. 30B וידוע דשערי בינה הם נקראים שערי קדושה, דהם זה לעומת זה של נו"ן שערי טומאה.

[48] B.T. *Nedarim* 38A רב ושמואל אמרו: חֲמִשִּׁים שַׁעֲרֵי בִּינָה נִבְרְאוּ בָּעוֹלָם וְכֻלָּם נִתְּנוּ לְמֹשֶׁה חוּץ מֵאֶחָד שֶׁנֶּאֱמַר, "וַתְּחַסְּרֵהוּ מְעַט מֵאֱ-לֹהִים" (תהלים ח', ו'). (note 97 explains this translation)

[49] Exodus 33:20 וַיֹּאמֶר לֹא תוּכַל לִרְאֹת אֶת פָּנָי כִּי לֹא יִרְאַנִי הָאָדָם וָחָי

[50] Isaiah 52:8 קוֹל צֹפַיִךְ נָשְׂאוּ קוֹל יַחְדָּו יְרַנֵּנוּ כִּי עַיִן בְּעַיִן יִרְאוּ בְּשׁוּב ה' צִיּוֹן

[51] *Midrash Tanchuma*, Numbers 17 אבל לעתיד לבוא כשאחזיר שכינתי לציון אני נגלה בכבודי על כל ישראל, והן רואין אותי וחיים לעולם, שנאמר, "כִּי עַיִן בְּעַיִן יִרְאוּ בְּשׁוּב ה' צִיּוֹן" (ישעיה נ"ב, ח').

The fiftieth level of impurity is the exact opposite — an illogical denial of God's existence even when He clearly reveals Himself.[52]

ഇൽ The Ten Plagues

When the ten plagues struck Egypt, the *Torah* states that *Hashem* hardened Pharaoh's heart. The *Maharal* explains this to mean that *Hashem* caused Pharaoh not to fear the terrible consequences of the plagues. Instead of freeing the Jews because he feared punishment, Pharaoh would have to do so because he recognized that God exists and that he must obey Him.[53]

But even if Pharaoh did not fear the plagues, why did he not understand them as evidence of *Hashem's* existence and His desire to free the Jews? Why did Pharaoh stubbornly refuse to obey God?

Pharaoh was a quasi-atheist. He admitted that there is a Creator but denied that the Creator directs and controls every detail of the universe.[54]

---

[52] There is an opinion that there is no fiftieth level of impurity and that the forty-ninth level is the greatest level of impurity (*Leshem Shevo Ve'achlamah*, *Sefer Hadeah* II 5:2:5 בעניין שער הנ׳ דשערי טומאה. הנה הגם שהזכיר אותה גם כן הרמ״ק ז״ל בספר הפרדס שער השערים פ״א. אמנם הגר״א ז״ל במשלי ט״ז ד׳... אמר שם כי להסטרא אחרא אינו רק מ״ט שערי טומאה ושער הנ׳ אין לו). However, even according to this view, one may say that the ultimate level of impurity is an irrational denial of God.

[53] *Gevuroth Hashem*, chapter 31 וכאשר התחיל לבא המכות האחרונות שהם מעליונים, דבר שהוא יותר מן כוחו של אדם, ובוודאי היה משלח את ישראל לא בשביל שהוא חוזר בתשובה רק שהמכות כל כך קשות עליו, והקדוש ברוך הוא רוצה שלא יהיה האדם מוכרח במעשיו על ידי מכות. לכך הקדוש ברוך הוא החזיק את ליבו נגד זה שהיו המכות באות עליו להכריח שישלח ישראל. כנגד זה החזיק את ליבו להכריח אותו שלא ישלח והיה מכריע אותו לצד אחר, ולפיכך יפה ויפה הוא שהקשה לבבו כנגד המכות שהיו מכריעות אותו לשלוח ועכשיו המשקל שווה.

[54] *Rabbeinu Bachye* on Exodus 8:18 פרעה הרשע שהיה כופר בהשגחה; *Kithvei Ha'arizal*, *Shaar Hapesukim, Parashath Bo* הנה פרעה לא היה מכיר בשם ההוי״ה, והיה ח״ו כופר בשם זה, וכמש״ה, "לֹא יָדַעְתִּי אֶת ה׳" (שמות ה׳, ב׳). האמנם היה מכיר בשם א-להים, וכמש״ה, "אֶצְבַּע אֱ-לֹהִים הוּא" (שם ח׳, ט״ו).

The term *Elo-him* (אֱ-לֹהִים) in Hebrew alludes to how *Hashem* works through the laws of nature. Indeed, the numeric value of *Elo-him* (אֱ-לֹהִים) is the same as "Nature" (הַטֶּבַע).[55] When Pharaoh's sorcerers told him that "the finger of God" (אֶצְבַּע אֱ-לֹהִים) was at work during the plague of lice, he adopted a position similar to that of a diehard atheist, namely, that the plague was a natural phenomenon, but that his sorcerers were unfamiliar with the natural processes that caused it.[56]

If that was how Pharaoh thought, then what was different about the plague of the firstborn? What suddenly convinced him that God supervises worldly affairs and that he must obey His command to free the Jews?

During the plague of the firstborn, *Hashem* appeared "not through a messenger, not through an angel, and not through an agent, but the Holy One, Blessed be He, in all His glory, directly."[57] Pharaoh could explain away other miracles as having some unknown natural explanation, but faced with a direct revelation of God, he was forced to admit the existence of Divine Providence.

Even so, Egypt's underlying inclination to reject this idea remained. After a few days, Pharaoh and his servants wondered, "What have we done that we have sent away Israel from serving us?"[58] Incredibly, Pharaoh and his people reasoned that the

---

[55] *Be'er Mayim Chayim, Parashath Yithro* 18 כי נודע אשר שם הוי"ה יתברך הוא המכונה בעשות הדברים אשר למעלה מטבע העולם, כי הוא המהוה את (ה)כל ובידו לשדדם ולשברם ולהכניעם. מה שאין כן שם א-להים שמכונה על שם הטבע שהוא גימטריא 'הטבע', ועל כן אמר פרעה, 'לא יָדַעְתִּי אֶת ה' ', (שמות ה', ב') כלומר איני יודע יודע בחינה המהוה שלמעלה מהטבע. אבל משם א-להים ידע...

[56] *Chomath Anach* on Exodus 8:15 דכל עצמו דפרעה לומר דכל מעשה משה ואהרן היה על ידי כשוף ולא ה' פעל כל זאת... אמנם ודאי דהחרטומים לא הגיעו למדרגת משה ואהרן בכשוף

[57] *Haggadah Shel Pesach* לֹא עַל יְדֵי מַלְאָךְ וְלֹא עַל יְדֵי שָׂרָף וְלֹא עַל יְדֵי שָׁלִיחַ, אֶלָּא הַקָּדוֹשׁ בָּרוּךְ הוּא בִּכְבוֹדוֹ וּבְעַצְמוֹ.

[58] Exodus 14:5 וַיֻּגַּד לְמֶלֶךְ מִצְרַיִם כִּי בָרַח הָעָם וַיֵּהָפֵךְ לְבַב פַּרְעֹה וַעֲבָדָיו אֶל הָעָם וַיֹּאמְרוּ מַה זֹּאת עָשִׂינוּ כִּי שִׁלַּחְנוּ אֶת יִשְׂרָאֵל מֵעָבְדֵנוּ.

revelation of *Hashem* during the plague of the firstborn was not a revelation at all. Pharaoh began to think that perhaps his mind had played a trick on him. Perhaps the Egyptians had been victims of some form of mass hysteria or power of suggestion that led them to believe that a Supreme Being had intervened on Israel's behalf. Perhaps *Moshe Rabbeinu* had engaged in some clever chicanery which had a natural explanation. Pharaoh and his people "knew" that it could not really have been God because they remained convinced that there is no such thing as Divine Providence.

Hashem reveals Himself in different ways and to different degrees. He revealed Himself at the Reed Sea in a much clearer and even more direct way than He did during the plague of the firstborn.[59] Only then did Pharaoh finally admit without reservation that God intervenes in worldly affairs in supernatural ways. It was not just some peculiar natural phenomenon. It was not his mind playing tricks on him or a clever deception foisted upon him by a wily *Moshe Rabbeinu*. It was God.

✣✣ The End of Days

A form of denial even more radical than Pharaoh's will take place in the end of days. The sages teach that, "All civilization will turn to atheism, and no proof [to the contrary will help]."[60]

When God finally reveals Himself, the other nations will initially accept Him and regret their earlier rejection of His

---

[59] Israel saw more at the Reed Sea than the Prophet Ezekiel saw in his vision of the workings of the Divine Chariot (*Mechilta, Parashath Hashirah* 3 רבי אליעזר אומר... שֶׁרָאֲתָה שִׁפְחָה עַל הַיָּם מַה שֶׁלֹּא רָאָה יְחֶזְקֵאל וְכָל שְׁאָר הַנְּבִיאִים).

[60] *Mishnah Sotah* 9:15 וְהַמַּלְכוּת תֵּהָפֵךְ לְמִינוּת וְאֵין תּוֹכֵחָה

commandments. After a short time, however, their new-found faith will falter. They will not merely leave the *Sukkah*. They will kick it down because they will reason that no revelation really happened. They will convince themselves that there must be some other explanation for what seemed like a revelation of God.

Gog and his followers will interpret all of the miracles which happen in the end of days — even the revelation of the Divine Presence — as nothing more than natural phenomena with a scientific explanation that remains to be discovered.

No wonder that *Hashem* will find such blind atheism amusing and, as it were, mock the other nations. Imagine the absurdity of introducing yourself to another person and having that person insist not only that you do not exist but that your existence is an impossibility!

ೞೞೞ Anti-Semitism

If the reader thinks such extremely irrational behavior sounds far-fetched, anti-Semites even now display the same irrational attitude towards the Jewish nation, a nation which represents faith in *Hashem*.

There are, for example, anti-Semites who believe that Jews control the world banking system. If someone points out that most of the people who sit on the board of directors or serve as officers in almost every major bank are not Jewish, anti-Semites respond that either: (a) These people do not openly admit it, but secretly they are Jewish, or (b) Although they are not Jewish, they are secretly controlled by Jews.

No amount of rational argument or straightforward evidence can convince anti-Semites of the truth. Similarly, even when *Hashem* reveals Himself in the end of days, the nations will continue to insist that He does not exist.

The Sadducees: Divine Providence versus Random Chance

ঙ Their Origin

The *Mishnah* states:

Antigonos of Socho received [the Oral *Torah*] from Shimon the *Tzaddik*. [Antigonos] used to say, "Do not be like servants who serve the Master in order to receive reward. Rather, be like servants who serve the Master not for the sake of receiving reward. And let the fear of Heaven be upon you."[61]

---

[61] *Pirkei Avoth* 1:3 אַנְטִיגְנוֹס אִישׁ סוֹכוֹ קִבֵּל מִשִּׁמְעוֹן הַצַּדִּיק. הוּא הָיָה אוֹמֵר: "אַל תִּהְיוּ כַּעֲבָדִים הַמְשַׁמְּשִׁין אֶת הָרַב עַל מְנָת לְקַבֵּל פְּרָס, אֶלָּא הֱווּ כַּעֲבָדִים הַמְשַׁמְּשִׁין אֶת הָרַב שֶׁלֹּא עַל מְנָת לְקַבֵּל פְּרָס, וִיהִי מוֹרָא שָׁמַיִם עֲלֵיכֶם".

The sages explain that Antigonos was not suggesting that *Hashem* does not reward the righteous and punish the wicked. He merely meant that ideally a person should not serve *Hashem* because of that. Nevertheless, Antigonos had two disciples, Zadok and Boethius, who repeated this teaching to their disciples, and those disciples repeated it to still others. Eventually, some of those who heard it misinterpreted Antigonos's statement to mean that God does not reward the righteous or punish the wicked. They then founded the deviant sects known as Sadducees and Boethusians.[62]

This account seems strange. Antigonos's teaching does not seem to be particularly complex or confusing, so those who heard it should have had no trouble understanding it.

Even more puzzling is the assertion of some later commentators that the Sadducees adopted the position they did because they accepted only the Written *Torah* and rejected the Oral *Torah*.[63]

The idea that God rewards the righteous and punishes the wicked is mentioned numerous times throughout the *Torah*, with an extensive list of blessings for the obedient and curses for the rebellious. Furthermore, the *Torah* relates many instances in which God acted accordingly, such as the destruction of Sodom and Gomorrah, the plagues visited upon the Egyptians, and the splitting of the Reed Sea so that the Jews could escape. Thus, even someone who accepts only the Written *Torah* must accept the doctrine of reward and punishment. Furthermore, even if the

---

[62] *Avoth D'Rabbi Nathan* 5:2 אנטיגנוס איש סוכו היו לו שני תלמידים שהיו שונין בדבריו והיו שונים לתלמידים ותלמידים לתלמידיהם. עמדו ודקדקו אחריהן ואמרו: 'מה ראו אבותינו לומר [דבר זה]? אפשר שיעשה פועל מלאכה כל היום ולא יטול שכרו ערבית? אלא אילו היו יודעין אבותינו שיש עולם [אחר] ויש תחיית המתים לא היו אומרים כך'. עמדו ופירשו מן התורה ונפרצו מהם שתי פרצות – צדוקין וביתוסין. צדוקים על שום צדוק, ביתוסין על שום ביתוס.

[63] *Rashi* on B.T. *Eruvin* 61B צדוקי ישראל הוא ונהפך למינות ואינו מודה בתורה שבעל פה

Sadducees were troubled by the fact that one does not often observe reward and punishment in this world, the *Tanach* repeatedly states that the soul survives death,[64] with reward and punishment occurring then.[65]

Rabbi Yitzchak Abarbanel clarifies that the corrupt views of the Sadducees came from Greek beliefs.[66] Aristotle and other Greek philosophers taught that God only pays attention to the spiritual worlds and does not supervise anything that happens in the physical world, instead leaving matters to random chance. This explains why the righteous sometimes suffer and the wicked sometimes prosper.[67] Once people die, their souls return

---

[64] For example, "The dust shall return to the ground as it was, and the spirit shall return to God who gave it" (Ecclesiastes 12:7 וְיָשֹׁב הֶעָפָר עַל הָאָרֶץ כְּשֶׁהָיָה וְהָרוּחַ תָּשׁוּב אֶל הָאֱ-לֹהִים אֲשֶׁר נְתָנָהּ)

[65] There is an opinion that the Sadducees denied that a person's soul survives his death (*Sefer Ha'ikarim* 4:31 הצדוקים והכותיים הכופרים בהשארות הנפש ואומרים שהנפש תמות במות הגוף). However, it seems that such a conclusion would be impossible in light of the verse from Ecclesiastes cited in the previous footnote as well as the repeated promises of the *Torah* concerning reward and punishment which usually go unfulfilled in this world. Perhaps there were several subsects among the Sadducees — some accepted the principle of a spiritual afterlife whereas others rejected even this.

[66] *Yeshuoth Meshicho*, Part 2, *Iyun Rishon*, 3 שבבית שני רבו הפריצים, המינים והאפיקורסים והצדוקים ונשרשה ביניהם אמונת יון שהחריבה את העולם. This is also the view of *Pri Tzaddik*, *Parashath Vayishlach* 11 כי אז בימי שמעון הצדיק לאחר שפסקו כבר התגלות נביאים והיה זמן אנשי כנסת הגדולה שביטלו יצרא דעבודה זרה וגזרו גזירות לעשות סייג לתורה, ואז נגד זה הייתה חכמת יון והצדוקים

The *Alshich* states that the Greek exile was caused by the Sadducees (*Alshich* on Numbers 14:11 וגלות יון שהיה על שפרחה צרעת צדוקים שהוא העדר האמנה). This punishment was measure for measure because they adopted the views of the Greeks.

[67] *Torath Haminchah* by Rabbi Yaakov Scili 49 אריסטו סובר כי הנהגת הגלגלים וחילוף הזמנים וסידור הכוכבים הכל בהנהגה א-לוהית ודעת עליון, ומה שיש למטה מגלגל הירח הכל במקרה... ואין חילוק בין מין האנושי למין הבהמי... אם פגעה חיה רעה בנביא והמיתו, או... נפלה כותל על אנשי חסד ומתו, או שטבעה ספינה ובה אנשים צדיקים ומתו, הכל במקרה.

As noted above in the chapter titled *The Philosophers of Athens*, the position of the Greek philosophers is untenable. Why would God create a lower realm if He has no interest in it and abandons it to random chance?

to the spiritual realm where reward and punishment are meted out.

According to the Greek view, it would make no sense for *Hashem* to resurrect the dead and restore the union between the body and the soul so that He may reward the righteous and punish the wicked because He never involves Himself in the physical realm.[68]

The Sadducees agreed with the opinion of the Greek philosophers. Accordingly, they accepted the idea that the soul is rewarded or punished in the afterlife, but they rejected the doctrine of resurrection.[69] At the same time, they realized that complete reward or punishment requires resurrection so that a person's physical and spiritual components can both participate in the final reckoning. They did not understand Antigonos's statement to mean that no reward and punishment exist at all, but only that complete reward and punishment, which can only be achieved through resurrection, does not exist.

This explains why a Sadducee asked Rabbi Ami, "You say that the dead shall live, yet they become dust, and how can dust

---

[68] Certain Romans asked Rabbi Yeshoshua ben Chananya, "From where [do you know] that the Holy One, Blessed be He, will revive the dead and knows what will happen in the future?" (B.T. *Sanhedrin* 90B מְנַּיִן שֶׁהַקָּדוֹשׁ בָּרוּךְ הוּא מְחַיֶּה מֵתִים וְיוֹדֵעַ מַה שֶּׁעָתִיד לִהְיוֹת?). At first glance, the two parts of this question appear unrelated. However, the Romans, who adopted Greek philosophy, held that after Creation, *Hashem* abandoned the physical realm to the vagaries of chance. Accordingly, He does not know what will happen to people in the future. He also will not resurrect the dead because He never concerns Himself with the physical realm. (*Maharsha* on B.T. *Sanhedrin* 90B "מְנַּיִן שֶׁהַקָּדוֹשׁ בָּרוּךְ הוּא מְחַיֶּה מֵתִים וְיוֹדֵעַ מַה שֶּׁעָתִיד לִהְיוֹת?" — הפילוסופים הם מן הכופרים בידיעה ובתחיית המתים והם שאלו על שניהם מנין מן התורה).

[69] *Rashi* on B.T. *Berachoth* 54A התקינו — עזרא וסיעתו שיהו אומרים מן העולם ועד העולם, לומר ששני עולמות יש, להוציא מלב הצדוקים הכופרים בתחיית המתים.

live?"[70] The rabbi responded to the effect that if God could create the entire universe from nothing, then certainly He can resurrect the dead from their remains.[71]

Another time, a Sadducee declared to Geviah ben Pesisa, "Woe unto you sinners who claim that the dead shall live. If those who are alive die, shall the dead live?"[72] The rabbi answered that if those who did not exist at all can be brought to life, then surely those who once lived can return to life.[73]

The Sadducees repeatedly challenged the doctrine of resurrection but not the more general idea that God rewards the righteous and punishes the wicked.[74]

৵৵ Refuting Aristotle's Heresy

The sages teach that if someone claims there is wisdom among the nations, believe him, but if someone claims there is *Torah* among the nations, do not believe him.[75] The Greek philosophers were brilliant thinkers, but their ancestors did not stand

---

[70] B.T. *Sanhedrin* 91A, according to the version found in *Ein Yaakov* אָמַר לֵיהּ הַהוּא (מינא) [צְדוֹקִין] לְרַבִּי אַמִי, "אַמְרִיתוּ דְּשַׁכְבֵי חַיֵּי. הָא הֲווּ עַפְרָא וְעַפְרָא מִי קָא חַיֵּי?!" which states that a Sadducee was involved. The Romm Vilna text of the Babylonian *Talmud* states that a "heretic" (מִין) confronted Rabbi Ami, but this term also sometimes denotes Sadducees. (See, for example, *Tifereth Yisrael, Yachin* on *Rosh Hashanah* 2:1, note 5 הצדוקים – המינין).

[71] This accords with the second comment of *Rashi* ad. loc. אי נמי, כל העולם כולו יצר מתוהו

[72] B.T. *Sanhedrin* 91A, again according to the version found in *Ein Yaakov* אָמַר לֵיהּ הַהוּא (מינא) [צְדוֹקִין] לִגְבִיהָא בֶּן פְּסִיסָא, "אוֹי לְכוֹן חַיָּבַיָּא דְּאַמְרִיתוּ מֵיתֵי חַיִּין. דְּחַיִּין מֵיתֵי, דְּמֵיתֵי חַיִּין?!"

[73] Rashi ad. loc. אותן שלא היו מעולם נוצרין ונולדין וחיין, אותן שהיו כבר לא כל שכן שחוזרין וחיין

[74] Their devotion to Greek philosophy was such that they apparently were not bothered by the fact that this view contradicts Daniel 12:2, which states, "Many of those who sleep in the dust shall awaken — some to eternal life and some to eternal shame and disgrace" (וְרַבִּים מִיְּשֵׁנֵי אַדְמַת עָפָר יָקִיצוּ אֵלֶּה לְחַיֵּי עוֹלָם וְאֵלֶּה לַחֲרָפוֹת לְדִרְאוֹן עוֹלָם).

[75] *Eichah Rabbah* 2:13 אם יאמר לך אדם יש חכמה בגוים תאמן... יש תורה בגוים אל תאמן

at Mount Sinai and interact directly with God, so it is only natural that their investigations led them to conclusions contrary to the teachings of the *Torah*.

What caused the Greeks to think that *Hashem* does not involve Himself with the physical realm?

The Greek philosophers observed the seemingly random operation of the universe. In particular, they were struck by the fact that people appear to suffer and die randomly. For instance, if an epidemic strikes a certain region, it typically kills a certain percentage of people seemingly without regard for who is righteous and who is not. If God is intimately involved in the physical universe, they wondered, then why does this happen?[76]

In contrast to this, the sages teach that people must have faith that whatever happens comes from *Hashem*. Even seemingly minor matters are controlled by God, as Rabbi Chanina said, "A person does not bump his finger below unless it is decreed upon him from above."[77]

Although many events appear random, *Hashem* controls them so that when good or evil befall a person it is through His will. Despite appearances, *Hashem* is directly involved in each person's life.[78]

---

[76] *Mogen Avoth L'Rashbatz*, ch. 2 *Behashgachah Vegemul Ve'onesh* אמנם הפילוסוף אריסטו מלאו לבו להכחיש זה. לא שהביאו לזאת ההכחשה מופת שכלי כי אם עניינים מוחשים לפי דעתו. וזה מכוח קושיא קדמונית מפני מה צדיק ורע לו, רשע וטוב לו. כי לפי מה שהונח מהשגחה, היה ראוי שיסודרו העניינים סדור יותר נאות ממה שאנו רואים... על כן החליט המאמר שכל אלה הפרטים אינם משולחים מהא-ל יתברך, אבל משולחים אל הקרי וההזדמן. ואין הבדל אצלו בין חסיד טרפו אריה ובין זבוב טרפו עכביש. והשגחת הא-ל יתברך אינם אלא בנמצאות הקיימות בשכלים הנבדלים והגלגלים אשר בהשגחתו היא סיבת קיומם. ומהשפע השופע מהם ביסודות הם מתקיימים המינים, אבל האישים ההוים ונפסדים משולחים אל המקרה. ולזה הוא אומר כי השגחת הא-ל יתברך תכלה ותפסק אצל גלגל הירח.

[77] B.T. *Chullin* 7B וְאָמַר רַבִּי חֲנִינָא: אֵין אָדָם נוֹקֵף אֶצְבָּעוֹ מִלְמַטָּה אֶלָּא אִם כֵּן מַכְרִיזִין עָלָיו מִלְמַעְלָה

[78] If *Hashem's* involvement in the world would be obvious, people would not have free will, so *Hashem* permits events to appear random.

When *Hashem* was about to destroy Sodom and Gomorrah, Abraham argued that He should not do so if a minimum number of righteous people lived there, saying, "Shall not the Judge of all the Earth do justice?" (Genesis

ജ୪ଔ Statistics Don't Lie, but They also Don't Tell the Entire Truth

The Greek philosophers and their Sadducee admirers were dissatisfied with this approach. Statistics show that a certain number of people die each year. In fact, more precise statistics show that each year a certain number of women will die in childbirth, a certain number of people from lung cancer, a certain number from heart failure, a certain number in motor vehicle accidents, and so on. Like other laws of nature, the laws of chance seem stable and predictable. If so, how can it be that *Hashem* makes specific decisions about who will live and who will die?

Although it is not possible for human beings to fully understand how *Hashem* controls the universe, it is possible to understand why the laws of chance are deceptive and that statistics do not limit Him.

ജ୪ଔଔ The Gambler's Fallacy

If a person flips a coin one hundred times, then, on average, heads will come up fifty times and tails will come up fifty times. Many people think this means that if a person flips a coin nine times and heads come up every time, then there is a 10% chance that heads will appear on the next flip and a 90% chance that tails will come up. This is incorrect because there is no causal connection between any given flip of the coin and any other. Since each flip of the coin is causally independent of every other

---

חָלִלָה לְּךָ מֵעֲשֹׂת כַּדָּבָר הַזֶּה לְהָמִית צַדִּיק עִם רָשָׁע וְהָיָה כַצַּדִּיק כָּרָשָׁע חָלִלָה לָּךְ הֲשֹׁפֵט כָּל הָאָרֶץ לֹא 18:25 יַעֲשֶׂה מִשְׁפָּט). Although *Hashem* usually permits retribution to appear random to preserve free will, Abraham argued that the situation of Sodom and Gomorrah required a different approach. Since God planned to reveal Himself anyway by destroying them in a supernatural way, it made sense to differentiate between the righteous and the wicked.

flip, the chance that the tenth flip will come up heads remains 50%. This is true even though, in any given set of coin flips, on average, heads will come up half the time and tails half the time.

The Greek philosophers considered only the general principle of the law of probability — when looking at a large number of coin flips, on average, approximately 50% will come up heads and 50% tails. They therefore assumed that God allows the world to operate by random chance and that there is just as much chance that evil will befall one person as it will another.

In fact, *Hashem* guides the world with specific providence (הַשְׁגָּחָה פְּרָטִית). Since the chance of any particular coin flip coming up heads or tails is always 50/50, *Hashem* can intervene, if He chooses, and cause the coin to come up heads or tails at any time without changing the overall result that the coin will come up roughly half the time heads and half the time tails.

To explain further, if a coin is flipped one hundred times, results will sometimes be 51 times heads and 49 times tails (or the reverse), or 52 times heads and 48 times tails (or the reverse), or something else other than 50 times heads and 50 times tails. This means that no series of coin flips has a 100% probability of yielding the ideal 50/50 result unless the series is infinite. Since all worldly phenomena are finite, no event can ever be perfectly random, and *Hashem* can exercise Divine intervention without disturbing the statistical ideal.

෨෨෨ The Difficulty of Understanding Complex Phenomena

The above example of flipping coins is a very simple case. Most natural phenomena have many complex variables which allow far more leeway for Divine intervention. Moreover,

Hashem's ways are too complex for human beings to understand, and what may appear as random chance to people may really be something quite different.

King Solomon wrote, "I said in my heart concerning human beings who are [apparently] distinguished by God [because of their superior intelligence], that they should see that they are [nothing more than] animals [in comparison to Him]."[79]

Animals cannot speak and certainly cannot read or write. They do not understand anything about people flying to the moon nor are they even aware that such flights have taken place. In addition, there is no way to communicate such information to animals or cause them to understand it. King Solomon meant that human understanding of God is like an animal's understanding of human affairs.[80] For this reason, the expression "they are nothing more than animals" (בְּהֵמָה הֵמָּה) has the same numeric value as "faith" (אֱמוּנָה), hinting that some things are beyond the intellectual grasp of human beings.

To gain some insight into how this works, let the reader consider the following.

෨෨෨෨ The Monty Hall Problem

During the 1970's, a Jewish celebrity named Monty Hall hosted a popular game show in which a prize was placed behind one of three doors and contestants were given the opportunity to choose one of them. Before opening the door which the contestant chose, Mr. Hall, who knew where the prize lay hidden,

---

[79] Ecclesiastes 3:18 אָמַרְתִּי אֲנִי בְּלִבִּי עַל דִּבְרַת בְּנֵי הָאָדָם לְבָרָם הָאֱ-לֹהִים וְלִרְאוֹת שְׁהֶם בְּהֵמָה הֵמָּה לָהֶם according to *Metzudoth David.*

[80] Compare Psalms 73:22 — "I was like a fool and did not know, like animals with [respect to] You" וַאֲנִי בַעַר וְלֹא אֵדָע בְּהֵמוֹת הָיִיתִי עִמָּךְ

opened one of the remaining two doors where the prize was not. He then offered the contestant a choice: either keep the door originally chosen or switch to the remaining closed door.

Most people assume that it makes no difference whether the contestant changes his selection. Since only two doors remain unopened, it seems that there is just as much chance that the prize lies behind one as behind the other.

However, someone who observed this game at the time claimed that if the contestant kept his original choice, he would still only have a one-third chance of winning, whereas if he switched his choice, he would have a two-thirds chance of winning.

This claim became a matter of heated debate, and even expert mathematicians challenged it, but direct experimentation shows that it is correct.

Why is this so?

৯৩৯৩৯৩৯৩ The Rabbinic Method of Problem-Solving

There are advanced mathematical proofs which explain why switching doors increases a contestant's chance of winning from one-third to two-thirds, but the sages had a simple method of problem-solving which they applied to mathematical questions.

The Rabbinic method involves taking a complex problem and breaking it into smaller segments. Once people solve the smaller segments of the problem, they can then arrive at a solution for the entire problem.[81]

---

[81] See *Rashi* sub verba *"Mipnei Shemafsid"* (מפני שמפסיד) on B.T. *Eruvin* 56B for an example of how this method is applied.

This method can be applied to the Monty Hall problem as follows:

To make matters easier to understand, one can use a card game which follows the same rules.

STEP ONE:

Suppose that Reuven offers to play a simple game with Shimon. He takes three playing cards, one of which is an ace, shuffles them thoroughly, and places them face down on a table. He then offers Shimon to pick one of the cards, with the stipulation that if Shimon picks the ace, he wins a dollar.

Clearly, Shimon has a one-third chance of winning. Conversely, Reuven has a two-thirds chance of winning because there is a two-thirds chance that Shimon will pick a card other than the ace, as illustrated below.

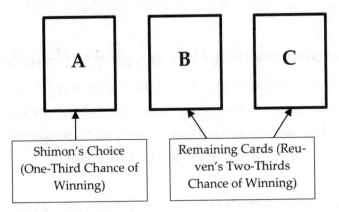

STEP TWO:

Before turning over the card Shimon chose, Reuven makes the following offer: "Instead of turning over the card you picked, you can turn over *both* of the other cards you did not pick."

If Shimon agrees, he now has a two-thirds chance of winning, whereas Reuven has only a one-third chance of winning. To put it another way, Shimon has exchanged his one-third chance of winning for Reuven's two-thirds chance of winning.

STEP THREE:

Suppose, instead, that Reuven is allowed to peek at the two cards Shimon did not pick. Of the two cards Shimon did not choose, at least one is not an ace, and Reuven turns over that card. Turning over the card, however, is irrelevant to the chances of winning or losing the game. Even after turning over the card, Reuven still has the same two-thirds chance of winning he started off with. If Shimon switches from the face-down card he originally chose to the face-down card he did not choose, he is still exchanging his original one-third chance of winning for Reuven's two-thirds chance of winning, as illustrated below.

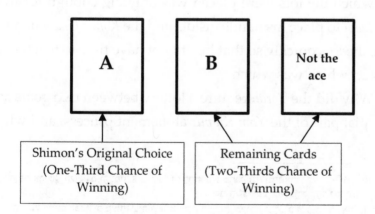

This demonstrates how even seemingly simple issues of probability and statistics can be tricky to resolve. Merely exposing one of the cards that is not the ace confuses most people. This makes it a bit easier to understand how *Hashem* "confuses"

people by disguising His Divine Providence (הַשְׁגָּחָה פְּרָטִית) in seemingly random natural processes.

෨ The Yom Kippur Lottery

In Temple times, the *Yom Kippur* service included a ceremony in which two goats were placed in front of the *Kohen Gadol*. One goat was sacrificed to *Hashem*, and the other was sent to the desert. The *Torah* required the *Kohen Gadol* to use a lottery to select which goat would be used for each purpose.[82]

The *Mishnah* states that, "It was a *Mitzvah* for both goats to be equal in appearance, height, and value, and for both to be purchased together."[83] Similarly, the lots for the goats were of the same size and made of the same material.[84]

It was considered a favorable sign when the lot for *Hashem* came up in the *Kohen Gadol's* right hand.[85] To ensure that the results of the lottery were untainted by any tampering, the box in which the lots were placed was only big enough for the *Kohen Gadol* to place his hands inside, and the *Kohen Gadol* had to remove the lots quickly so that he did not have time to feel them and detect which was which.[86]

Why did the *Torah* require a lottery between two goats as an essential part of the *Yom Kippur* atonement process, and why

---

[82] Leviticus 16:7-8 (ז) וְלָקַח אֶת שְׁנֵי הַשְּׂעִירִם וְהֶעֱמִיד אֹתָם לִפְנֵי ה' פֶּתַח אֹהֶל מוֹעֵד. (ח) וְנָתַן אַהֲרֹן עַל שְׁנֵי הַשְּׂעִירִם גֹּרָלוֹת גּוֹרָל אֶחָד לַה' וְגוֹרָל אֶחָד לַעֲזָאזֵל.

[83] Yoma 6:1 שְׁנֵי שְׂעִירֵי יוֹם הַכִּפּוּרִים מִצְוָתָן שֶׁיִּהְיוּ שְׁנֵיהֶן שָׁוִין בְּמַרְאֶה וּבְקוֹמָה וּבְדָמִים וּבִלְקִיחָתָן כְּאֶחָד

[84] B.T. Yoma 37A מה תלמוד לומר "גורלות"? שיהיו שוין – שלא יעשה אחד של זהב ואחד של כסף אחד גדול ואחד קטן.

[85] B.T. Yoma 39A אַרְבָּעִים שָׁנָה שֶׁשִּׁמֵּשׁ שִׁמְעוֹן הַצַּדִּיק הָיָה גוֹרָל עוֹלֶה בְּיָמִין. מִכָּאן וָאֵילָךְ פְּעָמִים עוֹלֶה בְּיָמִין פְּעָמִים עוֹלֶה בִשְׂמֹאל.

[86] B.T. Yoma 39A לָמָּה לִי "טָרַף בַּקַּלְפִּי"? כִּי הֵיכִי דְּלָא נִיכַוֵּין וְלִישְׁקוֹל. אָמַר רָבָא: קַלְפִּי שֶׁל עֵץ הָיְתָה... וְאֵינָהּ מַחֲזֶקֶת אֶלָּא שְׁתֵּי יָדַיִם... כִּי הֵיכִי דְּלָא לִיכַוֵּין וְלִישְׁקוֹל

Rashi ad. loc. "דְּלָא נִיכַוֵּין" – שלא ימשמש להבין במשמושו איזה של שם ויטלנו בימין לפי שהוא סימן יפה כשהוא עולה בימין.

was it so important to make sure that the process be as unbiased as possible?

The *Midrash* explains:

> Samael [another name for the Accuser] complained before the Holy One, Blessed be He, "You gave me permission [to prosecute] other [nations], but You did not give me permission [to prosecute] Israel."
>
> "Behold," He answered, "you have permission [to prosecute] them on *Yom Kippur*."
>
> Therefore, [the Jews] would give [Samael] a bribe — one [goat] for Azazel [selected by] lot with all the sins of Israel upon it.[87]

Other nations believe that everything happens randomly, as the *Torah* states concerning Amalek, who is called "chief among the nations"[88] — "He happened upon you on the way...and did not fear God."[89] The Amalekites viewed their confrontation with Israel as happenstance because they did not fear God and thought that all events are accidental.

Similarly, when God appeared to Balaam, the greatest prophet of the non-Jewish nations, the *Torah* states that, "God happened upon Balaam."[90] Although Balaam knew about God and even spoke with him, he did not believe in Divine Providence but in happenstance.

---

[87] *Yalkut Shimoni* on Leviticus 16, paragraph 578 אמר סמאל לפני הקדוש ברוך הוא, "על אחרים נתת לי רשות ועל ישראל אי אתה נותן לי רשות". אמר לו, "הרי יש לך רשות עליהן ביום הכפורים". לפיכך היו נותנין לו שוחד אחד לעזאזל וכל עונותיהן של ישראל עליו.

[88] Numbers 24:20 וַיַּרְא אֶת עֲמָלֵק וַיִּשָּׂא מְשָׁלוֹ וַיֹּאמַר רֵאשִׁית גּוֹיִם עֲמָלֵק וְאַחֲרִיתוֹ עֲדֵי אֹבֵד

[89] Deuteronomy 25:18 אֲשֶׁר קָרְךָ בַּדֶּרֶךְ וַיְזַנֵּב בְּךָ כָּל הַנֶּחֱשָׁלִים אַחֲרֶיךָ וְאַתָּה עָיֵף וְיָגֵעַ וְלֹא יָרֵא אֱ-לֹהִים

[90] Numbers 23:4 וַיִּקָּר אֱ-לֹהִים אֶל בִּלְעָם וַיֹּאמֶר אֵלָיו אֶת שִׁבְעַת הַמִּזְבְּחֹת עָרַכְתִּי וָאַעַל פָּר וָאַיִל בַּמִּזְבֵּחַ

Throughout the year, some Jews sin because, at least subconsciously, they think that chance guides the universe. If they had complete faith that everything happens according to Divine Providence, they would behave differently. When *Hashem* judges the world on *Yom Kippur*, the Accuser argues that the Jewish nation is no better than any other in this respect.

The lottery used to select which goat would be sacrificed to *Hashem* and which would be sent to the desert neutralized this argument. By guarding the ceremony from any taint of human interference, the Jews made it appear as random as possible. Nevertheless, they recognized that it was a favorable sign if the lot for *Hashem* came up in the *Kohen Gadol's* right hand. This stressed Israel's belief that *Hashem's* Divine Providence controls every detail of every event even when those events appear completely random. This atoned for those Jews who behaved during the year as if there were no Divine Providence.

৪৫৪৬ Hashem is One, but Chances Must be at Least Two

The *Kedushath Levi* notes that if only one outcome is possible, then random results cannot occur. Random outcomes which can be predicted by the laws of probability only exist when more than one outcome is possible.

Hashem is an absolute unity. All history is laid out before Him, with past, present, and future all occurring simultaneously. Accordingly, from His perspective random chance does not exist.

In the universe *Hashem* created, however, multiplicity exists, so from the perspective of His creatures, random occurrences whose probability can be predicted are possible.[91] From the human point of view, the possibility that the *Kohen Gadol* will select the lot for either goat appears random, but in reality, the result depends solely upon God's will.

This distinction reflects the essence of idolatry. If there are many gods, events ***must*** happen by chance because sometimes one god will overpower or outmaneuver another whereas on other occasions the opposite will occur. The expression "other gods" (אֱלֹהִים אֲחֵרִים) hints at this because it has the same numeric value as "happenstance" (מִקְרֶה).

✂ The Spies in the Wilderness

The *Midrash* states that the men *Moshe Rabbeinu* sent to spy out the Land of Israel were righteous people.[92] Why, then, did they sin by reporting that the land was unconquerable, and why did they advise their fellow Jews to turn back in spite of God's command to go forward? Surely, they did not doubt God's ability to perform whatever miracles were necessary for Israel to succeed?

The *Chiddushei Harim* explains that the spies did not doubt *Hashem's* ability to perform miracles. Indeed, the Jews had been living with supernatural miracles throughout their journey in the Sinai Desert. Their food fell from the sky, their water came from a rock which traveled with them, the Clouds of Glory protected them from sun and rain, and their clothing and shoes grew as they grew, never wearing out.

---

[91] *Kedushath Levi, Kedushah Rishonah, Purim* והנה אם אין רק דבר אחד אינו שייך גורל. רק אם יש שני דברים דומים זה לזה (ף) שבורר לו דבר אחד שייך גורל. שגורל אינו רק הבורר אחד משני דברים הדומים זה לזה. לכן, בעולם הזה אשר מלכותו והנהגותו מכוסה שייך גורל אחד לה׳ וכו׳... אבל למעלה ששם אחדותו נראה ואין רואין רק מלכותו יתברך שמו (אינו שייך מושג ההגדלה).

[92] *Bamidbar Rabbah* 16:5 שְׁלַח לְךָ אֲנָשִׁים" (במדבר י״ג, ב׳) ובכל מקום שנאמר "אֲנָשִׁים" בני אדם צדיקים הם.

The spies knew that all of this would change when they entered the Land of Israel. They would have to obtain food, water, clothing, shelter, and all their other needs in a natural way. They therefore reasoned that they would have to conquer the Land by natural means and could not rely on supernatural miracles. Since the Canaanites were bigger and stronger than they were, they doubted that they could succeed.[93]

But how could the spies think that *Hashem* could only cause them to succeed by use of supernatural miracles? Why did they not realize that *Hashem* could just as easily cause the Jews to succeed through natural means?

This may be compared to someone who creates a jigsaw puzzle. Such a person could start with blank board, print a picture of sheep grazing in a meadow on it, and then cut the board into sundry shapes. After the pieces are scrambled, one can reassemble them to form the picture. Suppose, however, that someone wanted to assemble the same scrambled pieces to form a picture of penguins on an iceberg diving for fish. Such a task is impossible.

The spies understood how *Hashem* could alter or override the laws of nature altogether, but how was *Hashem* going to act within the laws of nature to make the Jews victorious over the Canaanites? It was like trying to use pieces of a jigsaw puzzle made from a picture of sheep grazing in a meadow to form a picture of penguins on an iceberg diving for fish.

The *Ramchal* explains that *Hashem* is not only omnipotent in every way people can imagine, but also in every way they

---

[93] *Kethav Sofer* on Numbers 14:18 דטעות המרגלים והעם הייתה מאחר שראו כי הוצרכו למרגלים וילחמו בטבע חשבו כי יהיה הכל בטבע בלי עזרת ה׳, כי הורגלו עד עתה שה׳ עזר להם בלי פעולת אדם כלל וחשבו שכל עזרת אלוקי חוץ לטבע, ולכן יראו לנפשם כי בטבע לא יוכלו להם. אלא שבאמת לאו בכל יומא יעשה ה׳ נסים שלא בטבע, אלא מה שחסר הטבע ישלים עזרת אלוקי.

cannot imagine.[94] He can produce miraculous results within the confines of nature even though people cannot imagine how He will do so any more than they can imagine how to use the puzzle pieces from a picture of sheep grazing in a meadow to form a picture of penguins on an iceberg diving for fish.

In a similar way, *Hashem* directs the events of the world through seemingly chance events even though we do not understand how He does so.

[94] *Kelach Pithchei Hachochmah* 30 כי האין סוף ברוך הוא צריך להבין אותו – כל-יכול בכל מיני יכולת שהמחשבה תופסת, ושאינה תופסת.

HASHEM'S INFINITITUDE

The Backwards Nun (ꓩ): Faith in Hashem's Infinitude

The letter *Nun* (נ) appears in the *Torah* in a unique form. In addition to the bent *Nun* (נ) and the straight *Nun* (ן), two verses in the Book of Numbers are marked off from the rest of the *Torah* by backwards *Nuns* (ꓩ).[95] No other Hebrew letter is used in this way as a punctuation mark.

What is the significance of this special form?

❧ The Infinite One, Blessed be He

Nun (נ) has a numeric value of fifty. The *Talmud* teaches that, "Fifty gates of understanding were created in the world. All of them were given to *Moshe* except one, as it is stated, 'You made

---

[95] The two verses appear in Numbers 10:35-36   (לה) וַיְהִי בִּנְסֹעַ הָאָרֹן וַיֹּאמֶר מֹשֶׁה קוּמָה ה' וְיָפֻצוּ אֹיְבֶיךָ וְיָנֻסוּ מְשַׂנְאֶיךָ מִפָּנֶיךָ. (לו) וּבְנֻחֹה יֹאמַר שׁוּבָה ה' רִבְבוֹת אַלְפֵי יִשְׂרָאֵל.

him less than God.'[96]"[97] The fiftieth gate of understanding represents full comprehension of God's absolute infiniteness. No created being, not even an angel, can achieve that level of understanding.[98]

Even so, human beings can relate to this exalted level through faith because it is possible to believe something without fully understanding it. For example, people can believe that a motor causes an automobile to move even if they do not understand exactly how it does so and are not even familiar with all of its parts or their functions.

৪৩৪৩ Faith in Hashem's Absolute Infinitude

One can form a diagram with all three *Nuns* which resembles the linear configuration of the supernal spheres:

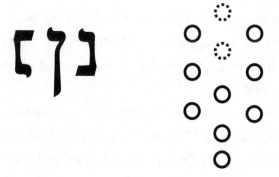

---

[96] Psalms 8:6 וַתְּחַסְּרֵהוּ מְּעַט מֵאֱ-לֹהִים וְכָבוֹד וְהָדָר תְּעַטְּרֵהוּ

[97] B.T. *Rosh Hashanah* 21B, חֲמִשִּׁים שַׁעֲרֵי בִינָה נִבְרְאוּ בָעוֹלָם, וְכוּלָן נִיתְּנוּ לְמֹשֶׁה חָסֵר אֶחָד שֶׁנֶּאֱמַר, "וַתְּחַסְּרֵהוּ מְּעַט מֵאֱ-לֹהִים" (תהלים ח', ו').

Although most commentators interpret מֵאֱ-לֹהִים in this verse to mean "than the angels," it is translated here as "than God" consistent with the understanding of *Ma'or Einayim* in the following footnote.

[98] *Ma'or Einayim, Parashath Vayelech* הכוונה ...ונודע כי מ"ט שערי בינה נמסרו למשה חוץ מאחד שהשיג את מ"ט שערי בינה שאפשר לנבראים להשיג. משם ולמעלה אי אפשר לשום נברא להשיג מחמת ששער הנו"ן הוא עצם א-להותו של אין סוף ברוך הוא שאי אפשר בשום פנים להשיגו מלאכי מעלה כמו שנאמר, "אַיֵּה מְקוֹם כְּבוֹדוֹ" (*בקדושה שבתפילת מוסף*). ולפי זה השיג משה רבינו ע"ה כל מה שאפשר להשיג לנברא.

The bent *Nun* (נ) represents a bent person of faith — one whose faith is imperfect — whereas the straight Nun (ן) represents an upright person of faith — one whose faith is whole.[99]

The backwards *Nun* (ׂ) represents a third level of faith — faith in *Hashem's* absolute infinitude.

Hashem initiated Creation by creating various spiritual forces which correspond to the letters of the alphabet. The *Book of Formation* (סֵפֶר יְצִירָה) explains that *Hashem* expressed these forces through "text, tally, and tale" (סֵפֶר סְפַר סִפּוּר),[100] that is, through methods analogous to three forms of human communication — writing, numbering, and speech.

Text, tally, and tale do not apply to the backwards *Nun*. They have no meaning as part of the text of the *Torah* because they are merely markers which separate two verses from the rest of the text. Also, unlike the bent *Nun* (נ) or the straight *Nun* (ן), the backwards *Nun* (ׂ) has no numeric value. Finally, unlike other letters of the alphabet, the backwards *Nun* (ׂ) does not correspond to any sound and therefore has nothing to do with speech, or tale.

In light of the unique nature of the backwards *Nuns* (ׂ), Rabbi Yitzchak Isaac Chaver wrote, "These two *Nuns* are literally the glory of the Holy One, Blessed be He, and they are the mainstay of the world."[101]

The backwards *Nun* (ׂ) stands for a type of faith utterly divorced from those types of faith which have at least a partial connection to human intellect, just as the backwards *Nun* (ׂ) has

---

[99] B.T. *Shabbath* 104A נוּן כְּפוּפָה, נוּן פְּשׁוּטָה – נֶאֱמָן כָּפוּף, נֶאֱמָן פָּשׁוּט

[100] *Sefer Yetzirah* 1:1 וברא את עולמו בשלשה ספרים: בְּסֵפֶר וּסְפַר וְסִפּוּר

[101] *Siach Yitzchak* 1, *Derush Be'inyan Beth Nunin* citing *Zohar Chadash* דאלו ב׳ נונין הם כבודו של הקב״ה ממש והן עיקרו של עולם.

no connection to any form of human communication but serves merely as a symbol of demarcation.

The verses which the backwards *Nuns* mark off describe the way in which the Ark of the Covenant traveled through the Sinai Desert:

> When the Ark traveled, Moses would say, "Arise, *Hashem*, and let Your enemies scatter and Your opponents flee from before You." And when it rested, he would say, "Return, *Hashem*, to the myriads of thousands of Israel."[102]

The rabbis state that although the room in which the Ark stood was twenty cubits by twenty cubits, one could measure ten cubits from each wall to the Ark. Thus, miraculously, the Ark itself took up no space.[103] It was an aspect of infinity that was revealed in the finite world.

Likewise, the backwards *Nuns* "take up no space" because they are not really part of the text of the *Torah*, nor can they be expressed as sounds or numbers like the other letters of the alphabet.

Just as the other forms of the letter *Nun* represent different levels of faith, the backwards *Nun* (נ) symbolizes faith in the absolute infinitude of *Hashem* — a faith which can never be fully perfected.

Other kinds of faith can be complete. For example, it is possible to have complete faith in an ultimate redemption because Jews have experienced redemptions throughout history, such as the Exodus from Egypt or the deliverance from Haman

---

[102] Numbers 10:35-36 ‏(לה) וַיְהִי בִּנְסֹעַ הָאָרֹן וַיֹּאמֶר מֹשֶׁה, קוּמָה ה' וְיָפֻצוּ אֹיְבֶיךָ וְיָנֻסוּ מְשַׂנְאֶיךָ מִפָּנֶיךָ.‏
‏(לו) וּבְנֻחֹה יֹאמַר, שׁוּבָה ה' רִבְבוֹת אַלְפֵי יִשְׂרָאֵל.‏

[103] B.T. *Megillah* 10B ‏וְאָמַר רַבִּי לֵוִי: דָּבָר זֶה מַסֹּרֶת בְּיָדֵינוּ מֵאֲבוֹתֵינוּ – מְקוֹם אָרוֹן אֵינוּ מִן הַמִּדָּה‏

on *Purim*. By contrast, infinity is something which goes on forever without end. Human beings, who are limited creatures, can never fully experience infinity and can only understand it in a theoretical sense.

As a result, even those among the righteous who merit the level of the straight *Nun* (ן), i.e., faith unburdened by any doubts, cannot have absolutely perfect faith in *Hashem's* infinitude.

Even so, it is human faith in this concept which permits *Hashem's* infinite Divine light to pass through the system of spheres and create the physical world, as will be explained.[104]

◈ The Properties of Physical Light Allude to Those of Divine Light

When facing one another, the backwards *Nun* (כ) and the bent *Nun* (נ) resemble two concave mirrors facing one another.

To understand the significance of this, one must analyze how concave mirrors reflect light.

When the light rays which strike a concave mirror reflect away from its surface, they converge at a focal point along an imaginary line called the optical axis which runs through the center of the concave mirror, as illustrated below.

---

[104] The numeric value of "infinity" (אֵין סוֹף) hints at this because it is the same as "light" (אוֹר).

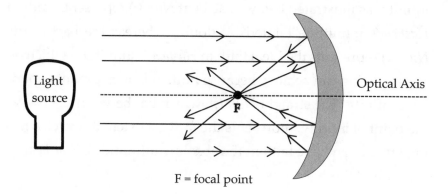

F = focal point

When an object lies on a point along the optical axis between the focal point and the mirror, its reflection appears larger than the actual object, as shown in the next diagram.

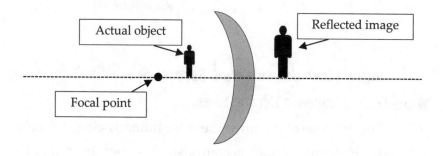

As an object moves away from the mirror towards the focal point, its reflected image grows larger, and when the object reaches the focal point, its reflection becomes infinitely large. Physicists therefore call the focal point the point of infinity.

When the three *Nuns* are used to depict the system of supernal worlds, the bent *Nun* (ב) and the backwards *Nun* (ﬢ) may be viewed as functioning like concave mirrors which focus the Divine light onto the straight *Nun* (ן) which lies at the point of infinity, as illustrated below. The bent *Nun* (נ) represents faith in *Hashem's* infinitude tainted by doubt, whereas the backwards *Nun* (ז) represents the ideal faith in *Hashem's* infinitude which no human being can achieve because human beings cannot experience infinity. The straight *Nun* (ן), which lies between the two at the point of infinity, represents the farthest extent to which a human being can have faith in the absolute infinitude of *Hashem* — the faith of the righteous.

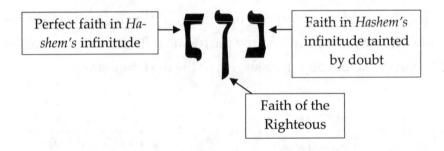

Perfect faith in *Hashem's* infinitude

Faith in *Hashem's* infinitude tainted by doubt

Faith of the Righteous

ജ്ജ How the Supernal Spheres Symbolized by these Nuns Focus Hashem's Divine Light

The purpose of the universe is for human beings to recognize God. If people cannot accomplish this, then by rights the universe should cease to exist. Recognition of God includes grasping His infinite nature, yet there are aspects of that infiniteness which people can never fathom. How, then, does the universe exist?

The set of spheres on the right side of the linear system of supernal worlds are referred to as the "Side of Kindness" (סִטְרָא דְחֶסֶד), while the set of spheres on the left side are referred to as the "Side of Judgment" (סִטְרָא דִגְבוּרָה).[105] The middle set of spheres is called "the Righteous One" (צַדִּיק),[106] as illustrated below.

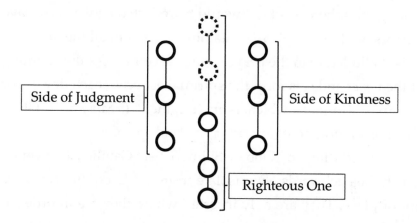

Sefer Habahir explains:

A single pillar [stretches] from the Earth to the Heavens, and its name is Righteous One (צַדִּיק), corresponding to the righteous. When there are righteous people in the world, it becomes powerful, and when not, it becomes weak. [This pillar] bears the entire world, as it is written, "The righteous one is the foundation of the world."[107] If it becomes [too] weak, then the world cannot endure. Therefore, even if there is but one righteous person in the world, that person causes the world to survive.[108]

---

[105] See *Zohar* III 179A. מִסְטַר דִּימִינָא דְּאִיהוּ חֶסֶד... מִסְּטְרָא דִּשְׂמָאלָא דְּאִיהוּ גְבוּרָה.

[106] *Otzar Eden Haganuz* 1:1 צדיק יסוד עולם באמצע והוא יוצא ממקומו של עולם והוא שר על אלה השניים.

[107] Proverbs 10:25 וְצַדִּיק יְסוֹד עוֹלָם

[108] *Sefer Habahir* 102 תנא: עמוד אחד מן הארץ לרקיע וצדיק שמו על שם הצדיקים. וכשיש צדיקים בעולם מתגבר ואם לאו מתחלש. והוא סובל כל העולם דכתיב, "וְצַדִּיק יְסוֹד עוֹלָם" (משלי י, כ"ה). ואם חלש לא יוכל להתקיים העולם. הלכך אפילו אין בעולם אלא צדיק אחד מעמיד העולם.

Although the spheres are depicted as arrays of straight lines, the Divine light does not descend into Creation through straight arrays of spheres. Rather, it reflects back and forth among the spheres, as light would be reflected between concave mirrors, with each sphere containing aspects of all the others.[109] This is alluded to in the prayer which accompanies the counting of the *Omer* and sets forth the spiritual aspect of each day — for example, Kindness which is in Judgment (חֶסֶד שֶׁבִּגְבוּרָה), Glory which is in Judgment (תִּפְאֶרֶת שֶׁבִּגְבוּרָה), and so on.[110]

According to Rabban Shimon ben Gamliel, the verses which the backwards *Nuns* isolate from the rest of the *Torah* are out of place. They are only inserted where they are in order to separate between two misdeeds deserving of punishment.[111] The verses which precede them report how the Jewish nation ran away from Mount Sinai as a child flees from school.[112] The verses which follow them describe how the Jews fabricated bogus complaints in order to find excuses to distance themselves from *Hashem*.[113]

Rabban Shimon ben Gamliel's statement hints that the backwards *Nun* (נ) mitigates judgment. This is true even though it lies on the "Side of Judgment" (סִטְרָא דִגְבוּרָה) because the judgment it represents is mixed with and modified by other Divine Attributes.

---

[109] *Shelah Hakadosh, Masecheth Chullin, Torah Ohr* כִּי הַמַּשְׁפִּיעַ חוֹזֵר לִהְיוֹת מְקַבֵּל וְהַמְקַבֵּל מַשְׁפִּיעַ, וְהַפָּנִים אָחוֹר וְהָאָחוֹר פָּנִים, וְהַשְׂמֹאל יָמִין וְהַיָּמִין שְׂמֹאל.

[110] See Appendix C for illustrations of how the supernal spheres interact in a manner which resembles concave mirrors.

[111] B.T. *Shabbath* 116A. רַבָּן שִׁמְעוֹן בֶּן גַּמְלִיאֵל אוֹמֵר: עֲתִידָה פָּרָשָׁה זוֹ שֶׁתֵּיעָקֵר מִכָּאן וְתִכָּתֵב בִּמְקוֹמָהּ. וְלָמָּה כְּתָבָהּ כַּאן? כְּדֵי לְהַפְסִיק בֵּין פּוּרְעָנוּת רִאשׁוֹנָה לְפוּרְעָנוּת שְׁנִיָּיה.

[112] *Tosafoth* on B.T. *Shabbath* 116A, sub verba "*Puranuth Rishonah*" (פורענות ראשונה): שֶׁנָּסְעוּ מֵהַר סִינַי דֶּרֶךְ שְׁלֹשֶׁת יָמִים כְּתִינוֹק הַיּוֹצֵא מִבֵּית הַסֵּפֶר שֶׁבּוֹרֵחַ לוֹ וְהוֹלֵךְ לוֹ.

[113] *Rashi* on Numbers 11:1 sub verba "*Kemithonanim*" (כְּמִתְאוֹנְנִים): אֵין מִתְאוֹנְנִים אֶלָּא לְשׁוֹן עֲלִילָה — מְבַקְשִׁים עֲלִילָה הֵיךְ לִפְרוֹשׁ מֵאַחֲרֵי הַמָּקוֹם.

The bent *Nun* (נ) lies on the side of Kindness (סִטְרָא דְחֶסֶד), representing forgiveness. The *Torah* alludes to this in the verse, "He maintains kindness unto thousands [of generations] and tolerates iniquity,"[114] where the bent *Nun* (נ) which starts the verse is written larger than elsewhere in the *Torah* scroll (נֹצֵר חֶסֶד).[115]

If *Hashem* would apply strict judgment to humankind for its defective understanding of His infinite nature, Creation would cease to exist because Creation's purpose is for human beings to recognize Him, and perfect recognition of His infinite nature is not possible. On the other hand, if *Hashem* would apply absolute kindness and excuse humanity from any obligation to appreciate His infiniteness, Creation would also cease because, again, its purpose could not be achieved.

However, the side of Judgment is not pure judgment, nor is the side of Kindness pure kindness. The curvature of the *Nuns* represents how the vertical arrays of spheres do not behave as straight lines would, but rather like concave mirrors which direct the Divine light onto a focal point — the point of infinity. That point lies on the central pillar between them — the straight *Nun* (ן) which represents the absolute faith of *Tzaddikim* in *Hashem's*

---

[114] Exodus 34:7   נֹצֵר חֶסֶד לָאֲלָפִים נֹשֵׂא עָוֹן וָפֶשַׁע וְחַטָּאָה וְנַקֵּה לֹא יְנַקֶּה פֹּקֵד עֲוֹן אָבוֹת עַל בָּנִים וְעַל בְּנֵי בָנִים עַל שִׁלֵּשִׁים וְעַל רִבֵּעִים.

[115] *Otzar Hachayim* on *Parashath Titzaveh*   "נֹצֵר חֶסֶד" – נון רבתי להמתיק דיני הנחש נון כפופה הידוע.

infinite nature even though they cannot fully grasp it.[116] It is this acute awareness which keeps the world in existence.[117]

This explains the following passage from the *Zohar*:

> The letter *Samech* (ס) entered [God's presence] and declared before Him: Master of the Universe, it should be pleasing before You to create the world through me because I include the concept of supporting those who fall, as it is written, "*Hashem* supports all who fall,"[118] [and the word for "supports" (סוֹמֵךְ) resembles *Samech* (ס)].
>
> "It is precisely because of this that you must remain in your place and not move from it," explained *Hashem*. "If you leave your place, what will become of those who fall in as much as you support them?"
>
> Immediately, [*Samech* (ס)] departed from His presence.
>
> The letter *Nun* (נ) entered [God's presence] and declared before Him: Master of the Universe, it should be pleasing before You to create the world through me because it is written [that You are] "awesome of praises"[119] (נוֹרָא תְהִלֹּת), [a phrase that commences with the letter *Nun* (נ)], and praises pertain to the righteous, [as it is written, "Sing, righteous ones, for

---

[116] See *Emek Hamelech* 1:42 אות נון פשוטה... וכל ההתפשטות הוא חסד, להורות כי הצדיקים מהפכים דין לרחמים.

The understanding great scholars such as *Rashi* or the *Vilna Gaon* have of a *Torah* verse is much more profound than that of an ordinary Jew even though everyone has some understanding of the verse. Similarly, although every Jew can and should recognize that *Hashem's* infinitude is unfathomable, the grasp which *Tzaddikim* have of this concept is far clearer than that of ordinary Jews.

[117] See *Breishith Rabbah* 12:15 כך אמר הקב"ה: "אם בורא אני את העולם במידת הרחמים, הוי חטייה סגיאין. במידת הדין, היאך העולם יכול לעמוד? אלא הרי אני בורא אותו במידת הדין ובמידת הרחמים, והלואי יעמוד".

[118] Psalms 145:14 סוֹמֵךְ ה' לְכָל הַנֹּפְלִים וְזוֹקֵף לְכָל הַכְּפוּפִים

[119] Exodus 15:11 מִי כָמֹכָה בָּאֵלִם ה' מִי כָּמֹכָה נֶאְדָּר בַּקֹּדֶשׁ נוֹרָא תְהִלֹּת עֹשֵׂה פֶלֶא

Hashem; for the upright] "praise is fitting"[120] (נָאוָה תְהִלָּה), [and this expression also begins with a *Nun* (נ)].

"*Nun* (נ), return to your place," answered *Hashem*, "for it was for you that *Samech* (ס) returned to her place so that you can be supported by her [because the expression "those who fall" (נוֹפְלִים) begins with a *Nun* (נ)]."

Immediately, [*Nun*] returned to her place.[121]

If the Side of Kindness and the Side of Judgment represented by the bent *Nun* (נ) and the backwards *Nun* (ן) would remain separate from one another and never interact, they would fall, and Creation would collapse and disappear. However, these *Nuns* face one another and focus the Divine light on a focal point which lies equidistant between them. Therefore, it is as if they form between the two of them the letter *Samech* (ס), as illustrated below.[122]

---

[120] Psalms 33:1 רַנְּנוּ צַדִּיקִים בַּה' לַיְשָׁרִים נָאוָה תְהִלָּה

[121] *Zohar* I:2B-3A עָאלַת אָת ס'. אָמְרָה קַמֵּיה: "רִבּוֹן עָלְמִין, נִיחָא קַמָּךְ לְמִבְרֵי בִּי עָלְמָא, דְּאִית בִּי סְמִיכָא לְנָפְלִין, דִּכְתִיב, "סוֹמֵךְ ה' לְכָל הַנּוֹפְלִים" (תהלים קמ"ה, י"ד). אָמַר לָהּ: "עַל דָּא אַנְתְּ צָרִיךְ לְאַתְרָךְ וְלָא תָזוּז מִנֵּיהּ. אִי אַתְּ נָפִיק מֵאַתְרָךְ מַה תְּהֵא עֲלַיְיהוּ דְּאִנּוּן נְפִילִין הוֹאִיל וְאִנּוּן סְמִיכִין עֲלָךְ?" מִיָּד נָפְקַת מִקַּמֵּיהּ. עָאלַת אָת נ'. אָמְרָה קַמֵּיה: "רִבּוֹן עָלְמָא, נִיחָא קַמָּךְ לְמִבְרֵי בִּי עָלְמָא, דְּבִי כְּתִיב, "נוֹרָא תְהִלּוֹת" (שמות ט"ו, י"א), וּתְהִלָּה דְּצַדִּיקִים – "נָאוָה תְהִלָּה" (תהלים ל"ג, א'). אָמַר לָהּ: "נו"ן תּוּב לְאַתְרָךְ, דְּהָא בְגִינָךְ תָּבַת סַמָּ"ךְ לְאַתְרָהּ וְהֱוֵי סָמִיךְ עֲלָהּ". מִיָּד תָּבַת לְאַתְרָהּ וְנָפְקַת מִקַּמֵּיהּ.

Rashi on Exodus 15:11 comments that "awesome of praises" means that people should feel apprehensive about praising *Hashem* because they can never properly articulate His true greatness (נוֹרָא תְהִלֹּת – יראוי מלהגיד תהילותיך פן ימעטו כמו שכתוב, "לְךָ דֻמִיָּה תְהִלָּה" (תהלים ס"ה, ב'). Even the greatest people can neither understand nor express *Hashem's* infinitude to its fullest extent.

[122] See *Zera Kodesh, Parashath Beha'alothecha* "וַיְהִי בִּנְסֹעַ הָאָרֹן" – כבר כתבתי בעניין הב' נוני"ן הסובבים, שהם דוגמת ב' עפעפי עינא, וזהו דוגמת אות סמ"ך.

The circular shape of the *Samech* (ס) symbolizes infinity, as the *Shelah Hakadosh* states, "The circle indicates that which goes around and around without end."[123] The bent *Nun* "falls" as does the backwards *Nun* because from the perspective of either pure kindness or pure judgment the universe cannot endure. Only when they blend together and are, so to speak, supported by the *Samech* (ס) can the world survive.

ಬ Another Way of Understanding the Backwards Nun (ן) ಬಬ Everything the Merciful One Does is for the Best[124]

As stated above, the rabbis do not attribute any numeric value to the backwards *Nun* (ן). Nevertheless, because an ordinary *Nun* (נ) has a numeric value of fifty, perhaps a backwards *Nun* (ן) may be viewed as symbolizing the opposite — negative fifty (-50).

Although people commonly speak of negative numbers, such numbers are really imaginary because there cannot be less than nothing. As a simple example, suppose that Reuven owes his bank $100,000.00. That is a positive number. If Reuven's assets are only $75,000.00, that is also a positive number. Even so, Reuven is said to have a negative net worth of $25,000.00. There is, however, no such thing as negative $25,000.00, and this is merely a convenient way of describing how Reuven's debt exceeds his assets. If Reuven wins the lottery and then mistakenly pays $110,000.00 to the bank to settle his debt, he might be said to have negative debt, but that is just another way of saying that

---

[123] *Shelah Hakadosh, Toldoth Ha'adam, Rimzei Otioth Lechathimath Hahakdamah* הָעִגּוּל מוֹרֶה עַל דָּבָר הַחוֹזֵר חָלִילָה וְאֵין לָהּ סוֹף.
[124] B.T. *Berachoth* 60B ."לְעוֹלָם יְהֵא אָדָם רָגִיל לוֹמַר, "כָּל דְּעָבִיד רַחֲמָנָא לְטָב עֲבִיד

the bank owes him a $10,000.00 refund. He cannot really owe the bank less than zero.

The *Malbim* notes that *Hashem* created light in such a way that when it is absent, there is darkness.[125] When light is present, one can speak of it in comparative terms — more light or less light. Although darkness is not a substance, but merely the absence of light, one can also speak of it in comparative terms. As long as some light is present there can be more darkness or less darkness. If light is totally absent, however, such comparisons cannot be made. No greater amount of darkness can exist than when there is no light at all. There is no such thing as "negative light."

ೞೞೞೞ The Darkness in Egypt

The *Torah* states:

Hashem told Moses, "Stretch forth your hand over the heavens, and there shall be darkness in the Land of Egypt — and they shall feel the darkness." Moses stretched his hand over the heavens, and there was deep darkness in all the Land of Egypt for three days. A man could not see his brother, and no man could rise from his place for three days, but for all the Children of Israel there was light wherever they were.[126]

---

[125] *Malbim* ad. loc. אם היה עניין האור עצם בלתי מקבל מקרים, לא היה משתנה ולא יצוייר חושך, אבל ע״י שיצר אור, והוא שעצם האור הוא עצם בעל מקרים, עי״כ ימצא החושך שהוא העדר האור.

[126] Exodus 10:21-23. (כא) וַיֹּאמֶר ה׳ אֶל מֹשֶׁה נְטֵה יָדְךָ עַל הַשָּׁמַיִם וִיהִי חֹשֶׁךְ עַל אֶרֶץ מִצְרָיִם וְיָמֵשׁ חֹשֶׁךְ. (כב) וַיֵּט מֹשֶׁה אֶת יָדוֹ עַל הַשָּׁמָיִם וַיְהִי חֹשֶׁךְ אֲפֵלָה בְּכָל אֶרֶץ מִצְרַיִם שְׁלֹשֶׁת יָמִים. (כג) לֹא רָאוּ אִישׁ אֶת אָחִיו וְלֹא קָמוּ אִישׁ מִתַּחְתָּיו שְׁלֹשֶׁת יָמִים וּלְכָל בְּנֵי יִשְׂרָאֵל הָיָה אוֹר בְּמוֹשְׁבֹתָם.

The *Midrash* elaborates: "How much was that darkness? Our sages say it was thick as a *Dinar*, as it states, 'they shall feel the darkness' — darkness that had substance."[127]

At first glance, this seems to mean that there is such a thing as "negative light" — a darkness which is palpable and has substance.

How can this be?

When *Hashem* initiated Creation, He said, "Let there be light,"[128] referring to the Divine light which is the source of all created things. The darkness in Egypt did not consist of "negative light," but of a complete absence of Divine light during which the statement "Let there be light" was removed.[129]

Human beings can interact with their surroundings because all of Creation consists of various manifestations of *Hashem's* Divine light, the same substance from which they themselves are composed. When this light was completely removed from their environment, the Egyptians found themselves surrounded by non-existence, something with which they could not interact. This is what prevented them from moving from their places, and this is what gave the darkness what seemed to be a quality of substance and solidity.

ஐஒஐ Negative Good Does Not Exist

Just as darkness is nothing more than the absence of light, evil is merely the absence of good. One can speak of the presence

---

[127] *Shemoth Rabbah* 14:1 — "וְיָמֵשׁ חֹשֶׁךְ", שנאמר, עבה כדינר היה: רבותינו אמרו ? כמה היה אותו חשך שהיה בו ממש.

[128] Genesis 1:3 וַיֹּאמֶר אֱ-לֹהִים יְהִי אוֹר וַיְהִי אוֹר

[129] *Shem Mishmuel, Parashath Bo* 5674 ,"יְהִי אוֹר" שבמכת חושך נסתלק מהמצרים המאמר ולעומתם זכו ישראל לאור שנברא ביום ראשון.

of more good or less good, but there is no such thing as "negative good." Evil has no true existence.

The backwards *Nun* (נ) symbolizes the faith of the Jewish nation in this concept. No matter how negative matters appear, Jews believe that everything comes from *Hashem's* Divine light. Accordingly, there are really only degrees of good, but there is never evil.

May we merit to perceive this clearly with the coming of *Mashiach* speedily and in our days!

The Letter Kaf (כ): Connecting the Finite to the Infinite

80 Each Letter of the Alphabet Wanted Hashem to Use it to Initiate Creation

The *Zohar* describes how each letter of the Hebrew alphabet came before the Master of the Universe in reverse order starting from *Tav* (ת) and requested that He use it to commence Creation. The Holy One, Blessed be He, rejected each letter until *Beth* (ב) appeared and became both the beginning of creation and the first letter of the *Torah*.

Kaf (כ) descended before Him, a letter from His Throne of Glory. It trembled and said, "Master of the Universe, it should be pleasing before You to create the world through me, for I am Your honor."[130]

When *Kaf* (כ) descended from [the] Throne of Glory, two hundred thousand worlds quaked, the Throne [itself] shook, and all the worlds wobbled [on the verge of] collapse.

The Holy One, Blessed be He, said, "*Kaf, Kaf,* what are you doing here? I shall not create the world from you! Return to your place, for you include [the concept of] annihilation[131]... Return to your Throne and stay there!"

At that moment, [*Kaf* (כ)] departed from before Him and returned to its place.[132]

Although *Hashem* rejected all the other letters except *Beth* (ב), He did not warn of cataclysmic consequences if He used them to commence Creation. *Kaf* (כ) is the only letter concerning which the *Zohar* states that the universe was about to disintegrate when it appeared before the Holy One, Blessed be He.

What is so unique about this letter?

In the above passage, the *Kaf* (כ) stated that it represents God's honor (כָּבוֹד). Honor cannot exist without at least two parties — one to give the honor and one to receive it. The Hebrew for "honor" (כָּבוֹד) alludes to this. If the *Kaf* (כ) at its beginning is

---

[130] *Kaf* (כ) alludes to *Hashem's* Throne of Glory, or Honor, because both "throne" (כִּסֵּא) and "honor" (כָּבוֹד) start with this letter (*Kithvei Ha'arizal, Sha'ar Maamarei Rashbi, Parashath Breishith* ואות כ"ף רומזת אל כסא הכבוד).

[131] The word used here for "annihilation" (כְּלָיָה) starts with *Kaf* (כ).

[132] *Zohar* I:3A נְחֵתָא כ׳ מִן קֳדָמוֹהִי, אָת מֵעַל כּוּרְסֵי יְקָרֵיהּ. אִזְדַּעְזָעַת וְאַמְרָה קַמֵּיהּ: "רִבּוֹן עָלְמָא, נִיחָא קַמָּךְ לְמִבְרֵי בִּי עָלְמָא דְּאֲנָא כְּבוֹדָךְ". וְכַד נְחֵתַת כ׳ מֵעַל כּוּרְסֵי יְקָרֵיהּ, אִזְדַּעְזָעוּ מָאתָן אֶלֶף עָלְמִין, וְאִזְדַּעְזָע כֻּרְסָיָּא, וְכֻלְּהוּ עָלְמִין אִזְדַּעְזָעוּ לְמִנְפַּל. אָמַר לַהּ קוּדְשָׁא בְּרִיךְ הוּא: "כ"ף כ"ף, מָה אַתְּ עָבִיד הָכָא? דְּלָא אִבְרֵי בָּךְ עָלְמָא. תּוּב לְאַתְרָךְ דְּהָא בָּךְ כְּלָיָה... תּוּב לְכָרְסָיָיךְ וְהֱוֵי תַּמָּן". בְּהַהִיא שַׁעֲתָא נָפְקַת מִקַּמֵּיהּ וְתָבַת לְדוּכְתַּהּ.

A similar passage appears in *Batei Midrashoth* II, *Midrash Othioth D'Rabbi Akiva Hashalem, Nosach* 2.

removed, the remaining letters (בוד) mean "single" or "isolated,"[133] a condition in which honor is not possible.

The rabbis teach that *Hashem* has an Attribute of Kingship but that there cannot be a king without a people over whom to rule.[134] *Kaf* (כ) represents honor and the purpose of Creation, which is to have human beings honor the King of Kings. This purpose preceded the creation of all the worlds. If *Kaf* (כ) would leave its place — if this purpose could not be fulfilled — then all that would remain of "honor" (כָּבוֹד) would be "isolation" (בוד). God would remain alone, and Creation would cease to exist.

All of this is true only from a human perspective. In reality, *Hashem* is completely independent of Creation and has no need for it. When the letter *Kaf* (כ) appears in front of a word, it indicates similarity or likeness (כַּף הַדִּמְיוֹן). Human beings cannot fathom God's purpose in creating the universe, and the idea that He did so to receive honor from His creatures merely gives human beings a vague insight into this matter — a semblance of the purpose of Creation.[135]

≈≈≈ The Throne of Glory

Hashem is infinite but Creation is finite. The Throne of Glory stands between the two.[136] The shape of the letter *Kaf* (כ)

---

[133] *Rabbeinu Bachye* on Leviticus 16:4 שכן לשון "בד" יחידי; *Gur Aryeh* on Exodus 30:34 כי לשון "בד" הוא לשון "בדד".

[134] *S'fath Emeth, Vayikra Lepesach* 5654 כי אין מלך בלא עם ולתכלית זה נברא כל העולם להיות מלכותו יתברך שמו מתגלה.

[135] See *Arvei Nachal, Parashath Va'era* מצינו לרז"ל בכמה מקומות שנשנה במשנה או בברייתא כ"ף הדמיון. אמרו הם שאינו דומה בכל צד, אלא דומה בצד זולת צד, כאומרם בכמה דוכתי כשהקשה דבמתניתין תני שדבר זה כזה והאמורא אומר שיש חילוק דין ביניהם. השיב על זה המתרץ כזה ולא כזה דאלו בהא כך ובהא אינו כך.

[136] *Chatham Sofer* on Genesis 32:2 ישראל סבא הוא יעקב בעצמו שצורתו חקוקה בכיסא הכבוד הוא עומד בין ה' וביננו; *Sefer Habrith,* Part II, Discourse 14 *Ha'ahavah Vehasimchah,* chapter 5 בשם ספר הקדוש ברית מנוחה שאם היה רשות לעין לראות, היו רואים איך כיסא הכבוד עומד על ראש כל צדיק, וזה סוד אמרם ז"ל האבות הן הן המרכבה.

symbolizes the finite because it is a semicircle with clearly defined beginning and end points. *Samech* (ס), on the other hand, is a full circle, and a circle represents infinity because it has no beginning or end points.[137] Together these two letters spell "throne" (כֵּס) in the verse, "for the hand [of *Hashem*] is on the throne (כֵּס) of God [to pledge] war for *Hashem* against Amalek from generation to generation."[138] Ordinarily, "throne" is spelled with an *Alef* (א) (כִּסֵּא), but this verse uses a shortened form (כֵּס) because "as long as the offspring of Amalek is in the world, neither the Name nor the throne is complete."[139]

The Throne of Glory, which represents the connection between the infinite and the finite, is perfected by faith in God. This faith is represented by the letter *Alef* (א) which has a numeric value of one. Faith in God's absolute oneness and infinitude powers and perfects the connection between the infinite and the finite.

When traveling through the Sinai Desert, the Jews asked, "Is *Hashem* in our midst or not?"[140] The word "not" (אָיִן) in this verse may be understood as alluding to infinity (אֵין סוֹף), so that this question can be taken to mean, "Can *Hashem*, who is infinite, be in the midst of we who are finite?" This doubt provoked an attack by Amalek, as the next verse states, "And Amalek came to make war with Israel in Rephidim."[141] Amalek represents

---

[137] *Shelah Hakadosh, Toldoth Ha'adam, Rimzei Otioth Lechathimath Hahakdamah*
הָעִגּוּל מוֹרֶה עַל דָּבָר הַחוֹזֵר חָלִילָה וְאֵין לָהּ סוֹף.

[138] Exodus 17:16 וַיֹּאמֶר כִּי יָד עַל כֵּס יָהּ מִלְחָמָה לַה' בַּעֲמָלֵק מִדֹּר דֹּר

[139] *Rashi* on Exodus 17:16 quoting *Midrash Tanchuma, Parashath Kee Theitzei* 11
רבי לוי בשם רבי אחא בר חיננא אומר: כל זמן שזרעו של עמלק בעולם לא השם שלם ולא הכיסא שלם.

[140] Exodus 17:7 וַיִּקְרָא שֵׁם הַמָּקוֹם מַסָּה וּמְרִיבָה עַל רִיב בְּנֵי יִשְׂרָאֵל וְעַל נַסֹּתָם אֶת ה' לֵאמֹר הֲיֵשׁ ה' בְּקִרְבֵּנוּ אִם אָיִן.

[141] Exodus 17:8 וַיָּבֹא עֲמָלֵק וַיִּלָּחֶם עִם יִשְׂרָאֵל בִּרְפִידִם; *Zohar* II:65A אָתוּן אָמַר קוּדְשָׁא בְּרִיךְ הוּא: אֲמַרְתּוּן: "הֲיֵשׁ ה' בְּקִרְבֵּנוּ אִם אָיִן !" חַיֵּי אֲנִי מוֹסֵר אֶתְכֶם לַכֶּלֶב. מִיָּד "וַיָּבֹא עֲמָלֵק".

doubt,[142] including doubt about how the Infinite One, Blessed be He, can create a finite universe and yet be present in it. Since doubt is the opposite of faith, the Throne of Glory cannot be perfected as long as Amalek exists.

ഇൽഇൽഇൽ How Faith (אֱמוּנָה) Maintains the Connection between the Infinite and the Finite

The sages call the Divine Light which God projects into the physical universe "direct light" (אוֹר יָשָׁר). By having faith in God, performing good deeds, and studying the *Torah*, people reflect the Divine Light back to its Source. This is called "returning light" (אוֹר חוֹזֵר).[143]

The semicircular *Kaf* (כ), which symbolizes finiteness, represents the direct light which the Infinite One projects to create a finite universe. Its mirror image looks like the English letter "C" and represents the reflected light which people propel back into the spiritual realm.[144] As illustrated below, when these two events occur simultaneously, the *Kaf* (כ) and its mirror image (ɔ) join to form a circle, or *Samech* (ס), which symbolizes infinity.

ס

---

[142] The numeric value of "Amalek" (עֲמָלֵק) equals "doubt" (סָפֵק). (*Tzemach Tzaddik, Parashath Beshalach* פירוש (שמות י"ז, ז'-ח'). וַיָּבֹא עֲמָלֵק וגו'" "הֲיֵשׁ ה' בְּקִרְבֵּנוּ אִם אָיִן.
(שעל ידי שהיה ספק להם אם יש ה' בקרבם, בא עמל"ק שגימ' ספ"ק).

[143] *Mavoh Lechochmath Hakabbalah* 2:5:2 וגם תכלית הכלים היה בשביל הגבול, שעל ידי זה נעשתה בחירה ורצון לעבודה, עד שעל ידי זה יהיה בחינת שכר ועונש שלהם העולים בבחינת מיין נוקבין בסוד אור חוזר.

[144] *Shelah Hakadosh, Masecheth Pesachim, Matzah Ashirah* 401 שֶׁהָאוֹר הַחוֹזֵר הוּא כְּמוֹ חוֹתָם הַמִּתְהַפֵּךְ.

The Infinite One's effort to reveal Himself in the finite universe and the willingness of humanity to accept and believe in Him perfect the Throne of Glory (כִּסֵּא הַכָּבוֹד) and allow the physical realm to exist.

Although all human effort to serve *Hashem* reflects the Divine Light back into the spiritual realm, it is the highest level of faith held by a very few exceptional *Tzaddikim* which ensures the connection between Creation and the Infinite One, Blessed be He, as the *Talmud* explains:

> Rav Yehudah said in the name of Rav: At the time when *Moshe Rabbeinu* ascended on high, he found the Holy One, Blessed be He, sitting and tying crowns to letters [of the alphabet].[145]
>
> *Moshe Rabbeinu* inquired, "Why must You have these [crowns]?"
>
> "There is one person who will live after several generations," answered God, "and Akiva ben Yosef is his name. In the future he will derive from each and every strand [of these crowns] piles upon piles of *Halachoth*."
>
> …"Show me his reward."
>
> "Turn behind you."
>
> *Moshe Rabbeinu* turned around and saw [how the Romans brutally tortured Rabbi Akiva to death and] weighed his flesh in the market. He declared, "Master of the Universe, is this the *Torah*, and is this its reward!?!"

---

[145] When written in *Torah* scrolls, *Tefillin,* and *Mezuzoth,* some letters have flourishes called crowns — שִׁעְטְנֵז גֵּץ (B.T. *Menachoth* 29B אמר רבא: שבעה אותיות צריכות זיונין, ואלו הן: שעטנ"ז ג"ץ). Jewish scribes also customarily add one or two flourishes to certain other letters (*Shulchan Aruch, Orach Chaim* 36:3 צריך לתייג שעטנ"ז ג"ץ והסופרים נהגו לתייג אותיות אחרות).

God answered, "Be silent, for so it arose in thought before Me."[146]

This passage may be understood as follows.

Hashem uses spiritual forces symbolized by the letters of the Hebrew alphabet to create and maintain the universe. Crowns refer to the infinite[147] because they are circular like the letter *Samech* (ס). *Moshe Rabbeinu* observed *Hashem* tying crowns to the letters — creating and maintaining the connection between the finite and the infinite.

Hashem's purpose in creating the universe is for people to recognize and serve Him, so He fashioned this connection in such a way that it could only continue to exist by virtue of human faith.

Moshe Rabbeinu asked *Hashem* who would have sufficient faith to maintain this connection. God then revealed that *Tzaddikim* such as Rabbi Akiva, whose faith was so powerful that he recited *Shema* while being tortured to death,[148] would maintain the connection between the finite and the infinite. This is why the Holy One, Blessed be He declared, "so it arose in thought before Me." "So" (כָּךְ) is written with two *Kafs*, hinting at

---

[146] B.T. *Menachoth* 29B אָמַר רַב יְהוּדָה אָמַר רַב: בְּשָׁעָה שֶׁעָלָה מֹשֶׁה לַמָּרוֹם מְצָאוֹ לְהַקָּדוֹשׁ בָּרוּךְ הוּא שֶׁיּוֹשֵׁב וְקוֹשֵׁר כְּתָרִים לָאוֹתִיּוֹת. אָמַר לְפָנָיו: "רִבּוֹנוֹ שֶׁל עוֹלָם, מִי מְעַכֵּב עַל יָדְךָ ?" אָמַר לוֹ: "אָדָם אֶחָד יֵשׁ שֶׁעָתִיד לִהְיוֹת בְּסוֹף כַּמָּה דוֹרוֹת וַעֲקִיבָא בֶּן יוֹסֵף שְׁמוֹ שֶׁעָתִיד לִדְרוֹשׁ עַל כָּל קוֹץ וְקוֹץ תִּילִין תִּילִין שֶׁל הֲלָכוֹת"...אָמַר לְפָנָיו: "רִבּוֹנוֹ שֶׁל עוֹלָם...הַרְאֵנִי שְׂכָרוֹ." אָמַר לוֹ: "חֲזוֹר [לַאֲחוֹרֶךָ]". חָזַר לַאֲחוֹרָיו. רָאָה שֶׁשּׁוֹקְלִין בְּשָׂרוֹ בְּמָקוּלִין. אָמַר לְפָנָיו: "רִבּוֹנוֹ שֶׁל עוֹלָם, זוֹ תּוֹרָה וְזוֹ שְׂכָרָהּ ?" אָמַר לוֹ: "שְׁתֹק ! כָּךְ עָלָה בְּמַחֲשָׁבָה לְפָנַי".

[147] *Zohar* III:258A states that the term "crown" refers to the infinite דְּכֶתֶר אֵין סוֹף אִתְקְרֵי. In addition, *Kithvei Ha'arizal, Sha'arei Tzedek* 10 states that the crowns which appear on the letters of the *Torah* scroll allude to the infinite ודע כי בסוד הכתר הזה נאחזים כל הסודות הפנימיים של קוצי האותיות שבספר תורה וכתריהם. וכולם נרמזים ונאחזים בכתר ואומם הקוצות והכתרים מורין שאין לתורה סוף וגבול בחכמה מצד הכתר העליון. כמו שקוצו של יוד הוא סוד הכתר העליון שאינו מושג ואין לו סוף וקץ וכן כל קוצי האותיות והתגין וכתרים הם סודדות הכתר הנאחזים בעולם העליון שאין לו סוף וגבול וקץ.

[148] B.T. *Berachoth* 61B בְּשָׁעָה שֶׁהוֹצִיאוּ אֶת רַבִּי עֲקִיבָא לַהֲרִיגָה זְמַן קְרִיאַת שְׁמַע הָיָה וְהָיוּ סוֹרְקִים אֶת בְּשָׂרוֹ בְּמַסְרְקוֹת שֶׁל בַּרְזֶל וְהָיָה מְקַבֵּל עָלָיו עוֹל מַלְכוּת שָׁמַיִם.

the combination of two semicircular *Kafs* to form a circle, as described above.

The *Zohar* explains that Adam was "a formation of God's hands" (יְצִיר כַּפָּיו), an expression which can be taken to mean "a formation of two *Kafs*." God instilled in Adam the power of the two *Kafs* — the ability to maintain the connection between finite Creation and the Infinite One through faith. Prior to sinning, Adam's faith in *Hashem* kept the connection between the finite and the infinite intact. Later, Jacob attained a level of faith comparable to that of Adam before the sin, and he too maintained this connection.[149]

The forces of evil represented by Esau oppose Jacob's faith. They do not realize that the universe would cease to exist without this connection, and they wish to sever it, thinking to free themselves of *Hashem's* dominion. As the *Torah* records, Esau's guardian angel touched "the curve of Jacob's thigh" (בְּכַף יְרֵכוֹ).[150] The term the *Torah* uses here for "curve" is *Kaf* (כַּף), hinting that the angel wanted to damage the connection between the finite and the infinite represented by the letter *Kaf* (כַּף). In addition, the numeric value of the term the verse uses for "curve" (בְּכַף) is the same as that of "faith" (אֱמוּנָה). Esau's guardian angel sought to break the connection between the finite and the infinite by damaging Jacob's faith.

---

149 *Zohar* II:70A וְהָא כְּגַוְונָא דְּאָדָם קַדְמָאָה דְּאִיהוּ קֶדֶם לַיְצִירָה, יְצִיר כַּפָּיו שֶׁל הַקָּדוֹשׁ בָּרוּךְ הוּא, אוּף הָכִי יַעֲקֹב רֵאשׁוֹן רֵאשׁוֹן לִשְׁלֵימוּ.

How did the universe remain in existence between the time of Adam and that of Jacob and between the time of *Moshe Rabbeinu* and that of Rabbi Akiva?

Hashem transcends time, so past, present, and future are all the same to Him. The fact that Jacob and Rabbi Akiva would live in the future was therefore sufficient to keep the universe in existence even before they were born.

150 Genesis 32:26 וַיַּרְא כִּי לֹא יָכֹל לוֹ וַיִּגַּע בְּכַף יְרֵכוֹ וַתֵּקַע כַּף יֶרֶךְ יַעֲקֹב בְּהֵאָבְקוֹ עִמּוֹ

More than anything else, it is specifically the faith displayed by a person who dies for the sanctification of God's Name which maintains the connection between the infinite and the finite. Intellect has limitations, so the appreciation of *Hashem* which a person acquires through reasoning is also limited. By contrast, the faith shown by those willing to sacrifice their lives for their belief in God and His *Torah* exceeds the limitations of intellect and has a quality of limitlessness. This attracts and arouses the infiniteness of the Divine Presence and connects it to the finite realm.[151]

Without *Tzaddikim* such as Rabbi Akiva who are willing to die for the sake of the *Torah*, the world could not exist. This is expressed in the *Yom Kippur Musaf* prayer which lists ten exceptionally great sages who were cruelly murdered by idolaters. When the angels asked the Holy One, Blessed be He, "Is this the *Torah*, and is this its reward?" *Hashem* answered, "If I hear another sound, I will turn the universe to water. I will cause the lower realms to revert to emptiness and nothingness."[152] Without the faith of those who are willing to sacrifice their lives for *Hashem's* sake, the connection between the finite and infinite would fail, and the finite universe would cease to exist.

---

[151] See *Shelah Hakadosh, Toldoth Adam, Hasha'ar Hagadol* כִּי בִּזְכוּת הַצַּדִּיק הַמְדַּמֶּה הַצּוּרָה לְיוֹצְרָהּ, שְׁכִינָה שׁוֹרָה בַּתַּחְתּוֹנִים, וְיוֹתֵר עַל הַצּוּרָה הַטְּהוֹרָה, כִּי מָצָא מִין אֶת מִינוֹ וְנֵעוֹר.

[152] *Mussaf* of *Yom Kippur* אִם אֶשְׁמַע קוֹל אַחֵר אֶהֱפֹךְ אֶת הָעוֹלָם לְמַיִם. לְתֹהוּ וָבֹהוּ אֲשִׁית הָדוֹמַיִם; This prayer is also recited on *Tisha B'Av*.

෩෩෩෩ Why Jews Must Sacrifice their Lives Rather than Deny Hashem

A Jew may not declare himself an idolater to avoid being put to death.[153] The same applies to denying God's existence or stating that one believes in God and also in idolatry.

Why does the *Halachah* require this? If people know the truth, what difference does it make what they say?

The *Rambam* explains that *Hashem* is one in a unique sense:

> This Deity is one, and not two, or more than two. Rather, one [in the sense that] there is no unity like Him among the "ones" found in the world. Not one [in the sense of] a type [of one] which includes many units, and not one like an entity which may be divided into subunits or [various] dimensions. Rather, a unity concerning which no other unity is like it in the world.[154]

> ...Once it has been clarified that He is neither a body nor a physical entity, it also becomes clear that no bodily incidents apply to Him — not connection, not division, not ascending, not descending, not right, not left, not front, not back, not sitting, and not standing. Furthermore, He is not present in time such that He has beginning or end, or any age, and He does not change.[155]

---

[153] *Shulchan Aruch, Yoreh Deah*157:2 אסור לאדם לומר שהוא עובד כוכבים כדי שלא יהרגוהו

[154] *Hayad Hachazakah, Hilchoth Yesodei Hatorah* 1:7 א-לוה זה אחד הוא ואינו שניים ולא יתר על שניים. אלא אחד שאין כיחודו אחד מן האחדים הנמצאים בעולם. לא אחד כמין שהוא כולל אחדים הרבה ולא אחד כגוף שהוא נחלק למחלקות ולקצוות. אלא יחוד שאין יחוד אחר כמותו בעולם.

[155] *Hayad Hachazakah, Hilchoth Yesodei Hatorah* 1:11 וכיוון שנתברר שאינו גוף וגוייה יתברר שלא יארע לו אחד ממאורעות הגופות לא חיבור ולא פירוד לא מקום ולא מידה לא עלייה ולא ירידה ולא ימין ולא שמאל ולא פנים ולא אחור ולא ישיבה ולא עמידה ואינו מצוי בזמן עד שיהיה לו ראשית ואחרית ומניין שנים ואינו משתנה.

Jews cannot declare outwardly that they deny *Hashem* while inwardly thinking that He is one because such an act in and of itself contradicts *Hashem's* unity, which has no inner or outer aspects or divisions of any kind.

৪০ Kaf (כַּף) and Prophecy

As mentioned above, when the letter *Kaf* (כ) appears in front of a word, it indicates similarity or likeness (כַּף הַדִּמְיוֹן), but the Hebrew for "similarity" (דִּמְיוֹן) also means "imagination." How are the concepts of similarity and imagination related?

The *Rambam* teaches that imagination is the opposite of logical analysis.

Part of the process of scientific investigation involves clearly defining various phenomena by describing them ever more precisely. For example, one could start off with the statement, "Fifi is a dog." One could then proceed to be more precise by adding that, "Fifi is a dog with brown fur," narrow things down further by saying that, "Fifi is a dog with brown fur and floppy ears," and so on. The more one breaks down Fifi's characteristics, the clearer the picture becomes of what Fifi is.

By contrast, imagination often involves joining together matters which are unrelated. For example, people know what a man is, what a horse is, and what a bird is, so they may imagine a man with the head of a horse and the wings of a bird even though no such thing exists.[156]

---

[156] *Moreh Nevuchim* I:73 ואין פועל הדמיון פועל השכל, אבל הפכו. וזה כי השכל יפרק המורכבות ויבדיל חלקיהם ויפשיטם ויצירם באמיתתם ובסיבותיהם(ף) וישיג מן הדבר האחד עניינים רבים מאוד... ואין לדמיון פועל דבר מאלו הפעולות שהדמיון לא ישיג אלא האיש המורכב בכללו, לפי מה שהשיגוהו החושים, או ירכיב הדברים המפוזרים במציאות וירכיב קצתם על קצתם... כמו שידמה המדמה איש אדם וראשו ראש סוס ולו כנפים, וכיוצא בזה.

From a certain perspective, logical analysis is more valuable than imagination. Scientific research demands that its practitioners make observations and then carefully describe and define those observations. They must then use logical analysis to try to explain what they have observed. Science would make very little progress if its practitioners spent their time daydreaming about things which have no basis in reality.

On the other hand, imagination does play an important role in the development of human understanding and technology. For example, had people simply stuck to the factual observations they find in the world and never imagined being able to fly, airplanes might never have been invented.

This feature of imagination — the ability to think beyond the reality one knows — gives it an advantage over logical analysis provided that it is properly controlled and directed. The *Rambam* explains that once a person has developed his intellect sufficiently, God may grant him prophecy. Prophecy works through the imagination, permitting prophets to perceive spiritual phenomena which they cannot grasp intellectually.[157]

What makes imagination a better vehicle for receiving prophecy than rational intellect?

First, people limit the use of rational thought processes to what they have experienced. Since a person with the head of a horse and the wings of a bird has never been observed, such a concept lies outside the scope of rational thought.

Imagination does not have this limitation. Since spiritual matters are not part of human experience, they cannot be

---

[157] *Moreh Nevuchim* II:36 דע כי אמיתת הנבואה ומהותה הוא שפע שופע מאת הא-לוה יתברך ויתעלה באמצעות השכל הפועל על הכוח הדברי תחילה ואחר כן ישפע על הכוח המדמה... והעניין ההוא הוא תכלית שלמות הכוח המדמה, וזה עניין אי אפשר בכל איש בשום פנים, ואינו עניין יגיע אליו בשלמות בחכמות העיוניות והטבת המידות. ואפילו יהיו כולם בתכלית מה שיוכלו להיות מן הטוב והנאה שבהם עד שיחוברו אל זה שלמות הכוח המדמה בעיקר היצירה בתכלית מה שאפשר.

grasped by rational thought. They can, however, be grasped with the help of imagination.

Secondly, as the *Rambam* explains, intellectual inquiry typically involves categorizing information and dissecting it into ever finer distinctions. By contrast, imagination entails bringing disparate matters together.

Hashem is the only true reality, and He underlies all Creation. Objects and events which appear to have nothing to do with one another nevertheless have their source in *Hashem*. Imagination is the best vehicle for understanding *Hashem* because it joins together matters which have nothing to do with one another or which may even appear to oppose one another. The Hebrew language uses the same word for both "imagination" and "similarity" (דִמְיוֹן) because imagination permits a person to understand that despite outward appearances all physical phenomena are similar at their root.

A well-known children's story illustrates this point:

> Four blind men came upon an elephant — something they had never before encountered — and each one tried to identify it.
>
> The first blind man felt the elephant's trunk and concluded that an elephant is a type of snake.
>
> The second man touched the elephant's ear and concluded that the elephant is a type of bat.
>
> The third man felt the elephant's tusk and concluded that elephants must resemble mollusks with hard shells.
>
> The fourth man touched the elephant's wrinkled skin and concluded that elephants must be some sort of very elderly animals.

Each of the blind men in the story tried to classify the elephant according to an experience he had had with something he knew. If these men were suddenly able to see, however, they would immediately understand what an elephant is and that their prior assumptions were wrong.

Similarly, those who try to employ logic to understand the spiritual realm fall short. Only when God grants people the sight of prophecy (חֲזוֹן הַנְּבוּאָה) through the faculty of imagination do they recognize the true nature of spirituality and realize that their prior understanding was wrong.

Prophecy, powered by imagination, permits a person to attain an especially acute insight into the concept of absolute infinitude which lies beyond human experience and understanding. This is why the test for determining whether a person is a prophet is whether he or she can foretell the future.[158] Since the infinite is not limited by time, a true prophet has the power to foresee the future.[159]

---

[158] *Hayad Hachazakah, Hilchoth Yesodei Hatorah* 10:1 כל נביא שיעמוד לנו ויאמר שה' שלחו אינו צריך לעשות אות כאחד מאותות משה רבינו או כאותות אליהו ואלישע שיש בהם שינוי מנהגו של עולם אלא האות שלו שיאמר דברים העתידים להיות בעולם ויאמנו דבריו... לפיכך כשיבוא אדם הראוי לנבואה במלאכות השם ולא יבוא להוסיף ולא לגרוע אלא לעבוד את ה' במצוות התורה אין אומרין לו, "קרע לנו הים" או "החיה מת" וכיוצא באלו ואחר כך נאמין בך. אלא אומרים לו, "אם נביא אתה, אמור דברים העתידים להיות", והוא אומר ואנו מחכים לראות היבואו דבריו אם לא יבואו. ואפילו נפל דבר קטן בידעו שהוא נביא שקר ואם באו דבריו כולן יהיה בעינינו נאמן.

[159] *Tifereth Sh'lomo, Parashath Behar* ישראל עלו במחשבה. הפירוש בזה כי הודיעו לנו בזה מהיכן יזכו הצדיקים להסתכל ולדעת מה שהיה ומה שעתיד להיות. ופירשו לנו כי זהו ע"י מעלות קדושת המחשבה של הצדיקים שלא נפגמה והם תמיד במחשבות קדושות לה'. על כן יתעלו במחשבה ההיא לדביקות העליון אין סוף ב"ה שלמעלה העבר והעתיד הכל שווה. לכך יזכו לאור הרוח הקודש ולנבואה בהמשך אור אין סוף ב"ה במחשבתו כנ"ל.

The Clouds of Glory Connected Israel to Hashem's Infiniteness

❧ General Description

The *Midrash* records:

> How many Clouds of Glory surrounded Israel [when they journeyed] in the [Sinai] Desert? Rabbi Hoshaya and Rabbi Yoshaya [had different opinions on the subject].
>
> Rabbi Yoshaya said: [There were] five — four [stationed] at each of the four directions, [i.e., front, back, right, and left,] and one that traveled ahead of them.
>
> Rabbi Hoshaya said: [There were] seven — four [stationed] at each of the four directions [mentioned above] plus one above them, one below them, and one which traveled ahead of them at a distance of three days [journey] that destroyed snakes, scorpions, [other] venomous creatures, and boulders. In addition, if there was a depression, it raised it, and

if there was an elevation, it flattened it, converting these [uneven places] into a level plain.[160]

The Clouds of Glory also prevented the Jews' garments from wearing out and cleaned and pressed them.[161]

Just as God conducted the Jews out of the Egyptian exile with Clouds of Glory, so will He conduct them out of the present exile with Clouds of Glory.[162] Moreover, He will fashion a canopy out of Clouds of Glory for each *Tzaddik*.[163]

ৰু Blended Light

Nothing in Creation can exist independently from God, and since God is infinite, everything in Creation must possess an aspect of infinity so that it does not become detached from Him and cease to exist.

Emek Hamelech elaborates on this idea by describing three types of infinity which may be understood by analogy to a circle, as illustrated below.

---

[160] *Bamidbar Rabbah* 1:2 וכמה ענני כבוד היו מקיפין את ישראל במדבר? רבי הושעיה ורבי יאשיה. רבי יאשיה אמר: חמישה — ארבע לארבע רוחות וא' מהלך לפניהם. רבי הושעיה אמר: שבעה — ארבעה לארבע רוחות השמים וא' מלמעלן וא' מלמטן ואחד שהיה מהלך לפניהם רחוק ג' ימים והיה מכה לפניהם את הנחשים ואת העקרבים ואת השרפים ואת הסלעים. ואם היה מקום נמוך, היה מגביהו ואם היה מקום גבוה, היה משפילו ועושה אותם מישור...

[161] *Pesikta D'Rav Kahana* 11:21 רבי לעזר ברבי שמעיה שאל את רבי שמעיה ברבי יוסי בר לקוניא חמויי: ...מה הוא דין דכתיב, "שִׂמְלָתְךָ לֹא בָלְתָה מֵעָלֶיךָ" (דברים ח', ד')? ...אמר ליה: ענני כבוד היו מעטפין אותם ולא היו בלים. אמר ליה: ...ולא היו צריכין תכבוסת? אמר ליה: ענני כבוד היו מגחצין אותן.

[162] *Midrash Tehillim* 48 אמר רב נחמן: "מַה שֶׁהָיָה הוּא שֶׁיִּהְיֶה" (קהלת א', ט') — כשם שנטל הקב"ה את ישראל ממצרים בענני כבוד ונשאם, שנאמר, "וָאֶשָּׂא אֶתְכֶם עַל כַּנְפֵי נְשָׁרִים" (שמות י"ט, ד') כך הוא עושה להם...

[163] *Bamidbar Rabbah* 21:22 ועתיד הקב"ה לעשות לכל צדיק וצדיק חופה של ענני כבוד

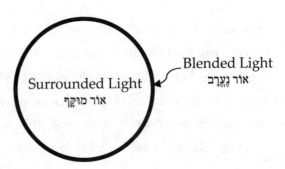

Light of the Infinite One
אוֹר אֵין סוֹף בָּרוּךְ הוּא

Blended Light
אוֹר נֶעֱרָב

Surrounded Light
אוֹר מוּקָף

The area outside the circle may be viewed as consisting of unlimited space which extends forever in every direction. This represents *Hashem* Himself who has no limitations of any kind and whom the human mind cannot fathom.

The interior of the circle represents "surrounded light" (אוֹר מוּקָף), the infinite aspect of Creation. This is a limited form of infinity, a concept which can be understood by considering the diameter of a circle. According to Euclidean geometry, a circle consists of an infinite number of points. An infinite number of lines can therefore be drawn to represent the diameter of a circle, and each of these lines in turn consists of an infinite number of points. Nevertheless, each line has a definite length and therefore is limited. This represents Creation in which the Infinite One exists, but His infinitude is perceived only in a limited way.

Finally, there is the circumference of the circle which serves as the boundary between its interior and its exterior and is called "blended light" (אוֹר מְעוּרָב). It is not a boundless infinity as is the circle's exterior. Nonetheless, because a circle has no beginning or end, it represents a broader concept of infinity than the confined space it encompasses.[164]

The Clouds of Glory represent this "blended light" (אוֹר נֶעֱרָב) — the circumference of the circle[165] and the interface between the Infinite One and Creation. As the *Torah* states, at the time of Creation, "A cloud rose from the earth and watered all the surface of the land."[166] *Rabbeinu Bachye* comments that this refers to the Clouds of Glory through which *Hashem's* Divine influence passes to all the lower realms.[167]

During their journey through the Sinai Desert, the Jews were surrounded by this "blended light" — the Clouds of Glory — which serve as an intermediary between Creation and the Infinite One, Blessed be He. Rabbi Yehudah taught that one of the reasons *Hashem* took the Jews out of Egypt was so that they could ride upon the Clouds of Glory.[168] *Hashem* wanted Israel to experience the greatest possible understanding of His infinite nature.

Ma'or Vashamesh explains that the faith of the Jews caused them to merit the Clouds of Glory.[169] As noted above, human intellect can only grasp so much of *Hashem's* infinitude. To go

---

[164] *Emek Hamelech* I:57, ויש בזה העיכוב ג׳ בחינות: האחת היא בחינת אור אין סוף המקיף המלכות, ובחינה ב׳ היא בחינת אור אין סוף המוקף בתוך העיגול, ובחינה הג׳ היא אור אין סוף ב״ה מה שבין המקיף והמוקף... ונקרא אור נערב.

[165] Rabbi Tzadok Hakohen of Lublin, *Likutei Amarim* on the Book of Joshua, chap. 1 ומן הוא אור פנימי וענני כבוד מקיף

[166] Genesis 2:6 וְאֵד יַעֲלֶה מִן הָאָרֶץ וְהִשְׁקָה אֶת כָּל פְּנֵי הָאֲדָמָה.

[167] *Rabbeinu Bachye* on Genesis 2:6 ועל דרך המדרש אלו ענני כבוד שהיו מתגברים ועולין... ענני כבוד רמז לקבלת שפע הכבוד שהוא מקבל מאת ה׳ יתברך... "וְהִשְׁקָה אֶת כָּל פְּנֵי הָאֲדָמָה" – אלו הגלגלים וכל מה שלמטה מהם שהם פועלים באדמה.

[168] *Shemoth Rabbah* 24:2 רבי יהודה אומר: אמרו ישראל באותה שעה: כלום הוציאנו הקב״ה ממצרים אלא בשביל ה׳ דברים – אחת לתת לנו ביזת מצרים שנית להרכיבנו על ענני כבוד...

[169] *Ma'or Vashamesh, Parashath Ha'azinu* וגם אבותינו בצאתם ממצרים זכו לענני כבוד בזכות האמונה שהאמינו בה׳ ויצאו לארץ לא זרועה ולמדבר שמם. Jews sit in the *Sukkah* in memory of the Clouds of Glory, and the *Zohar* calls the *Sukkah* "the shadow of faith" (*Zohar* III:103A כָּל מַאן דְּאִיהוּ מְשָׁרְשָׁא וְגִזְעָא קַדִּישָׁא דְּיִשְׂרָאֵל יֵשְׁבוּ בַּסֻּכּוֹת תְּחוֹת צֵלָּא דִּמְהֵימְנוּתָא).

beyond that level requires faith. The great faith of the Jews enabled them to achieve that maximum possible perception.

This highest level of comprehension is symbolized by clouds because, just as clouds cover and hide the sky, so too, even the greatest revelation of God leaves Him hidden and unknown. Even when *Hashem* gave the *Torah*, He appeared "in the thickness of the cloud,"[170] meaning that He remained hidden.

❧❧ How the Clouds of Glory Affected Objects they Touched

In as much as the Clouds of Glory formed a border between the infinite and the finite, they affected whatever they touched in one of two opposite ways depending upon which of the two benefited Israel.

The Clouds of Glory had the ability to transform finite objects and give them an infinite quality when such a result was desirable. For example, the Jews' garments, which would ordinarily not last very long in the harsh conditions of the desert, never wore out. Instead, they gained a quality of everlastingness and remained clean and fresh.

How did the Clouds of Glory do this?

The sages refer to the world to come as "a day which is completely good" and "a day which is completely long."[171] Good therefore possesses an aspect of everlastingness. Accordingly, when something with the potential to be good for Israel came into contact with the Clouds of Glory it connected to their infinite nature and acquired the quality of infinitude.

---

[170] Exodus 19:9.

[171] B.T. *Kiddushin* 39B ‏(שם) "לְמַעַן יַאֲרִיכֻן יָמֶיךָ", "לְעוֹלָם שֶׁכּוּלוֹ טוֹב, – (דברים ה', ט"ז) "לְמַעַן יִיטַב לָךְ"‏
‏שם) – לְעוֹלָם שֶׁכּוּלוֹ אָרוֹךְ.)‏

By contrast, evil will cease to exist in the world to come, as the Prophet Isaiah said, "death will be swallowed up forever."[172] Evil is ephemeral and not connected to infiniteness. Accordingly, that which was harmful to Israel, such as venomous snakes or boulders that impeded the nation's path, could not tolerate contact with the infinitude of the Clouds of Glory and vanished.

৪৩ The Clouds of Glory and Amalek

The *Torah* records that, "The Canaanite heard — the king of Arad who dwelled in the south — that Israel came by the route of the spies, and he attacked Israel and captured a prisoner from among them."[173]

The *Gemara* explains the phrase "the Canaanite heard" as meaning that the enemy heard that Aaron had died and that the Clouds of Glory had departed, leaving the Jews exposed.[174]

Although the *Midrash* states that it was Amalek who attacked the Jews,[175] Amalek was not one of the Canaanite nations. *Rashi* clarifies that the *Torah* calls Amalek "the Canaanite" because the Amalekites changed their language to confuse Israel and to cause them to pray for victory over the Canaanites. When the Jews observed that their enemies dressed like Amalekites but

---

[172] Isaiah 25:8 בִּלַּע הַמָּוֶת לָנֶצַח וּמָחָה ה' אֱ-לֹנָי ה' דִּמְעָה מֵעַל כָּל פָּנִים וְחֶרְפַּת עַמּוֹ יָסִיר מֵעַל כָּל הָאָרֶץ כִּי ה' דִּבֵּר.

[173] Numbers 21:1 וַיִּשְׁמַע הַכְּנַעֲנִי מֶלֶךְ עֲרָד יֹשֵׁב הַנֶּגֶב כִּי בָּא יִשְׂרָאֵל דֶּרֶךְ הָאֲתָרִים וַיִּלָּחֶם בְּיִשְׂרָאֵל וַיִּשְׁבְּ מִמֶּנּוּ שֶׁבִי.

[174] B.T. *Rosh Hashanah* 3A מַה שְׁמוּעָה שָׁמַע? שָׁמַע שֶׁמֵּת אַהֲרֹן וְנִסְתַּלְּקוּ עַנְנֵי כָבוֹד, וּכְסָבוּר נִתְּנָה רְשׁוּת לְהִלָּחֵם בְּיִשְׂרָאֵל.

[175] *Yalkut Shimoni* on Numbers 21, continuation of paragraph 764 "וַיִּשְׁמַע הַכְּנַעֲנִי מֶלֶךְ עֲרָד" — זה עמלק שנאמר, "עֲמָלֵק יוֹשֵׁב בְּאֶרֶץ הַנֶּגֶב" (במדבר י"ג, כ"ט). והיה יושב על הפרצה. כיוון ששמע שמת אהרן ונסתלקו עננֵי כבוד, מיד נתגרה בה.

spoke the Canaanite language, they were unsure of their identity, so they prayed that they defeat their enemies generally.[176]

What did the Amalekites think they were doing? Why did they think it so crucial for the Jews to pray for the defeat of a specific enemy? Surely *Hashem* could discern which nation the Jews were praying to defeat even if they did not identify it correctly in their prayers!

The Hebrew for "prayer" (תְּפִלָּה) means connection.[177] Prayer is effective when it connects a person to *Hashem*, and the force which creates that connection is faith. The stronger the faith, the more effectively the prayer connects a person to *Hashem* and the greater the prayer's power.

Even a slight doubt can contaminate prayer and reduce its effectiveness. Although the Jews did not doubt *Hashem* in any way, the Amalekites sought to create uncertainty about their true identity to contaminate the Jews with doubt. In as much as the prayers of the Jews were on an incredibly lofty spiritual level, any relationship to doubt, however slight or remote, could ruin them.

Why was this so?

ೞೞ Infinite Doubt

Hashem is called "the Infinite One, Blessed be He" (אֵין סוֹף בָּרוּךְ הוּא), and for every holy concept there is a corresponding impure concept.[178]

---

[176] *Rashi* on Numbers 21:1 ושנה את לשונו לדבר בלשון כנען כדי שיהיו ישראל מתפללים להקב״ה לתת כנענים בידם והם אינם כנענים. ראו ישראל לבושיהם כלבושי עמלקים ולשונם לשון כנען. אמרו: נתפלל סתם, שנאמר, 'אם נָתֹן תִּתֵּן אֶת הָעָם הַזֶּה בְּיָדִי' (במדבר כ״א, ב')".

[177] *Kedushath Levi, Parashath Shemoth* תפלה לשון התחברות

[178] *Be'er Mayim Chayim, Parashath Breishith* 6 כי "אֶת זֶה לְעֻמַּת זֶה עָשָׂה הָאֱ-לֹהִים" (קהלת ז', י"ד), וכל מה שיש בקדושות יש נגדו בקליפה.

But how can this apply to the concept of infinity which describes God Himself? How can there be an infinite form of impurity?

The answer is that doubt has an infinite aspect.

The *Mishnah* teaches that before *Yom Kippur* those in charge of the Temple service used to prepare a substitute *Kohen Gadol* in case the regular *Kohen Gadol* became ritually impure and therefore disqualified from serving. Rabbi Yehudah suggested that since an unmarried man may not serve as *Kohen Gadol*, a substitute wife should also be prepared in case the *Kohen Gadol's* wife suddenly died. The other rabbis rejected this idea, stating that, "If so, the matter has no end."[179] If one is going to worry about every possibility that can ever arise, then his doubt and uncertainty will never stop.

Infinite uncertainty is the antithesis of faith. If one permits even a minor doubt to bother him, it will soon be followed by another and yet another.

The Amalekites realized that they could not shake Israel's faith by trying to foster doubt that *Hashem* exists or that He created and supervises the universe, because the Jews would immediately reject such ideas. Rather, the Amalekites sought to introduce doubt indirectly by creating uncertainty about which nation the Jews were fighting. Since doubt has an infinite aspect, with one doubt leading to another and yet another, the Amalekites reasoned that this doubt, however minor and seemingly irrelevant, would eventually weaken the faith of the Jews and interfere with the efficacy of their prayers. In other words, they

---

[179] *Yoma* 1:1 וּמַתְקִינִין לוֹ כֹהֵן אַחֵר תַּחְתָּיו שֶׁמָּא יֶאֱרַע בּוֹ פְּסוּל. רַבִּי יְהוּדָה אוֹמֵר: אַף אִשָּׁה אַחֶרֶת מַתְקִינִין לוֹ, שֶׁמָּא תָמוּת אִשְׁתּוֹ שֶׁנֶּאֱמַר, "וְכִפֶּר בַּעֲדוֹ וּבְעַד בֵּיתוֹ" (ויקרא ט״ז, ר׳) (*משמעות*) "בֵּיתוֹ" זוֹ אִשְׁתּוֹ. אָמְרוּ לוֹ: אִם כֵּן, אֵין לַדָּבָר סוֹף !

tried to fight faith in the Infinite One, Blessed be He, with infinite doubt.

The Clouds of Glory combined with Israel's faith to provide the Jews with an extremely high appreciation of God's infinitude.

However, clouds can also symbolize doubt. For example, one may not perform any labor at the conclusion of the Sabbath until three small stars appear together in the sky. The *Shulchan Aruch* rules that "if it is a cloudy day, [a person] should wait until doubt leaves his heart."[180]

The Amalekites disguised themselves as Canaanites because the letters of "Canaan" (כְּנַעַן) can be rearranged to mean "like a cloud" (כְּעָנָן). When the Clouds of Glory departed, they saw an opportunity to contaminate the Jews with clouds of doubt.

ကြသသ Infinite Hatred

The behavior of the Amalekites is puzzling. If they believed in God and the effectiveness of prayer, why did they oppose Israel in the first place?

Indeed, Amalek's irrationality is striking. The *Torah* states that Amalek attacked Israel "and did not fear God."[181] The Amalekites knew that God exists and knew that He protects Israel, yet they attacked anyway.

Moreover, as noted above, the *Midrash* states that Amalek was not a Canaanite nation.

---

[180] *Shulchan Aruch, Orach Chayim* 293:2, צריך ליזהר מלעשות מלאכה עד שיראו ג' כוכבים קטנים. ולא יהיו מפוזרים אלא רצופים, ואם הוא יום מעונן ימתין עד שיצא הספק מליבו. Similarly, see *Shulchan Aruch, Orach Chayim* 235:1 זמן קריאת שמע בלילה משעת יציאת שלושה כוכבים קטנים, ואם הוא יום מעונן ימתין עד שיצא הספק מליבו.

[181] Deuteronomy 25:18 according to *Rashi*.

The Canaanite nations were wicked and corrupt. *Hashem* had decreed that the Jews would acquire the Land of Israel and that the Canaanites would be driven from it.[182] Nevertheless, it is understandable that the Canaanites opposed what they viewed as a Jewish invasion.

Since Amalek was not a Canaanite nation, however, the Jews posed no threat to them. Why, then, did Amalek attack?

Amalek was a descendant of Esau, who complained bitterly that Jacob had stolen his firstborn rights and Isaac's blessings. He even plotted to murder Jacob because of that perceived injustice.[183]

The irony of Esau's hatred is that the purpose of the firstborn status and blessings was to continue Isaac's mission of serving *Hashem*, but Esau was only interested in enjoying the pleasures of this world.[184] Thus, Esau had no use for the firstborn status or its attendant blessings. Nevertheless, Esau adopted the attitude that if he could not have them, then no one else should have them. Since it was God's will that Jacob receive the firstborn rights and blessings, Esau's resentment was ultimately directed against God Himself.[185]

---

[182] Deuteronomy 9:5 -אֶ ה' הָאֵלֶּה הַגּוֹיִם בְּרִשְׁעַת כִּי אַרְצָם אֶת לָרֶשֶׁת בָּא אַתָּה לְבָבְךָ וּבְיֹשֶׁר בְּצִדְקָתְךָ לֹא לְהָקִים וּלְמַעַן מִפָּנֶיךָ מוֹרִישָׁם לֹהֶיךָ הַדָּבָר אֲשֶׁר נִשְׁבַּע ה' לַאֲבֹתֶיךָ לְאַבְרָהָם לְיִצְחָק וּלְיַעֲקֹב.

[183] Genesis 27:41 וַיִּשְׂטֹם עֵשָׂו אֶת יַעֲקֹב עַל הַבְּרָכָה אֲשֶׁר בֵּרְכוֹ אָבִיו וַיֹּאמֶר עֵשָׂו בְּלִבּוֹ יִקְרְבוּ יְמֵי אֵבֶל אָבִי וְאַהַרְגָה אֶת יַעֲקֹב אָחִי.

[184] Genesis 25:34 וְיַעֲקֹב נָתַן לְעֵשָׂו לֶחֶם וּנְזִיד עֲדָשִׁים וַיֹּאכַל וַיֵּשְׁתְּ וַיָּקָם וַיֵּלַךְ וַיִּבֶז עֵשָׂו אֶת הַבְּכֹרָה; *Rashi* ad. loc. וַיִּבֶז עֵשָׂו – הֵעִיד הַכָּתוּב עַל רִשְׁעוֹ שֶׁבִּזָּה עֲבוֹדָתוֹ שֶׁל מָקוֹם

[185] Esau told Jacob that he wanted to eat from "this red, red stuff" (Genesis 25:30 הָאָדֹם הָאָדֹם הַזֶּה). The numeric value of the expression "red, red" (הָאָדֹם הָאָדֹם) is the same as "faith" (אֱמוּנָה) if one is added for each word. (Note 197 explains why numeric values can be calculated this way.) This hints at Esau's rejection of faith in *Hashem*. Moreover, the *Torah* writes the words "red" without the letter *Vav* (ו), so this expression may be taken to mean "humanity, humanity," (הָאָדָם הָאָדָם), alluding to Esau's belief that people are in charge, not God.

It was this vicious attitude that Amalek inherited. The Amalekites attacked Israel because they figured that if they were not interested in serving *Hashem*, then no one else should.

This is why *Hashem* swore that His Name and His Throne will not be complete until Amalek is utterly eradicated.[186] In the future, other nations may come to realize the truth of the *Torah* and support Israel's mission, but the Amalekite nation is irredeemable.

---

[186] Exodus 17:16 וַיֹּאמֶר כִּי יָד עַל כֵּס יָ-הּ מִלְחָמָה לַה׳ בַּעֲמָלֵק מִדֹּר דֹּר

Pesikta Rabethai 12 comments: אמר רבי לוי בשם רבי חמא בי רבי חנינא: כביכול כל זמן שזרעו של עמלק בעולם לא השם שלם ולא הכיסא שלם. נעקר זרעו של עמלק, הכיסא שלם והשם שלם.

HASHEM'S OMNISCIENCE

Balaam's Donkey

૨૦ Balaam's Conversation with His Donkey

Balaam was a non-Jewish prophet who wanted to curse the Jewish people. When he rode his donkey to meet King Balak of Moab to arrange to do so, *Hashem* sent an angel to block the donkey's way. Balaam could not see the angel, but the donkey could. When the donkey refused to proceed, Balaam became enraged and hit it. The *Torah* then states:

God opened the mouth of the donkey, and it asked Balaam, "What have I done to you that you have beaten me these three times?"

Balaam answered, "Because you mocked me. If only I had a sword in my hand, I would slaughter you now!"

"Am I not your donkey upon whom you have ridden from the beginning of your existence until today?" asked the donkey. "Have I ever been accustomed to do this to you?"

"No," admitted Balaam.[187]

At that moment *Hashem* revealed the angel to Balaam, and the donkey died.[188]

The mouth of the donkey was one of ten things *Hashem* created at twilight on the first *Shabbath* eve.[189]

৪৩৪৩ Did the Donkey Really Speak?

There are three main opinions about whether the donkey literally spoke to Balaam: a) Miraculously, God gave the donkey the ability to speak just as the text plainly states;[190] b) The donkey itself never spoke. Instead, the angel which blocked Balaam's way spoke to him through the donkey.[191] According to the *Zohar*, the angel's name was Kamriel (קַמְרִיאֵל);[192] c) No conversation took place at all. Instead, Balaam had a dream-like prophetic vision in which he saw himself speaking with the donkey.[193]

Tifereth Yehonathan adopts the view that the donkey literally spoke and explains that at the time of Creation animals could speak intelligently. The superiority of humans over animals was

---

[187] Numbers 22:28-30 (כח) וַיִּפְתַּח ה' אֶת פִּי הָאָתוֹן וַתֹּאמֶר לְבִלְעָם מֶה עָשִׂיתִי לְךָ כִּי הִכִּיתָנִי זֶה שָׁלֹשׁ רְגָלִים. (כט) וַיֹּאמֶר בִּלְעָם לָאָתוֹן כִּי הִתְעַלַּלְתְּ בִּי לוּ יֶשׁ חֶרֶב בְּיָדִי כִּי עַתָּה הֲרַגְתִּיךְ. (ל) וַתֹּאמֶר הָאָתוֹן אֶל בִּלְעָם הֲלוֹא אָנֹכִי אֲתֹנְךָ אֲשֶׁר רָכַבְתָּ עָלַי מֵעוֹדְךָ עַד הַיּוֹם הַזֶּה הַהַסְכֵּן הִסְכַּנְתִּי לַעֲשׂוֹת לְךָ כֹּה וַיֹּאמֶר לֹא.

[188] Numbers 22:31 וַיְגַל ה' אֶת עֵינֵי בִלְעָם וַיַּרְא אֶת מַלְאַךְ ה' נִצָּב בַּדֶּרֶךְ וְחַרְבּוֹ שְׁלֻפָה בְּיָדוֹ וַיִּקֹּד וַיִּשְׁתַּחוּ ; *Bamidbar Rabbah* 20:15 מיכן את למד (במדבר כ״ב, ל״ג) – "גַּם אֹתְכָה הָרַגְתִּי וְאוֹתָהּ הֶחֱיֵיתִי" ;לְאַפִּיו שהרג את האתון

[189] *Pirkei Avoth* 5:6 עֲשָׂרָה דְבָרִים נִבְרְאוּ בְּעֶרֶב שַׁבָּת בֵּין הַשְּׁמָשׁוֹת, וְאֵלּוּ הֵן... וּפִי הָאָתוֹן

[190] Rabbi Yitzchak Abarbanel on Genesis 3:1-7 פלא דרך ועל כפשוטו האתון דיבור שהיה

[191] *Rabbeinu Bachye* on Numbers 22:28 האתון דיבור כי הפרשה בעניין בנסתר תשכיל ואם כדיבור הנחש, וזה וזה לא מדעת עצמן כי אין בהם נפש מדברת...כי נטייתה מן הדרך ולחיצת הרגל והרביצה, שהם שלושה סימנים, כל אחד ואחד היה מצד המלאך, ואין צריך לומר הסימן הרביעי שהוא הדיבור.

[192] *Zohar* III 201B קַמְרִיאֵל דְּאִקְרֵי פִּי הָאָתוֹן

[193] *Rambam, Moreh Nevuchim* II:42 הנבואה במראה הכל האתון ודברי. According to this view, it would have been Balaam's prophetic experience which was created during the twilight of the first Sabbath eve.

that humans had a greatly enhanced understanding and recognition of the Divine. When Adam and Chavah lost that recognition, the animals correspondingly lost their ability to speak.[194]

This view would explain why some animals, such as parrots, can imitate human speech even though they do not understand what they are saying, while others, such as chimpanzees, can be trained to recognize and use certain symbols to communicate with each other or with people in a rudimentary way.

According to this view, although animals lost the ability to speak as humans do, a remnant of that ability remained and resurfaced when Balaam's donkey spoke.

Rabbi Yitzchak Caro offers a slightly different explanation. When *Hashem* created donkeys on the sixth day of Creation, He stipulated that they would be able to speak whenever He chose. Light symbolizes the actual occurrence of a phenomenon whereas darkness symbolizes its non-occurrence. Twilight represents potential — a condition between the two. The donkey's potential to speak was therefore created at twilight.[195]

Indeed, the *Torah* states that, "*Hashem* **opened** the mouth of the donkey"[196] when it spoke to Balaam, implying that the potential for the donkey to speak already existed and that *Hashem* merely activated it when needed. Moreover, the Hebrew for "stipulation" (תְּנַאי) has almost the same letters as "the donkey" (הָאָתוֹן) and the same numeric value if one is added for the word

---

[194] *Tifereth Yehonathan* on Numbers 22:28 דקודם חטא אדם הראשון כל בהמה וחיה הייתה במעלה זו לדבר כפי כל האדם, ומעלת האדם מן הבהמה אין בדבר זה, רק בהשגה להשיג אור העליון. רק אחר כך כשסרח נתהוה בדוגמא בהמה לעניין השגה ובהמה היה הלוך וחסור לפי ערך האדם.

[195] *Toldoth Yitzchak* on Numbers 22:21 שכשברא הקב״ה הבעלי חיים ביום השישי ואמר ״תּוֹצֵא הָאָרֶץ נֶפֶשׁ חַיָּה לְמִינָהּ״ ובְרא מין החמורים, התנה עמהם שבכל זמן שירצה הקב״ה שידברו ידברו. והדבר שהוא בכוח מצד שבזמן מה יצא לפועל דומה ליום שהוא דבר בפועל והוא אור. ומצד שכשאינו בפעל והוא בכוח דומה להעדר ובזה דומה ללילה. פי האתון פירוש[ון] דיבור האתון, שהאתון עצמו לא נברא, אלא בזמן בלעם נולדה. אבל הדבר נברא בכוח ערב שבת בין השמשות, ולכן דימהו לבין השמשות שהוא ספק יום ספק לילה.

[196] Numbers 22:28 וַיִּפְתַּח ה׳ אֶת פִּי הָאָתוֹן, וַתֹּאמֶר לְבִלְעָם, מֶה עָשִׂיתִי לְךָ כִּי הִכִּיתָנִי זֶה שָׁלֹשׁ רְגָלִים

itself,[197] hinting that *Hashem* stipulated at the time donkeys were created that they would speak whenever He wanted them to.

ౠ How Balaam Became a Rasha

Balaam's story seems strange. He had prophetic powers and spoke with God, who ordered him not to curse the Jews.[198] Nevertheless, Balaam remained steadfast in his desire to destroy Israel and advised King Balak of Moab to command the women of his kingdom to seduce the Jewish men in order to anger God against Israel.[199]

How is such a thing possible? How could any human being possessing clear and direct knowledge of God's will rebel against Him?

ౠౠ Balaam's Heresy

When God speaks to people, He does so in a manner that resembles human conversation so that people will not become frightened out of their wits. As an example, when God spoke to Adam after the latter sinned, He asked, "Where are you?"

---

[197] The rules for calculating numeric values (גִּמַטְרִיָה) permit this for the following reason. Although each letter of a Hebrew word represents a particular spiritual force, the totality of the letters which form a word represents an overarching spiritual force which is greater than the sum of its constituent letters. The number one may therefore be added to the numeric value of a word to represent its totality. (See *Ohr Hameir, Parashath Emor* עניין ראשי תיבות כי הנה נתבאר לנו... וסופי תיבות. והכוונה כלליות הארה ותענוגים של כללות אותיות, צירוף התיבה, המה מקובצים תחילה באות ראשונה. ולכן אות ב' דבראשית רברבא).

[198] Numbers 22:12 וַיֹּאמֶר אֱ-לֹהִים אֶל בִּלְעָם לֹא תֵלֵךְ עִמָּהֶם לֹא תָאֹר אֶת הָעָם כִּי בָרוּךְ הוּא

[199] B.T. *Sanhedrin* 106A אָמַר לוֹ: אֱ-לֹהֵיהֶם שֶׁל אֵלוּ שׂוֹנֵא זִימָה הוּא, וְהֵם מִתְאַוִּים לִכְלֵי פִּשְׁתָּן. בּוֹא וַאֲשִׂיאֲךָ עֵצָה, עֲשֵׂה לָהֶן קְלָעִים וְהוֹשִׁיב בָּהֶן זוֹנוֹת...

Although God knew where Adam was, He did not want to startle him.[200]

The *Torah* records how King Balak sent emissaries to Balaam to ask him to curse Israel. "God came to Balaam and asked, 'Who are these men with you?'"[201] The *Midrash* states that Balaam should have replied, "Master of the Universe, all is revealed before You, and nothing is hidden from You, yet You ask me?!?" Instead, Balaam took this as proof that *Hashem* does not know everything.[202]

If one combines the last two letters of Balaam (בִּלְעָם) with the last two letters of Balak (בָּלָק), they spell Amalek (עֲמָלֵק).[203] The numeric values of "Amalek" (עֲמָלֵק) and "doubt" (סָפֵק) are identical, and this was the essence of Balaam and Balak. Even though Balaam was in direct contact with the Creator, he doubted His omniscience.

৪৩৪৩ The Difference between Holy Knowledge and Impure Knowledge

For everything in the realm of holiness there is a counterpart in the realm of impurity. Balaam boasted that he possessed supreme knowledge,[204] but Balaam's knowledge came from the realm of impurity.[205]

---

200 *Rashi* on Genesis 3:9 "אַיֶּכָּה ?" – יודע היה היכן הוא, אלא ליכנס עמו בדברים שלא יהא נבהל להשיב אם יענישהו פתאום...וכן בבלעם, "מִי הָאֲנָשִׁים הָאֵלֶּה עִמָּךְ" (במדבר כ"ב, ט').

201 Numbers 22:9 וַיָּבֹא אֱ-לֹהִים אֶל בִּלְעָם וַיֹּאמֶר מִי הָאֲנָשִׁים הָאֵלֶּה עִמָּךְ

202 *Bamidbar Rabbah* 20:6 אמר לו הקב"ה, "מִי הָאֲנָשִׁים הָאֵלֶּה עִמָּךְ ?" (במדבר כ"ב, ט'), (ובלעם) היה צריך לומר, "רבש"ע הכל גלוי לפניך ואין כל דבר נעלם ממך ולי את שואל ! ? !" אלא אמר לו, "בָּלָק בֶּן צִפֹּר מֶלֶךְ מוֹאָב שָׁלַח (אותם) אֵלָי" (במדבר כ"ב, י').

203 *Zohar* I:25A בִּלְעָם וּבָלָק מִסִּטְרָא דַעֲמָלֵק הֲוֵוֹ. טוֹל ע"ם מִן בִּלְעָם ל"ק מִן בָּלָק

204 Numbers 24:16 נְאֻם שֹׁמֵעַ אִמְרֵי אֵ-ל וְיֹדֵעַ דַּעַת עֶלְיוֹן מַחֲזֵה שַׁ-דַּי יֶחֱזֶה נֹפֵל וּגְלוּי עֵינָיִם

205 *Emek Hamelech* 5:48 כמו שמשה רבינו ע"ה הוא סוד הדעת בסטרא דקדושה, כן בלעם הוא בסוד הדעת בסטרא אוחרא.

At first glance, it is difficult to fathom how a distinction can exist between holy knowledge and impure knowledge. After all, facts are facts, and logic is logic. For example, if it is a fact that a person was born on a certain date, then that fact is settled and not subject to varying interpretations. Moreover, valid inferences from facts always yield true results. For instance, if Reuben was born on 10 *Adar*, 5776, and Shimon was born on 10 *Adar*, 5776, then it follows that Reuben and Shimon were born on the same day, and there is no room for doubt about this conclusion.

What, then, is "impure knowledge?"

To understand the answer requires understanding the source of Balaam's doubts about *Hashem's* omniscience and why he did not realize that *Hashem* knows everything and only spoke to him as He did so as not to overwhelm him.

An ancient philosophical belief was that God did not create time,[206] and Balaam adhered to this opinion. Accordingly, he held that *Hashem* is subject to time just like everything else and that His knowledge changes over time.

This false belief is hinted at by Balaam's description of himself as one "who knows the mind of the Supreme One" (דַּעַת עֶלְיוֹן).[207] With a slight change in vowels, this expression means that "time is supreme" (דְּעֵת עֶלְיוֹן).

This idea was also the source of Amalek's heretical doubts. If the letters of Amalek (עֲמָלֵק) are spelled out (עי"ן מ"ם למ"ד קו"ף), their combined numeric value is the same as "time" (עֵת), and if four is added for the four letters of Amalek's name, the total equals "knowledge" (דַּעַת).[208] Balak, Balaam, and Amalek

---

[206] *Moreh Nevuchim* 2:13 והדעת השלישי, הוא דעת אריסטו... שהזמן והתנועה עולמיים תמידיים

[207] Numbers 24:16 נְאֻם שֹׁמֵעַ אִמְרֵי אֵ-ל וְיֹדֵעַ דַּעַת עֶלְיוֹן מַחֲזֵה שַׁ-דַּי יֶחֱזֶה נֹפֵל וּגְלוּי עֵינָיִם

[208] See *Mavoh Lechochmath Hakabbalah* 2:1:2 למ"ד. עשר פעמים אהי"ה. עי"ן מ"ם, עשר פעמים אהי"ה. למ"ד לכן במילוי, קו"ף, עשר פעמים הוי"ה. בסך הכל עת ועם הד' אותיות הרי 'דעת'.

derive from the realm of impure Knowledge which is tainted with doubts that come from the belief that God did not create time.[209]

Rashi comments that the Amalekites used astrology to determine a favorable time for attacking the Jews, but *Moshe Rabbeinu* stopped the sun in its course and "mixed up the hours."[210] *Moshe Rabbeinu* thereby demonstrated that God controls time and is not subject to it.

The heretical thinking of Amalek, Balak, and Balaam based upon impure knowledge was the same as that of the mixed multitude (עֵרֶב רַב) who accompanied the Jews out of Egypt and who were responsible for the sin of the golden calf.[211] That sin was related to time — the erroneous idea that *Moshe Rabbeinu* failed to descend from Mount Sinai at the time he promised he would. Two of Balaam's sons were leaders of the mixed multitude and inspired them to fashion the golden calf. The numeric value of "mixed multitude" (עֵרֶב רַב) equals that of "knowledge" (דַּעַת), implying that these people were contaminated with the same uncertain, doubtful knowledge as Balaam.[212]

Using this information, a further analysis of the logic laid out above about when Reuben and Shimon were born will clarify

[209] *Baal Shem Tov Al Hatorah, Parashath Vayetzei* משה ובלעם הם סוד הדעת – זה בקדושה וזה בטומאה.

Yisrael Kedoshim 5 וידוע דבלעם ועמלק הם משורש אחד מן הדעת דסיטרא אחרא נגד משה רבינו ע"ה.

[210] *Rashi* on Exodus 17:12 referencing *Midrash Tanchuma, Parashath Beshalach* 28 "עַד בֹּא הַשֶּׁמֶשׁ" – שהיו עמלקים מחשבין את השעות באצטרולוגיאה (אסטרולוגיה) באיזו שעה הם נוצחים והעמיד להם משה חמה וערבב את השעות.

[211] *Midrash Tanchuma, Parashath Kee Tisa* 30 "אמר לו הקב"ה לאותו העגל: "מי עשה אותך?" אמר לו: "...הערב רב שיצאו עם ישראל ממצרים".

[212] *Chessed L'Avraham* 5:17 וכבר ידעת כי ערב רב הם עשו את העגל, וראשי ערב רב הם יוניס וימבוריס, הם שני בניו של בלעם הרשע... כי הלא נודע כבר אצלינו כי בלעם הוא פסולת הזוהמא שיצא מדעת שהוא שורש משה רבינו ע"ה, וזהו שאמר "וְיֹדֵעַ דַּעַת עֶלְיוֹן". גם ערב רב הם סוד הפסולת של הדעת, כי כן ערב רב בגימטריא דע"ת, אך אינם כל כך זוהמא כמו בלעם.

the difference between Holy Knowledge and impure Knowledge.

Suppose Reuben and Shimon were born at twilight at the beginning of 10 *Adar*, 5776. Rabbi Yossi taught that the moment when one day ends and the next day begins occurs in a single instant which is impossible for a person to discern.[213] Accordingly, in this case, no one can be certain whether Reuben and Shimon were indeed born on the same day. On the other hand, since *Hashem* created time, He knows when twilight occurs and therefore knows with certainty whether or not Reuben and Shimon were born on the same day.

Holy Knowledge means recognizing that *Hashem* possesses this type of absolute knowledge. Impure Knowledge refers to the doubt people such as Balaam have — a doubt based on their erroneous belief that *Hashem* did not create time and has the same limited knowledge as human beings.

ಜಜಜ The Moment of Rage

The *Gemara* records that:

[Balaam] knew how to pinpoint the time when the Holy One, Blessed be He, is angry, [and he tried to curse the Jews at that time].

Does anger exist before the Holy One, Blessed be He? Yes, as it is learned [in a *Braitha*]: "God rages forth every day."[214] And how long does His rage last? A moment. And how long is a moment? One 58,888th of an hour, and no one could pinpoint that moment except for the wicked Balaam.

---

[213] B.T. *Berachoth* 2B. אָמַר רַבִּי יוֹסֵי: בֵּין הַשְּׁמָשׁוֹת כְּהֶרֶף עַיִן – זֶה נִכְנָס וְזֶה יוֹצֵא, וְאִי אֶפְשָׁר לַעֲמֹד עָלָיו.

[214] Psalms 7:12 אֱ-לֹהִים שׁוֹפֵט צַדִּיק וְאֵ-ל זֹעֵם בְּכָל יוֹם

...Rabbi Elazar said: The Holy One, Blessed be He, told Israel, "Take note of how compassionately I dealt with you, for I did not become angry [each day as I usually do] during the time of the wicked Balaam."[215]

The rabbis teach that certain times are predisposed for good or for bad, and Rabbinic literature is replete with references to auspicious times (עֵת רָצוֹן).[216] Balaam was aware of this concept, but because he believed that God did not create time and that it is independent from Him, he maintained that God cannot control or alter these times. To the contrary, God is bound to behave in certain ways at certain times and cannot cancel the daily moment of rage.

This was incorrect. King David said, "As for me, may my prayer to You, *Hashem*, [be] at an auspicious time (עֵת רָצוֹן)."[217] King David requested that *Hashem* make the time of his prayer an auspicious one.[218] Since *Hashem* created time, including certain favorable and unfavorable times, He can convert an inauspicious time into a favorable one or a moment of rage into a moment of compassion.

৪৩৪৩৪৩ What Led Balaam to this False Conclusion?

As a prophet, Balaam knew that *Hashem* claimed that He

---

215 B.T. *Berachoth* 7A שֶׁהָיָה יוֹדֵעַ לְכַוֵּן אוֹתָהּ שָׁעָה שֶׁהַקָּדוֹשׁ בָּרוּךְ הוּא כּוֹעֵס בָּהּ... וּמִי אִיכָּא רִתְחָא קַמֵּיהּ דְּקוּדְשָׁא בְּרִיךְ הוּא ? אִין, דְּתַנְיָא: "וְאֵל זֹעֵם בְּכָל יוֹם" (תהלים ז', י"ב). וְכַמָּה זַעְמוֹ ? רֶגַע. וְכַמָּה רֶגַע ? אֶחָד מַחֲמֵשֶׁת רִבּוֹא וּשְׁמוֹנַת אֲלָפִים וּשְׁמוֹנֶה מֵאוֹת וּשְׁמוֹנִים וּשְׁמוֹנֶה בְּשָׁעָה, וְזוֹ הִיא רֶגַע, וְאֵין כָּל בְּרְיָה יְכוֹלָה לְכַוֵּן אוֹתָהּ הַשָּׁעָה, חוּץ מִבִּלְעָם הָרָשָׁע... אָמַר רַבִּי אֶלְעָזָר: אָמַר לָהֶם הַקָּדוֹשׁ בָּרוּךְ הוּא לְיִשְׂרָאֵל: "דְּעוּ כַּמָּה צְדָקוֹת עָשִׂיתִי עִמָּכֶם שֶׁלֹּא כָּעַסְתִּי בִּימֵי בִּלְעָם הָרָשָׁע".

216 For example, B.T. *Berachoth* 69B; B.T. *Ta'anith* 24B; B.T. *Yevamoth* 72A.

217 Psalms 69:14 וַאֲנִי תְפִלָּתִי לְךָ ה' עֵת רָצוֹן אֱ-לֹהִים בְּרָב חַסְדֶּךָ עֲנֵנִי בֶּאֱמֶת יִשְׁעֶךָ

218 *Metzudoth David* ad. loc. רוצה לומר: ברוב חסדך יהיה עת רצון

created time. He nevertheless accepted the view of the ancient philosophers that this was not so and that time always existed.

What led him to this conclusion?

Balaam reasoned that if at some point Creation did not exist and at a later point it did, then time must have existed before Creation.

The *Rambam* explains that the doctrine that God existed before Creation for an infinite period of time even though time did not exist prior to Creation uses time in a metaphorical sense and does not refer to time as human beings know it.[219]

Hashem is infinite and encompasses both Creation and the absence of Creation — both time and the absence of time. *Hashem* alluded to this through the miracle of Balaam's donkey speaking. The mouth of the donkey was created at twilight on the first Sabbath eve — the precise moment between the act of Creation and its cessation. It was also a moment of both time and the absence of time because human beings cannot pinpoint the exact moment when one day ends and another begins.[220]

Concerning people like Balaam the sages teach, "As for whoever contemplates four things, it would be fitting for him if he never entered the world — what is above, what is below, what was before, and what will be afterwards."[221] Even the smartest and most capable people cannot grasp how it is that time did not exist prior to Creation because an existence without time is not within human experience. This was Balaam's downfall. He tried

---

[219] *Moreh Nevuchim* 2:13 'ושזה אשר יאמר, היה הא-לוה קודם שיברא העולם אשר תורה מילת 'היה על זמן, וכן כל מה שיעלה בשכל מהמשך מציאותו קודם בריאת העולם המשך אין תכלית לו, כל זה שיעור זמן או דמות זמן, לא אמתת זמן.

[220] B.T. *Berachoth* 2B אָמַר רַבִּי יוֹסֵי: בֵּין הַשְּׁמָשׁוֹת כְּהֶרֶף עַיִן – זֶה נִכְנָס וְזֶה יוֹצֵא וְאִי אֶפְשָׁר לַעֲמֹד עָלָיו.

[221] *Mishnah Chagigah* 2:1 כָּל הַמִּסְתַּכֵּל בְּאַרְבָּעָה דְּבָרִים, רָאוּי לוֹ כְּאִלּוּ לֹא בָּא לָעוֹלָם – מַה לְּמַעְלָה, מַה לְּמַטָּה, מַה לְּפָנִים, וּמַה לְאָחוֹר.

to delve into what existed before Creation and arrived at a false conclusion.

The donkey's question to Balaam alluded to this. "Am I not your donkey upon whom you have ridden from the beginning of your existence (מֵעוֹדְךָ) until today?"[222] When *Hashem* created the universe, He created the potential for everything destined to come into existence, including the souls of all human beings. The donkey explained to Balaam that as great a prophet as he was, he could only grasp as far as the beginning of Creation. No human being can grasp "what was before."

Even though no one can fully understand existence without time, it is possible to get a better grasp of this phenomenon. If the reader stares for several seconds at the square in the center of the following optical illusion from a distance of about twelve inches (thirty centimeters), it appears to move even though it is perfectly stationary. In a similar manner, it appears to human beings that time moves and changes. From God's perspective, however, which is the true reality, time does not move or change at all.

---

[222] Numbers 22:30 וַתֹּאמֶר הָאָתוֹן אֶל בִּלְעָם, הֲלוֹא אָנֹכִי אֲתֹנְךָ אֲשֶׁר רָכַבְתָּ עָלַי מֵעוֹדְךָ עַד הַיּוֹם הַזֶּה, הַהַסְכֵּן הִסְכַּנְתִּי לַעֲשׂוֹת לְךָ כֹּה, וַיֹּאמֶר לֹא.

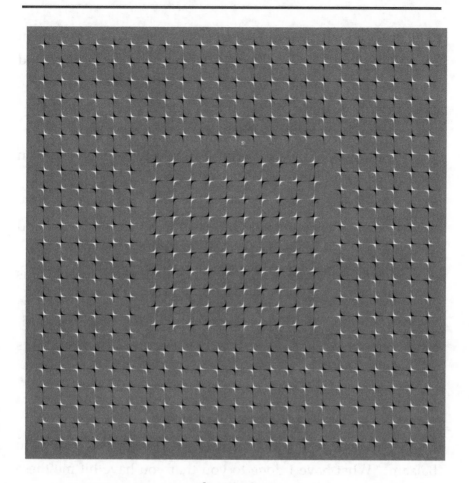

৪৩ Feet and Faith (אֱמוּנָה) ৎ৩

Regel (רֶגֶל) has two seemingly unrelated meanings. It means "foot" or "leg," but also "time" in the sense of an instance or occasion.

The passage of the *Torah* which recounts the story of Balaam and his donkey uses *Regel* (רֶגֶל) in both of these senses. One verse states that, "The donkey saw *Hashem's* angel, and pressed itself to the wall, crushing Balaam's foot (רֶגֶל)."[223] As a result,

---

[223] Numbers 22:25 וַתֵּרֶא הָאָתוֹן אֶת מַלְאַךְ ה׳ וַתִּלָּחֵץ אֶל הַקִּיר וַתִּלְחַץ אֶת רֶגֶל בִּלְעָם אֶל הַקִּיר וַיֹּסֶף לְהַכֹּתָהּ

Balaam became lame and walked with a limp.[224] A subsequent verse states that, "*Hashem* opened the mouth of the donkey, and it said to Balaam, 'What have I done to you that you have hit me these three times (רְגָלִים)?'"[225]

What is the relationship between feet and time?

Feet symbolize faith because just as feet support a person physically, so faith supports a person spiritually.[226]

Moreover, the sages teach that "falsehood has no feet."[227] Just as a person with an injured foot walks unsteadily, falsehood is supported by shaky principles. Truth, however, is well-grounded in principles which are absolute and immutable. It is surefooted and constant.[228]

Balaam's foot injury matched his shaky, uncertain attitude concerning *Hashem's* knowledge and how He transcends time.

ೞೱ The Three Pilgrim Festivals

The *Midrash* states that when the donkey complained to Balaam, "What have I done to you that you have hit me these three times (רְגָלִים)?" she hinted to Balaam that, "You want to uproot a nation which celebrates three pilgrim festivals (רְגָלִים), [and therefore you cannot succeed]."[229]

---

[224] *Maharsha* on B.T. *Sotah* 10A "וְאָמַר רַבִּי יוֹחָנָן: בִּלְעָם חִיגֵּר בְּרַגְלוֹ אַחַת הָיָה שֶׁנֶּאֱמַר, וַיֵּלֶךְ שֶׁפִי" (במדבר כ"ג, ג')". אמרו בזה שעל ידי שנלחץ רגלו אל הקיר היה מכותת וחיגר באותו רגל.

[225] Numbers 22:28 וַיִּפְתַּח ה' אֶת פִּי הָאָתוֹן וַתֹּאמֶר לְבִלְעָם מֶה עָשִׂיתִי לְךָ כִּי הִכִּיתַנִי זֶה שָׁלֹשׁ רְגָלִים

[226] *Orach Lechayim, Parashath Bechukothai* ובחינת אמונה נקרא בספרים 'רגלים' – כמו שרגלים מעמידין את האדם כן אמונה ברוחניות

[227] *Rashi* on Proverbs 12:19 שהשקר אין לו רגלים

[228] See B.T. *Shabbath* 104A וּמַאי טַעְמָא שִׁיקְרָא אַחֲדָא כַּרְעֵיהּ קָאֵי וְאֱמֶת מְלַבֵּן לְבוּנֵי? קוּשְׁטָא קָאֵי, שִׁיקְרָא לָא קָאֵי.

[229] *Bamidbar Rabbah* 20:14 "...וַתֹּאמֶר לְבִלְעָם מֶה עָשִׂיתִי לְךָ כִּי הִכִּיתַנִי זֶה שָׁלֹשׁ רְגָלִים" (במדבר כ"ב, כ"ח) – רמזה לו, "אתה מבקש לעקור אומה החוגגת שלש רגלים".

Why was the merit of the three pilgrim festivals so great that it protected the Jews more than any other merit?

The observance of these festivals was a tremendous demonstration of faith because it required the Jews to go to Jerusalem, leaving their homes and property vulnerable to plundering heathens.[230]

It was their faith in *Hashem* that distinguished the Jews from Balaam. The Jews were willing to believe in *Hashem* and His *Torah* even when faced with questions about His omniscience and providence which seem to defy logic. By contrast, Balaam was lame and unsteady. He refused to believe something that the limited human mind cannot grasp.

[230] *Shir Hashirim Rabbah* 7:3 אמר רבי פנחס: מעשה בשני אחים עשירים שהיו באשקלון. והיו להם שכנים רעים מאומות העולם והוון אמרין: "אימתי אילין יהודאין סלקין למצלייה בירושלם ואנן עלין מקפחין ביתיהון ומחרבין להון?" מטא זמנא וסלקין. זימן להם הקב"ה מלאכים כדמותן והוו נכנסין ויוצאין בתוך בתיהם. מן דאתיין מן ירושלם פלגין מן מה דאייתון עמהון לכל מגיריהון. אמרון לון: "אן הויתון?" אמרון לון: "בירושלם". "אימת סליקתון?" "ביום פלן". "ואימת אתיתון?" "ביום פלן". אמרין: "בריך אלההון דיהודאין דלא שבקון ולא שבק יתהון אינון...".

RESTORING CREATION TO ITS ORIGINAL STATE

Seth

The *Torah* states that, "Adam knew his wife again, and she bore a son and called his named Seth (שֵׁת), for [she said], 'God placed (שָׁת) other offspring for me instead of Abel, because Cain killed him.'"[231]

Seth (שֵׁת) means "placed" or "founded," and the world's population was founded from Seth.[232] Just as the Foundation Stone (אֶבֶן שְׁתִיָּה) is the transitional point between the upper spiritual realms and the physical world,[233] Seth served as the transitional point between Adam and Chavah, who originally lived in the Garden of Eden, and the rest of humanity, who lived afterwards.

---

[231] Genesis 4:25 וַיֵּדַע אָדָם עוֹד אֶת אִשְׁתּוֹ וַתֵּלֶד בֵּן וַתִּקְרָא אֶת שְׁמוֹ שֵׁת כִּי שָׁת לִי אֱ-לֹהִים זֶרַע אַחֵר תַּחַת הֶבֶל כִּי הֲרָגוֹ קָיִן.

[232] *Bamidbar Rabbah* 14:11 שת, שממנו הושתת העולם

[233] *Understanding Emunah*, Rabbi Yehuda Cahn (2016, Ohr Nissan Talmud Center, Inc., Baltimore) pp. 60-66.

Tikunei Zohar elaborates:

The letters of Seth (שֵׁת) are at the end of the alphabet. Father (אָב) is at the beginning of the alphabet. This is the secret of *Aht Bash* (אַ"תְּ בַּ"שׁ), [the principle that one may interpret a word by exchanging the first letter of the alphabet with the last letter of the alphabet, the second letter with the second to last, and so on]. In this instance, a father was rectified together with a son. Wherever they went, they did not separate from one another. [The phrase] "In the beginning" (בְּרֵאשִׁית) includes [the letters of] *Aht Bash* (אַ"תְּ בַּ"שׁ) and [also] father and Seth (אַ"ב שֵׁ"ת).[234]

∞ How *Aht Bash* (אַ"תְּ בַּ"שׁ) works

The *Talmud* and *Midrash* frequently use *Aht Bash* (אַ"תְּ בַּ"שׁ) to interpret words from the *Tanach*,[235] but what connection does the first letter of the alphabet have with the last one, the second letter with the second to last, and so on? Why are they interchangeable?

When people have a certain objective in mind, they usually need to take many steps to achieve it. Although in practice many things precede the final objective, that objective is the first thing the person thought about before doing anything else. The first step towards a final goal may therefore be viewed as the last one and vice versa.

This concept applies to the creation of the universe. Even though the *Torah* lists *Shabbath* as the last thing God created, it came first in His plan of Creation. As the *Lechah Dodi* (לְכָה דוֹדִי) hymn states, "[*Shabbath* was] last in execution but first in

---

[234] *Tikunei Zohar* 112A   וְהַיְינוּ "בְּרֵאשִׁית בָּרָא" אִשְׁתַּלִּים בְּשִׁית. שֵׁת סִיּוּמָא דְאַלְפָּא בֵּיתָא, אב רֵישָׁא דְאַלְפָּא בֵּיתָא, וְדָא הוּא רָזָא דְאַ"תְּ בַּ"שׁ. הָכָא אִתְתַּקַּן אָב עִם בֵּן, תַּרְוַיְיהוּ דָא עַל גַּב דָא. בְּכָל אֲתַר דְּאָזְלוּ לָא אִתְפָּרְשׁוּ דָא מִן דָא. בְּרֵאשִׁית תַּמָּן אַ"תְּ בַּ"שׁ, אַ"ב שֵׁ"ת.

[235] B.T. *Shabbath* 104A; *Bamidbar Rabbah* 13:15.

thought" (סוֹף מַעֲשֶׂה בְּמַחֲשָׁבָה תְּחִלָּה). Accordingly, the beginning of Creation may be viewed as its end and vice versa.

Hashem created the universe using spiritual forces which correspond to the letters of the Hebrew alphabet.[236] Since these letters parallel the forces *Hashem* used to create the universe, the first one may also be viewed as the last one and vice versa.

৪৩৪৩ Seth Rectified the Damage His Parents Caused

The goal of Creation was for Adam and Chavah to enjoy the Garden of Eden, but their sin thwarted that goal and damaged their sons Cain and Abel. Cain became a murderer. Abel was also not completely blameless, for had he been perfectly righteous, Cain would not have succeeded in harming him.

Seth (שֵׁת) partially rectified this damage. When the principle of *Aht Bash* (א"ת ב"ש) is applied, the letters of his name (שֵׁת) spell "father" (אָב) because he fulfilled the goal of creation that was intended for his father, Adam.

৪৩৪৩ Seth Rectified the Shattered Vessels

A person is a miniature universe,[237] and what happened to the universe in the process of Creation also befell humankind.

Hashem created the universe by filtering His Divine light through a chain of supernal worlds. Initially, He organized those worlds in an arrangement analogous to a set of concentric spheres, with each inner sphere being less spiritual than the one outside it, as depicted on the following page. Just as concentric spheres do not touch one another, these spiritual worlds did not interact with one another. This made it impossible for the lower

---

[236] *Pirkei Avoth* 5:1 בַּעֲשָׂרָה מַאֲמָרוֹת נִבְרָא הָעוֹלָם
[237] *Midrash Tanchuma, Parashath Pekudei* 3 האדם שהוא עולם קטן

spiritual realms to contain the intense Divine light transmitted to them from the higher ones. As a result, the lower spheres shattered, a phenomenon the rabbis refer to as the "breaking of the vessels" (שְׁבִירַת הַכֵּלִים).[238]

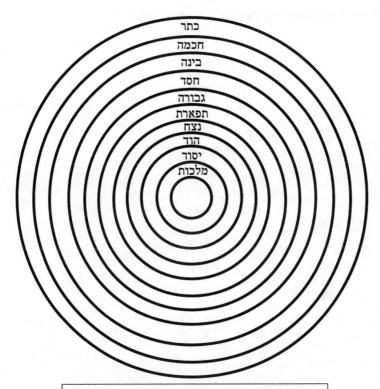

The supernal worlds, or spheres, organized as concentric circles

---

[238] This configuration of the spiritual worlds is called *Iggulim* (עָגּוּלִים) — circles.

Hashem then reorganized the supernal worlds into a new configuration corresponding to the human body, as shown on the following page. Although the head is higher than the other parts of the body and controls them, it is also connected to and interacts with them. Similarly, this new system of supernal worlds functioned harmoniously and transmitted the Divine light without damaging the lower worlds.[239]

---

[239] The rabbis refer to this reconfigured system as *Yosher* (יוֹשֶׁר) — straightness. *Avodath Yisrael, Parashath Shelach* והוא על פי מה שאמר האר״י ז״ל בעולמות העגולים שאין עיגול נוגע בחבירו, ושם היה השבירה עד שניתקן בעולם היושר.

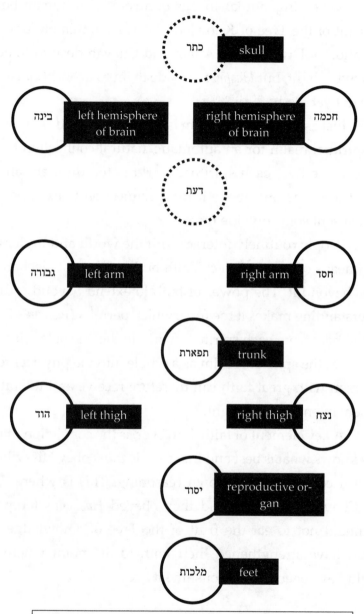

The supernal worlds, or spheres, organized in a configuration paralleling the human body

Something similar to this occurred with human beings. The fruit of the Tree of Knowledge was an extremely powerful revelation of Divine light. Adam and Chavah desired to access this Divine light, but *Hashem* forbade them to do so because they were not yet ready for it.[240]

Just as the physical realm is too different and remote from the spiritual realm for an automatic, natural connection to exist between the two, each spiritual world is too different and detached from the one above it for a connection to exist between them absent some outside force.

People routinely interact with the world and understand it by means of their intellect. Faith builds upon intellect and extends beyond it. The power of faith to extend beyond ordinary understanding makes it the force which permits *Hashem's* Divine light to pass from each spiritual world to the one below it and to flow from the spiritual realm as a whole into the physical realm. A person with great faith can therefore receive and tolerate extremely intense Divine light.

A key element of faith, however, is the conviction that *Hashem* knows what is best and that people must obey His will even when it contradicts their own reasoning. This is where Adam and Chavah fell short. Had they obeyed *Hashem's* temporary command not to eat the fruit of the Tree of Knowledge, they would have strengthened their faith to the point where they would have been able to consume it later on.[241]

---

[240] *Kedushath Levi, Parashath Breishith*   מחמת שבחינת עץ הדעת אורו גדול כל כך אשר אין
ביכולתם להמשיך עליהם אור גדול כל כך כי לא יסבולו אור גדול כזה.

[241] *Be'er Mayim Chayim, Parashath Breishith 2, Hemshech* לא נאסר באכילת עץ הדעת כי אם
לבו ביום, ואילו היה ממתין עד שבת משחשכה היה מצוהו ה' שיאכל דווקא בכדי לידע ברע ובטוב ויבחר בטוב
ויבחר אוכל מן הפסולת. אך היה צריך מקודם להדביק ולהשריש עצמו בקדושה יפה יפה בכדי שלא ימשיכנו
הסטרא אחרא והרע הלוך אחריהם.

Just as the lower spiritual worlds suffered damage when they could not contain the Divine light transmitted to them from the higher ones, Adam and Chavah suffered damage when they attempted to access the Divine light of the fruit of the Tree of Knowledge before being capable of tolerating it.[242]

Masculinity represents the flow of Divine light while femininity represents the reception of that light.[243] Originally, Adam and Chavah — male and female — functioned harmoniously as if they were one and the same person, as the *Torah* states, "Male and female He created them, and He blessed them, and He called their name Adam on the day they were created."[244] The transmission of Divine light and its reception functioned smoothly. Had Adam and Chavah obeyed *Hashem*, they would have reached the point where they would have been able to tolerate the higher spiritual level represented by the fruit of the Tree of Knowledge, and *Hashem* would have permitted them to enjoy it.

This explains the teaching of the sages that, "[The serpent] observed [Adam and Chavah] together and became desirous [of

---

[242] *Imrei Noam Al Hatorah, Parashath Vayetzei*, ותפסו בלשונם הדך מי שיבר כלי ואכל תאנים,
רומז על חטא הקדמוני הנקרא שבירת הכלים, ואילן שאכל אדם הראשון תאנה הייתה (עיין ברכות מ', ע"א).

This resembles the episode recorded in the *Talmud* about four great scholars who entered the spiritual realm. Although they were exceptional people, one died, one became insane, and one became a heretic. Only Rabbi Akiva entered in peace and left in peace (B.T. *Chagigah* 14B תָּנוּ רַבָּנַן: אַרְבָּעָה נִכְנְסוּ לְפַרְדֵּס
וְאֵלּוּ הֵן: בֶּן עַזַאי וּבֶן זוֹמָא, אַחֵר, וְרַבִּי עֲקִיבָא... בֶּן עַזַאי הֵצִיץ וָמֵת... בֶּן זוֹמָא הֵצִיץ וְנִפְגַּע... אַחֵר קִיצֵץ בַּנְטִיעוֹת.
(רַבִּי עֲקִיבָא יָצָא בְשָׁלוֹם.).

[243] *Aruch Lanair* on B.T. *Sukkah* 29A דהחמה היא המשפיע האור והארץ החשוכה היא הנשפעת
המקבלת שפע. וכן הזכר הוא המשפיע והנקבה המקבלת השפע.
Sefer Gerushin L'Rabbi Moshe Cordovero, האור מצד הזכר המשפיע יורד ומכה,
והניצוץ חוזר אל מקורו מצד הנקבה המקבלת.

[244] Genesis 5:2 זָכָר וּנְקֵבָה בְּרָאָם וַיְבָרֶךְ אֹתָם וַיִּקְרָא אֶת שְׁמָם אָדָם בְּיוֹם הִבָּרְאָם
According to some, Adam and Chavah were originally created as one unit and then split apart (B.T. *Berachoth* 61A דְּאָמַר רַבִּי יִרְמְיָה בֶּן אֶלְעָזָר: דּוּ פַּרְצוּפִין בָּרָא
הַקָּדוֹשׁ בָּרוּךְ הוּא בְּאָדָם הָרִאשׁוֹן). Nevertheless, they remained united spiritually prior to sinning.

Chavah]."[245] The serpent, who is identical with the *Satan*,[246] was jealous of the unity of Adam and Chavah which permitted them to attain a higher spiritual level than any angel could. He therefore provoked them to disobey God.[247]

As a result of their sin, Adam and Chavah, the masculine and the feminine, separated from one another.[248] The flow of Divine light (the masculine) no longer had a fit receptacle (the feminine), and the harmony of the universe was shattered. When Adam repented, he reunited with Chavah and produced Seth. This partially restored the harmony between masculinity and femininity.[249]

Seth's name (שֵׁת) has a numeric value of seven hundred. In calculating the numeric values of the letters of the Hebrew alphabet, the five final forms (מנצפ"ך) may be viewed as following *Tav* (ת) so that final *Kaf* (ך) is five hundred, final *Mem* (ם) is six hundred, final *Nun* (ן) is seven hundred, and so on.[250] Final *Nun* (ן) therefore corresponds to Seth (שֵׁת).

As mentioned above, the bent *Nun* (נ) represents the bent faithful whereas the straight final *Nun* (ן) represents the faithful standing upright.[251] The straight final *Nun* (ן) symbolizes the

---

[245] *Yalkut Shimoni* on Genesis 2, paragraph 25 (מתוך שראה אותם מתעסקין בדרך ארץ נתאווה לה), cited by *Rashi* on Genesis 3:1

[246] B.T. *Baba Bathra* 16A אָמַר רַבִּי שִׁמְעוֹן בֶּן לָקִישׁ: הוּא שָׂטָן, הוּא יֵצֶר הָרָע, הוּא מַלְאַךְ הַמָּוֶת and דִּנְחָשׁ דָּא אִיהוּ שָׂטָן Zohar I:35B

[247] *Ben Ish Chai, Halachoth, Shanah Rishonah, Parashath Breishith* הנחש שנתקנא באדם הראשון קודם החטא, ונתגרה בו להחטיאו, כי נתקנא מכתונת אור שלו, שראה שיש עליו אור מקיף גדול כפי ערך הכתונת אור, והוא אין לו אחיזה באור מקיף בסוד "וְהַנָּחָשׁ הָיָה עָרוּם" (בראשית ג', א').

[248] *Breishith Rabbah* 24:6... דא"ר סימון: כל ק"ל שנה שפרשה חוה מאדם

[249] *Zohar* II 168A כֵּיוָן דְּאִתְבְּרִיר פְּסוֹלֶת, שָׁרִיאוּ אַתְוָון לְאוֹלָדָא מֵרָזָא דְּאָת ש"ת. תִּקּוּנָא דְּכַר וְנוּקְבָּא. בְּאָסְתַּכְּמוּתָא כַּחֲדָא. וּכְדֵין כְּתִיב בְּדִמוּתוֹ כְּצַלְמוֹ וַיִּקְרָא אֶת שְׁמוֹ שֵׁת, וְלָא כְּתִיב וַתְּקְרָא. וַיִּקְרָא אִיהוּ, וְלָא אִיהִי. אִיהוּ קָרָא שְׁמֵיהּ שֵׁת, תִּקּוּנָא דְּכַר וְנוּקְבָּא כַּחֲדָא, דַּהֲווֹ בְּאָסְתַּכְּמוּתָא חֲדָא.

[250] *Shelah Hakadosh, Parashath Korah* אַחַר כָּךְ אוֹתִיּוֹת מנצפ"ך, ך' חֲמֵשׁ מֵאוֹת, ם' שֵׁשׁ מֵאוֹת, ן' שֶׁבַע מֵאוֹת.

[251] B.T. *Shabbath* 104A נון כְּפוּפָה, נון פְּשׁוּטָה – נֶאֱמָן כָּפוּף, נֶאֱמָן פָּשׁוּט.

harmonious vertical integration of the supernal worlds caused by faith in *Hashem*. This was the power of Seth whose name (שֵׁת) resembles the Hebrew for "vertical" (שְׁתִי).[252]

৪০ Restoring the Broken Circuit

The spiritual worlds function in a manner analogous to an electric circuit which must be completed for electricity to flow through it. This is the meaning of the repetition of the word "light" in the verse, "God said, 'Let there be light,' and there was light."[253] There are two lights — (a) the Divine light which flows from *Hashem* through all the spiritual worlds, and (b) that same light reflected back through those worlds by the *Torah* learning and good deeds people perform.[254]

Adam and Chavah's sin interfered with this system, but Seth partially restored it. This is what the sages mean by stating that Seth (שֵׁת) rectified his father (אָב) according to the secret of *At Bash* (אַ"תְּ בַּ"שׁ). Just as *At Bash* (אַ"תְּ בַּ"שׁ) entails exchanging the last letter of the alphabet with the first one, so Seth (שֵׁת) completed the circuit through which the Divine light flows by reflecting that light from its terminal point in the physical realm back to its beginning point in the spiritual one.

God told the serpent, "I will place (אָשִׁית) enmity between you and between the woman and between your offspring and

---

[252] The expression "he paid attention" (שָׁת לִבּוֹ) implies connecting to something. Just as one who notices something connects to it, Seth (שֵׁת) represented the connection between the upper and lower realms.

[253] Genesis 1:3 וַיֹּאמֶר אֱ-לֹהִים יְהִי אוֹר וַיְהִי אוֹר

[254] *Kithvei Hagaon M.M. Mi'Shklov, Biur Mishnath Chassidim,* p. 241 באור ישר ואור חוזר, בסוד (הֵשָׁנוֹת) ב' (פְּעָמִים) אוֹר — אחד של "יְהִי אוֹר" ואחד של "וַיְהִי אוֹר".

her offspring. He will strike you [on your] head, and you will strike him [on his] heel (עָקֵב)."[255]

The term "I will place" (אָשִׁית) alludes to Seth (שֵׁת), whose name means "placement" and whose faith in *Hashem* partly corrected the damage caused by the sin which the serpent provoked. The *Yud* (י) is missing from Seth (שֵׁת) because the rectification was incomplete.

The root of Jacob's name (יַעֲקֹב) is heel (עָקֵב). Jacob continued the rectification process and, metaphorically, struck the serpent (the *Satan*) with his heel. The *Yud* (י) which should have appeared in Seth's name (שֵׁת) therefore became the first letter of Jacob's name (יַעֲקֹב).[256] As the *Tikunei Zohar* explains, "[The rectification process initiated by] Seth was drawn out until Jacob."[257]

ೞೲ The Covenant between Shin (ש) and Tau (ת)

The *Zohar* teaches:

> Come and see: When the Holy One, Blessed be He, created the world, He made a covenant and stood the world upon it. From where [do we know this]? It is written ["In the beginning" (בְּרֵאשִׁית), which can be interpreted to mean] "He created a foundation (בְּרָא שִׁית)." This [foundation] is the covenant upon which the world stands — a foundation from which blessings flow and go forth to the world, and upon which the world was created. Adam violated this covenant and shifted it from its place.

---

255 Genesis 3:15 וְאֵיבָה אָשִׁית בֵּינְךָ וּבֵין הָאִשָּׁה וּבֵין זַרְעֲךָ וּבֵין זַרְעָהּ הוּא יְשׁוּפְךָ רֹאשׁ וְאַתָּה תְּשׁוּפֶנּוּ עָקֵב

256 *Kithvei Ha'arizal, Sefer Halikutim, Parashath Vayetzei* 32 כל העניין היה על אות יו"ד המורשם לשם יעקב, כי היה שמו עקב, ובא לתקן חטא אדם הראשון ולבסמו, נכתב ביו"ד.

Jacob got his name because he held onto Esau's heel (עָקֵב) when they were born. The *Arizal's* comment explains why a *Yud* (י) was added to it (יַעֲקֹב).

257 *Tikunei Zohar* 112A שֵׁת אִתְפַּשְּׁטוּתֵיהּ הֲוָה עַד יַעֲקֹב, דְּפָרַח בֵּיהּ י' מִן שִׁית וְאִשְׁתְּאַר שֵׁת, וְאִשְׁתְּאַר יַעֲקֹב עָקֵב, דְּיַעֲקֹב דְּיוֹקְנֵיהּ דְּאָדָם קַדְמָאָה הֲוָה, כְּמָה דְּאוּקְמוּהָ שׁוּפְרֵיהּ דְּיַעֲקֹב כְּצֵין שׁוּפְרֵיהּ דְּאָדָם הָרִאשׁוֹן.

This covenant is alluded to by the letter *Yud* (י), a tiny letter which is the root and foundation of the world. When [Adam] produced [a third] son, he confessed his sin, and named him Seth (שֵׁת). He did not mention *Yud* (י) with respect to [Seth] to make him into a "foundation" (שִׁית), because [Adam] had violated [that covenant]. Accordingly, the Holy One, Blessed be He, planted the world from [Seth], and all [subsequent] meritorious generations are related to him.[258]

ଊଊଊ What was Adam's Covenant?

In a plain sense, God's original covenant with humankind was simply that Adam and Chavah observe the commandment not to eat the fruit of the Tree of Knowledge.

On a deeper level, the *Gemara* states that *Shin* (ש) stands for falsehood (שֶׁקֶר) whereas *Tav* (ת) stands for truth (אֱמֶת).[259] One may therefore understand the *Zohar's* statement to mean that *Hashem* created the world with truth and falsehood united through a covenant represented by *Yud* (י).

But how can truth and falsehood — diametrically opposed concepts — be connected, and how can both serve as a foundation for the universe?

Hashem created the universe for the purpose of benefiting humankind. Everything that happens serves that purpose, including evil. Accordingly, evil is merely a hidden form of good.

Everything that exists, whether good or evil, has its spiritual source in God's Divine light, and that source is reflected in its Hebrew name. For example, in the realm of holiness, the

---

[258] *Zohar* I:56A תָּא חֲזֵי: כַּד בָּרָא קוּדְשָׁא בְּרִיךְ הוּא עָלְמָא, עֲבַד הַאי בְּרִית וְקַיְּימָא עֲלֵיהּ עָלְמָא. מְנָלָן? דִּכְתִיב "בָּרָא שִׁית." דָּא בְּרִית דְּעָלְמָא קָיְימָא עֲלֵיהּ. שִׁית דְּמִנֵּיהּ נְגִידִין וְנָפְקָא בִּרְכָאן לְעָלְמָא וְעָלֵיהּ אִתְבְּרֵי עָלְמָא. וְאָדָם עֲבַר עַל הַאי בְּרִית וְאַעֲבַר לֵיהּ מֵאַתְרֵיהּ (ס"א מעמיה). הַאי בְּרִית אִתְרְמִיזַת בְּאָת יו"ד, אָת זְעֵירָא עִקָּרָא וִיסוֹדָא דְּעָלְמָא. כַּד אוֹלִיד בַּר, אוֹדִי עַל חֶטְאוֹ וְקָרָא שְׁמֵיהּ ש"ת. וְלָא אַדְכַּר בֵּיהּ יו"ד לְמֶהֱוֵי שִׁית, בְּגִין דְּעָבַר עֲלֵיהּ. וּבְגִין כַּךְ קוּדְשָׁא בְּרִיךְ הוּא (מהכא) מִינֵּיהּ אַשְׁתִּיל עָלְמָא וְאִתְיַחֲסוּ כָּל דָּרֵי זַכָּאֵי דְּעָלְמָא (משת).

[259] B.T. *Shabbath* 104A שִׁין – שֶׁקֶר, תָּיו – אֱמֶת

highest level is called "delight" (עֹנֶג), but in the realm of impurity the letters are transposed so that the lowest level is called "plague" (נֶגַע).[260]

Yosher Divrei Emeth explains that the forces of good and evil share the same letters because they share the same spiritual source. They only differ in how that source manifests itself in the world. In the realm of holiness, there is a concept of "connection" (קֶשֶׁר), but in the realm of impurity the letters are transposed to mean "falsehood" (שֶׁקֶר).[261]

People ordinarily think of truth as the opposite of falsehood. How is "connection" (קֶשֶׁר) its opposite?

At their source in *Hashem*, all aspects of the universe are united and connected. As the Divine light descends through the spiritual worlds it appears to split apart until it forms the physical universe where many things seem to have no connection between them. This misleading appearance of disconnectedness is "falsehood" (שֶׁקֶר).

৪৩৪৩৪৩ How Connection (קֶשֶׁר) Became Falsehood (שֶׁקֶר)

Rabbi Elazar said: A person could see from one end of the world to the other with the light which the Holy One, Blessed be He, created on the first day. Once the Holy One, Blessed be He, foresaw that the deeds of the Generation of the Flood and the Generation of the Dispersion would be destructive, He

---

[260] אין בטובה למעלה מענג ואין ברעה למטה מנגע *Sefer Yetzirah* 2:4

[261] *Yosher Divrei Emeth* 28 וכל, אבל "זֶה לְעֻמַּת זֶה עָשָׂה הָאֱ-לֹהִים" (קהלת ז', י"ד), טוב לעומת רע כו', המידות שיש בטוב יש ברע, רק בטוב הם לטוב, וברע הם לרע... ואותיות השמות של קדושה ושל קליפה שווים, רק הצירוף היא להיפוך. למשל בקדושה יש "כֶּתֶר" ובקליפה "כָּרֵת" – אותיות שווים. בקדושה "קֶשֶׁר" ובקליפה "שֶׁקֶר"... בקדושה " עֹנֶג" ובקליפה "נֶגַע" והרבה כדומה, ומדת הקליפה להפוך כל דבר אמת, ולעשות מטוב רע, ומרע טוב, כמו שאמר הכתוב, "הוֹי הָאֹמְרִים לָרַע טוֹב וְלַטּוֹב רָע וגו'" (ישעיה ה', כ').

arose and hid it from them, as it says, "He withheld their light from the wicked."[262] For whom did He hide it? For the righteous in the future to come...."[263]

Hashem created the world to come with the letter *Yud* (י),[264] so this letter represents the Divine light hidden for the future enjoyment of the righteous.

Originally, Adam and Chavah lived in the Garden of Eden, a spiritual realm where good and evil — truth and falsehood — were not fully differentiated. At that time, falsehood (שֶׁקֶר) had not fully developed. It still had a relationship to connection (קֶשֶׁר) — the concept that all Creation is joined at its source.

Although God hid the Divine light because He foresaw the deeds of the wicked, He would not have done so had Adam and Chavah not sinned.[265] Their sin damaged the covenant — it caused the connection between good and evil to become so completely hidden that good and evil now appear to be completely separate from one another.

Although *Hashem* hid His Divine light for the righteous to enjoy in the future, He also did so for the benefit of the wicked. If the shared source of good and evil were obvious, the wicked might reason that there is nothing wrong with what they do because, at its source, evil is no different from good. By hiding this

---

[262] Job 38:15   וְיִמָּנַע מֵרְשָׁעִים אוֹרָם וּזְרוֹעַ רָמָה תִּשָּׁבֵר

[263] B.T. *Chagigah* 12A   דָּאמַר רַבִּי אֶלְעָזָר: אוֹר שֶׁבָּרָא הַקָּדוֹשׁ בָּרוּךְ הוּא בַּיוֹם רִאשׁוֹן, אָדָם צוֹפֶה בּוֹ מִסּוֹף הָעוֹלָם וְעַד סוֹפוֹ. כֵּיוָן שֶׁנִּסְתַּכֵּל הַקָּדוֹשׁ בָּרוּךְ הוּא בְּדוֹר הַמַּבּוּל וּבְדוֹר הַפַּלָּגָה וְרָאָה שְׁמַעֲשֵׂיהֶם מְקוּלְקָלִים, עָמַד וּגְנָזוֹ מֵהֶם, שֶׁנֶּאֱמַר, "וַיִּמָּנַע מֵרְשָׁעִים אוֹרָם" (איוב ל"ח, ט"ו). וּלְמִי גְּנָזוֹ? לַצַּדִּיקִים לֶעָתִיד לָבֹא.

[264] B.T. *Menachoth* 29B   "בְּטְחוּ בַה' עֲדֵי עַד כִּי בְּיָ-הּ ה' צוּר עוֹלָמִים" (ישעיה כ"ו, ד')... כְּדְדָרַשׁ רַבִּי יְהוּדָה בְּרַבִּי אִלְעָאי: אֵלּוּ שְׁנֵי עוֹלָמִים שֶׁבָּרָא הַקָּדוֹשׁ בָּרוּךְ הוּא, אֶחָד בְּהֵ"א, וְאֶחָד בְּיוֹ"ד... הָעוֹלָם הַזֶּה בְּהֵ"א וְהָעוֹלָם הַבָּא בְּיוֹ"ד.

[265] *Gur Aryeh* on Genesis 1:14   קודם שנברא אדם הראשון לא נגנז, וכאשר נברא אדם וחטא בסוף יום ו' והיה סמוך לשבת, ומפני כבוד השבת לא נגנז האור הראשון עד מוצאי שבת.

from the wicked, *Hashem* gives them the opportunity to mend their ways.

Although Adam and Chavah repented and produced Seth, and although Jacob continued the rectification they began, the final rectification will not occur until the end of days — the world to come. At that time the *Yud* (י) of "He created a foundation" (בָּרָא שִׁית) will be fully restored, the Divine light will be revealed in the physical universe, and people will recognize that what appears to be evil is really nothing more than good in disguise.

The Spiral

ಐ The Size of the Oral Torah
ಐ೩ Limited and yet Unlimited

To the extent that the Oral *Torah* sets out certain *Halachoth* not mentioned in the Written *Torah* and prescribes rules for interpreting the *Halachah* it is limited to certain information. On the other hand, because the Oral *Torah* includes the application of the *Halachoth* to any set of circumstances which may arise, it is infinite.

For instance, the Oral *Torah* defines thirty-nine general categories of activity forbidden on *Shabbath*. As circumstances arise, *Torah* scholars apply accepted principles of interpretation to determine whether an activity is permitted or forbidden on *Shabbath*. The Oral *Torah* is limited because it lists a specific number of categories of forbidden activity yet unlimited because

Torah scholars apply it to every new situation which occurs, or which may theoretically occur.

໑໐໐໐໐ The Torah Serves as the Blueprint for the Universe

Hashem looked into the *Torah* and created the world, but there are two *Torahs* — one written and one oral. As described earlier, *Hashem* originally created the universe through a system of spiritual worlds called *Iggulim* (עִגּוּלִים) which resembled concentric spheres. Since these worlds did not interact harmoniously, the Divine light from the upper worlds could not pass smoothly to the lower ones, and those lower worlds shattered. *Hashem* then reconfigured the spiritual worlds in a pattern resembling three straight lines. This second system, called *Yosher* (יוֹשֶׁר), did not fully replace the first one, but supplemented it.

These two systems are connected in an imperfect way, and the Divine light flows through them into the world according to the merit of the Jewish nation.[266] The inability of the Divine light to flow smoothly into the world is what permits evil and death to exist. The ultimate rectification of the universe will take place when the systems of *Iggulim* (עִגּוּלִים) and *Yosher* (יוֹשֶׁר) become perfectly harmonized.[267] The Divine light will then flow into the world in a revealed manner, putting an end to death and evil.[268] When this occurs, the two systems will blend together in

---

[266] *Pithchei She'arim, Nethiv Iggulim Veyosher* 4 הספירות דעיגולים קשורים בפנימיותם אל הספירות דיושר, ולפי זכותם של ישראל כך מתגלת או נעלמת בחינת היושר שלהם, ומשנה בכך את הסדר הטבעי.
[267] *Leshem Shevo Ve'achlamah, Sefer Hadeah* 1, Introduction והכוונה הוא על האלף דור המשמשים בעוה"ז שהם האלף דור דמלכי העיגולים ועל האלף דור דמלכי יושר אשר יתחדשו לעתיד לבוא ואז יתוקנו ויחזרו ויתחדשו גם האלף דור דהעוה"ז ויתייחדו זב"ז וישמשו אז השני אלפים דור ביחד. and see *Pri Tzaddik, Parashath Korach* 1 שאמר האריז"ל שיש מדרגות הנקראים בחינת עיגולים ויש הנקראים בחינת יושר. ובעלמא דאתחרבן קודם בריאת העולם היה אז בבחינת עיגולים ובעולם התיקון התחיל מדרגה בחינת יושר ולעתיד יתגלה גם כן בחינת עיגולים. וזה סוד מה שאמרו (ב)סוף (מסכת) תענית (דף ל"א, ע"א), "עָתִיד הַקָּדוֹשׁ בָּרוּךְ הוּא לַעֲשׂוֹת מָחוֹל לַצַּדִּיקִים" – לשון "מָחוֹל" הוא בעיגול.
[268] *Ma'or Vashamesh, Parashath Beshalach* ויעלו לעתיד יתקן כל אחד חלק נשמתו עד שורשו הניצוצין הקדושים והחיצוניות יתבטלו מכל וכל, ויופיע אז אור בהירות א-להותו בכל העולמות ויהיה העיגול

a configuration resembling a spiral. The Prophet Isaiah alluded to this when he declared that, "the curved will become straight."[269] Unlike a set of concentric circles which have no connection to one another, a spiral is one long curve and therefore bears some resemblance to a straight line:

∞∞∞ Why both Systems are Necessary

As discussed above, the force which joins the physical realm to the spiritual realm is faith, but faith cannot be complete when people are uncertain about how matters will ultimately turn out. In the end of days, people will finally see how everything is for the best, their faith will be perfected, and the Divine light will flow into the world in a revealed manner.

The letters of the alphabet symbolize this concept. *Ohev Yisrael* explains that when the letters are placed in a straight row, *Alef* (א) is very distant from *Tav* (ת), as shown below:

$$\text{א ב ג ד ה ו ז ח ט י כ ל מ נ ס ע פ צ ק ר ש ת}$$

והקו שווה ולא יהיה אז בחינת דכר ונוקבא כי כולם בשווה ישיגו אור א-להותו יתברך שמו כמו בדבר עגול שאין ראש וסוף.

[269] Isaiah 40:4 כָּל גֶּיא יִנָּשֵׂא וְכָל הַר וְגִבְעָה יִשְׁפָּלוּ וְהָיָה הֶעָקֹב לְמִישׁוֹר וְהָרְכָסִים לְבִקְעָה

In a similar manner, although people believe *Hashem's* promise that everything will work out in the end, doubt lingers because the connection between what happens now and how matters will eventually turn out seems remote.

The sages teach that in the future, the righteous will form a circle, the center of which will be occupied by the Holy One, Blessed be He. Then, in a manner of speaking, the righteous will be able to point to Him just as one points to an acquaintance.[270]

If the letters of the alphabet are arranged in a circle, then *Alef* (א) and *Tav* (ת) stand next to one another, as illustrated below.

---

270 B.T. *Ta'anith* 31A אָמַר עוּלָּא בִּירָאָה, אָמַר רַבִּי אֶלְעָזָר: עָתִיד הַקָּדוֹשׁ בָּרוּךְ הוּא לַעֲשׂוֹת מָחוֹל לַצַּדִּיקִים וְהוּא יוֹשֵׁב בֵּינֵיהֶם בְּגַן עֵדֶן, וְכָל אֶחָד וְאֶחָד מַרְאֶה בְּאֶצְבָּעוֹ.

At the time of the ultimate redemption, the relationship of the beginning of history to the end of history will become clear,[271] human faith will be perfected, and the Divine light will be revealed in the physical realm in the strongest and clearest form humans can tolerate.

The linear arrangement of the supernal spheres is necessary so that history can follow a straightforward progression. In fact, the very inability to see the final outcome gives human beings the opportunity to gain merit by having faith that everything *Hashem* does is for the best.

The circular arrangement of the spiritual worlds is also necessary because the ultimate revelation of the Divine Presence will permit people to see their faith vindicated.

ೞೞೞೞ Moshe Rabbeinu Merited this Revelation

Moshe Rabbeinu had a unique relationship with *Hashem*, who stated, "Mouth to mouth I speak with him."[272] The Hebrew for "mouth" (פֶּה) is the same as the name of the letter *Pay* (פ), which consists of a spiral. This expression therefore hints that *Moshe Rabbeinu* merited glimpsing the ultimate rectification of the spiritual worlds and how the Divine light will be revealed in the physical realm.

The *Torah* states that when fashioning the golden calf, "The people removed the gold rings in their ears and brought

---

[271] *Ohev Yisrael, Parashath Vayeitzei* אז כסדר היינו ביושר כשהם באמת התורה באותיות ודאי הא׳ קודמת לתי״ו בכ״ב דרגין. אבל אם תסדרם בעגולה, אז כולם שווים, הא׳ עם תי״ו כי הם עומדים זה אצל זה. וזהו בחינת א״ב ש שהא׳ סמוכה להתי״ו. וזהו שהקב״ה יעשה מחול כו׳, היינו שלעתיד לבוא יתנשאו כל העולמות וכל המידות ולא יהא שום מיעוט בשום דבר — אור הלבנה כאור החמה. ואז לא יהיה קנאה בשום דבר. כי השם יתברך ישפיע אור צח ובהיר אשר ממנו יתנוצץ אור לכל העולמות בשווה. וכל הצדיקים ירגישו זה התענוג בשווה. כי לעתיד לבא יתאחדו האותיות ריש דרגין — הוא אלף — עד סוף דרגין — הוא תי״ו. ואז יהיה האור מופיע ומקיף את כל מכל צד בשווה. וזהו כמו מחול.

[272] Numbers 12:8 פֶּה אֶל פֶּה אֲדַבֶּר בּוֹ וּמַרְאֶה וְלֹא בְחִידֹת וּתְמֻנַת ה׳ יַבִּיט וּמַדּוּעַ לֹא יְרֵאתֶם לְדַבֵּר בְּעַבְדִּי בְמֹשֶׁה.

them to Aaron."[273] The ear is the counterpart of the mouth (פֶּה) because the ear hears what the mouth says. In addition, the auricle of the ear has a shape which resembles the letter *Pay* (פ), and the inner ear has a spiral-shaped organ called a cochlea, as shown below.

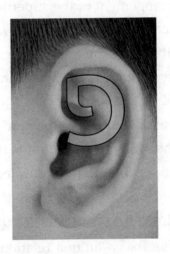

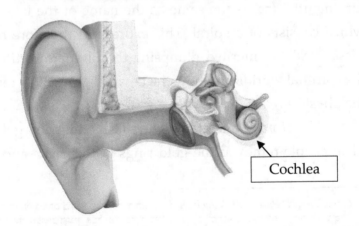

Cochlea

[273] Exodus 32:3 וַיִּתְפָּרְקוּ כָּל הָעָם אֶת נִזְמֵי הַזָּהָב אֲשֶׁר בְּאָזְנֵיהֶם וַיָּבִיאוּ אֶל אַהֲרֹן

The use of earrings for the golden calf alluded to how the Jews lacked the faith necessary to share the "mouth to mouth" (פֶּה אֶל פֶּה) revelation *Moshe Rabbeinu* enjoyed, and that revelation will never be regained by any human being until the end of days.[274]

᥅ᥩ᥅ᥩ᥅ᥩ᥅ How *Torah* Study Hastens the Redemption

The Written *Torah* corresponds to the original set of circle-like spheres called *Iggulim* (עֲגוּלִים).[275] Like that system, the Written *Torah* cannot directly interact with the physical world. Without the guidance of the Oral *Torah* it cannot be correctly put into practice by itself because the details and implications of its laws are not apparent from a casual reading of its text.

The Oral *Torah* corresponds to the linear set of spiritual worlds called *Yosher* (יוֹשֶׁר). Just as the system of *Yosher* (יוֹשֶׁר) enables harmonious interaction between the upper spiritual worlds and the lower ones, so the Oral *Torah* permits the Written *Torah* to be given practical effect in the physical world by supplementing it and by providing rules for applying its laws to new situations.

At present, the Oral *Torah* only performs this function imperfectly. That is why the *Gemara* records many doubts and disputes about how to correctly interpret and apply its principles.

---

[274] See *Rashi's* comment on Exodus 34:30 (וַיִּרְאוּ מִגֶּשֶׁת אֵלָיו – בוא וראה (וְהִנֵּה קָרַן עוֹר פָּנָיו)) כמה גדולה כוחה של עבירה שעד שלא פשטו ידיהם בעבירה מהו אומר? "וּמַרְאֵה כְּבוֹד ה' כְּאֵשׁ אֹכֶלֶת בְּרֹאשׁ הָהָר לְעֵינֵי בְּנֵי יִשְׂרָאֵל" (שמות כ"ד, י"ז), ולא יראים ולא מזדעזעים. ומשעשו את העגל, אף מקרני הודו של משה היו מרתיעים ומזדעזעים.)

[275] The rabbis refer to the Written *Torah* as "the crown of *Torah*" (*Sefer Hapliah*, sub verba "*Nun Yesh Lah Gimel*" (נ' יש לה ג' זיונין) – כתר תורה הוא תורה שבכתב), and a crown is circular, as the *Tanach* states, "They surrounded Benjamin like a crown" (Judges 20:43 כִּתְּרוּ אֶת בִּנְיָמָן). See also *Likutei Halachoth, Orach Chaim, Hilchoth Tefillath Aravith* 4 וְזֶהוּ בְּחִינַת הַהַקָּפוֹת שֶׁעוֹשִׁין עִם הַסֵּפֶר תּוֹרָה. זֶה בְּחִינַת מַקִּיפִים וַעֲגוּלִים.

The Hebrew for Oral *Torah* (תּוֹרָה שֶׁבְּעַל פֶּה) can be interpreted homiletically to mean "*Torah* with the characteristics of the letter *Pay* (פ),"[276] whose shape resembles a spiral. In the end of days, all disputes and doubts concerning the correct understanding and application of the Oral *Torah* (תּוֹרָה שֶׁבְּעַל פֶּה) will be resolved, and its spiral-like characteristic of harmonization will be perfected. The Written and Oral *Torahs* and the systems of *Iggulim* (עִגּוּלִים) and *Yosher* (יוֹשֶׁר) which they represent will be fully integrated.[277]

When a *Torah* scholar renders a correct *Halachic* decision, he helps rectify both of these systems because he clarifies the correct interpretation of the Written *Torah* and resolves the disputes among earlier authorities concerning the Oral *Torah*. The study of *Halachah* therefore hastens the ultimate redemption.[278]

৵ The Snail

The sages teach that *Hashem's* relationship to Creation resembles that of a snail to its shell. Although its shell appears to be separate from the snail's body, it is actually part and parcel of it just as *Hashem* pervades Creation even though He appears to be separate from it.[279] In addition, a snail's shell has a spiral

---

[276] Compare expressions such as "בַּעַל גַּאֲוֶה," literally meaning "one who possesses the trait of conceit," and "בַּעַל נִסָּיוֹן," literally meaning "one who possesses experience."

[277] See *Iggra D'pirka* 20 פ׳ רומז לתורה שבעל פ״ה, שעל ידה נגלה האור הגנוז. וזהו "גנזו לצדיקים" [חגיגה י״ב, ע״א]

[278] See *Likutei Moharan, Mahadura Kama* 62 עִקַּר הִתְהַוּוּת מַחֲלֹקֶת הַיֵּצֶר הָרָע, שֶׁרָשׁוּ מִן הַמַּחֲלֹקֶת שֶׁבְּקְדֻשָּׁה. כְּשֶׁהַשְׁתַּלְשָׁלָה מִן דַּרְגָּא לְדַרְגָּא, עַד שֶׁנִּשְׁתַּלְשֵׁל לְמַטָּה, נִתְהַוֶּה מִמֶּנּוּ מַחֲלוֹקֶת הַיֵּצֶר הָרָע בִּבְחִינַת "חֵלַק לָבָם"... וּמַחֲלֹקֶת שֶׁבִּקְדֻשָּׁה הוּא מַחֲלֹקֶת תַּנָּאִים וַאֲמוֹרָאִים שֶׁבַּגְּמָרָא שֶׁזֶּה אוֹסֵר וְזֶה מַתִּיר. וּמֵהִשְׁתַּלְשְׁלוּתָם לְמַטָּה נִתְהַוֶּה מִמֶּנּוּ מַחֲלֹקֶת הַיֵּצֶר הָרָע. וּכְשֶׁמְּתַקֵּן הַמַּחֲלֹקֶת שֶׁבִּקְדֻשָּׁה, אֲזַי מִמֵּילָא נִתְבַּטֵּל מַחֲלֹקֶת הַיֵּצֶר הָרָע כִּי אֵין אֲחִיזָתוֹ אֶלָּא מִשָּׁם. וְתִקּוּן הַמַּחֲלֹקֶת שֶׁבִּקְדֻשָּׁה הֵן הֲלָכוֹת פְּסוּקוֹת. כִּי פְּסַק הֲלָכָה הוּא הַשָּׁלוֹם וְהַכְרָעָה שֶׁל מַחֲלוֹקַת הַתַּנָּאִים וְאָמוֹרָאִים. וְעַל יְדֵי לִמּוּד הַפּוֹסְקִים הוּא נִתְקָשֵׁר לְהַשָּׁלוֹם שֶׁבִּקְדֻשָּׁה וּמְתַקֵּן הַמַּחֲלֹקֶת שֶׁבִּקְדֻשָּׁה.

[279] *Likutei Amarim Tanya*, chapter 21 שאין הצמצומים והלבושים דבר נפרד ממנו יתברך ח״ו, אלא כהדין קמצא דלבושיה מיניה וביה.

shape, as illustrated below, alluding to the harmonization of the systems of *Iggulim* (עֲגוּלִים) and *Yosher* (יוֹשֶׁר).

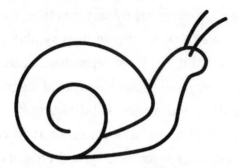

ೞೞ Reconciling Differences

Hashem is an absolute indivisible unity, but Creation appears separate from Him, with many divisions. To produce Creation, *Hashem* therefore first created the possibility of differentiation. He did so by creating a circular configuration of spheres (*Iggulim* עֲגוּלִים), but this configuration took differentiation to an extreme because it did not permit harmonious interaction among its different elements. It therefore had to be modified by reconfiguring the spheres into a straight line (*Yosher* יוֹשֶׁר).

The Hebrew for "snail" (שַׁבְּלוּל) alludes to the spiral shape of its shell — שָׁב means to "return" or "repeat" while לוּלָאָה means "loop," and a spiral consists of a repeating loop.

An object's Hebrew name refers to its spiritual essence, and the snail symbolizes the blending of the circular configuration of spheres with the straight one.

৪০৪০৪০ The Role of the Jewish Nation in Reconciling these Concepts

The sages refer to the snail by its Aramaic name, *Kamtza* (קַמְצָא), which can also refer to any tiny creature, such as an ant.[280] The *Maharal* explains that such creatures symbolize the concept of division and separation. They reproduce in the extreme and form huge swarms, symbolizing a radical degree of splitting apart — repeatedly dividing and subdividing.[281]

The concept of division or differentiation can be good or evil. The initial act of Creation was a good type of differentiation because Creation cannot exist without seeming to be separate from *Hashem*. Likewise, those who seek to become *Tzaddikim* must separate themselves to some degree from worldly matters.[282]

At the beginning of Creation, *Hashem* fashioned a system of primordial spiritual forces from which the rest of Creation emerged. This system of spiritual forces corresponds to all the two-letter combinations of the Hebrew alphabet, the total number of which is four hundred sixty-two, but these combinations include duplicates. For example, the first two-letter combination is אב. When reversed, the same two-letter combination is בא. The total number of unique two-letter combinations, without any such duplicates, is half that amount, i.e., two hundred thirty-

---

[280] *Rashi* on B.T. *Yevamoth* קמצא בעלמא" – חגב או נמלה"; *Kisei David, Derush* 18, *Derush Leshabbath Hagadol* "מַאי טַעְמָא קַרְנָא דְּקַמְצָא רְכִיכָא?" הוא השבלול

[281] *Netzach Yisrael*, chapter 5 וכאשר תדקדק בלשון "קמצא", כי השם הזה מורה על חילוק, שקורא "קמצא" על שם החילוק והפירוד, כי זה הוא לשון קמיצה, כמו "וְקָמַץ מִשָּׁם" (ויקרא ב', ב'). ובלשון חכמים גבי האחים שחלקו, ובא בעל חוב וטרף חלקו של אחד מהם, ואמר שם "מקמצים" (בבא בתרא ק"ז, ע"א), כלומר שגובין מעט מכל אחד. ולפיכך הנפרד והנחלק מהכל נקרא "קמצא"... ובלשון חכמים נקרא החגב "קמצא" (עדיות ח', ד')... וזה מפני כי יש בהם ריבוי גדול, ולכך נקרא "ארבה" על שם הריבוי. והריבוי הוא מכוח חילוק ופירוד, כי הדבר אשר הוא מתאחד אין שייך בו ריבוי, כי לא יתרבה רק המחולק והנפרד.

[282] See *Gur Aryeh* on Numbers 21:35 השם יתברך הוא שהביא עליהם קמצא, הם כוח אלוקי נבדל מן הגשמיּ)ות.

one.[283] The numeric value of "snail" (קַמְצָא) is also two hundred thirty-one, hinting that despite outward appearances, *Hashem* and His creation are not truly separate just as a snail's shell is part and parcel of the snail itself and grows together with it.

The aforesaid primordial forces of Creation correspond to the Jewish nation, as Rabbi Chanina explained, "Among those things which, [so to speak], arose in thought before the Holy One, Blessed be He, created His world, Israel arose because it was fit to receive the *Torah*."[284] The name "Israel" (יִשְׂרָאֵל) hints at this because its letters can be rearranged to mean "there are two hundred thirty-one" (יש רל"א).[285]

When Jews study the *Torah* and are united, they keep the primordial forces of Creation in equilibrium so that *Hashem* is at once both hidden so that Creation can exist and also sufficiently revealed so that the Divine Presence can manifest itself in the Temple.

When the concept of division and separation is carried to an extreme, however, the Divine Presence becomes so hidden that it cannot be revealed in the Temple. This occurred in the dispute which the *Gemara* records concerning Kamtza and Bar Kamtza, whose names mean "snail" (קַמְצָא).

When a wealthy Jerusalemite hosted a banquet, he told his servant to invite his friend Kamtza, but the servant mistakenly invited the host's adversary, Bar Kamtza. When Bar Kamtza appeared at the banquet, the host forced him to leave in a very

---

[283] To calculate how many possible two-letter combinations exist in the Hebrew alphabet, one must multiply the total of twenty-two letters by the number of other letters with which they may combine, i.e., twenty-one. (*Perush Hagra Al Sefer Yetzirah* 4:16   בכ"ב אותיות יש רל"א שערים פנים רל"א אחור כמנין כפל כ"ב עם כ"א).

[284] *Zohar Chadash*, Margolioth Edition, 88B   רבי חנינא אומר: מאותם דברים שעלו במחשבה קודם שברא הקב"ה את עולמו ישראל עלה במחשבה מפני שהוא ראוי לקבל התורה.

[285] *Shelah Hakadosh, Parashath Vayishlach, Torah Ohr* 5   יש רל"א – ישראל וזהו עניין

rude and humiliating way. Bar Kamtza then turned traitor and incited the Romans to destroy the Temple.[286]

The term *"Bar"* (בַּר) in Hebrew can mean "wild."[287] The name Bar Kamtza (בַּר קַמְצָא) therefore suggests a "wild snail," alluding to differentiation spreading in an uncontrolled, wild fashion beyond the confines which allow the Divine Presence to manifest itself in the Temple.

Once the divisions among Jews went wild, becoming so extreme that they extended beyond all reasonable bounds, the Divine Presence could no longer reveal itself in the Temple. Unable to serve its purpose, the Temple was certain to be destroyed. The numeric value of Bar Kamtza (בַּר קַמְצָא) hints at this because it is the same as "exile" (גָּלַת).

---

[286] B.T. *Gittin* 55B-56A אַקַּמְצָא וּבַר קַמְצָא חָרוּב יְרוּשְׁלַיִם. דְּהַהוּא גַּבְרָא דִּרְחֲמֵיהּ קַמְצָא וּבַעֵל דְּבָבֵיהּ בַּר קַמְצָא. עָבֵד סְעוּדָתָא. אָמַר לֵיהּ לְשַׁמְעֵיהּ: "זִיל אַיְיתִי לִי קַמְצָא". אָזַל אַיְיתֵי לֵיהּ בַּר קַמְצָא. אָתָא אַשְׁכְּחֵיהּ דַּהֲוָה יָתֵיב. אָמַר לֵיהּ: "מִכְּדֵי הַהוּא גַּבְרָא בַּעֵל דְּבָבָא דְּהַהוּא גַּבְרָא הוּא, מַאי בָּעֵית הָכָא? קוּם פּוּק!" אָמַר לֵיהּ: "הוֹאִיל וְאָתָאי, שִׁבְקָן וְיָהֵיבְנָא לָךְ דְּמֵי מַה דְּאָכִילְנָא וְשָׁתֵינָא". אָמַר לֵיהּ: "לָא!" אָמַר לֵיהּ: "יָהֵיבְנָא לָךְ דְּמֵי פַּלְגָא דִּסְעוּדָתִיךְ". אָמַר לֵיהּ: "לָא!" אָמַר לֵיהּ: "יָהֵיבְנָא לָךְ דְּמֵי כּוּלַּהּ סְעוּדָתִיךְ". אָמַר לֵיהּ: "לָא!" נַקְטֵיהּ בִּידֵיהּ וְאוֹקְמֵיהּ וְאַפְּקֵיהּ. אָמַר: "הוֹאִיל וַהֲווּ יָתְבֵי רַבָּנָן וְלָא מְחוּ בֵיהּ, שְׁמַע מִינָהּ קָא נִיחָא לְהוּ. אֵיזֵיל אֵיכוּל בְּהוּ קוּרְצָא בֵּי מַלְכָּא".

[287] For example, *"Tarnegol"* (תַּרְנְגוֹל) means "rooster," and *"Tarnegol Bar"* (תַּרְנְגוֹל בַּר) means "wild rooster."

Tzedakah, a Unique Mitzvah

✥ Tzedakah Makes One Wealthy and Saves from Death

The *Mitzvah* of giving charity (צְדָקָה) has two beneficial consequences for the donor: a) those who contribute to *Tzedakah* become wealthy,[288] and b) *Tzedakah* saves from death.[289]

These benefits sometimes manifest themselves openly, sometimes not.

The *Mishnah* teaches, "Who is wealthy? One who is satisfied with his portion."[290] Thus, the reward for giving to charity may sometimes be a feeling of satisfaction with what one has rather than an improvement in finances.

---

[288] B.T. *Shabbath* 119A עָשֵׁר בִּשְׁבִיל שֶׁתִּתְעַשֵּׁר

[289] Proverbs 10:2 לֹא יוֹעִיל הוֹן בְּיוֹם עֶבְרָה וּצְדָקָה תַּצִּיל מִמָּוֶת and 11:4 לֹא יוֹעִילוּ רֶשַׁע וּצְדָקָה תַּצִּיל מִמָּוֶת תַּצִּיל מִמָּוֶת.

[290] *Pirkei Avoth* 4:1 אֵיזֶהוּ עָשִׁיר ? הַשָּׂמֵחַ בְּחֶלְקוֹ.

Likewise, even people who contribute to charity eventually die, but giving to charity protects them from judgment and assures them eternal life in the world to come.[291]

Nevertheless, in some instances the rewards for donating to charity manifest themselves even in this world as many stories in the *Talmud* and *Midrash* show. One famous passage is the following:

> Sh'muel and [a non-Jewish astrologer named] Ablat were sitting together when some men passed on their way to a pasture [to cut wood].
>
> Ablat commented to Sh'muel, "That man will go and not return, for a snake will bite him, and he will die."
>
> "If he is a Jew," replied Sh'muel, "he will go and return [safely]."
>
> While they were still sitting together, the same person went and returned. Ablat arose and threw down the man's load [of wood to examine it]. He discovered a snake which had been cut in two.
>
> "What did you do?" Sh'muel asked [the man].
>
> "Every day we [workers] pool our food together and eat it. Today there was one among us who had no food and was embarrassed [by his poverty]. I said [to the others], 'I'll go and collect [the food from everyone].' When I reached that person, I pretended to take from him, [but substituted from my own food] in order not to shame him."
>
> "You performed a charitable act."
>
> [As a result of this incident,] Sh'muel went forth and expounded, "'Charity saves from death,' and not only from a

---

[291] *Midrash Mishlei* 10 שנאמר, "לֹא יוֹעִיל הוֹן בְּיוֹם עֶבְרָה, וּצְדָקָה תַּצִּיל מִמָּוֶת" (משלי י"א, ד') ונאמר "לֹא יוֹעִילוּ אוֹצְרוֹת רֶשַׁע, וּצְדָקָה תַּצִּיל מִמָּוֶת" (משלי י', ב'). שתי צדקות למה? אחת שמצלת מדינה של גיהנם ואחת שמצלת ממיתה משונה.

gruesome death, but from death itself," [i.e., even from judgment in *Gehinnom*].

...Rabbi Akiva had a daughter concerning whom the astrologers said, "On the day she enters the wedding hall, a snake will bite her, and she will die."

Rabbi Akiva was very worried about her. On the day [of the wedding], she took a hairpin and stuck it into [a crack in] the wall [for safekeeping]. It so happened that it struck the eye of a snake, [killing it]. In the morning, when she removed [the hairpin], the snake came trailing along after it.

"What did you do?" inquired her father.

"In the evening, [during the wedding celebration], a beggar came and called at the gate, but everyone was preoccupied with the feast, so no one paid him any mind. I got up, took the portion that had been given me, and gave it to him."

"You performed a charitable act."

[As a result of this incident,] Rabbi Akiva went forth and expounded, "'Charity saves from death,' and not only from a gruesome death, but from death itself," [i.e., even from judgment in *Gehinnom*].[292]

৪৩৪৩ How Does Tzedakah Have the Power to Do This?

No other *Mitzvah* has such power that its promised reward often comes about even in this world.

What is unique about *Tzedakah*?

According to the original laws of nature ordained by the Creator, human beings were to live forever in the Garden of Eden where all their needs would have been met without any effort on their part. When Adam and Chavah sinned, God

---

[292] B.T. *Shabbath* 156B. The full Hebrew text appears in Appendix D.

altered the laws of nature so that people must work for a living and eventually die.

When a person contributes to the poor, he eases the burden of their livelihood and extends their lives. In this way, the donor partially restores the recipients to the initial state of affairs which existed in the Garden of Eden. Measure for measure, God sometimes rewards those who give *Tzedakah* by providing them with a bountiful livelihood just as if they resided in the Garden of Eden. Alternatively, He rescues them from death and they ultimately merit life in the Garden of Eden.

When God does this, He is not performing a miracle in the usual sense. Rather, He is merely reinstating the original laws of nature. This is why the Prophet Malachi declared:

> Bring all the tithes to the storehouse, and let there be food in My House, and test Me with this, says *Hashem*, [Master] of Multitudes, if I do not open for you the windows of Heaven and empty out for you an endless blessing.[293]

One may not test *Hashem* with respect to other *Mitzvoth* because He would have to change the laws of nature to achieve a supernatural result. With *Tzedakah*, however, the reward is not supernatural. Instead, matters merely revert to the original state of affairs in the Garden of Eden where poverty and death did not exist.[294]

---

[293] Malachi 3:10 הָבִיאוּ אֶת כָּל הַמַּעֲשֵׂר אֶל בֵּית הָאוֹצָר וִיהִי טֶרֶף בְּבֵיתִי וּבְחָנוּנִי נָא בָּזֹאת אָמַר ה׳ צְ-בָאוֹת אִם לֹא אֶפְתַּח לָכֶם אֵת אֲרֻבּוֹת הַשָּׁמַיִם וַהֲרִיקֹתִי לָכֶם בְּרָכָה עַד בְּלִי דָי.

[294] There is a difference of opinion about whether one may test *Hashem* with any *Tzedakah* or only specifically when tithing produce (*Shulchan Aruch, Yoreh Deah* 247:4 הצדקה דוחה את הגזירות הקשות, וברעב תציל ממות... הגה... ואסור לנסות הקב״ה כי אם בדבר (זה... ויש אומרים דווקא בנתינת מעשר מותר לנסות הקב״ה, אבל לא בשאר צדקה.

✿✿✿ Understanding this on a Deeper Level

How does charity restore the original configuration of spiritual forces which existed prior to Adam and Chavah's sin?

The paradigm for charitable giving is the tithe (מַעֲשֵׂר). The *Torah* requires farmers to donate one-tenth of their produce to the Levites.[295] The Levites, in turn, must give one-tenth of what they receive to the *Kohanim* — the *Torah* calls this "a tithe of a tithe" (מַעֲשֵׂר מִן הַמַּעֲשֵׂר) — with the result that the *Kohanim* received one-hundredth of the total crop.[296]

Corresponding to the concept of tithing, there is a method of calculating the numeric value of words called "small number" (מִסְפָּר קָטָן), which involves eliminating the tens and hundreds units.

The logic behind this method is that all Creation derives from ten spiritual worlds which combine and recombine to produce all created things. Each spiritual world, or sphere, has aspects of all the others in it. For this reason, as mentioned above, when counting the *Omer*, reference is made to the sub-world of Kindness which is in Glory (חֶסֶד שֶׁבְּתִפְאֶרֶת), the sub-world of Might which is in Glory (גְּבוּרָה שֶׁבְּתִפְאֶרֶת), and so on. Each of these sub-worlds, in turn, has aspects of each other sub-world in it so that there are an infinite number of sub-worlds, sub-sub-worlds, sub-sub-sub-worlds and so on. However, all of these spiritual realms derive from one of the original ten spheres, so that at their source they are only ten. Accordingly, when calculating a word's

---

[295] Numbers 18:21   וְלִבְנֵי לֵוִי הִנֵּה נָתַתִּי כָּל מַעֲשֵׂר בְּיִשְׂרָאֵל לְנַחֲלָה חֵלֶף עֲבֹדָתָם אֲשֶׁר הֵם עֹבְדִים אֶת עֲבֹדַת אֹהֶל מוֹעֵד.

[296] Numbers 18:26 and 28   (כו) וְאֶל הַלְוִיִּם תְּדַבֵּר וְאָמַרְתָּ אֲלֵהֶם כִּי תִקְחוּ מֵאֵת בְּנֵי יִשְׂרָאֵל אֶת הַמַּעֲשֵׂר אֲשֶׁר נָתַתִּי לָכֶם מֵאִתָּם בְּנַחֲלַתְכֶם וַהֲרֵמֹתֶם מִמֶּנּוּ תְּרוּמַת ה' מַעֲשֵׂר מִן הַמַּעֲשֵׂר... (כח) כֵּן תָּרִימוּ גַם אַתֶּם תְּרוּמַת ה' מִכֹּל מַעְשְׂרֹתֵיכֶם אֲשֶׁר תִּקְחוּ מֵאֵת בְּנֵי יִשְׂרָאֵל וּנְתַתֶּם מִמֶּנּוּ אֶת תְּרוּמַת ה' לְאַהֲרֹן הַכֹּהֵן.

numeric value, one may ignore the tens and hundreds units and count only the single digits.[297]

Since seemingly unrelated phenomena of the physical world have the same source, one who accesses that source can cause those phenomena to interchange with one another.

In the case of "death" (מָוֶת), the usual numeric value is four hundred forty-six, calculated as follows:

$$
\begin{array}{lll}
\textit{Mem} \ (\text{מ}) & = & 40 \\
\textit{Vav} \ (\text{ו}) & = & 6 \\
\textit{Tav} \ (\text{ת}) & = & \underline{400} \\
& & 446
\end{array}
$$

According to the "small number" (מִסְפָּר קָטָן) system, however, the numeric value of "death" (מָוֶת) is fourteen, calculated by removing the tens and hundreds units:

$$
\begin{array}{lll}
\textit{Mem} \ (\text{מ}) & = & 4 \\
\textit{Vav} \ (\text{ו}) & = & 6 \\
\textit{Tav} \ (\text{ת}) & = & \underline{4} \\
& & 14
\end{array}
$$

The Hebrew for "life" (חַיִּים) ordinarily has a numeric value of sixty-eight, calculated as follows:

---

[297] In practice, there are only nine digits because zero is not counted in this system. This is because the highest sphere in any lower set of worlds is also the lowest sphere in the set above it. (*Nefesh Hachayim* 1:17 וכידוע בכתבי האריז"ל שחיצונית מלכות של כל עולם ופרצוף נעשה פנימיות כתר להעולם או הפרצוף שתחתיו).

```
Cheth (ח) =      8
Yud  (י) =     10
Yud  (י) =     10
Mem  (ם) =     40
                68
```

According to the "small number" (מִסְפָּר קָטָן) system, however, "life" (חַיִּים) also has a numeric value of fourteen:

```
Cheth (ח) =      8
Yud  (י) =      1
Yud  (י) =      1
Mem  (ם) =      4
                14
```

Strange as it may seem, life and death have the same spiritual root. When people contribute to *Tzedakah,* they connect the spiritual forces which generate death to their source and convert them to life.

In the case of growing rich as a result of donating to *Tzedakah,* the same principle applies because the Hebrew for "poor" (עָנִי) has the same "small number" (מִסְפָּר קָטָן) value as the Hebrew for "rich" (עָשִׁיר):

```
              Standard    Small Number
                Value         Value
Ayin (ע) =       70     =       7
Nun  (נ) =       50     =       5
Yud  (י) =       10     =       1
                130            13
```

		Standard Value		Small Number Value
Ayin (ע)	=	70	=	7
Shin (ש)	=	300	=	3
Yud (י)	=	10	=	1
Raish (ר)	=	200	=	2
		580		13

One who donates to *Tzedakah* accesses the spiritual source of "poor" (עָנִי) and converts it to "rich" (עָשִׁיר).

In addition, the sages note the similarity between the words for "tithe" (מַעֲשֵׂר) and "wealth" (עוֹשֶׁר), and instruct Jews to, "Tithe so that you may grow wealthy."[298] One who donates to charity causes the spiritual configuration of "tithe" (מַעֲשֵׂר) to transform into "wealth" (עוֹשֶׁר).

Tzedakah has the power to do this because the usual way to accumulate wealth is to keep one's money, not to give it away. Since people who donate to *Tzedakah* behave in a manner which is the reverse of the way in which people ordinarily accumulate wealth, measure for measure, *Hashem* reverses the laws of nature for them at their source.

Furthermore, those who contribute to *Tzedakah* show their belief that the material world is less important to them than the spiritual world, which is the source of the commandment to give to *Tzedakah*. Measure for measure, *Hashem*, in a manner of speaking, adopts the position that the current laws of nature are not too important and sets them aside for the donor.

---

[298] B.T. *Shabbath* 119A עַשֵּׁר בִּשְׁבִיל שֶׁתִּתְעַשֵּׁר

Reincarnation

෨ The Source of the Doctrine of Reincarnation

Hashem told Adam, "By the sweat of your face shall you eat bread until your return to the earth, for from it you were taken; for you are dust, and to the dust shall you return."[299]

The end of this verse seems redundant. Once God told Adam that he would die and return to the earth, why repeat the exact same idea by saying "for you are dust, and to the dust shall you return"? The *Shelah Hakadosh* explains that these extra words hint that Adam and his progeny would undergo repeated reincarnations, returning to the dust over and over again.[300]

---

[299] Genesis 3:19 בְּזֵעַת אַפֶּיךָ תֹּאכַל לֶחֶם עַד שׁוּבְךָ אֶל הָאֲדָמָה כִּי מִמֶּנָּה לֻקָּחְתָּ כִּי עָפָר אַתָּה וְאֶל עָפָר תָּשׁוּב

[300] *Shelah Hakadosh, Parashath Mishpatim* דְּהַיְנוּ "כִּי עָפָר אַתָּה וְאֶל עָפָר תָּשׁוּב" (בראשית ג', י"ט), דְּהַיְנוּ סוֹד הַגִּלְגּוּל שֶׁיִּתְגַּלְגֵּל מֵעָפָר לְעָפָר דְּהַיְנוּ מִגּוּף לְגוּף וְיָמוּת וְיַחֲזֹר וְיָמוּת.

Rabbeinu Bachye notes that the wording of the verse, "A generation goes, and a generation comes,"[301] contradicts common observation. Since people are first born and later die, the verse should say, "a generation *comes* [into the world], and a generation *goes* [out of the world]." The reversed order hints that after a generation dies out it will return.[302]

৪৩৪৩ A Person's Worldly Success Depends upon What He Did in a Previous Lifetime

The *Gemara* records a parable told by Rabbah bar bar Chana:

> [A certain Arab guide] said to me, "Come, I will show you where the Earth and the sky kiss one another."
>
> [Upon arriving there], I took up my basket and placed it in the window of the sky while I recited my prayers. I sought [to retrieve it], but I could not find it, [so] I said, "There must be thieves here."
>
> [The guide] told me, "This is the wheel of the sky which turns. Wait here until tomorrow, and you will find it."[303]

Rabbi Nachman of Breslov explains that when Rabbah bar bar Chana said that he placed his basket in the window of

---

301 Ecclesiastes 1:4 דּוֹר הֹלֵךְ וְדוֹר בָּא וְהָאָרֶץ לְעוֹלָם עֹמָדֶת

302 *Rabbeinu Bachye* on Exodus 34:7 לפי "דור בא ודור הולך" כי על דרך הפשט היה ראוי שיאמר שהנולדים הם באים והמתים הם הולכים, אבל אמר "דור הולך ודור בא" כי ההולך הוא בא.

    Rabbeinu Bachye also relates the Hebrew for "generation" (דוֹר) to "ball" (כַּדּוּר) ((י"ח כ"ב, (ישעיה רַחַבַת יָדָיִם" אֶל אֶרֶץ מלשון "כַּדּוּר שהוא "דוֹר לשון (וזהו. Just as a ball repeatedly touches the ground as it rolls along, a person's soul repeatedly visits the Earth.

303 B.T. *Baba Bathra* 74A אָמַר לִי (ההוא טייעא): "תָּא וְאַחֲוֵי לָךְ הֵיכָא דְּנָשְׁקֵי (ואמר רבה בר בר חנה): אַרְעָא וּרְקִיעָא אַהֲדָדֵי". שַׁקְלְתָא לְסִילְתָּאי, אִתְנָחֲתָה בְּכַוְּותָא דִּרְקִיעָא אַדְּמַצְּלֵינָא. בָּעִיתֵיהּ וְלָא אַשְׁכַּחִיתֵהּ. אֲמִינָא לֵיהּ: "אִיכָּא גַּנְּבֵי הָכָא !" אֲמַר לִי: "הַאי גַּלְגַּלָּא דִּרְקִיעָא הוּא דַּהֲדַר. נְטַר עַד לִמְחָר הָכָא וּמַשְׁכַּחַת לָהּ".

the sky and prayed, he meant that he prayed for his livelihood. After finishing his prayers, he looked for his basket — his livelihood — but could not find it, so his prayers seemed ineffective. His guide explained that the reason a righteous person does not have a sufficient livelihood is due to the wheel of the sky, meaning reincarnation.[304] Something he did in a previous lifetime impaired his ability to earn a living in his present lifetime.

ഇഇ Rectifying Wrongdoing among Jews

The *Zohar* states that the verse, "These are the statutes [governing financial disputes] which you shall place before them,"[305] means, "These are the adjustments [brought about by] reincarnations."[306]

Degel Machneh Ephraim asks why the *Zohar* relates the laws governing financial disputes to the seemingly unrelated topic of reincarnation?

He explains that sometimes the *Halachah* is not applied correctly. A deceptive person may succeed in misleading a Jewish court with false claims backed by false proofs or even false witnesses. Alternatively, a party who by rights should win his case sometimes fails to do so because he lacks acceptable proof to support his claim.[307]

Although a Jewish court may rule incorrectly, the *Torah* is absolutely true and cannot be subverted. Such injustices are

---

[304] *Likutei Moharan, Mahadura Kama* 14:9 שֶׁקֶל – "וְשָׁקְלִית לְסַלְתָּאִי וְאַנַּחְתֵּיהּ בְּכַוָתָא דִרְקִיעָ"
לַתְפִלָּה שֶׁהוּא לְצֹרֶךְ הַגּוּף וְאַנָחָה בִּתְפִלָּה, הַכֹּל לְצֹרֶךְ נִשְׁמָתוֹ, כִּי מִמֵּילָא כְּשֶׁנִּתְקַן שָׁם בְּרוּחָנִיּוֹת, נִתְקָן גַּם בְּגַשְׁמִיּוֹת.
"וְעַד דִּמְצַלֵּינָא בָּעוּתִי לָא אַשְׁכְּחָה" – הַיְנוּ אַחַר כָּךְ לֹא מָצָא כְּדֵי פַּרְנָסָתוֹ אַף עַל פִּי שֶׁתִּקֵּן אַף עַל פִּי כֵן
לֹא נִמְשַׁךְ לוֹ שֶׁפַע בְּגַשְׁמִיּוֹת. אָמַר: "אִיכָּא גַּנְבָא הָכָא" – שֶׁגּוֹנְבִים הַשֶּׁפַע שֶׁלִּי. הֵשִׁיב לוֹ: "גַּלְגַּלָּא דִּרְקִיעָא דְּהַדְרָא"
– הַיְנוּ גִּלְגּוּלִין דִּנְשָׁמָתִין הִיא הַגּוֹרֶמֶת שֶׁאֵין לַצַּדִּיק כְּדֵי פַּרְנָסָתוֹ.

[305] Exodus 21:1 וְאֵלֶּה הַמִּשְׁפָּטִים אֲשֶׁר תָּשִׂים לִפְנֵיהֶם

[306] *Zohar* II:94A אִלֵּין אִינוּן סִדּוּרִין דְּגִלְגּוּלָא

[307] As the rabbis teach, "A judge has nothing to go on but what his eyes see" (B.T. *Sanhedrin* 6B אֵין לוֹ לַדַּיָּין אֶלָּא מַה שֶּׁעֵינָיו רוֹאוֹת).

corrected when the parties to the case are reincarnated and matters work out so that the person who was wronged retrieves his loss from the opposing party.[308]

At first glance it seems strange that *Hashem* would create a system of reincarnation primarily for the purpose of setting financial matters straight. One would think that such worldly matters are trivial and have nothing to do with spirituality. Why is it so important to fix them?

In addition, it is difficult to understand how this system corrects wrongdoings when those who live in a later generation are unaware of anything that happened in their previous lifetimes.

The answer is that it is true that financial matters have little to do with spirituality, but it is for that very reason that wronging another person financially damages the soul. People who cheat others demonstrate that they care more about the trivialities of this world than they do about spiritual matters.

In addition, a key element of faith in *Hashem* is the belief that poverty and wealth flow from His will. One who takes something to which he is not *Halachically* entitled demonstrates lack of faith in *Hashem*. As a result, such individuals damage their souls. Just as such damage is not perceptible to people because it is spiritual in nature, so the rectification of that damage is not recognized by those who are reincarnated.

---

[308] Based on *Degel Machneh Ephraim, Parashath Mishpatim* sub verba *"Ve'eleh"* (ואלה):

והוא תמוה לכאורה. הא בפסוק מפרש ואזיל דיני ממונות ! ...וזה יש לומר שרימז הזוהר הקדוש ואלה המשפטים שהם דיני ממונות אף על פי שמן הנראה הם נגד האמת לפעמים אך דהאמת הוא אילין סדורין דגלגולא והיינו הבורא הכל ובורא כל הנשמות הוא היודע איך היה בגלגולים הקודמים בין איש לחבירו ככה יסובב המסבב ומנהיג על פי התורה את עולמו בחסד וברחמים ובצדק ובמשפט.

ೞಣೞ Keeping Creation in Existence

On a deeper level, *Hashem* is one simple undifferentiated and indivisible Being,[309] whereas Creation has many divisions and differentiations. When Jews unite and eliminate the differences among themselves, they attain a degree of indivisibility and thereby some similarity to *Hashem*. This helps bridge the gap between Creation and *Hashem*, and since nothing can exist without some connection to Him, it keeps Creation in existence. Moreover, in the end of days this bond will be strengthened to the point where the Divine Presence will be revealed in the physical realm.

When one Jew wrongs another, his actions cause disunity among the Jewish nation, and this has cosmic consequences that delay the ultimate redemption. When the parties to a miscarriage of justice are reincarnated and pass through circumstances that correct it, they repair the damage caused to the spiritual unity of Israel.

ೞಣೞಣ The Punishment of the Slingshot

Abigail was a prophet who became one of King David's wives. On one occasion, she told him, "May the soul of my master be bound in the bond of life with *Hashem*, your God, and may the souls of your enemies be spun in the pocket of a slingshot."[310] According to the *Vilna Gaon*, the punishment of being "spun in the pocket of a slingshot" refers to repeated reincarnations.[311]

---

[309] *Hayad Hachazakah, Hilchoth Yesodei Hatorah* 1:7 א-לוה זה אחד הוא ואינו שניים ולא יתר על שניים. אלא אחד שאין כיחודו אחד מן האחדים הנמצאים בעולם. לא אחד כמין שהוא כולל אחדים הרבה ולא אחד כגוף שהוא נחלק למחלקות ולקצוות. אלא יחוד שאין יחוד אחר כמותו בעולם.

[310] I Samuel 25:29 -אֶ 'וְהָיְתָה נֶפֶשׁ אֲדֹנִי צְרוּרָה בִּצְרוֹר הַחַיִּים אֵת ה' וְלְבַקֵּשׁ אֶת נַפְשֶׁךָ וַיָּקָם אָדָם לְרָדְפְךָ לְהֶיךָ וְאֵת נֶפֶשׁ אֹיְבֶיךָ יְקַלְעֶנָּה בְּתוֹךְ כַּף הַקָּלַע.

[311] *Biur Hagra* on Proverbs 11:4 כף הקלע שבזה נכלל סוד הגלגול

The type of slingshot referred to in the *Tanach* had a stone placed inside a pocket attached to strap. The person using the slingshot whirled it over his head and, when it gained enough speed, he released the stone so that it flew off in the desired direction.

To understand the analogy between a slingshot and reincarnation one must understand the principles of physics involved in its use.

Although Sir Isaac Newton publicized the principle of inertia and gave it a scientific formulation in 1687, it was well-known to the rabbis centuries beforehand. The *Radak*, who lived about five hundred years before Sir Isaac, explains that, "If a person rolls a ball over the surface of the Earth and there is no barrier or anything else to stop it, it will continue to roll until it encounters something that stops it."[312]

When a person spins a slingshot, inertia causes the stone to pull away and travel in a straight line. By holding the slingshot firmly, the person using it counteracts the stone's inertia and keeps it traveling in a circular path. When the user releases his grip, the stone flies off, as illustrated below.

See also *Biurei Aggadoth* (*Afikei Yam*) by Rabbi Yitzchak Isaac Chaver on B.T. *Shabbath* 152B בסוד הגלגול והוא כף הקלע

[312] *Radak* on Isaiah 22:18 כמו שמשליך אדם הכדור בארץ רחבת ידיים שאין שם גדר או דבר מעכבו שהוא מתגלגל והולך עד שימצא דבר שיעכבנו. Friction between the ball and the Earth's surface is the "anything else" which slows the ball and eventually stops it.

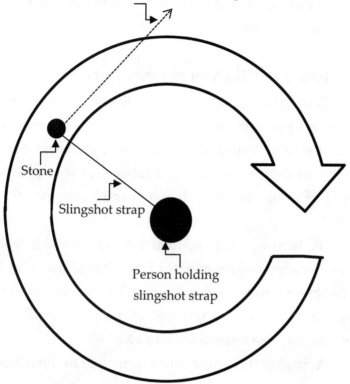

Direction in which the stone will travel
due to inertia if released at this point

Stone

Slingshot strap

Person holding
slingshot strap

Just as a stone inside the pocket of a slingshot tends to fly away from the person holding it, the souls of the Jewish nation have a natural tendency to fly off towards the higher spiritual worlds. Their physical bodies, however, resemble the person holding the strap of the slingshot, connecting them to the physical realm and preventing them from doing so.[313]

---

[313] See *Toldoth Yaakov Yosef, Parashath Mishpatim* 2, בכל נשימה הנשמה רוצה לצאת מהגוף,
שהם ב׳ הפכים – הנשמה מצד הקדושה חושקת) לדברים קדושים והגוף עכור חושק לגשמיים, היפך הקדושה.

This is hinted at in the verse, "A generation goes, and a generation comes, but the Earth stands forever."[314] The souls of Israel rotate through repeated cycles of reincarnation in generation after generation, but the Earth — the physical realm — holds them fast.

ఴఴఴఴఴ The Year of Jubilee (יוֹבֵל)

During the Jubilee year (יוֹבֵל), Jewish slaves were set free, and whoever sold his ancestral landholdings got them back, as the *Torah* states, "You shall proclaim liberty throughout the land to all its inhabitants. It shall be a Jubilee for you, and you shall return [each] man to his landholding and [each] man to his family."[315]

In Hebrew, when the final letter of a word is repeated, it makes the word more emphatic. For instance, the term *Mar* (מַר) means "bitter," so *Maror* (מָרוֹר) means "excessively bitter."[316] Similarly, *Sar* (סָר) means "to turn away," and *Sorer* (סוֹרֵר) means "to rebel," an extreme form of turning away.[317]

Applying this grammatical principle to this verse, if *Dor* (דוֹר) means "generation," then *D'ror* (דְּרוֹר) — "liberty" — has the enhanced meaning of referring to the combined force of all generations of Jews throughout history sufficient to liberate the nation from the physical world.[318]

---

[314] Ecclesiastes 1:4 דּוֹר הֹלֵךְ וְדוֹר בָּא וְהָאָרֶץ לְעוֹלָם עֹמָדֶת

[315] Leviticus 25:10 וְקִדַּשְׁתֶּם אֵת שְׁנַת הַחֲמִשִּׁים שָׁנָה וּקְרָאתֶם דְּרוֹר בָּאָרֶץ לְכָל יֹשְׁבֶיהָ יוֹבֵל הִוא תִּהְיֶה לָכֶם וְשַׁבְתֶּם אִישׁ אֶל אֲחֻזָּתוֹ וְאִישׁ אֶל מִשְׁפַּחְתּוֹ תָּשֻׁבוּ.

[316] *Mishnah B'rurah*, note 35 on *Shulchan Aruch, Orach Chayim* 473:5 ומרור – הוא גם כן מין ירק מר הידוע להם בשם מרור על שם שהוא מר ביותר.

[317] *Rashi* on Deuteronomy 21:18 סורר – סר מן הדרך

[318] See *Ramban* on Leviticus 25:10 ועל דרך האמת, "דרור" מלשון "דוֹר הֹלֵךְ וְדוֹר בָּא" (קהלת א', ד').

In addition, *Rabbeinu Bachye* comments that besides meaning "generation," *Dor* (דוֹר) can mean to "spin like a ball."[319] *D'ror* (דְּרוֹר) refers to "liberty" in the sense that an extreme form of spinning — numerous repeated reincarnations — will enable Israel to break away from the physical realm.

This future time corresponds to the Jubilee (יוֹבֵל) as implied by the phrase "you shall return [each] man to his landholding and [each] man to his family."[320] Eventually, the cycle of reincarnation will cease,[321] and the souls of all the generations of the Jewish nation will return to their spiritual root and source.[322]

ഇരുഇരുഇരു The Mechanism that will Cause the Cycle of Reincarnation to Cease

Releasing the strap of the slingshot is not the only way in which a stone can break away from the circular path it follows and fly off in the direction dictated by inertia.

A sudden extreme gain in the stone's mass would cause it to break away from the pull of the person holding the strap. Furthermore, if the strap would be strong enough and the stone massive enough, it could even drag the person holding the strap along with it.

To understand this principle, consider how the Earth revolves around the Sun. The Earth does not fly away from its orbit because the Sun, which contains more than three hundred thousand times more mass than the Earth, has a gravitational pull

---

[319] *Rabbeinu Bachye* on Exodus 34:7 "וזהו לשון "דור" שהוא מלשון "כַּדּוּר אֶל אֶרֶץ רַחֲבַת יָדָיִם" (ישעיה כ"ב, י"ח).

[320] Leviticus 25:10 וְשַׁבְתֶּם אִישׁ אֶל אֲחֻזָּתוֹ וְאִישׁ אֶל מִשְׁפַּחְתּוֹ תָּשֻׁבוּ

[321] *Perush Harekanati Al Hatorah, Parashath Behar* יש עוד מן המקובלים אחרונים שפירשו בסוד היובל כי אז יכלה גלגול הנשמות ויחזרו כל הנשמות לאצילותן וזהו "וְשַׁבְתֶּם אִישׁ אֶל אֲחֻזָּתוֹ".

[322] *Ramban* on Leviticus 25:10 וכן "יובל" שישוב אל היובל אשר שם שרשיו

strong enough to prevent the Earth from doing so. If matters were suddenly reversed and the Earth had hundreds of thousands of times more mass than the Sun, it would not only stop revolving around the Sun and fly out of its orbit, but its gravitational force would pull the Sun along with it.

Reincarnation rectifies injustices among Jews and thus perfects the connections among them. In the end of days, after repeated reincarnations, the souls of all members of the Jewish nation will be completely harmonized and united. The nation will then achieve the spiritual "critical mass" necessary for its drive toward spirituality to overcome its attachment to the physical realm. This attachment will not be broken, however. Rather, the Jewish nation will drag the physical realm along with it. Jewish souls will elevate their bodies so that their bodies will acquire a spiritual quality and live forever.

This explains the many statements of the sages that in the future all physical things will be elevated and take on an enhanced spiritual character. For example, Rabbi Levi said, "In the future Jerusalem will encompass the Land of Israel, and the Land of Israel will encompass the entire world,"[323] and Rabbi Shimon ben Elazar declared that non-Jews will convert.[324]

෨ Sod Ha'ibur (סוֹד הָעִבּוּר) ෨

The Jewish calendar uses lunar months, but twelve lunar months have only 354 days, whereas the solar year has 365 days. If no adjustment were made to the calendar, the holidays would occur during different seasons of the year. The *Torah*, however,

---

[323] *Pesikta Rabbethai* 1 אמר רבי לוי: עתידה ירושלים להיות כארץ ישראל וארץ ישראל ככל העולם כולו

[324] B.T. *Berachoth* 40B, citing Zephaniah 3:9 כִּי אָז אֶהְפֹּךְ אֶל עַמִּים שָׂפָה בְרוּרָה לִקְרֹא כֻלָּם בְּשֵׁם ה'; and see also Zachariah 2:15 וְנִלְווּ גוֹיִם רַבִּים אֶל ה' בַּיּוֹם הַהוּא וְהָיוּ לִי לְעָם ה', לְעָבְדוֹ שְׁכֶם אֶחָד

states that Passover must fall during springtime.[325] To ensure that this happens, the calendar is adjusted by making some months twenty-nine days and some thirty days, and by adding an extra month every two or three years.

The sages refer to the calculations used to determine when to insert these extra days and months as *Sod Ha'ibur* (סוד הָעִבּוּר), literally the "secret of the pregnancy."[326] Just as a pregnant woman's abdomen becomes extended, so the year becomes extended through the insertion of additional days or an additional month.[327]

The ordinary understanding of reincarnation is that when a person dies with issues which require rectification, he is reincarnated in a different body so that he can make that rectification.

Rabbi Chayim Vital explains that there is another kind of reincarnation that may occur while a person is still alive.

When a person performs a *Mitzvah* with proper intent and devotion, the soul of a *Tzaddik* who performed the same *Mitzvah* in a previous generation may join that person to assist him with his spiritual rectification.[328] Just as a day or month is added to the calendar to adjust it to achieve the proper result, a spiritual component from the soul of a deceased *Tzaddik* may assist a person in completing his spiritual rectification. The recipient of the *Tzaddik's* help is not consciously aware of it, and this phenomenon is also called *Sod Ha'ibur* (סוד הָעִבּוּר).

---

[325] Exodus 23:15 אֶת חַג הַמַּצּוֹת תִּשְׁמֹר שִׁבְעַת יָמִים תֹּאכַל מַצּוֹת כַּאֲשֶׁר צִוִּיתִךָ לְמוֹעֵד חֹדֶשׁ הָאָבִיב כִּי בוֹ יָצָאתָ מִמִּצְרָיִם וְלֹא יֵרָאוּ פָנַי רֵיקָם.

[326] *Malbim* on Exodus 12:2 סוד" שנקרא והעיבורים החודשים קביעת פה בעל למשה אז מסר 'שה העיבור" וחישוב תקופות ומזלות.

[327] *Ma'or Vashamesh, Parashath Pekudei* שנות עם הלבנה שנות להשוות כדי הם העיבור חודשי כי החמה... וגם נקרא חודש העיבור כי בעיבור כלול כל הולד כמו אישה עוברה.

[328] *Sha'ar Hagilgulim, Hakadamah* 3 ואז כתקנה, ויעשנה מצוה, איזו האדם ליד יזדמן לפעמים כי מצווה בעניין יחד שנתדמו וכיוון כתקנה, עצמה המצווה אותה שעשה קדמון צדיק איזה מן אחד נפש לו יזדמן זאת, יתעבר בו נפש הצדיק ההוא.

This is what the rabbis meant when they taught that, "The Holy One, Blessed be He, observed that the righteous are few, [so He] arose and planted them in each and every generation."[329] When *Hashem* foresaw that few people would succeed in becoming righteous on their own, He "planted the righteous in each and every generation," enabling the souls of the *Tzaddikim* to influence people and help them develop spiritually.

Rabbi Tarfon taught that, "You are not obligated to complete the work, but you are also not free to desist from it."[330] People usually are not able to complete the work of spiritual rectification on their own and therefore are not obligated to do so. Nevertheless, they must make some effort to merit assistance in completing that rectification. A component from the soul of a *Tzaddik* then joins them to make up the remainder.

This process also functions conversely — part of the soul of a dead individual who requires rectification may join a living *Tzaddik* who rectifies and elevates it, as seen in the following passage of the *Gemara*:

> Rav Yosef used to cry when he reached this verse: "There is one who perishes [prematurely] although there is no judgment, [meaning that he has not yet completed the preordained term of his lifespan]."[331]
>
> Asked [the *Gemara*], "Is there one who goes before his time?"
>
> Indeed [there is], as was [witnessed by] Rav Bibi bar Abaye whom the Angel of Death frequented.

---

[329] B.T. *Yoma* 38B. [וְאָמַר] רַבִּי חִיָּא בַּר אַבָּא (ש)אָמַר רַבִּי יוֹחָנָן: רָאָה הַקָּדוֹשׁ בָּרוּךְ הוּא שֶׁצַּדִּיקִים מוּעָטִין, עָמַד וּשְׁתָלָן בְּכָל דּוֹר וָדוֹר.

[330] *Pirkei Avoth* 2:16 לֹא עָלֶיךָ הַמְּלָאכָה לִגְמוֹר וְלֹא אַתָּה בֶן חוֹרִין לִבָּטֵל מִמֶּנָּה

[331] Proverbs 13:23 רָב אֹכֶל נִיר רָאשִׁים וְיֵשׁ נִסְפֶּה בְּלֹא מִשְׁפָּט

[The Angel of Death] told his agent, "Go bring me Miriam the women's hair-braider."

[The agent] went and brought him Miriam the childcare provider.[332]

"I told you Miriam the hair-braider!" exclaimed [the Angel of Death].

"In that case I'll return her," replied [his agent].

"As long as you brought her, let her be included in the quota [of those who must die], but how did you overpower her, [seeing as she was not yet destined to die]?"

"She had taken a poker in her hand and was stirring up [coals] in the oven. She took it and [accidentally] put it on her leg. [Her leg] burned, her *Mazal* went bad, and I brought her."[333]

Rav Bibi bar Abaye asked [the Angel of Death], "Do you have permission to do so?"

He responded, "Is it not written, 'There is one who perishes [prematurely] although there is no judgment'?"[334]

"But," [objected Rav Bibi bar Abaye], "is it not [also] written, 'A generation goes, and a generation comes,'[335] [implying that each generation must consist of a given number of people, and this cannot be the case if someone destined to live in a certain generation dies prematurely]?"

"I take charge of [the souls of] such individuals until they fill out the generation, [i.e., until the time they were destined to live and be part of the generation passes], and I then

---

[332] Apparently, the agent was confused because the Aramaic words for braiding hair and raising children are similar (מְגַדְלָא).

[333] Generally, a person's *Mazal* determines how long he or she will live. Nevertheless, the Heavenly Tribunal judges people in times of danger and may permit retribution to occur then (B.T. *Shabbath* 32A וּמַאי שְׁנָא בִשְׁעַת לֵידָתָן? אָמַר רָבָא: נָפַל תּוֹרָא, חַדֵּד לְסַכִּינָא.).

[334] Proverbs 13:23 רַב אֹכֶל נִיר רָאשִׁים וְיֵשׁ נִסְפֶּה בְּלֹא מִשְׁפָּט

[335] Ecclesiastes 1:4 דּוֹר הֹלֵךְ וְדוֹר בָּא וְהָאָרֶץ לְעוֹלָם עֹמָדֶת

turn them over to Dumah, [the angel in charge of the dead]." [Since her soul continued to roam the Earth with the Angel of Death, she was still counted among the members of that generation.]

"Even so, what do you do with her years [that she should have lived]?"

"If there is a young *Torah* scholar who [has been wronged, but] does not stand on his rights, I add them to [his lifetime], and it counts as a [valid] substitution."[336]

Rav Bibi bar Abaye pointed out to the Angel of Death that when people die prematurely, they cannot accomplish the rectification they were meant to accomplish during their sojourn in a given generation.[337] The Angel of Death responded that when people die prematurely, their spiritual rectification is achieved by a *Tzaddik* who takes over the remaining years they were destined to live. Rather than the soul of a departed *Tzaddik* joining and assisting someone else, a living *Tzaddik* takes on a spiritual component from a less righteous person who died and performs the rectification that person was meant to achieve.[338]

The sages state that when a young *Torah* scholar becomes angry it is because the *Torah* makes him hotheaded.[339] By this they mean that a young scholar who studies intensely and with zeal recognizes the truth of the *Torah* and feels more deeply

---

[336] B.T. *Chagigah* 4B-5A. See Appendix E for the full text.

[337] As mentioned above, the phrase "A generation goes, and a generation comes" refers to reincarnation.

[338] As *Rashi* comments on this passage, the souls of those who die prematurely "roll about and roam the world until their years are completed," an expression which implies that a form of reincarnation (גִּלְגּוּל) is involved (אֵינִי מוֹסְרָן לְשׁוֹמֵר הַמֵּתִים שֶׁשְּׁמוֹ דוּמָה, אֶלָּא מִתְגַּלְגְּלִין עֲמִי וְשָׁטִין בָּעוֹלָם עַד שֶׁיִּתְמַלְאוּ שְׁנוֹתָיו, וְהוּא קָרוּי "דוֹר").

[339] B.T. *Ta'anith* 4A וְאָמַר רָבָא: הַאי צוּרְבָא מֵרַבָּנָן דְּרָתַח, אוֹרָיְיתָא הוּא דְּקָא מַרְתְּחָא לֵיהּ, שֶׁנֶּאֱמַר, "הֲלוֹא כֹה דְבָרִי כָּאֵשׁ נְאֻם ה'" (ירמיה כ"ג, כ"ט).

offended than others when he is mistreated or his rights are violated. In addition, a young person tends to be more hot-blooded than an older one, so if a young *Torah* scholar is forbearing, then he is an exceptionally righteous person.[340]

This is especially important to the ultimate rectification of the world which cannot happen until the souls of all Jews are united with one another through the process of eliminating all injustices among them. As mentioned above, such injustices can be corrected through reincarnation. However, they can also be corrected if the victims of wrongdoing forgive those who have offended them. The Angel of Death revealed to Rav Bibi bar Abaye that when a righteous young *Torah* scholar forgives those who wrong him, he achieves the same effect as reincarnation. Accordingly, awarding the years of a person who died prematurely to such a scholar accomplishes the same spiritual rectification which the deceased would have accomplished had he or she lived.

๛ Time and Reincarnation
๛๛ Circles and Squares Symbolize the Supernal Worlds

The sages teach that "the same image that fits inside a circle fits perfectly inside a square."[341] This sounds like a mathematical impossibility because the area of a circle equals πr^2, and since π (3.14159...) cannot be calculated to its last decimal place, there is no way anyone can determine the exact area of a circle and

---

[340] *Benayahu ben Yehoyada* on B.T. *Chagigah* 5A נראה לי בס"ד תרתי בעי – חדא עודנו בחור וקטן בשנים דדמו רותח ונוח לכעוס ולהקפיד, ועוד דהוא חכם דאורייתא מרתחא ליה. ועם כל זה מעביר במיליה.
[341] *Tikunei Zohar Chadash, Tikuna Kadma'ah* כְּדְיֹקְנָא דְּאָעֵיל בְּעִגּוּלָא הַהוּא דְיֹוקְנָא מַמָּשׁ אָעֵיל בְּרִבּוּעָא.

fashion a square with an area precisely equal to it. Accordingly, the sages' statement should be understood as follows.

It is true that one cannot equate the *areas* of a circle and a square, but the rabbis spoke of equating their *images*, and there is an aspect of their images which is identical.

If one divides a square from its centerpoint into four quadrants, the angle of each is ninety degrees, for a total of 360 degrees, as shown below.

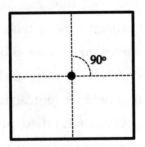
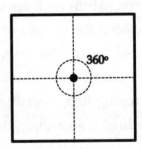

The same is true of a circle divided into four quadrants diverging from its center:

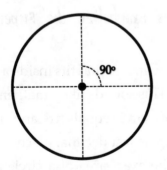
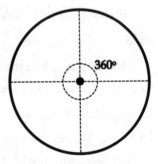

Despite their different shapes, squares and circles share the same 360-degree range of angles emanating from their centers.

The spiritual worlds are classified into four general categories which are, from highest to lowest, Emanation (אֲצִילוּת), Creation (בְּרִיאָה), Formation (יְצִירָה), and Action (עֲשִׂיָּה). The highest of these, Emanation (אֲצִילוּת), is so close to *Hashem* that no meaningful concept of separation or differentiation between *Hashem* and His Creation exists. Among the lower categories, Creation (בְּרִיאָה) is said to resemble a square, Formation (יְצִירָה) a circle, and Action (עֲשִׂיָּה) a square.[342]

This arrangement resembles a set of two squares and a circle inscribed in one another, as illustrated below.

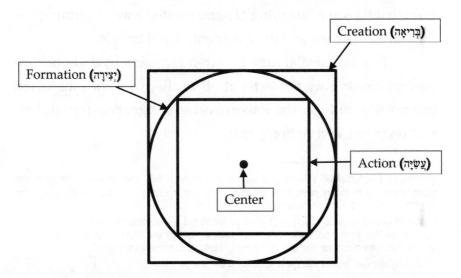

∞∞∞ The Source of Division is Primordial Time

Although these three shapes share the same center, if the relationship of each to the center is considered separately, the total of their center angles equals 1080 degrees (3 x 360).

---

[342] *Tikunei Zohar Chadash* פִּירוּדָא וְלָא חַשְׁבְּנָא תַּמָּן לָאו אֲצִילוּת,; *Kithvei Harama Mifano*, *Maamar Meah Kesita* 63 לבריאה רמז בתוכו שהעיגול העליון והרבוע בעשיה רבועה ביצירה, עגולא.

The *Rambam* explains that the sages divided each hour into 1080 parts because 1080 divides easily into many different whole numbers.[343] Time therefore symbolizes division.

Hashem is one simple undifferentiated and indivisible unit,[344] but Creation has many divisions and differentiations. Accordingly, one of the first things *Hashem* created was the concept of division. He did so by creating time, which may be divided into past, present, and future as well as into many subunits. As the sages taught, "In the beginning" (בְּרֵאשִׁית) counts as one of the ten expressions *Hashem* used to create the universe.[345] This implies that the very first thing *Hashem* created was "beginning" — the concept of time and the fragmentation it entails.[346]

This primordial time is extremely subtle and almost imperceptible. It does not exist at all in the world of Emanation (אֲצִילוּת)[347] — only in the lower worlds of Creation (בְּרִיאָה), Formation (יְצִירָה), and Action (עֲשִׂיָּה).

---

[343] *Hayad Hachazakah, Hilchoth Kiddush Hachodesh* 6:2 והשעה מחולקת לאלף ושמונים חלקים. ולמה חלקו השעה למניין זה? לפי שמניין זה יש בו חצי ורביע ושמין ושליש ושתות ותשיע וחומש ועישור והרבה חלקים יש לכל אלו השמות.

[344] *Hayad Hachazakah, Hilchoth Yesodei Hatorah* 1:7 א-לוה זה אחד הוא ואינו שניים ולא יתר על שניים. אלא אחד שאין כיחודו אחד מן האחדים הנמצאים בעולם. לא אחד כמין שהוא כולל אחדים הרבה ולא אחד כגוף שהוא נחלק למחלקות ולקצוות. אלא יחוד שאין יחוד אחר כמותו בעולם.

[345] B.T. *Rosh Hashanah* 32A בְּרֵאשִׁית נָמֵי מַאֲמָר הוּא

[346] This explains why the seventy-two elders who translated the *Torah* into Greek for King Ptolemy reversed the wording of this verse to read, "God created in the beginning." (B.T. *Megillah* 9A מַעֲשֶׂה בְּתַלְמַי הַמֶּלֶךְ שֶׁכִּינֵס שִׁבְעִים וּשְׁנַיִם זְקֵנִים וְהִכְנִיסָן בְּשִׁבְעִים וּשְׁנַיִם בָּתִּים וְלֹא גִּילָּה לָהֶם עַל מַה כִּנְּסָן. וְנִכְנַס אֵצֶל כָּל אֶחָד וְאֶחָד וְאָמַר לָהֶם: "כִּתְבוּ לִי תוֹרַת מֹשֶׁה רַבְּכֶם!" נָתַן הַקָּדוֹשׁ בָּרוּךְ הוּא בְּלֵב כָּל אֶחָד וְאֶחָד וְהִסְכִּימוּ כּוּלָּן לְדַעַת אַחַת וְכָתְבוּ לוֹ, "אֱ-לֹהִים בָּרָא בְּרֵאשִׁית"). Although they were concerned that the king would misunderstand a literal translation of the text, they did not alter the wording of the verse in a false manner. Their translation is valid because *Hashem* indeed created "beginning," i.e., time, before the rest of Creation.

[347] *Shefa Tal, Chelek Tal* 6:1 אין האצילות נופל תחת הזמן

According to *Pithchei She'arim, Nethiv Seder Hapartzufim* 7 this is only true in the three highest levels of the realm of Emanation (אֲצִילוּת): כדי להבין מה ההבדל בין שתי בחינות שבעתיק שהן א) בחינות הג' ראשונות שלו הקשורים להנהגת הנצחיות, ב) ובחינות הז' תחתונות שלו שהם במדרגת הנהגת הזמן, צריך להבין מה הוא עניין הזמן עצמו.

೮೦೮೦ Unity among Jews Imitates Hashem's Unity

The *Midrash* teaches that God created the universe for the sake of the Jewish nation which is called "first" (רֵאשִׁית).[348] Israel therefore corresponds to time. Just as the 1080 units of an hour may be divided into many different whole numbers, so Israel may be divided into many different subunits as well as into its individual members. In fact, such division is often commendable as when Jethro advised *Moshe Rabbeinu* to divide the nation into subunits to ease the burden of attending to their needs.[349]

However, God's purpose in creating humankind was to have a dwelling place in the physical world.[350] This occurs when human beings bear some resemblance to their Creator and thereby draw His Presence into the world. This is why Abba Shaul said, "Just as He is gracious and merciful, so you be gracious and merciful."[351] Just as God is indivisible, so Jews must overcome the differences between them and become, to some extent, indivisible. Their unity then serves as an interface between *Hashem* and the physical realm.

In the spiritual realm, the opposing worlds of Kindness (חֶסֶד) and Judgment (גְּבוּרָה) are harmonized and melded together in the world of Glory (תִּפְאֶרֶת).[352] This synthesis of opposites corresponds to the way in which Jews must overcome their differences to connect the physical realm to *Hashem*. The numeric value of Glory (תִּפְאֶרֶת) is 1081, alluding to the 1080 subunits of an

---

[348] *Yalkut Shimoni* on Genesis 1, paragraph 2 אמר ר' יהודה בר שלום: ...בראשית – בזכות ישראל שנקראו ראשית שנאמר, "קֹדֶשׁ יִשְׂרָאֵל לַה' רֵאשִׁית תְּבוּאָתֹה" (ירמיה ב, ג').

[349] Exodus 18:21 וְאַתָּה תֶחֱזֶה מִכָּל הָעָם אַנְשֵׁי חַיִל יִרְאֵי אֱ-לֹהִים אַנְשֵׁי אֱמֶת שֹׂנְאֵי בָצַע וְשַׂמְתָּ עֲלֵהֶם שָׂרֵי אֲלָפִים שָׂרֵי מֵאוֹת שָׂרֵי חֲמִשִּׁים וְשָׂרֵי עֲשָׂרֹת.

[350] *Midrash Tanchuma, Parashath Nasso* 16 אמר רבי שמואל בר נחמן: בשעה שברא הקב"ה את העולם נתאווה שיהא לו דירה בתחתונים כמו שיש בעליונים.

[351] B.T. *Shabbath* 133B הֱוֵי דוֹמֶה לוֹ – מַה הוּא חַנּוּן וְרַחוּם אַף אַתָּה הֱיֵה חַנּוּן וְרַחוּם.

[352] *Kehillath Yaakov, Erech Lechem* התפארת הוא המכריע בין חסד וגבורה ומחבר החסד לגבורה להמתיקה.

hour — the concept of differentiation — combined with the absolute unity of the one God.

After the destruction of the Temple, Jeremiah lamented, "He cast down the glory of Israel from Heaven to Earth."[353] The "glory of Israel" (תִּפְאֶרֶת יִשְׂרָאֵל) which had risen to Heaven and connected the physical realm to the spiritual one was cast down, and the connection was damaged.

Reincarnation has a special relationship to this idea because its chief purpose is to rectify injustices among Jews and thereby unify the nation. As the sages teach, "There is no person who does not have his hour,"[354] and, "There are people who acquire their entire world in a single hour."[355] A person may live an entire lifetime primarily for the purpose of correcting an injustice that took place in a prior lifetime. He or she thereby rectifies the concept of an hour, i.e., time and the apparent differentiations which exist throughout Creation.

ೞೞೞೞ Primordial Time, Exile, and Redemption

The Hebrew language has several words for time. The sages state that one of these, "*Eth*" (עֵת), refers to the Divine Presence,[356] which is the corporate soul of the Jewish nation.[357]

What does time (עֵת) have to do with these other matters?

Eth (עֵת) connotes not ordinary time, but primordial time — the potential from which all past, present, and future events

[353] Lamentations 2:1 אֵיכָה יָעִיב בְּאַפּוֹ אֲ-דֹנָי אֶת בַּת צִיּוֹן הִשְׁלִיךְ מִשָּׁמַיִם אֶרֶץ תִּפְאֶרֶת יִשְׂרָאֵל וְלֹא זָכַר הֲדֹם רַגְלָיו בְּיוֹם אַפּוֹ.

[354] *Pirkei Avoth* 4:3 שֶׁאֵין לְךָ אָדָם שֶׁאֵין לוֹ שָׁעָה

[355] See *Be'er Mayim Chayim, Parashath Re'eh* 12 ...(אבות ד',ג'). "שֶׁאֵין לְךָ אָדָם שֶׁאֵין לוֹ שָׁעָה" הנה נודע הדבר מסוד גילגולי הנשמות כי לפעמים יתגלגל האדם...לתקן הקילקול מה שעיוות באחת ממצוות ה'... ועל זה אמרו חז"ל: "יֵשׁ קוֹנֶה עוֹלָמוֹ בְּשָׁעָה אַחַת" (מסכת עבודה זרה י', ע"ב; י"ז, ע"א).

[356] *Kehillath Yaakov, Erech Sal* "עת" נקרא השכינה כי

[357] *Zohar* I:116A "עת" דא כנסת ישראל

emerge. For this reason, there are three words which refer to "past," "present," and "future" that start with *Eth* (עֵת). They are "ancient" (עָתִיק), "now" (עַתָּה), and "future" (עָתִיד).

King Solomon writes that, "There is a season and time (עֵת) for everything under the sun."[358] He then goes on to list fourteen pairs of opposing times such as "a time (עֵת) for war and a time (עֵת) for peace," for a total of twenty-eight times. The Hebrew for "potential" (כֹּח) has a numeric value of twenty-eight, so these verses imply that all conflicting forces in the universe have their source in primordial time before it crystallizes into the time with which people are familiar.[359]

As mentioned, the Divine Presence (שְׁכִינָה) is identical to the corporate soul of Israel (כְּנֶסֶת יִשְׂרָאֵל).[360] *Rabbeinu Nissim* explains that, "The great attachment that a person has to his Creator is the Divine Presence (שְׁכִינָה)."[361] In other words, the Divine Presence (שְׁכִינָה) is the interface between *Hashem* and humanity. This interface includes all of the potential connections between humankind and God from the beginning of time until the end of days.

The sages state that, "The Holy One, Blessed be He, did not exile Israel among the nations except so that converts could be added to them."[362] The Divine Presence accompanies the Jewish nation in exile[363] because without the Divine Presence, which

[358] Ecclesiastes 3:1 לַכֹּל זְמָן וְעֵת לְכָל חֵפֶץ תַּחַת הַשָּׁמָיִם

[359] *Megaleh Amukoth, Parashath Vayera* רוצה (קהלת ג', א') "לַכֹּל זְמָן וְעֵת לְכָל חֵפֶץ תַּחַת הַשָּׁמָיִם" לומר עת הוא בכוח למעלה מהזמן שהוא מוכן ומזומן לצאת לפועל.

[360] *Kav Hayashar* 64 השכינה כוללת כלל נשמותיהן של ישראל, ולכן נקראת השכינה כנסת ישראל

[361] *D'rashoth Haran* 5 והנה הדבקות הגדול שיש בין האדם לבוראו היא השכינה

[362] B.T. *Pesachim* 87B וְאָמַר רַבִּי אֶלְעָזָר: לֹא הִגְלָה הַקָּדוֹשׁ בָּרוּךְ הוּא אֶת יִשְׂרָאֵל לְבֵין הָאוּמּוֹת אֶלָּא כְּדֵי שֶׁיִּתּוֹסְפוּ עֲלֵיהֶם גֵּרִים.

[363] B.T. *Megillah* 29A רַבִּי שִׁמְעוֹן בֶּן יוֹחַאי אוֹמֵר: בּוֹא וּרְאֵה כַּמָּה חֲבִיבִין יִשְׂרָאֵל לִפְנֵי הַקָּדוֹשׁ בָּרוּךְ הוּא שֶׁבְּכָל מָקוֹם שֶׁגָּלוּ שְׁכִינָה עִמָּהֶן.

includes all potential connections between God and humanity, Israel could not fulfill its mission of gathering converts.[364]

Since the Divine Presence includes all the potential connections between God and humankind, it is intertwined with primordial time (עֵת), which includes the potential of all of history from beginning to end.

The connection between *Hashem* and humankind can only be perfected when all of the souls included in the corporate soul of Israel, i.e., the Divine Presence, are perfectly united over the course of time. Hence, the final redemption can only occur after all the souls included in the Divine Presence are invested in human bodies as many times as necessary for this to occur.[365]

---

[364] *Aruch Lanair* on B.T. *Makoth* 24B דאמרו רז"ל כל מקום שגלו ישראל שכינה שנקראת כנסת ישראל גלתה עמהם.

[365] See *Pithchei She'arim, Nethiv Partzuf Zeir Anpin* 23 וכל אדם מישראל יש לו דרך ומדרגה בפני עצמו בתיקוני המאורות העליונים, שאין צדיק דומה לחברו ואין לך יום ושעה דומה לחברתה. רק כל א' לפי שורש נשמתו יש לו מדרגה בפני עצמו בזער אנפין, והוא כולל אילן שלם שבו נמצאים כל המדרגות שכתבנו, וגם משתנה לפי הזמן המתחלף בכל עת שעושה תמיד תיקונים חדשים בסוד גלגולי תתר"ף רגעים שבכל שעה, שבכל רגע הוא צירוף משם הוי"ה שכולל כל האילן וכל המדרגות, הכל ע"פ צירוף הנקודות והאותיות של רל"א שערים פנים ואחור.

The Cherubim
הַכְּרוּבִים

The *Torah* commands: "You shall make two gold *Cherubim*. Make them beaten out from the two ends of the lid [of the Ark]. Make one *Cherub* from one end and one *Cherub* from the other end; from the lid [of the Ark] make *Cherubim* on its two ends."[366]

In addition to these golden *Cherubim*, King Solomon installed ten-cubit tall wooden *Cherubim* on either side of the Ark,[367] and images of *Cherubim* were embroidered into the

---

[366] Exodus 25:18-19 וְעָשִׂיתָ שְׁנַיִם כְּרֻבִים זָהָב מִקְשָׁה תַּעֲשֶׂה אֹתָם מִשְּׁנֵי קְצוֹת הַכַּפֹּרֶת. וַעֲשֵׂה כְּרוּב אֶחָד מִקָּצָה מִזֶּה וּכְרוּב אֶחָד מִקָּצָה מִזֶּה מִן הַכַּפֹּרֶת תַּעֲשׂוּ אֶת הַכְּרֻבִים עַל שְׁנֵי קְצוֹתָיו.

   Rashi explains that rather than first fashioning the *Cherubim* and then soldering them onto the lid of the Ark, the artisans left extra gold at the ends of the lid when they cast it. They then used mallets to beat the extra gold into the shape of *Cherubim* (*Rashi* ad. loc. שלא תעשם בפני עצמם ותחברם בראשי הכפרת לאחר עשייתם כמעשה צורפים שקורין שולדיר"ן אלא הטיל זהב הרבה בתחילת עשיית הכפורת והכה בפטיש ובקורנס באמצע וראשין בולטין למעלה וצייר וציר הכרובים בבליטת קצוותיו).

[367] I Kings 6:23 וַיַּעַשׂ בַּדְּבִיר שְׁנֵי כְרוּבִים עֲצֵי שָׁמֶן עֶשֶׂר אַמּוֹת קוֹמָתוֹ

curtain which hung between the sanctuary (קֹדֶשׁ) and the Holy of Holies (קֹדֶשׁ הַקֳּדָשִׁים).[368]

๛ The Function of the Cherubim

All of these *Cherubim* correspond to angels in the spiritual realm of the same name. These angels compose part of the Divine Chariot — the system of spiritual worlds through which *Hashem's* Divine light passes to form the physical realm.[369] This is suggested by their name (כְּרֻב), which has the same letters as the grammatical root of "chariot" (מֶרְכָּבָה). The Prophet Samuel also hinted at this by stating that God "rode upon a *Cherub*."[370]

The prophets envisioned the *Cherubim* as having faces that resemble a baby's face.[371] A new-born baby is an entirely unknown potential. No one knows what personality a baby will have, what experiences he or she will undergo, or what decisions he or she will need to make. The prophets perceived the *Cherubim* as looking like babies because these angels represent the unknown potential of Creation — an intermediate state between the infinite Source of Creation and finite Creation.[372] This

---

According to Rabbi Moshe Feinstein, ten cubits is about 21.5 feet, or roughly 6.5 meters. Other estimates range from eighteen to twenty-four feet, or about 5.5 to 7.5 meters.

[368] Exodus 26:31 וְעָשִׂיתָ פָרֹכֶת תְּכֵלֶת וְאַרְגָּמָן וְתוֹלַעַת שָׁנִי וְשֵׁשׁ מָשְׁזָר מַעֲשֵׂה חֹשֵׁב יַעֲשֶׂה אֹתָהּ כְּרֻבִים; Exodus 26:33 וְנָתַתָּה אֶת הַפָּרֹכֶת תַּחַת הַקְּרָסִים וְהֵבֵאתָ שָׁמָּה מִבֵּית לַפָּרֹכֶת אֵת אֲרוֹן הָעֵדוּת וְהִבְדִּילָה הַפָּרֹכֶת לָכֶם בֵּין הַקֹּדֶשׁ וּבֵין קֹדֶשׁ הַקֳּדָשִׁים.

[369] *Malbim* on Exodus 32:1 המרכבה שיחזקאל ראה במרכבה הראשונה צורת שור משמאל, ובמרכבה השניה ראה תמורתו צורת כרוב

Rashi on I Chronicles 28:18 הם הכרובים שהשכינה רוכבת עליהם

[370] II Samuel 22:11 וַיִּרְכַּב עַל כְּרוּב וַיָּעֹף וַיֵּרָא עַל כַּנְפֵי רוּחַ

[371] *Rashi* on Exodus 25: 18 דמות פרצוף תינוק להם

[372] See *Malbim, Mashal Umelitzah* on Song of Songs 1:17 שתדבק הנפש עם האין סוף יתברך כפי הציור שציווה ה' לעשות בבית המקדש שהוא אמצעי בין האין סוף ובין הצמצום – בין הבלתי גבול ובין הגבול – כי ברצות ה' האין סוף ובלתי בעל תכלית לשכון כבוד על נפשות ישראל אשר הם מוגבלים ומצומצמים בתכלית כי מושב הנפש בעליית קיר קטנה כפף איש היה כען כעין פשר שיבנו לו בית ארזים כאילו הא-ל הנשגב

clarifies why God chose to communicate with *Moshe Rabbeinu* from the space between the gold *Cherubim* on the Ark's lid.[373]

The word *Cherub* (כְּרֻב) also alludes to the intermediating function of the *Cherubim*. The number one symbolizes the Creator who is one absolute unity. The letters of *Cherub* (כְּרֻב) indicate the first step away from the Creator and towards Creation because *Beth* (ב) has a numeric value of two, the second in the series of the ones units, *Kaf* (כ) has a numeric value of twenty, the second in the series of the tens units, and *Raish* (ר) has a numeric value of two hundred, the second in the series of the hundreds units.[374]

These three letters symbolize three elements of Creation — time, the spiritual, and the physical.

When *Kaf* (כ) appears before a word it sometimes means "when" as in, "It was when Abram came (כְּבוֹא אַבְרָם) to Egypt."[375] *Kaf* (כ) therefore alludes to time.

Beth (בֵּית) means "house," a reference to the spiritual structures (worlds) which house the Divine light when it emerges from the Infinite One, Blessed be He.[376]

יעזוב ענייניו שהוא בלתי בעל גבול ובלתי מתקומם במקום לשכון במקום מוגבל על כנפי הכרובים תחת קורות ארזים.

[373] Exodus 25:22 וְנוֹעַדְתִּי לְךָ שָׁם וְדִבַּרְתִּי אִתְּךָ מֵעַל הַכַּפֹּרֶת מִבֵּין שְׁנֵי הַכְּרֻבִים אֲשֶׁר עַל אֲרוֹן הָעֵדֻת אֵת כָּל אֲשֶׁר אֲצַוֶּה אוֹתְךָ אֶל בְּנֵי יִשְׂרָאֵל.

[374] See *Ohev Yisrael, Parashath Bo* 'א והנה הצירוף של בכ"ר הוא אותיות שניות היינו ב' שניה לאות שהיא תחילת יחידית. כ' הוא שניה לאות יו"ד שהוא התחלת העשיריות. ר' היא שניה לאות ק' שהוא תחילת המאות. והגם שהם אותיות שניות עם כל זאת המה דבוקים בשורשם ואחדותם באלופו של עולם.

[375] Genesis 12:14 וַיְהִי כְּבוֹא אַבְרָם מִצְרָיְמָה וַיִּרְאוּ הַמִּצְרִים אֶת הָאִשָּׁה כִּי יָפָה הִוא מְאֹד

[376] *Zohar* II:43B states that the commandment, "Sanctify for Me every firstborn," (Exodus 13:2) alludes to four overarching spiritual houses, or realms, that emerge from nothingness ('קַדֶּשׁ לִי כָל בְּכוֹר" דָּא אִיהוּ רָזָא עִלָּאָה דְּכָלִיל כָּל ד" בָּתִּים בְּרָזָא דִּנְהִירוּ עִלָּאָה דְּנָפְקָא מֵאַיִן). Parenthetically, the Hebrew for "firstborn" (בְּכֹר) has the same letters as *Cherub* (כְּרֻב).

Raish (רֵישׁ) denotes "head" (ראש)[377] and hints at the expression "the head of all outlying areas" (ראש כָּל חוּצוֹת).[378] This refers to the physical realm which lies far away from the spiritual realm even though its head, or source, is there.

All of Creation — time, the physical realm, and the spiritual realm — emanate from *Hashem*, who produces them by means of the *Cherubim*. The Hebrew *Olam* (עוֹלָם) encompasses all three because it can refer to the physical world or to a spiritual world and also means "forever." When spelled without a *Vav* (ו), *Olam* (עֹלָם) can be read to mean "child" (עֶלֶם), alluding to the *Cherubim*, which resemble small children or babies and connect between the Infinite One, Blessed be He, and all aspects of Creation.

The Prophet Ezekiel stated concerning the *Cherubim* that "their feet are [one] straight foot."[379] All aspects of Creation are rooted in a single Source. The *Cherubim* are the intermediaries through which the one unique Creator produces and maintains a diverse Creation.

The root of the term the *Torah* uses for the ends of the Ark (קְצוֹתָיו)[380] where the golden *Cherubim* stood also means "timespan" (קֵץ), as King David said, "Inform me of my end (קִצִּי) and what the measure of my days is."[381] The *Cherubim* represented the entire span of history from beginning to end. The numeric value of the expression "from one end" (מִקָּצָה) is two hundred thirty-five. It appears twice in the verse cited above which describes the placement of the *Cherubim*, yielding a total

---

[377] *Pardes Rimonim* 27:23 רִי״שׁ פִּירוּשׁוֹ רֹאשׁ

[378] Isaiah 51:20; Nahum 3:10; Lamentations 2:19 and 4:1.

[379] Ezekiel 1:7 וְרַגְלֵיהֶם רֶגֶל יְשָׁרָה -אֶ תַּחַת רָאִיתִי אֲשֶׁר הַחַיָּה הִיא as clarified by Ezekiel 10:20 לְהֵי יִשְׂרָאֵל בִּנְהַר כְּבָר וָאֵדַע כִּי כְרוּבִים הֵמָּה

[380] Exodus 25:19 וַעֲשֵׂה כְּרוּב אֶחָד מִקָּצָה מִזֶּה וּכְרוּב אֶחָד מִקָּצָה מִזֶּה מִן הַכַּפֹּרֶת תַּעֲשׂוּ אֶת הַכְּרֻבִים עַל שְׁנֵי קְצוֹתָיו.

[381] Psalms 39:5 הוֹדִיעֵנִי ה' קִצִּי וּמִדַּת יָמַי מַה הִיא אֵדְעָה מֶה חָדֵל אָנִי

numeric value of four hundred seventy, the same as "primordial time" (עֵת).

The Divine Presence, which is identical to the corporate soul of Israel, dwelled between the two *Cherubim* atop the Ark.[382] Thus, the fusion of the corporate soul of Israel and primordial time manifested itself there.

This explains the teaching of the sages that Joshua fit the entire nation between the poles which were mounted on either side of the Ark next to the *Cherubim*.[383] This was possible because the space between them represented the combined efforts of all Jews throughout history to serve *Hashem* and to cling to Him.

This also explains why the *Midrash* states that the *Cherubim* were among five things which were not destroyed or carried off by the Babylonians when the First Temple was destroyed. Instead, they were hidden away and will be restored at the time of the final redemption.[384] Since the world cannot exist without a nexus between the infinite and the finite, the *Cherubim* had to remain intact.

---

[382] *Yalkut Shimoni* on Zachariah 6, paragraph 574 שהייתה שכינה שרויה בין שני הכרובים

[383] *Breishith Rabbah* 5:7 זָקֵן אָמַר: רַב הוּנָא אָמַר (יהושע ג׳, ט׳). "וַיֹּאמֶר יְהוֹשֻׁעַ אֶל בְּנֵי יִשְׂרָאֵל גֹּשׁוּ הֵנָּה וגו׳" בֵּין שְׁנֵי בַּדֵּי הָאָרוֹן. רַבִּי אַחָא בְּרַבִּי חֲנִינָא: סְמָכָן בֵּין שְׁנֵי בַּדֵּי הָאָרוֹן. וְרַבָּנָן אַמְרִין: צִמְצְמָן בֵּין שְׁנֵי בַּדֵּי הָאָרוֹן. אָמַר לָהֶן יְהוֹשֻׁעַ: "מִמַּה שֶׁהֶחֱזִיקוּ שְׁנֵי בַּדֵּי הָאָרוֹן אֶתְכֶם אַתֶּם יוֹדְעִים שֶׁשְּׁכִינָתוֹ שֶׁל הַקָּדוֹשׁ בָּרוּךְ הוּא בֵּינֵיכֶם". (*Imrei Emeth, Parashath T'rumah* attributes this feat to *Moshe Rabbeinu* משה רבינו ע״ה כלל כל ישראל בין שני הכרובים.)

[384] *Bamidbar Rabbah* 15:10 כשחרב בית המקדש, נגנזה המנורה. וזה אחד מחמשה דברים שנגנז – הארון והמנורה והאש ורוח הקדש והכרובים. וכשישוב הקב״ה ברחמיו ויבנה ביתו והיכלו הוא מחזירן למקומן.

FAITH (אֱמוּנָה) HAS THE POWER TO ALTER NATURE

The Heaven Called "Curtain" (וִילוֹן)

✺ Curtain (וִילוֹן) Represents Faith

Raish Lakish stated: [There are] seven [heavens], and they are: curtain (וִילוֹן), firmament, highest heavens,[385] dwelling, habitation, abode, and expanses. Curtain (וִילוֹן) does nothing but enter in the morning and leave at night and renew the work of Creation.[386]

Raish Lakish's statement seems self-contradictory. First, he declares that Curtain (וִילוֹן) does nothing, but then he states that it renews the act of Creation daily.

What does he mean?

---

[385] Yonathan ben Uziel on Jeremiah 51:9 translates שְׁחָקִים as שמי שמיא.

[386] B.T. *Chagigah* 12B. רֵישׁ לָקִישׁ אָמַר: שִׁבְעָה וְאֵלוּ הֵן: וִילוֹן, רָקִיעַ, שְׁחָקִים, זְבוּל, מָעוֹן, מָכוֹן, עֲרָבוֹת. וִילוֹן אֵינוֹ מְשַׁמֵּשׁ כְּלוּם, אֶלָּא נִכְנָס שַׁחֲרִית וְיוֹצֵא עַרְבִית וּמְחַדֵּשׁ בְּכָל יוֹם מַעֲשֵׂה בְרֵאשִׁית.

Curtain (וילון) has the same numeric value as faith (אֱמוּנָה). Unlike other *Mitzvoth*, believing in *Hashem* entails no action, not even the intellectual effort that *Torah* learning requires. In as much as Curtain (וילון), meaning faith, entails no action, it "does nothing." On the other hand, the spiritual realm and the physical realm are too different from one another to be able to interact without something linking them. Faith forms the thin Curtain (וילון) that connects them. Thus, ironically, although faith "does nothing," it constantly keeps Creation in existence.[387]

The Hebrew for creating "something out of nothing" (יֵשׁ מֵאַיִן) reflects this idea because "out of nothing" (מֵאַיִן) also has the same numeric value as "faith" (אֱמוּנָה) if one is added for the word itself.[388] Unlike learning *Torah* and performing *Mitzvoth*, faith entails no action, so it is like nothing. On the other hand, the entire universe exists because of it.

ೞಬೞ The Torah's View of Astrology

"God said, 'Let there be luminaries in the expanse of the heavens to distinguish between day and night, and to be for signs, seasons, days, and years.'"[389]

The *Torah* does not state that the heavenly bodies *control* what happens in the world, but that they are *signs*. Their positions and movements correspond to spiritual forces that

---

[387] *Sha'arei Haleshem* 1:7:2, *Emunath Yisrael* כל האצילות כולו, שהוא גילוי שמותיו, הנה הוא תלוי באמונת ישראל, כי על ידי שהם מאמינים שהוא יתברך שמו מהוה הכל ומשגיח בכל ומנהיג את הכל הנה הם מעמידים את גילוייו אשר באצילות ומתקיימים ומתנהגים בהם – רוצה לומר באותן הגילויים – כל העולמות (של) בריאה, יצירה (ו)עשיה על מציאותם ובכל תהלוכותיהם והנהגתם. אבל בלתי האמונה חס ושלום היו חוזרים כל הגילויים למקורן ולהעלמתן שבאין סוף והרי היה חוזר האצילות שהוא גילוי א-להותו יתברך שמו לשורשו ואז הנה היה מתבטל תיכף כל העולמות בריאה, יצירה (ו)עשיה כרגע

[388] See note 197 for an explanation about why the rules for calculating numeric values (גִּמַטְרִיָא) permit this permit this.

[389] Genesis 1:14 וַיֹּאמֶר אֱ-לֹהִים יְהִי מְאֹרֹת בִּרְקִיעַ הַשָּׁמַיִם לְהַבְדִּיל בֵּין הַיּוֹם וּבֵין הַלָּיְלָה וְהָיוּ לְאֹתֹת וּלְמוֹעֲדִים וּלְיָמִים וְשָׁנִים.

influence earthly events. Those who know how to interpret these signs may be able to predict the future. However, few people, if any, currently possess this ability.

ജ‍ജ‍ജ The Accuracy of Astrological Predictions

The heavenly bodies shine through a thin Curtain (וִילוֹן) — the Earth's upper atmosphere — which corresponds to the spiritual Curtain (וִילוֹן) that lies between the physical and spiritual realms.

The way in which *Hashem's* Divine light flows into the universe depends upon how it flows through the supernal spheres. This flow corresponds to time which also flows in a certain sequence. People measure time by the movements and positions of the sun, moon, and stars. The configuration of the heavenly bodies at any given time therefore mirrors the flow of Divine light into the universe.

Curtain (וִילוֹן) has the same numeric value as "time" (הַזְּמָן). In ancient times, skilled astrologers could see the order of world history by observing the celestial bodies through the thin curtain of the Earth's upper atmosphere. Their predictions were not definite, however. The heavenly bodies, like the letters of the alphabet, symbolize the spiritual forces of Creation. Just as combinations of letters and words can have more than one meaning, the positions of the luminaries allude to multiple meanings.

For instance, Potiphar's wife tried to entice Joseph because she knew by means of astrology that she would have offspring through him. She failed to realize that those offspring would come through her daughter, who later married him.[390]

---

[390] *Breishith Rabbah* 85:2 דאמר רבי יהושע בן לוי: רואה הייתה באסטרולוגין שלה שהיא עתידה להעמיד ממנו בן ולא הייתה יודעת אם ממנה אם מבתה.

Similarly, the *Midrash* states:

Why did [the Egyptians] issue a decree to cast [the baby boys] into the [Nile] River? Because they foresaw through astrology that Israel's redeemer would be stricken by means of water. They figured [this meant] that he would drown in water, but it was [really] through a spring of water that a decree of death was issued against him. [When *Moshe Rabbeinu* struck a rock to produce water instead of speaking to it as *Hashem* had instructed him, *Hashem* decreed that he must die before the Jews entered the Land of Israel].[391]

֍ Faith (אֱמוּנָה) Alters the Preordained Flow of Spirituality into the Universe in Two Ways
֍֍ Reinterpretation

Rabbi Yochanan taught that astrology does not apply to Israel.[392] When Jews have faith in *Hashem*, their faith alters the meaning of the spiritual forces reflected by the position of the heavenly bodies.

Curtain (וִילוֹן), faith, "does nothing" on its own because it does not filter or configure the Divine light. Nonetheless, it is the screen through which that light passes into the physical realm. It recreates the act of Creation daily because faith can alter how the spirituality which flows through it affects the world.

How does it do so?

Imrei Emeth explains that shadows symbolize faith. When people see a shadow, they know that some object must be blocking a light source even if they cannot see that object and do not

---

[391] *Shemoth Rabbah* 1:18 למה גזרו להשליכן ליאור? לפי שהיו רואין האסטרולוגין שמושיען של ישראל ע״י מים ילקה, והיו סבורין שבמים יטבע ולא היה ע״י אלא ע״י באר מים נגזר עליו גזירת מוות.
[392] B.T. *Shabbath* 156A רַבִּי יוֹחָנָן אוֹמֵר: אֵין מַזָּל לְיִשְׂרָאֵל

know its exact dimensions. Similarly, faith means believing in something one does not fully understand.[393]

Just as people can surmise the general contours of an object by seeing its shadow, they can gain an indirect and incomplete understanding of God from what He has revealed of Himself. The *Tanach* states that, "He who occupies himself with the supreme secrets [of the *Torah*] lodges in the shadow of the Almighty."[394] The righteous reside in the shadow of the Almighty because their great faith gives them a vague idea about His nature.

A shadow only reveals the outer contours of an object, so objects consisting of different thicknesses, materials, and colors cast the same shadow. The configuration of the heavenly bodies resembles a shadow — it forms an outline which matches a configuration of spiritual forces. Just as someone looking at a shadow might surmise that it reveals the contours of one object when in reality a different object produced it, so a configuration of the stars understood to predict one event may predict another.

Because the configuration of the spiritual worlds can presage more than one outcome, *Hashem* tailors the outcome according to the deeds of human beings. It is as if a person would use a set of objects to cast a shadow, but if he wished to do so, he could rearrange those objects or replace them with others to produce the same shadow.

---

[393] *Imrei Emeth, Yamim Rishonim Shel Sukkoth* הצל הוא האמונה כי עיקר אמונה היא שמאמין במה שאינו רואה.

[394] Psalms 91:1 יֹשֵׁב בְּסֵתֶר עֶלְיוֹן בְּצֵל שַׁ-דַּי יִתְלוֹנָן

෨෨෨ The Exodus from Egypt

The departure from Egypt demonstrates how *Hashem* sometimes reinterprets the configuration of spiritual forces.

At the covenant between the pieces (בְּרִית בֵּין הַבְּתָרִים), "[*Hashem*] told Abram, 'Know for a certainty that your offspring will be strangers in a land which is not theirs, and [foreigners] will enslave them and torment them for four hundred years.'"[395] When the redemption from Egypt finally arrived, however, the *Torah* states that, "The [period] of the Children of Israel's dwelling which they dwelled in Egypt was four hundred thirty years."[396] Despite the numbers cited in these two verses, the rabbis calculated that the period the Jews stayed in Egypt was only two hundred ten years.[397]

To make matters even more puzzling, one could argue that the Egyptian exile did not end on the day that the Jews left Egypt because they did not enter the Land of Israel until forty years later. Accordingly, other calculations of the length of the Egyptian exile are possible.

How can all these different calculations be reconciled?

Although the original decree would have required Israel to stay in Egypt for the entire four hundred years, due to the merit of the ancestors of the Jewish people and the nation's faith in *Hashem*, *Hashem* calculated the duration of the Egyptian exile as starting from Isaac's birth. Although the Jews stayed in Egypt

---

[395] Genesis 15:13 וַיֹּאמֶר לְאַבְרָם יָדֹעַ תֵּדַע כִּי גֵר יִהְיֶה זַרְעֲךָ בְּאֶרֶץ לֹא לָהֶם וַעֲבָדוּם וְעִנּוּ אֹתָם אַרְבַּע מֵאוֹת שָׁנָה.

[396] Exodus 12:40 וּמוֹשַׁב בְּנֵי יִשְׂרָאֵל אֲשֶׁר יָשְׁבוּ בְּמִצְרָיִם שְׁלֹשִׁים שָׁנָה וְאַרְבַּע מֵאוֹת שָׁנָה

[397] *Shir Hashirim Rabbah* 2:21 on Song of Songs 2:8 ? אמרו לו: "משה רבינו היאך אנו נגאלין הלא אמר הקב"ה לאברהם, 'וַעֲבָדוּם וְעִנּוּ אֹתָם אַרְבַּע מֵאוֹת שָׁנָה' (בראשית ט"ו, י"ג), ועדיין אין בידינו אלא מאתים ועשר שנה?" אמר להם: "הואיל והוא חפץ בגאולתכם אינו מביט בחשבונותיכם אלא 'מְדַלֵּג עַל הֶהָרִים (מְקַפֵּץ עַל הַגְּבָעוֹת)' (שיר השירים ב', ח'). אין הרים וגבעות האמורין כאן אלא קצים ועיבורין. מדלג על החשבונות ועל הקצים ועיבורין ובחודש הזה אתם נגאלין".

only two hundred ten years, from Isaac's birth until they left was four hundred years.[398] On the other hand, *Hashem* told Abraham about the Egyptian exile thirty years prior to Isaac's birth. Counting from that time yields a total of four hundred thirty years.[399]

This demonstrates how even a prophecy can be reinterpreted when people merit it. In this instance, *Hashem* recalculated the amount of time the Jews were to remain in Egypt from a longer period of time to a shorter one. The same principle applies to astrological predictions.

Had the Jews been worthy, they would have entered the Land of Israel shortly after leaving Egypt. Only because they accepted the evil report of the spies were they detained in the Sinai Desert for forty years. The Jews should have had faith in *Hashem's* promise that they would succeed in conquering the Land of Israel regardless of the great strength of the Canaanites. Just as having faith in *Hashem* shortened their stay in Egypt, lack of faith lengthened their stay in the Sinai Desert.

The three time periods ascribed to the Egyptian exodus — 400, 430, and 210 — total 1040. If one adds in the additional forty years during which the Jews wandered in the desert before entering the Land of Israel, the total becomes 1080, the same as the number of divisions Jewish tradition assigns to each hour.[400]

Arvei Nachal explains that each hour includes 1080 combinations and permutations of the supernal spiritual realms. The sequence in which the Divine influence is destined to enter the

---

[398] *Pirkei D'Rabbi Eliezer* 47 אמר רבי אלעזר בן ערך: לא אמר לו הקב"ה לאברהם אלא משעה שהיה לו זרע שנאמר, "כִּי גֵר יִהְיֶה זַרְעֲךָ בְּאֶרֶץ לֹא לָהֶם" (בראשית ט"ו, י"ג) וכתיב, "כִּי בְיִצְחָק יִקָּרֵא לְךָ זָרַע" (בראשית כ"א, י"ב). ומשנולד יצחק עד שיצאו ישראל ממצרים ארבע מאות שנה.

[399] *Rashi* on Exodus 12:40, citing *Midrash Tanchuma, Parashath Bo* 9 "שְׁלשִׁים שָׁנָה וְאַרְבַּע מֵאוֹת שָׁנָה" — בין הכל משנולד יצחק עד עכשיו היו ארבע מאות שנה משהיה לו זרע לאברהם נתקיים כי גר יהיה זרעך ושלשים שנה היו משנגזרה גזירת בין הבתרים עד שנולד יצחק.

[400] *Mishnah B'rurah*, note 19 on *Shulchan Aruch, Orach Chaim* 426:3 דשעה מתחלק על תתר"ף חלקים.

world has been predetermined since the beginning of Creation.[401] Nevertheless, human faith can alter the consequences of this flow.

৪৩৪৩ Reaching above the System of Spiritual Worlds

There is a second and more powerful way in which faith affects the spiritual realm.

When human faith is very strong, it can affect a region of the spiritual realm above time, i.e., a level where the spiritual flow has not yet been divided and formed into any sequence. It can therefore cause the sequence to yield a different result than it otherwise might. As the blessing recited before the evening *Shema* states, "[God] alters seasons, switches times, and arranges the stars in their paths in the sky according to His will."[402] Since God's will is that human beings should obey Him and have faith in Him, He alters the way in which His Divine light affects the world when they do so.

The *Torah* states that the additional forty years the Jews were condemned to wander through the Sinai Desert corresponded to the forty days the spies spent on their mission.[403] The predestined history of the world has its root in a spiritual realm where time does not exist and can therefore change as a result of human behavior. When the Jews faltered in their faith, what should have been forty days became forty years.

---

[401] *Arvei Nachal, Derush 3 Leshabbath Hagadol* תתר"ף רגעי השעה – יש לכל רגע כוכב ומזל המנהיג העולם באותה רגע. וכן גבוה מעל גבוה עד שתתר"ף צירופי הוי"ה וצירופי רל"א שערים ורל"א אחור כל צירוף משפיע ומושל בכוכב ההוא והצירופים מתחלפין – יש לדין ויש לרחמים. ואותם הצירופים הם מתגלגלים ובאים מששת ימי בראשית עד סוף כל העולמות.

[402] מְשַׁנֶּה עִתִּים וּמַחֲלִיף אֶת הַזְּמַנִּים וּמְסַדֵּר אֶת הַכּוֹכָבִים בְּמִשְׁמְרוֹתֵיהֶם בָּרָקִיעַ כִּרְצוֹנוֹ

[403] Numbers 14:34 בְּמִסְפַּר הַיָּמִים אֲשֶׁר תַּרְתֶּם אֶת הָאָרֶץ אַרְבָּעִים יוֹם יוֹם לַשָּׁנָה יוֹם לַשָּׁנָה תִּשְׂאוּ אֶת עֲוֹנֹתֵיכֶם אַרְבָּעִים שָׁנָה וִידַעְתֶּם אֶת תְּנוּאָתִי.

෨෨෨෨ Why Faith (אֱמוּנָה) Has this Power ෨෨෨෨

Human logic follows certain rules, such as the thirteen principles through which the *Torah* is interpreted.[404] By contrast, faith entails comprehending something without using logic. Since faith transcends logical processes, it can reach a level that precedes the chain of supernal worlds and alter the way in which *Hashem's* Divine light is processed by them.[405]

Panim Yafoth explains that as a result of Adam and Chavah's sin, two hundred eighty-eight holy sparks from the Tree of Knowledge fell into the physical realm as a mixture of good and evil. Two hundred eighty-eight is the combined numeric value of "good" (טוב) and "evil" (רע) with the addition of one, representing the connection between the two.[406] *Kedushath Levi* elaborates that, "The principal service of humankind in this world is to convert darkness to light — to elevate those sparks high above to their root and source."[407]

"Past" (עָבָר) and "present" (הֹוֶה) also have a combined numeric value of two hundred eighty-eight. Originally, Adam and Chavah lived in the Garden of Eden in the same condition as will exist the world to come (עוֹלָם הַבָּא). Since all past and present events lead to the final state of happiness in the world to come, it may be said that the future world includes within it all of the past and present. Furthermore, in as much as Adam and Chavah originally lived in the same condition as will exist in the future

---

[404] These thirteen principles are enumerated in *Sifra, Parashath Vayikra* רַבִּי יִשְׁמָעֵאל אוֹמֵר: בִּשְׁלֹשׁ עֶשְׂרֵה מִדּוֹת הַתּוֹרָה נִדְרֶשֶׁת.

[405] *Likutei Halachoth, Orach Chaim, Hilchoth Masa Umatan* 4 כִּי עַל יְדֵי אֱמוּנָה שְׁלֵמָה יָדַלֵּג וְיִקְפּׂץ עַל כָּל הַמְּנִיעוֹת וְהַהַסָתוֹת וְהַפִּתּוּיִים וְהַדִּחִיוֹת וַחֲלִישׁוּת הַדַּעַת שֶׁהַיֵּצֶר הָרָע וְחֵילוֹתָיו רוֹצִים לְהַפִּילוֹ כְּאִלּוּ אֵין לוֹ עוֹד שׁוּם תִּקְוָה (עֲדַיִן). כִּי עַל יְדֵי אֱמוּנָה עוֹבְרִים וּמְדַלְּגִים עַל הַכֹּל.

[406] *Panim Yafoth* on Genesis 31:24 הניצוצות שנפלו הם רפ"ח, והוא מספר טוב ורע עם הכולל המחברם.

[407] *Kedushath Levi, Parashath Breishith* עיקר עבודת האדם בעולם הזה לאתהפכא חשוכא לנהורא להעלות הניצוצות ההם להעלותם למעלה מעלה לשורשם ומקורם.

world (עוֹלָם הַבָּא), it may be said that for them only future existed. Past and present had no meaning until after the sin because the rest of history only became necessary for the purpose of rectifying the sin's effects.

The sages hint at this when they state that before Adam and Chavah sinned, a special light existed which gave them the ability to see from one end of the world to the other,[408] meaning that they could see all of history from beginning to end at one glance.[409] This light will be restored at the time of the ultimate redemption so that past, present, and future will coalesce into one unit.

As Rabbi Yitzchak Isaac Chaver explains, time is a concept of ranking. Each heavenly body corresponds to a spiritual force which controls a certain aspect of Creation. When its function is completed, control is passed to another spiritual force, and this process continues until all the spiritual forces are activated throughout the six thousand years of Creation. In the seven thousandth millennium, all of the luminaries will shine simultaneously so that no ranking will exist, and time will cease to exist.[410]

Intense human faith reaches above and beyond this system even now and therefore has the power to override it. This is why the great faith of *Tzaddikim* enables them to give effective blessings.

---

[408] B.T. *Chagigah* 12 A דְּאָמַר רַבִּי אֶלְעָזָר: אוֹר שֶׁבָּרָא הַקָּדוֹשׁ בָּרוּךְ הוּא בַּיּוֹם רִאשׁוֹן, אָדָם צוֹפֶה בּוֹ מִסּוֹף הָעוֹלָם וְעַד סוֹפוֹ. כֵּיוָן שֶׁנִּסְתַּכֵּל הַקָּדוֹשׁ בָּרוּךְ הוּא בְּדוֹר הַמַּבּוּל וּבְדוֹר הַפַּלָּגָה וְרָאָה שֶׁמַּעֲשֵׂיהֶם מְקוּלְקָלִים, עָמַד וּגְנָזוֹ מֵהֶן... וּלְמִי גְּנָזוֹ? לַצַּדִּיקִים לֶעָתִיד לָבֹא.

[409] B.T. *Sanhedrin* דְּאָמַר רֵישׁ לָקִישׁ: מַאי דִּכְתִיב, "זֶה סֵפֶר תּוֹלְדֹת אָדָם" (בראשית ה', א')? מְלַמֵּד שֶׁהֶרְאָהוּ הַקָּדוֹשׁ בָּרוּךְ הוּא דּוֹר דּוֹר וְדוֹרְשָׁיו, דּוֹר דּוֹר וַחֲכָמָיו.

[410] *Pithchei She'arim, Nethiv Seder Hapartzufim* 7 עניין הזמן הוא דבר שנברא ולא שהיה קיים תמיד. הזמן מורה על עניין ההדרגה. הדרגה זו נבראה כשניתן לכל מאור (שהוא כוח רוחני פרטי של ההנהגה) גבול מסוים שעליו הוא שולט. כשתפקיד אותו מאור נשלם, שוב ניתנת השליטה למאור אחר, וכך ממשיך להיות עד שכל המאורות פועלים את פעולתם זה אחר זה בבריאה במשך כל השית אלפי שנין. באלף השביעי, כשהבריאה תגיע לתכליתה הרצויה(ה), אז יאירו כל המאורות בבת אחת, ומשום כך יתבטל מושג ההדרגה ועניין הזמן.

Reversing the Order of Cause and Effect

ಌ Rabbi Chanina ben Dosa

There was an incident in a certain place where there was a [venomous hybrid snake-lizard called an] *Arod* which used to injure people. The townsfolk came and informed Rabbi Chanina ben Dosa [about it].

"Show me where its burrow is," he instructed them.

When they showed him its burrow, the rabbi placed his heel at its entrance. The *Arod* emerged, bit him, and died.

[Rabbi Chanina ben Dosa] slung [the *Arod*] over his shoulder and brought it to the study hall, where he declared, "See, my sons, that it is not the *Arod* which kills, but sin which kills."

At that moment they proclaimed, "Woe to the person who meets up with an *Arod*, and woe to the *Arod* who meets up with Rabbi Chanina ben Dosa!"[411]

What was the secret behind this miracle?

Human beings cannot comprehend the way in which *Hashem* exists completely above and beyond time, but they can partially understand this phenomenon by contrasting intellect with faith.

Ordinary intellectual processes involve a sequence of reasoning. A person starts with some basic information (Wisdom חָכְמָה), analyzes that information (Understanding בִּינָה), and reaches a conclusion (Knowledge דַּעַת).[412] Since this intellectual process consists of a series of steps over a period of time, it can only take place where time exists.

Sometimes, however, people acquire knowledge instantaneously through simple observation rather than through a reasoning process. Suppose, for example, that a person observes a yellow flower with six petals. Knowledge of the flower requires no intellectual process and therefore no time need pass for it to occur. This is the concept of faith as it originally existed for Adam and Chavah who observed spirituality in the same way as a person can observe a yellow flower with six petals.

This type of faith may be said to comprise all three elements of the intellectual process described above collapsed and

---

[411] B.T. *Berachoth* 33A   מַעֲשֶׂה בְּמָקוֹם אֶחָד שֶׁהָיָה בּוֹ עָרוֹד וְהָיָה מַזִּיק אֶת הַבְּרִיּוֹת. בָּאוּ וְהוֹדִיעוּ לוֹ לְרַבִּי חֲנִינָא בֶּן דּוֹסָא. אָמַר לָהֶם: "הַרְאוּ לִי אֶת חוֹרוֹ". הֶרְאוּהוּ אֶת חוֹרוֹ. נָתַן עֲקֵבוֹ עַל פִּי הַחוֹר. יָצָא וּנְשָׁכוֹ וּמֵת אוֹתוֹ עָרוֹד. נְטָלוֹ עַל כְּתֵפוֹ וְהֶבִיאוֹ לְבֵית הַמִּדְרָשׁ. אָמַר לָהֶם: "רְאוּ בָּנַי ! אֵין עָרוֹד מֵמִית, אֶלָּא הַחֵטְא מֵמִית". בְּאוֹתָהּ שָׁעָה אָמְרוּ: "אוֹי לוֹ לְאָדָם שֶׁפָּגַע בּוֹ עָרוֹד וְאוֹי לוֹ לְעָרוֹד שֶׁפָּגַע בּוֹ רַבִּי חֲנִינָא בֶּן דּוֹסָא".

[412] *Emek Hamelech* 14:9   שמכוח חכמה ובינה מתהווה דעת. המשל בזה הוא כמו שאדם האנושי שלומד חכמה ומבין דבר מתוך דבר מכוח הבינה ומתוך ההבנה מסכים לדבר אחד, וזאת ההסכמה היא הדעת הנולד מחכמתו ובינתו.

consolidated into a single unit which occurs without the passage of time.

Most human knowledge, including belief in God, comes from intellectual reasoning and is therefore subject to the limitations of time. People on a lofty spiritual level, however, do not merely know about God and spirituality as a result of intellectual reasoning. Instead, they perceive spirituality akin to the way in which Adam and Chavah did before they sinned. Such people thereby connect themselves to timelessness.[413]

In the physical world, cause and effect take place within the context of time with a cause always preceding an effect. By contrast, time does not exist at the highest levels of the spiritual realm, so cause and effect are merged together, and there is no more reason for a cause to precede an effect than for an effect to precede a cause. There is, for example, no more reason that striking a match should cause a fire than that a fire should cause the striking of a match. Both possibilities exist equally.

When *Hashem's* Divine light descends from the upper spiritual worlds, it becomes subject to time, and *Hashem* created the universe in such a way that in those worlds where time exists certain effects always follow from certain causes. That is why in the physical world striking a match always causes a fire, but never the reverse.

---

[413] Adam and Chavah were originally immortal because they were not subject to time. (*Likutei Halachoth, Yoreh De'ah, Hilchoth Milah* 4 עָקַר הַהִתְקַשְׁרוּת וְהַבִּטּוּל שֶׁל הַזְּמַן בְּשָׁרְשׁוֹ בִּבְחִינַת לְמַעְלָה מֵהַזְּמַן הוּא עַל יְדֵי בְּחִינַת הַשֵּׁם שֶׁהוּא בְּחִינַת אֱמוּנָה... אֵלְיָהוּ זָכָה בְּחַיָּיו לַעֲלוֹת לַשָּׁמַיִם, כִּי זָכָה לְבַטֵּל הַזְּמַן בְּחַיָּיו. וְעַל כֵּן לֹא הָצְרַךְ לָמוּת, כִּי מֵחֲמַת זֶהֲמַת הַנָּחָשׁ מֵחֶטְא אָדָם הָרִאשׁוֹן אִי אֶפְשָׁר לְכִלֵל בִּשְׁלֵמוּת בָּזֶה הָעוֹלָם בִּבְחִינַת לְמַעְלָה מֵהַזְּמַן. וְעַל כֵּן צְרִיכִין לָמוּת וְאָז כְּשֶׁיּוֹצְאִין מֵהַגּוּף וְהַנְּשָׁמָה מִזְדַּכֶּכֶת, הוּא זוֹכֶה לַעֲלוֹת וְלִכְלֵל לְשָׁם לִבְחִינַת לְמַעְלָה מֵהַזְּמַן שֶׁזֶּהוּ בְּחִינַת חַיֵּי הָעוֹלָם הַבָּא כַּנַּ״ל, אֲבָל אֵלְיָהוּ זָכָה לִשְׁלֵמוּת (הַדַּעַת בְּחַיָּיו עַד שֶׁלֹּא הָצְרַךְ לָמוּת.)

The *Torah* states that, "God created man (אָדָם) upon the Earth, and from one end of the Heavens to the other,"[414] meaning that prior to sinning, Adam and Chavah were in contact with the spiritual worlds, including those where time does not exist.[415] Since cause and effect exist simultaneously at the highest spiritual levels, Adam and Chavah had the ability to reverse their sequence. They could have made fire cause the striking of a match had they wished to do so.

Although Adam and Chavah lost this ability after they sinned, there are *Tzaddikim*, such as Rabbi Chanina ben Dosa, who regained it. Although the venom of an *Arod* usually causes the death of the person it bites, Rabbi Chanina ben Dosa reversed the sequence of cause and effect so that biting him caused the *Arod* to die![416]

Parenthetically, some people raise a question about this incident. The sages teach that whenever injury is bound to happen, people should not rely on miracles.[417] If so, how could Rabbi Chanina ben Dosa place his heel at the mouth of the *Arod's* burrow?

The above explanation resolves this question because for a person such as Rabbi Chanina ben Dosa, this was not a miracle.

---

[414] Deuteronomy 4:32 כִּי שְׁאַל נָא לְיָמִים רִאשֹׁנִים אֲשֶׁר הָיוּ לְפָנֶיךָ לְמִן הַיּוֹם אֲשֶׁר בָּרָא אֱ-לֹהִים אָדָם עַל הָאָרֶץ וּלְמִקְצֵה הַשָּׁמַיִם וְעַד קְצֵה הַשָּׁמָיִם הֲנִהְיָה כַּדָּבָר הַגָּדוֹל הַזֶּה אוֹ הֲנִשְׁמַע כָּמֹהוּ.

[415] See B.T. *Chagigah* 12A דְּאָמַר רַבִּי אֶלְעָזָר: אָדָם הָרִאשֹׁון מִן הָאָרֶץ וְעַד לָרָקִיעַ הָיָה, שֶׁנֶּאֱמַר, "לְמִן הַיּוֹם אֲשֶׁר בָּרָא אֱ-לֹהִים אָדָם עַל הָאָרֶץ וּלְמִקְצֵה הַשָּׁמַיִם וְעַד קְצֵה הַשָּׁמָיִם)" (דברים ד', ל"ב).

[416] See *Gevuroth Hashem, Hakdamah Sheniah* for a related idea כי הטבע פועל בזמן ולפיכך צריך לכל פעל טבעי המשך זמן, אבל פעל אשר אינו טבעי אין צריך לפעולתו זמן, כי הטבעי כוח גשמי וכל כוח גשמי פעולתו בזמן, אבל הדברים הנבדלים פעולתם בלי זמן, שאינם כוח בגשם ולפיכך פועלים בלא זמן, ולכך ברגע אחד יתהפכו המים לדם שהוא פועל ברצונו בלבד, וברצונו נתהוה החומר והצורה לפי רגע אחד, ואין זה פעל טבעי שהוא פועל בזמן והוא צריך אל הכנת החומר, אבל בדבר ה' שמים נעשו וברוח פיו כל צבאם וזהו פעל הנבדל שהוא פועל בלי הכנת חומר כלל.

[417] B.T. *Kiddushin* 39B וְכָל הֵיכָא דִּקְבִיעַ הֶיזֵּקָא לָא סַמְכִינָן אַנִּיסָא

Rather, the *Arod's* death followed as natural consequence of biting the rabbi's heel.[418]

༄ The Splitting of the Reed Sea

After the Jews departed Egypt, *Hashem* commanded Israel to reverse course and camp at Pi Hahiroth (פִּי הַחִירֹת) in front of the Reed Sea.[419] Although the Jews complained on several other occasions, this time they had complete faith in *Hashem* and did as He commanded.[420] Measure for measure, because they obeyed Him and reversed course, *Hashem* performed a miracle which reversed the ordinary sequence of cause and effect.

The *Torah* states that *Hashem* caused a strong east wind to blow the entire night to dry up the sea and cause it to split,[421] but the sea did not actually part until Nahshon ben Aminadab jumped in.[422]

Why was this?

The root of the word the *Torah* uses for "east" (קָדִים) also means "ancient" or "primordial" (קֶדֶם), a reference to the spiritual realms where time does not exist.[423] *Hashem* revealed the spiritual source of the Reed Sea in those realms so that the usual

---

[418] *Sha'arei Haleshem* 2:11, *Bayith Sheni* הרי הכניסו את עצמם בסכנה מפני שהיו בטוחים על זה עד שלא היה נחשב להם לנס כלל וכלל. דאם לא כן הרי אסור להכניס את עצמו בסכנה ולסמוך על הנס.

[419] Exodus 14:2 דַּבֵּר אֶל בְּנֵי יִשְׂרָאֵל וְיָשֻׁבוּ וְיַחֲנוּ לִפְנֵי פִּי הַחִירֹת בֵּין מִגְדֹּל וּבֵין הַיָּם לִפְנֵי בַּעַל צְפֹן נִכְחוֹ תַחֲנוּ עַל הַיָּם.

[420] *Mechilta, Parashath Beshalach* 3 רבי אומר: כדי היא האמונה שהאמינו בי שאקרע להם את הים שנאמר, "וְיָשֻׁבוּ וְיַחֲנוּ וגו'".

[421] Exodus 14:21 וַיֵּט מֹשֶׁה אֶת יָדוֹ עַל הַיָּם וַיּוֹלֶךְ ה' אֶת הַיָּם בְּרוּחַ קָדִים עַזָּה כָּל הַלַּיְלָה וַיָּשֶׂם אֶת הַיָּם לֶחָרָבָה וַיִּבָּקְעוּ הַמָּיִם.

[422] B.T. *Sotah* 37A אָמַר לוֹ רַבִּי יְהוּדָה: לֹא כָּךְ הָיָה מַעֲשֶׂה, אֶלָּא זֶה אוֹמֵר, "אֵין אֲנִי יוֹרֵד תְּחִלָּה לַיָּם", וְזֶה אוֹמֵר, "אֵין אֲנִי יוֹרֵד תְּחִלָּה לַיָּם". קָפַץ נַחְשׁוֹן בֶּן עַמִּינָדָב וְיָרַד לַיָּם תְּחִלָּה. "נַחְשׁוֹן בֶּן עַמִּינָדָב לְמַטֵּה יְהוּדָה" *Bamidbar Rabbah* 13:7 (במדבר ז', י"ב) – למה נקרא שמו נחשון? על שם שירד תחלה לנחשול שבים.

[423] *Pituchei Chotham, Parashath Masa'ei*; *Imrei* הַשֶּׁפַע יוֹרֵד תְּחִלָּה מִקֶּדֶם שֶׁהוּא עוֹלָם הָאֲצִילוּת *Finchas* 4 *Shabbath Umo'adim*; *Yesod Ha'avodah* 2:19 מעולם האצילות והוא למעלה מהזמן ימי קדם מה שהוא למעלה מן הזמן.

sequence of cause and effect was reversed. Ordinarily, when water engulfs a person, he drowns. In this case, however, the opposite occurred — Nahshon ben Aminadab caused the sea to dry up![424]

ಶಿ The Prophet Elijah at Mount Carmel

At one point in history, the Jews could not make up their minds whether to follow *Hashem* or whether to follow the idol Baal. The *Tanach* records how Elijah confronted the people, saying, "'How long will you vacillate between two positions? If *Hashem* is God, go after Him, and if Baal [is real], go after him.' But the people could not answer a word."[425]

To prove that *Hashem* is the true God, Elijah arranged a contest in which the prophets of Baal attempted, but failed, to cause fire to descend from Heaven and consume a sacrifice they had prepared. Elijah then prayed, "Answer me, *Hashem*, answer me, and let this people know that You are *Hashem*, God, and that You turned their hearts backwards."[426]

The *Talmud* clarifies:

Rabbi Abahu said: Why did Elijah declare, "Answer me!" two times? This teaches that Elijah entreated the Holy One, Blessed be He, [saying], "Master of the Universe, answer me that fire descend from Heaven and consume everything on the altar, and answer me that their minds be set right so that they not

---

[424] *Moshav Zekeinim* on Numbers 7:12 כי היה נחשול של ים עולה ומתרברב ומיד שקפץ לים נח שנאמר, "הָיְתָה יְהוּדָה לְקָדְשׁוֹ" (תהלים קי"ד, ב'), כלומר שקדשו שמו של הקדוש ברוך הוא וקפץ תחילה. מיד "הַיָּם רָאָה וַיָּנֹס" (תהלים קי"ד, ג').

[425] I Kings 18:21 וַיִּגַּשׁ אֵלִיָּהוּ אֶל כָּל הָעָם וַיֹּאמֶר עַד מָתַי אַתֶּם פֹּסְחִים עַל שְׁתֵּי הַסְּעִפִּים אִם ה' הָאֱ-לֹהִים לְכוּ אַחֲרָיו וְאִם הַבַּעַל לְכוּ אַחֲרָיו וְלֹא עָנוּ הָעָם אֹתוֹ דָּבָר.

[426] I King 18:37 עֲנֵנִי ה' עֲנֵנִי וְיֵדְעוּ הָעָם הַזֶּה כִּי אַתָּה ה' הָאֱ-לֹהִים וְאַתָּה הֲסִבֹּתָ אֶת לִבָּם אֲחֹרַנִּית.

claim, 'This is an act of witchcraft,'" as it states, "You turned their hearts backwards."[427]

People have difficulty relating to a God who transcends cause and effect because they inhabit a world where everything is subject to sequences of cause and effect. The expression, "You turned their hearts backwards," refers to this problem. As the *Malbim* explains, *Hashem* created the universe in such a way that people can only understand it by looking backwards from effects to determine their causes.[428]

The people were attracted to Baal and other "gods" of nature, such as the sun god and the wind god, because these deities were depicted as behaving in ways that natural phenomena typically do, with effects following causes. They had difficulty believing in *Hashem*, who transcends this system.

To prove that he truly represented *Hashem*, that *Hashem* is the only true God, and that He transcends cause and effect, Elijah prayed to *Hashem* to perform a miracle which would reverse the usual roles of cause and effect. The *Tanach* records that, "Fire of *Hashem* fell and consumed the sacrifice, the wood, the stones, the dirt, and it drank up the water which was in the ditch [that surrounded the altar]."[429]

---

[427] B.T. *Berachoth* 9B אָמַר רַבִּי אַבָּהוּ: לָמָה אָמַר אֵלִיָּהוּ "עֲנֵנִי" שְׁתֵּי פְעָמִים? מְלַמֵּד שֶׁאָמַר אֵלִיָּהוּ לִפְנֵי הַקָּדוֹשׁ בָּרוּךְ הוּא: "רִבּוֹנוֹ שֶׁל עוֹלָם, עֲנֵנִי שֶׁתֵּרֵד אֵשׁ מִן הַשָּׁמַיִם וְתֹאכַל כָּל אֲשֶׁר עַל הַמִּזְבֵּחַ, וַעֲנֵנִי שֶׁתַּסִּיחַ דַּעְתָּם כְּדֵי שֶׁלֹּא יֹאמְרוּ, 'מַעֲשֵׂה כְשָׁפִים הֵם'". שֶׁנֶּאֱמַר, "וְאַתָּה הֲסִבֹּתָ אֶת לִבָּם אֲחֹרַנִּית" (מלכים-א, י"ח, ל"ז).

[428] *Malbim* on I Kings 18:37 אמר הטעם שישראל טועים ובלתי משיגים א-להותך הוא מצד שבראת את האדם באופן שלא ישיג שום דבר מן הקודם אל המאוחר ע"י מופת השכל, רק מן המאוחר אל הקודם — מן המסובב אל הסיבה — ולכן הוא מוכן אל הטעות והשגיאה בדברים העיוניים.

[429] I Kings 18:38 וַתִּפֹּל אֵשׁ ה' וַתֹּאכַל אֶת הָעֹלָה וְאֶת הָעֵצִים וְאֶת הָאֲבָנִים וְאֶת הֶעָפָר וְאֶת הַמַּיִם אֲשֶׁר בַּתְּעָלָה לִחֵכָה.

This translation follows the *Gemara*, which states that this was a type of fire which had the ability to consume water.[430] Although a sufficiently strong fire can dry up water, that is not what happened in this case. Instead, the qualities of fire and water were reversed so that the fire quenched the water. That is why the *Tanach* states that the fire "fell." Unlike ordinary fire which rises, this fire poured like water.[431] The chain of cause and effect was reversed. Rather than water extinguishing fire, fire extinguished water!

---

[430] B.T. *Yoma* 21B   תָּנוּ רַבָּנָן: שֵׁשׁ אֵשׁוֹת הֵן... אוֹכֶלֶת וְשׁוֹתָה – דְּאֵלִיָּהוּ, דִּכְתִיב, "וְאֶת הַמַּיִם אֲשֶׁר בַּתְּעָלָה לִחֵכָה".

[431] *Tifereth Yehonathan* on Genesis 1:7, וכן טבע מים דלמטה לירד לארץ ואש דלמטה לעלות, ולמעלה הוא בהיפוך.

The Burning Bush

❧ Moshe Rabbeinu's Reluctance to Approach Pharaoh

Moshe Rabbeinu asked *Hashem*, "Who am I to go to Pharaoh to take the Children of Israel out from Egypt?"[432] *Rashi* comments that *Moshe Rabbeinu* meant, "How am I important enough to speak to kings?"[433]

This seems strange. *Moshe Rabbeinu* grew up in Pharaoh's palace, knew Pharaoh personally, and must have been highly accustomed to addressing royalty. How can he have thought that he was not important enough to speak to kings?

Even more peculiar, despite God's repeated reassurances, *Moshe Rabbeinu* continued to express reservations about confronting Pharaoh, complaining that he stammered and could not

---

[432] Exodus 3:11 וַיֹּאמֶר מֹשֶׁה אֶל הָאֱ-לֹהִים מִי אָנֹכִי כִּי אֵלֵךְ אֶל פַּרְעֹה וְכִי אוֹצִיא אֶת בְּנֵי יִשְׂרָאֵל מִמִּצְרָיִם

[433] *Rashi* ad. loc. "מִי אָנֹכִי" — מה אני חשוב לדבר עם המלכים?

speak properly.[434] Once God ordered him to go, one would have expected *Moshe Rabbeinu* to trust that he would succeed. Why was he only reconciled to this task after God repeatedly told him that his brother Aaron would assist him?[435]

To understand the answer, one must examine *Moshe Rabbeinu's* very first prophetic experience. The *Torah* relates that while herding sheep, *Moshe Rabbeinu* observed a bush aflame, yet the fire did not destroy it.[436]

The spiritual source of all physical phenomena is analogous to speech.[437] *Hashem* revealed Himself to *Moshe Rabbeinu* by means of a burning bush that was not consumed[438] because He wanted him to understand that nature can be altered by reconfiguring the spiritual source of physical objects. In this case, if one rearranges the letters of "burning" (בֹּעֵר) they spell "passing" (עֹבֵר). The fire passed through the bush instead of consuming it.

When *Moshe Rabbeinu* repeatedly stated that he was of "uncircumcised lips" (עֲרַל שְׂפָתַיִם),[439] "heavy of mouth" (כְבַד פֶּה), and "heavy of tongue (כְבַד לָשׁוֹן),[440] he did not mean only that he

---

[434] Exodus 4:10 וַיֹּאמֶר מֹשֶׁה אֶל ה' בִּי אֲדֹנָי לֹא אִישׁ דְּבָרִים אָנֹכִי גַּם מִתְּמוֹל גַּם מִשִּׁלְשֹׁם גַּם מֵאָז דַּבֶּרְךָ אֶל עַבְדֶּךָ כִּי כְבַד פֶּה וּכְבַד לָשׁוֹן אָנֹכִי.

Exodus 6:12 וַיְדַבֵּר מֹשֶׁה לִפְנֵי ה' לֵאמֹר הֵן בְּנֵי יִשְׂרָאֵל לֹא שָׁמְעוּ אֵלַי וְאֵיךְ יִשְׁמָעֵנִי פַרְעֹה וַאֲנִי עֲרַל שְׂפָתָיִם.

Exodus 6:30 וַיֹּאמֶר מֹשֶׁה לִפְנֵי ה' הֵן אֲנִי עֲרַל שְׂפָתַיִם וְאֵיךְ יִשְׁמַע אֵלַי פַּרְעֹה

[435] Exodus 4:14-15 (יד) וַיִּחַר אַף ה' בְּמֹשֶׁה וַיֹּאמֶר הֲלֹא אַהֲרֹן אָחִיךָ הַלֵּוִי יָדַעְתִּי כִּי דַבֵּר יְדַבֵּר הוּא וְגַם הִנֵּה הוּא יֹצֵא לִקְרָאתֶךָ וְרָאֲךָ וְשָׂמַח בְּלִבּוֹ. (טו) וְדִבַּרְתָּ אֵלָיו וְשַׂמְתָּ אֶת הַדְּבָרִים בְּפִיו וְאָנֹכִי אֶהְיֶה עִם פִּיךָ וְעִם פִּיהוּ וְהוֹרֵיתִי אֶתְכֶם אֵת אֲשֶׁר תַּעֲשׂוּן.

Exodus 7:1-2 (א) וַיֹּאמֶר ה' אֶל מֹשֶׁה רְאֵה נְתַתִּיךָ אֱלֹהִים לְפַרְעֹה וְאַהֲרֹן אָחִיךָ יִהְיֶה נְבִיאֶךָ. (ב) אַתָּה תְדַבֵּר אֵת כָּל אֲשֶׁר אֲצַוֶּךָּ וְאַהֲרֹן אָחִיךָ יְדַבֵּר אֶל פַּרְעֹה וְשִׁלַּח אֶת בְּנֵי יִשְׂרָאֵל מֵאַרְצוֹ.

[436] Exodus 3:1-2 (א) וּמֹשֶׁה הָיָה רֹעֶה אֶת צֹאן יִתְרוֹ חֹתְנוֹ כֹּהֵן מִדְיָן וַיִּנְהַג אֶת הַצֹּאן אַחַר הַמִּדְבָּר וַיָּבֹא אֶל הַר הָאֱ-לֹהִים חֹרֵבָה. (ב) וַיֵּרָא מַלְאַךְ ה' אֵלָיו בְּלַבַּת אֵשׁ מִתּוֹךְ הַסְּנֶה וַיַּרְא וְהִנֵּה הַסְּנֶה בֹּעֵר בָּאֵשׁ וְהַסְּנֶה אֵינֶנּוּ אֻכָּל.

[437] *Pirkei Avoth* 5:1 בַּעֲשָׂרָה מַאֲמָרוֹת נִבְרָא הָעוֹלָם

[438] Exodus 3:2 וַיֵּרָא מַלְאַךְ ה' אֵלָיו בְּלַבַּת אֵשׁ מִתּוֹךְ הַסְּנֶה וַיַּרְא וְהִנֵּה הַסְּנֶה בֹּעֵר בָּאֵשׁ וְהַסְּנֶה אֵינֶנּוּ אֻכָּל

[439] Exodus 6:12 וַיְדַבֵּר מֹשֶׁה לִפְנֵי ה' לֵאמֹר הֵן בְּנֵי יִשְׂרָאֵל לֹא שָׁמְעוּ אֵלַי וְאֵיךְ יִשְׁמָעֵנִי פַרְעֹה וַאֲנִי עֲרַל שְׂפָתָיִם

Exodus 6:30 וַיֹּאמֶר מֹשֶׁה לִפְנֵי ה' הֵן אֲנִי עֲרַל שְׂפָתַיִם וְאֵיךְ יִשְׁמַע אֵלַי פַּרְעֹה

[440] Exodus 4:10 וַיֹּאמֶר מֹשֶׁה אֶל ה' בִּי אֲ-דֹנָי לֹא אִישׁ דְּבָרִים אָנֹכִי גַּם מִתְּמוֹל גַּם מִשִּׁלְשֹׁם גַּם מֵאָז דַּבֶּרְךָ אֶל עַבְדֶּךָ כִּי כְבַד פֶּה וּכְבַד לָשׁוֹן אָנֹכִי.

had a speech impediment. Rather, when God told him that he would have to perform miracles by reinterpreting the spiritual sources of natural phenomena in a manner analogous to interpreting speech, he questioned whether he had the merit to do so.

Hashem then reassured *Moshe Rabbeinu* that Aaron would assist him.

The sages teach that Aaron had a special talent for creating peace between husbands and wives and also between neighbors.[441]

People often quarrel as a result of a misunderstanding. A person says something intending one thing, but the listener interprets it differently. Moreover, even genuine differences of opinion usually stem from the fact that every person has a unique outlook on life. Sometimes, people cannot appreciate another person's perspective even when it is just as valid as their own.

Aaron had a special knack for identifying these issues, explaining them to people, and thereby fostering reconciliation. This talent enabled him to understand the different interpretations of the spiritual source of physical objects and thereby perform miracles.

---

[441] *Avoth D'Rabbi Nathan* 12:1 הֱוֵי מִתַּלְמִידָיו שֶׁל אַהֲרֹן – אוֹהֵב שָׁ-לוֹם וְרוֹדֵף שָׁ-לוֹם וּמֵשִׂים שָׁ-לוֹם בֵּין אִישׁ לְאִשְׁתּוֹ.

B.T. *Sanhedrin* 6B אַהֲרֹן אוֹהֵב שָׁלוֹם וְרוֹדֵף שָׁלוֹם וּמֵשִׂים שָׁלוֹם בֵּין אָדָם לַחֲבֵרוֹ

HASHEM NEVER CHANGES

Rabbi Meir's Insight into How Hashem Never Changes

ೞ Rabbi Meir's Teacher, Elisha ben Abuya

The *Talmud* records how Elisha ben Abuya became a heretic:

> He saw *Metatron*, who had been given permission to sit and record the merits of Israel. He then reasoned, "I have learned that above [the angels have] no sitting, no competition, no back [because they consist only of faces], and no fatigue, [which might cause them to need to sit and rest]. Perhaps, God forbid, there are two domains."[442]

Belief in monotheism is so fundamental for every Jew that it is inconceivable that a major *Torah* scholar such as Elisha ben

---

[442] B.T. *Chagigah* 15A חֲזָא מִיטַטְרוֹן דְּאִתְיְהִיבָא לֵיהּ רְשׁוּתָא לְמֵיתַב וּלְמִיכְתַּב זַכְוָותָא דְּיִשְׂרָאֵל. אָמַר: "גְּמִירָא דְּלְמַעֲלָה לֹא הֲוֵי לֹא יְשִׁיבָה וְלֹא תַּחֲרוּת וְלֹא עוֹרֶף וְלֹא עִיפּוּי. שֶׁמָּא חַס וְשָׁלוֹם שְׁתֵּי רָשׁוּיוֹת הֵן."

Abuya entertained a belief in polytheism. How, then, can one understand this story?

A basic tenet of Judaism is that *Hashem* never changes.[443] He is exactly the same after Creation as He was before Creation, even though the human mind cannot comprehend how this is possible. This is what troubled Elisha ben Abuya.

The sages teach that *Metatron's* name is like his Master's,[444] and Elisha ben Abuya therefore assumed that *Metatron's* behavior reflected God's nature. When Elisha ben Abuya observed an unexpected change in *Metatron's* behavior — sitting rather than standing — he wrongly assumed that *Hashem*, too, is subject to change. He did not think that there is more than one God. Instead, he thought that there are "two domains" — God as He was prior to Creation and God as He is after Creation.[445]

ഇരു Rabbi Meir's Secret Ingredient

The following *Talmudic* passage sheds light on the nature of this error:

> Rav Yehudah quoted Sh'muel, who [in turn] quoted Rabbi Meir [as saying]: When I was studying *Torah* under Rabbi Akiva, I would put [an ingredient called] *Kankantom*[446] into the ink [used for writing *Torah* scrolls to make it indelible], and he raised no objection.

---

[443] *Hayad Hachazakah, Hilchoth Yesodei Hatorah* 1:11 וכיוון שנתברר שאינו גוף וגוייה, יתברר שלא יארע לו אחד ממאורעות הגופות... ואינו משתנה שאין לו דבר שיגרום לו שינוי.

[444] B.T. *Sanhedrin* 38B זֶהוּ מְטַטְרוֹן שֶׁשְּׁמוֹ כְּשֵׁם רַבּוֹ

[445] For alternate explanations of Elisha ben Abuya's heresy, see *Understanding Emunah*, Rabbi Yehuda Cahn (2016, Ohr Nissan Talmud Center, Inc., Baltimore) pp. 212-220.

[446] The identity of *Kankantom* is a subject of dispute among the early authorities (*Tosafoth* on B.T. *Eruvin* 13A sub verba "*Kankantom*" (קנקנתום)). The *Rashbam*, among others, identifies it as vitriol (sulfuric acid).

When I came to [study under] Rabbi Yishmael, he asked me, "My son, what is your profession?"

I replied, "I am a scribe."

"My son," he said, "take care with your work, for your work is the work of Heaven. [Be careful] lest you omit a letter or add a letter, with the result that you destroy the entire world."

"I have an ingredient whose name is *Kankantom* that I put into the ink," I explained.

"Do we mix *Kankantom* into the ink?" asked Rabbi Yishmael. "Doesn't the *Torah* state, '[The *Kohen*] shall write [the curses of a suspected adulteress on parchment] and dissolve [them in the cursing water]',[447] implying that the writing must be capable of dissolving?"[448]

What was Rabbi Meir telling Rabbi Yishmael? [Rabbi Meir's response that he used indelible ink does not appear to address Rabbi Yishmael's admonition not to omit or add a letter when writing a *Torah* scroll.]

...This is what Rabbi Meir meant to say: Not only is there no need to worry about my omitting or adding letters, for I will not err because I am an expert [in my knowledge of the text], but even any concern that a fly might come and rest upon the projection of [the top line of] a *Dalet* (ד), thereby erasing it and converting it into a *Raish* (ר) [is unwarranted because] "I

---

[447] Numbers 5:23 וְכָתַב אֶת הָאָלֹת הָאֵלֶּה הַכֹּהֵן בַּסֵּפֶר וּמָחָה אֶל מֵי הַמָּרִים

[448] When a husband suspected his wife of infidelity, the *Torah* provided a way to test her. The *Kohen* would write the verses from this section of the *Torah* on parchment, erase them in water, and have the suspect drink the solution. A guilty wife became ill (Numbers 5:12-31). Rabbi Yishmael evidently held that this section of the *Torah* scroll should not be written with indelible ink which would not dissolve even though the parchment of a *Torah* scroll was never used for this purpose. The *Halachah* does not follow this opinion (*Shulchan Aruch, Yoreh Deah* 271:6 ואם כתבו במי עפצא וקנקנתום, כשר).

have an ingredient whose name is *Kankantom* that I put into the ink, [making it indelible]."[449]

Why did Rabbi Meir single out the example of a *Dalet* (ד) being transformed into a *Raish* (ר) when the same concern applies to many other letters? He could also have pointed out that, with a small erasure, a *Beth* (ב) can be transformed into a *Kaf* (כ), or a *Cheth* (ח) into a *Hay* (ה), or a *Kaf Sofith* (ך) into a *Dalet* (ד), and so on.

The answer is as follows.

A few letters throughout the *Torah* scroll must be written in extra-large script. One instance of this is the *Dalet* (ד) of the word *Echad* (אֶחָד), meaning "one," at the end of the first verse of *Shema* — "Listen, Israel, *Hashem* is our God, *Hashem* is one."[450] Another instance is the enlarged letter *Raish* (ר) in *Acher* (אַחֵר), meaning "another," in the verse "For you shall not bow to another god."[451]

The *Shulchan Aruch* rules that one must emphasize the *Dalet* (ד) when pronouncing the word *Echad* (אֶחָד) in *Shema* (שְׁמַע) to avoid accidentally saying *Acher* (אַחֵר) and thereby appear to blaspheme.[452] Although it is understandable that one should take care to pronounce the words of the *Shema* correctly, why would such a mistake be blasphemy when the resulting sentence makes no sense — "Listen, Israel, *Hashem* is our God, *Hashem* is

---

[449] B.T. *Eruvin* 13A. The full text appears in Appendix F.

[450] Deuteronomy 6:4 שְׁמַע יִשְׂרָאֵל ה' אֱלֹהֵינוּ ה' אֶחָד

[451] Exodus 34:14 כִּי לֹא תִשְׁתַּחֲוֶה לְאֵל אַחֵר

The difference between the numeric value of *Echad* (אֶחָד) and *Acher* (אַחֵר) is one hundred ninety-six. This is also the numeric value of *Kotz* (קוֹץ), which means "thorn" and refers to the tiny line which projects from the back of the *Dalet* (ד) and distinguishes it from *Raish* (ר).

[452] *Shulchan Aruch, Orach Chaim* 61:7 ידגיש בדלי"ת שלא תהא כרי"ש

another"? Is saying something self-contradictory or unintelligible blasphemy?

If the heresy of Elisha ben Abuya was a belief that *Hashem* changed and became different after Creation, then it is understandable why such a confusing sentence appears blasphemous — "*Hashem* is our God, but *Hashem* is also another God." He started off as one God but changed and therefore became like a different God.

God is absolutely One and never changes in any way. The concept of "another God" refers not only to idolatry, but also to the false idea that God changes and Himself becomes, so to speak, "another God." The small difference in appearance between *Dalet* (ד) and *Raish* (ר) represents the ease with which a person may fall into the erroneous belief that God changes, as did Elisha ben Abuya, who, incidentally, came to be known by the nickname "Another" (אַחֵר).

After Adam sinned, *Hashem* told him that "thorns and thistles shall [the Earth] sprout for you."[453] "Thistle" in Hebrew (דַרְדַּר) is composed of a repetition of the letters *Dalet* (ד) and *Raish* (ר). *Hashem* informed Adam not only that he and his descendants would have the frustrating experience of combating thorns and thistles when they farmed the land, but also that they would repeatedly face the spiritual challenge of recognizing that God's absolute unity never changes — of confusing the *Dalet* (ד) of "one" (אֶחָד) with the *Raish* (ר) of "another" (אַחֵר).[454]

---

[453] Genesis 3:18 וְקוֹץ וְדַרְדַּר תַּצְמִיחַ לָךְ

[454] *Pithchei She'arim, Nethiv Partzuf Nukva D'Zeir Anpin* 28 ועל ידי הקלקול היותר גדול שגרם חטאו בדורות העתידים כמו דור אנוש ודומיהם שכפרו בעיקר בסוד "אָז הוּחַל לִקְרֹא בְּשֵׁם ה'" (בראשית ד', כ"ו), הסירו קוצו של ד' דאח"ד ונעשה ר', והוא סוד ד"ר ד"ר.

See also *Bath Ayin* on *Parashath Vayera* for a related idea. שאברהם אבינו ע"ה הגביר כוח הקדושה על הסטרא אחרא, ועשה מן "אֶ-ל אַחֵר" שיהיה "אֵ-ל אֶחָד", שנעשה קרן לאות רי"ש ונעשה דלי"ת. וזהו "וַיִּשָּׂא אַבְרָהָם אֶת עֵינָיו וַיַּרְא וְהִנֵּה" מה שהיה "אֵיל אַחֵר" ברי"ש "נֶאֱחַז בַּסְּבַךְ בְּקַרְנָיו". פירוש שנאחז תג אחד בהקרן של הרי"ש ונעשה אח"ד.

ಶ಼ಶ಼ಶ಼ Rabbi Meir's Ability to Interpret Names

Although Rabbi Meir was a disciple of Elisha ben Abuya (אַחֵר), he remained steadfast in his belief that God never changes.

Kankantom (קַנְקַנְתּוֹם) — the ingredient he used to make indelible ink — hints at this. *Kankan* (קַנְקַן) can be interpreted to mean *Koneh Koneh* (קוֹנֶה קוֹנֶה) — "Creator Creator."[455] *Hashem* remains the same Creator of Heaven and Earth after Creation as He was before Creation.[456]

Moreover, the Hebrew for "ink" (דְּיוֹ) also means "two."[457] Rabbi Meir's statement that "I have an ingredient whose name is *Kankantom* that I put into the ink" may therefore be read to mean, "I have an ingredient of perfect faith in the God's immutability which I apply to the temptation to think that there are 'two' Gods — one before Creation and one after Creation."

Rabbi Meir used to interpret people's names to reveal their true nature. One time, he traveled to a village whose innkeeper was named *Kidor* (כִּידוֹר). Rabbi Meir refused to deposit his money with the innkeeper for safekeeping because *Kidor* (כִּידוֹר) resembles the first words in the phrase "for they are a wayward

---

[455] *Rashi* on Genesis 14:19 states that *Koneh* (קוֹנֶה) means "Creator" ("קֹנֵה שָׁמַיִם וָאָרֶץ" — כמו "עֹשֶׂה שָׁמַיִם וָאָרֶץ" (תהלים קמ"ו, ו). על ידי עשייתן קָנָאן להיות שלו.).

[456] *Perush Ba'alei Hatosafoth* on Exodus 34:6 expresses a similar idea concerning the repetition of God's Name. "ויעבור ה' על פניו ויקרא ה' ה'" — אני הוא שהייתי באין תחילה, אני הוא שהווה ואהיה באין סוף ותכלית.

The letters at the end of *Kankantom* (קַנְקַנְתּוֹם) — *Tom* (תּוֹם) — mean "whole" or "complete," implying that Rabbi Meir's faith in this principle was absolute.

[457] For example, the term דיומד is a contraction of דיו עמודין, referring to two boards attached to each other to form the corner of a *Sukkah* or other enclosure (B.T. *Eruvin* 18A מאי דיומדין? אמר רבי ירמיה בן אלעזר: דיו עמודין.).

generation" (כִּי דוֹר תַּהְפֻּכוֹת הֵמָּה),[458] and *Kidor* (כִּידוֹר) indeed turned out to be dishonest.[459]

The phrase "for they are a wayward generation" (כִּי דוֹר תַּהְפֻּכוֹת הֵמָּה) can be understood homiletically to refer to "those who switch around the *Dalet* and the *Raish*" (כִּי דל״ת ורי״ש תַּהְפֻּכוֹת הֵמָּה). Since Rabbi Meir carefully maintained the distinction between the *Dalet* (ד) of "one" (אֶחָד) with the *Raish* (ר) of "another" (אַחֵר), he merited the ability to detect *Kidor's* wicked nature.

ﮊﻭﮊﻭﮊﻭ Rabbi Yishmael's Objection

If this is what Rabbi Meir meant by saying that he mixed *Kankantom* into his ink, then why did Rabbi Yishmael object and state that it is forbidden to do so?

A different *Talmudic* story helps explain:

> When King David dug out the vents beneath the altar [in the place where the Temple was destined to stand], the [subterranean] depths surged up and were on the verge of flooding the world. Said King David, "Is there anyone who knows whether it is permitted to write [*Hashem's*] Name on a potsherd and cast it into the depths to calm them?"
>
> …Ahithophel devised an *a fortiori* argument: If to create peace between a husband and a wife [who is suspected of adultery] the *Torah* said, "Let My Name which is written in holiness be erased upon the water," how much more so to create peace for the entire world! [Ahithophel therefore told King David,] "It is permitted."

---

[458] Deuteronomy 32:20 וַיֹּאמֶר אַסְתִּירָה פָנַי מֵהֶם אֶרְאֶה מָה אַחֲרִיתָם כִּי דוֹר תַּהְפֻּכֹת הֵמָּה בָּנִים לֹא אֵמֻן בָּם.

[459] B.T. *Yoma* 83B רַבִּי מֵאִיר הֲוָה דָיֵיק בִּשְׁמָא. רַבִּי יְהוּדָה וְרַבִּי יוֹסֵי לָא הֲווֹ דָיְיקוּ בִּשְׁמָא. כִּי מָטוּ לְהַהוּא דוּכְתָּא, בָעוּ אוּשְׁפִּיזָא. יָהֲבוּ לְהוּ. אָמְרוּ לוֹ: "מַה שְׁמָךְ?" אֲמַר לְהוּ: "כִּידוֹר". אָמַר: "שְׁמַע מִינָהּ, אָדָם רָשָׁע הוּא שֶׁנֶּאֱמַר, 'כִּי דוֹר תַּהְפֻּכֹת הֵמָּה'". רַבִּי יְהוּדָה וְרַבִּי יוֹסֵי אַשְׁלִימוּ לֵיהּ כִּיסַיְיהוּ. רַבִּי מֵאִיר לָא אַשְׁלִים לֵיהּ כִּיסֵיהּ... לְמָחָר, אָמְרוּ לוֹ: "הַב לָן כִּיסָן". אָמַר לְהוּ: "לֹא הָיוּ דְבָרִים מֵעוֹלָם!"

The king wrote the Name upon a potsherd, cast it into the depths, and [the waters] descended....[460]

This story is puzzling. In the first place, how did King David know that writing *Hashem's* Name on a potsherd and casting it into the depths would calm them? Secondly, if he knew that such a procedure would work, how could he have been unsure whether it was allowed? One may violate every commandment in the *Torah* to save a life except for idolatry, immorality, and murder.[461] If saving the world required erasing *Hashem's* Name, surely it was permitted, and there should have been no need to deduce this from the case of a suspected adulteress (סוֹטָה).

ఴఴఴఴ People Cannot Fully Grasp Hashem's Immutability

If the entire purpose of Creation is for humanity to recognize God, it follows that it is a serious failing to hold false ideas about Him. Unfortunately, however, no human being can have a perfect understanding of how God remains the same after Creation as He was before Creation because this concept contradicts human logic.

The subterranean depths (תְּהוֹם) represent the strict Attribute of Judgment[462] which demands that even those who believe

---

[460] B.T. *Sukkah* 53A-B בְּשָׁעָה שֶׁכָּרָה דָּוִד שִׁיתִין, קָפָא תְּהוֹמָא וּבְעָא לְמִשְׁטְפָא עָלְמָא. אָמַר דָּוִד: "מִי אִיכָּא דְּיָדַע אִי שָׁרֵי לְמִיכְתַּב שֵׁם אַחַסְפָּא, וְנִשְׁדְּיֵה בִּתְהוֹמָא וּמְנַח?" ...נָשָׂא אֲחִיתוֹפֶל קַל וָחֹמֶר בְּעַצְמוֹ – וּמַה לַעֲשׂוֹת שָׁלוֹם בֵּין אִישׁ לְאִשְׁתּוֹ אָמְרָה תּוֹרָה: "שְׁמִי שֶׁנִּכְתָּב בִּקְדוּשָׁה יִמָּחֶה עַל הַמַּיִם", לַעֲשׂוֹת שָׁלוֹם לְכָל כָּל הָעוֹלָם כּוּלוֹ עַל אַחַת כַּמָּה וְכַמָּה?! אָמַר לֵיהּ: "שָׁרֵי". כָּתַב שֵׁם אַחַסְפָּא, וְשָׁדֵי לִתְהוֹמָא וְנָחִית תְּהוֹמָא.
[461] *Hayad Hachazakah, Hilchoth Yesodei Hatorah* 5:1-2 כשיעמוד עובד כוכבים ויאנוס את ישראל לעבור על אחת מכל מצות האמורות בתורה או יהרגנו, יעבור ואל יהרג... במה דברים אמורים בשאר מצות חוץ מעבודת כוכבים וגלוי עריות ושפיכת דמים.
[462] *Arvei Nachal, Parashath Breishith* מידת הדין נמשל לדבר עמוק והיינו "מִשְׁפָּטֶיךָ תְּהוֹם רַבָּה" (תהלים ל"ו, ז').
Tifereth Yehonathan on Genesis 1:2 ותהום הוא גם כן מידת הדין

in the Creator must suffer punishment because they do not fully grasp His nature despite their best efforts to do so.

Hashem does not accept this condemnation, however. Instead, in a manner of speaking, He allows His Name to be erased. He does not hold people accountable for having a less than perfect understanding of Him as long as they make a sincere effort to know Him.

King David dug the vents for the altar to prepare for building the Temple knowing that the Divine Presence would be more openly revealed in this permanent structure than it had been in the temporary Tabernacle. He feared that the strict Attribute of Judgment — the depths — would surge forth and demand retribution from the Jews because they did not have a full appreciation of the Divine Presence.

The law of the suspected adulteress (סוֹטָה) is unique in the *Torah*. In every other case, a Jewish court enforces *Torah* law by evaluating the testimony of witnesses together with other evidence to arrive at a decision. Had this procedure been followed in the case of a suspected adulteress (סוֹטָה), however, a court could never find a woman guilty because her case involved a situation in which she secreted herself with a man, but no one saw what they did. Such a result would not save her marriage because her suspicious husband would undoubtedly divorce her. To save the marriage, the *Torah* provides that the accused drink water in which verses containing *Hashem's* Name have been erased. If she is guilty, she dies a gruesome death. If she is innocent, her ability to bear children is enhanced.[463]

Ahithophel reasoned that if *Hashem* allows His Name to be erased to save a marriage, He would certainly overlook the

---

[463] Numbers 5:28 וְאִם לֹא נִטְמְאָה הָאִשָּׁה וּטְהֹרָה הִוא וְנִקְּתָה וְנִזְרְעָה זָרַע

fact that people do not understand Him perfectly even when the Divine Presence is highly revealed in the Temple.

This explains Rabbi Yishmael's response to Rabbi Meir.

The average Jew can and must believe that *Hashem* never changes and that He remains the same after Creation as He was before Creation. Nevertheless, this belief is not perfect because it is unintelligible to human beings.

By contrast, Rabbi Meir's understanding of this concept was vastly superior to that of other people. The *Gemara* states that in contrast to his fellow scholars, Rabbi Meir had the unique ability to grasp contradictory concepts. He could argue that something that was ritually impure was ritually pure and then argue equally well that something that was ritually pure was ritually impure, and his colleagues could not grasp his reasoning.[464] This unique ability gave Rabbi Meir a special insight into the seeming contradiction that *Hashem* is exactly the same after Creation as He was before Creation.[465] For him, this belief was as clear and absolute as if it were written with indelible ink.

With respect to the general public, however, the *Torah* must be written with ink that can dissolve. Although others cannot have the level of faith in *Hashem* that Rabbi Meir had, *Hashem* is willing to overlook this shortcoming. In a manner of speaking, He permits His Name to be erased to make peace between Himself and humankind.

---

[464] B.T. *Eruvin* 13B אָמַר רַבִּי אַחָא בְּרַבִּי חֲנִינָא: גָּלוּי וְיָדוּעַ לִפְנֵי מִי שֶׁאָמַר וְהָיָה הָעוֹלָם שֶׁאֵין בְּדוֹרוֹ שֶׁל רַבִּי מֵאִיר כְּמוֹתוֹ. וּמִפְּנֵי מַה לֹא קָבְעוּ הֲלָכָה כְּמוֹתוֹ? שֶׁלֹּא יָכְלוּ חֲבֵירָיו לַעֲמוֹד עַל סוֹף דַּעְתּוֹ, שֶׁהָיָה אוֹמֵר עַל טָמֵא טָהוֹר וּמַרְאֶה לוֹ פָּנִים, וְעַל טָהוֹר טָמֵא וּמַרְאֶה לוֹ פָּנִים.

[465] The rabbis state that Rabbi Meir was "a spark from *Metatron*" (*Kehillath Yaakov, Erech Meir* רבי מאיר היה ניצוץ מן מטטרון). Unlike Elisha ben Abuya who found *Metatron's* behavior confusing, Rabbi Meir's special connection to this angel gave him insight into how *Hashem* remains the same before and after the act of Creation.

The Tablets of the Ten Commandments

Of the ten items that *Hashem* created on the very first Sabbath eve, three pertain to the Tablets of the Ten Commandments: a) the power of the letters to form upon the Tablets without anyone chiseling them; b) the supernatural characteristics of the writing;[466] and c) the tablets themselves which were made from the primordial matter *Hashem* created ex nihilo (יֵשׁ מֵאַיִן) and from which He then fashioned the rest of Creation.[467]

---

[466] *Pirkei Avoth* 5:6. עֲשָׂרָה דְּבָרִים נִבְרְאוּ בְּעֶרֶב שַׁבָּת בֵּין הַשְּׁמָשׁוֹת, וְאֵלּוּ הֵן... וְהַכְּתָב וְהַמִּכְתָּב וְהַלּוּחוֹת. according to *Tifereth Yisrael, Yachin,* notes 36 and 37:

[לו] "וְהַכְּתָב" — צורת האותיות שבלוחות הראשונות, נברא בערב שבת בין השמשות, ובלוחות השניות גם כן כבר ניתן אז הכוח בהן שיתבקע בהם צורת האותיות מאליהן, אחר שיפסל משה את גוף הלוחות עצמן; [לז] "וְהַמִּכְתָּב" — הוא פנימיות האותיות, דמדהיו האותיות חרותים מעבר לעבר, מ"ם וסמ"ך המפולשין בלוחות בנס היו עומדין.

[467] *Rabbeinu Bachye* on Exodus 31:18 states that the Tablets were made of sapphire (וידוע כי הלוחות היו של סנפירינון ולוקחו מכסא הכבוד), and *Ma'asei Hashem, Chelek Ma'asei Torah* 10 states that sapphire is a metaphor for primordial matter (ברא החומר ההיולי שהמשילו ללבנת הספיר). *Ramban* on Genesis 1:1 comments that this was

ᴂ The Writing on the Tablets

The Tablets of the Ten Commandments were carved all the way through so that the letters could be seen from both sides,[468] but there are different opinions about how the letters appeared on the back of the Tablets.

According to Rav Chisda, the letters on the back of the Tablets were mirror images of those on the front so that the image of each was reversed. As an example, a *Kaf* (כ) carved into the front of the Tablets looked like the English letter "C" when viewed from the back of the Tablets. In addition, the order of the letters was reversed so that a word such as "בְּהַר" read "רַהַב." According to this view, the Tablets had a miraculous quality only because the centers of the *Samech* (ס) and the Final *Mem* (ם) hung suspended in midair unattached to the Tablets.[469]

Rabbeinu Bachye, however, holds that miraculously one could read the Ten Commandments the same way on both sides of the Tablets.[470] The letter *Kaf* (כ) looked the same on both sides, and a word such as "בְּהַר" appeared the same on both sides.

---

the only substance that was created ex nihilo and (יֵשׁ מֵאַיִן) that *Hashem* fashioned everything else from it (הוציא מן האפס הגמור המוחלט יסוד דק מאוד, אין בו ממש, אבל הוא כוח ממציא, מוכן לקבל הצורה, ולצאת מן הכוח אל הפועל, והוא החומר הראשון, נקרא ליוונים "היולי". (ואחר ההיולי לא ברא דבר, אבל יצר ועשה, כי ממנו המציא הכול).

[468] Exodus 32:15 וַיִּפֶן וַיֵּרֶד מֹשֶׁה מִן הָהָר וּשְׁנֵי לֻחֹת הָעֵדֻת בְּיָדוֹ לֻחֹת כְּתֻבִים מִשְּׁנֵי עֶבְרֵיהֶם מִזֶּה וּמִזֶּה הֵם כְּתֻבִים.

[469] B.T. *Shabbath* 104A אָמַר רַב חִסְדָּא: מֵ"ם וְסָמֶ"ךְ שֶׁבַּלּוּחוֹת בְּנֵס הָיוּ עוֹמְדִין. וְאָמַר רַב חִסְדָּא: כְּתָב שֶׁבַּלּוּחוֹת נִקְרָא מִבִּפְנִים וְנִקְרָא מִבַּחוּץ. כְּגוֹן, נְבוּב – בּוּבָן, (רהב בהר) [בָּהַר – רַהַב], סָרוּ – וּרָס.

[470] *Rabbeinu Bachye* on Exodus 32:15 זה היה פלא גדול שהכתב היה נקרא כסידורו משני העברים מה שאין כן בכתב שלנו כי מלפנים הוא כסידורו ומאחריו מהופך.

In the Jerusalem *Talmud*, Rabbi Shimon bar Yochai appears to hold the same opinion. Rabbi Simai goes a step further and states that the Tablets also had the Ten Commandments carved through their sides (J.T. *Shekalim* 6:1 (25A-B) according to the emendations of the Vilna *Gaon* : רבי שמעון בן יוחאי אומר עשרים על לוח זה ועשרים על לוח זה דכתיב, (וַיִּכָּתְבֵם עַל שְׁנֵי לֻחוֹת אֲבָנִים") "וּשְׁנֵי לֻחֹת הָעֵדֻת בְּיָדוֹ לֻחֹת כְּתֻבִים מִשְּׁנֵי עֶבְרֵיהֶם" (שמות ל"ב, ט"ו) – עשרים על לוח זה ועשרים על לוח זה. רבי סימאי אמר: ארבעים על לוח זה וארבעים על לוח זה דכתיב, ("מִזֶּה וּמִזֶּה הֵם כְּתֻבִים") "וּשְׁנֵי לֻחֹת הָעֵדֻת בְּיָדוֹ לֻחֹת כְּתֻבִים מִשְּׁנֵי עֶבְרֵיהֶם" (שם) – טטרוגה)).

The *Zohar* presents a third opinion. Each Tablet had the first five of the Ten Commandments carved on one side, and the very same letters which were carved all the way through the stone formed the words of the last five of the Ten Commandments on the opposite side. Thus, "I am *Hashem* your God" appeared on one side, but when people looked on the opposite side, they saw "Do not murder" in the place where the letters came through. "You shall have no other gods but Me" appeared on one side, while "Do not commit adultery" appeared opposite it on the other side, and so on.[471]

ಬಲ An Insight into How Hashem Never Changes

As mentioned earlier, human beings cannot fathom how *Hashem* created a changing universe and yet never changes.[472] He is exactly the same after Creation as He was before Creation, and He is unaffected by any changes which take place in Creation. This is true even though He exists everywhere throughout Creation. People cannot grasp this concept intellectually because it contradicts human logic.[473]

Nevertheless, people on a high spiritual level can grasp something of this concept by perceiving it directly. This resembles the way in which it is impossible to explain what sky-blue (תְּכֵלֶת) is to someone who cannot see. No amount of logical explanation can convey what a color looks like. On the other hand, one who sees a cloudless sky immediately understands what sky-blue is.

---

[471] *Zohar* II:84B הָא כֵּיצַד? מַאן דְּהֲוָה מִסְטְרָא דָא, הֲוָה קָרֵי בְּדָא, "אָנֹכִי ה' אֱ-לֹהֶיךָ", וּמֵאִלֵּין אַתְוָון הֲוָה חָמֵי וְקָרֵי, "לֹא תִּרְצַח" . הֲוָה קָרֵי, "לֹא יִהְיֶה לְךָ", וַהֲוָה חָמֵי וְקָרֵי, "לֹא תִּנְאָף".

[472] "For I am *Hashem*. I do not change." (Malachi 3:6) כִּי אֲנִי ה' לֹא שָׁנִיתִי

[473] *Mavoh Lechochmath Hakabalah* 2:2:1 ולא ניתנה לנו רשות לדרוש בזה כלל כי כאן סוד עצמותו כביכול הממלא הכל אחרי הבריאה כמו לפני הבריאה.

Prior to sinning, Adam and Chavah possessed a faith-sense (חוּשׁ הָאֱמוּנָה) which permitted them to perceive spirituality just as the sense of sight allows a person to perceive colors and images. If a person's eyes become damaged, God forbid, he can no longer see clearly or perhaps not at all. In a similar way, when Adam and Chavah sinned, they damaged their faith-sense (חוּשׁ הָאֱמוּנָה) and could no longer perceive spirituality.

When the Jews stood at Mount Sinai, their intense faith in *Hashem* caused them to merit the restoration of the faith-sense Adam and Chavah had lost. Using this restored faith-sense they could gaze upon the Tablets of the Ten Commandments and perceive how *Hashem* created a changing universe and yet never changes.

ೞೞೞ How the Tablets Provided this Insight

When a person writes with ink on paper, the ink and paper are independent of one another, with the ink forming the letters and the paper serving as a background for them. By contrast, when letters are carved through stone, the stone is not merely a background for the letters. Rather, the stone itself forms the letters by surrounding the hollow spaces.

This gives a very rough idea of how *Hashem*, in a manner of speaking, withdrew Himself to permit Creation to exist. Creation appears to have substance because *Hashem* surrounds it, just as the carved-out spaces in the Tablets appeared to form letters only because of the stone which surrounded them. At the same time, *Hashem* remains present in Creation but is invisible, just like the invisible air inside the hollow spaces. [474]

---

[474] The Hebrew for "hollow" (חָלָל) alludes to this because it is also the root for "generate" (לְחוֹלֵל).

Any material through which letters are carved could provide this insight, but the Tablets of the Ten Commandments permitted the Jews not merely to understand this but also to perceive it because the Tablets were made from the sapphire brickwork beneath the Throne of Glory — the same primordial matter from which all Creation comes — and they were filled with the speech *Hashem* used to create the universe.[475]

Just as air remains in the carved-out spaces of ordinary stone, Divine speech filled the hollow spaces of the Tablets. This speech gave the spaces it filled the ability to change so that they looked one way on the front but differently from the way ordinary carved stones would look on the back. It was this dynamic nature of the hollow spaces — their capability of changing instead of simply remaining inactive the way ordinary empty spaces do — that allowed the Jews to perceive with their restored faith-sense (חוּש הָאֱמוּנָה) how Creation appears dynamic and changing yet never affects *Hashem* so that He remains the unchanged.

The *Torah* states that "the writing was the writing of God carved upon the tablets."[476] According to *Kol Simchah*, the phrase "the writing of God" (מִכְתַּב אֱ-לֹהִים) implies that God was, so to speak, part of the writing.[477] The miraculous ability of the letters

---

[475] *Tziyuni, Parashath Yithro* היה הדבור ההוא כעין אש שחורה, כי נראית שחורה כלפי לבנת הספיר ונפלשה חקקים חקקים כצורות האותיות מפני שתחילתה הייתה חלשה למול אש הכבוד. ואז בהבקע הספיר ובהפלשה לחקקים באה אש הדבור ונהייתה כעין ממשות תוך פילוש החקיקה. ולפי שנראית כשחורה כלפי לבנת הספיר לכך נראות הלוחות כתובים כמכתב ספר ובדיו. ומפני שהחקקים היו מפולשין וממולאים באש שחורה, לכך נאמר "מִזֶּה וּמִזֶּה הֵם כְּתֻבִים" (שמות ל"ב, ט"ו).

Kithvei Ha'arizal, Sha'ar Hakavanoth, Drushei Tefillath Hashachar 1 ברכת יוֹצֵר אוֹר היא בלבנת הספיר, ולכן נאמר בו, "עֹשֶׂה שָׁלוֹם וּבוֹרֵא אֶת הַכּל".

[476] Exodus 32:16 וְהַלֻּחֹת מַעֲשֵׂה אֱ-לֹהִים הֵמָּה וְהַמִּכְתָּב מִכְתַּב אֱ-לֹהִים הוּא חָרוּת עַל הַלֻּחֹת

[477] See *Kol Simchah, Parashath Bamidbar*, "וְהַמִּכְתָּב מִכְתַּב אֱ-לֹהִים" – שהקב"ה הוא נכתב בתורה ויוכל האדם להשיג פעולת ה' על ידי עסק התורה.

In addition, the sages interpret the word "I" (אָנֹכִי) at the beginning of the Ten Commandments as an abbreviation for, "I Myself gave the writing"

to be formed from empty spaces and yet act differently from the way ordinary empty spaces do resulted from the fact that God revealed Himself in them.

ೞೞೞೞ Why the Jews Fashioned the Golden Calf

When *Hashem* revealed Himself and uttered the first two of the Ten Commandments, the Jews died, but He revived them.[478] The Jews therefore suspected that it was not possible for creatures who are subject to constant change to come into contact with an unchanging God without being destroyed. When *Moshe Rabbeinu* failed to return from Mount Sinai at the time when they expected him, they took this as confirmation of their suspicions. They then told Aaron, "Arise and make an intermediary for us who can lead us, for this Moses — the man who took us up from the Land of Egypt — we do not know what happened to him."[479] Obviously *Moshe Rabbeinu* was a man, so mentioning that fact was unnecessary. The Jews did so to emphasize that his failure to return from atop Mount Sinai proved that humans, who are subject to change, cannot survive contact with *Hashem*, who never changes.

The numeric value of "faith" (אֱמוּנָה) is the same as "calf" (עֵגֶל) if one is added for the word itself.[480] God had repeatedly demonstrated that He would remain connected to Israel through

---

(B.T. *Shabbath* 105A אֲנָא נַפְשִׁי כְּתִיבַת יְהָבִית), a phrase which may also be taken to mean, "I gave Myself as part of the writing."

[478] B.T. *Shabbath* 88B וְאָמַר רַבִּי יְהוֹשֻׁעַ בֶּן לֵוִי: כָּל דִּיבּוּר וְדִיבּוּר שֶׁיָּצָא מִפִּי הַקָּדוֹשׁ בָּרוּךְ הוּא יָצְתָה נִשְׁמָתָן שֶׁל יִשְׂרָאֵל... וּמֵאַחַר שֶׁמִּדִּבּוּר רִאשׁוֹן יָצְאָה נִשְׁמָתָן, דִּבּוּר שֵׁנִי הֵיאַךְ קִבְּלוּ? הוֹרִיד טַל שֶׁעָתִיד לְהַחֲיוֹת בּוֹ מֵתִים וְהֶחֱיָה אוֹתָם.

[479] Exodus 32:1 וַיַּרְא הָעָם כִּי בֹשֵׁשׁ מֹשֶׁה לָרֶדֶת מִן הָהָר וַיִּקָּהֵל הָעָם עַל אַהֲרֹן וַיֹּאמְרוּ אֵלָיו קוּם עֲשֵׂה לָנוּ אֱלֹהִים אֲשֶׁר יֵלְכוּ לְפָנֵינוּ כִּי זֶה מֹשֶׁה הָאִישׁ אֲשֶׁר הֶעֱלָנוּ מֵאֶרֶץ מִצְרַיִם לֹא יָדַעְנוּ מֶה הָיָה לוֹ.

[480] See note 197 for an explanation about why the rules for calculating numeric values (גִּמַטְרִיָּא) permit this permit this.

Moshe Rabbeinu, and the nation should have had faith that He would. Instead, they substituted the golden calf for that faith. Measure for measure, they lost their restored faith-sense (חוּשׁ הָאֱמוּנָה).

❧❧❧❧❧ The Difference between the First Tablets and the Second Ones

After *Hashem* accepted *Moshe Rabbeinu's* plea to forgive the Jews for the sin of the golden calf, He said, "Carve for yourself two stone tablets like the first ones, and I will write on those tablets the words that were on the first ones that you broke."[481]

Hashem had provided the primordial matter for the first Tablets, and the *Midrash* states that that material was carved from the sun.[482] The sun symbolizes absolute faith in *Hashem* free from any doubt because the sun's light and heat are plain for all to see and feel, and it would be foolish to doubt its existence. Israel's initial faith that *Hashem* is all powerful and that nothing is impossible for Him, including interacting with a changing universe yet remaining unchanged, gave the material from which the Tablets were fashioned the power to demonstrate this concept. Once the Jews lost that faith, they were no longer worthy of having Tablets with letters that had miraculous characteristics, so the letters flew away.[483]

Although the Jews repented, the second set of Tablets was made from sapphire that came from a quarry inside *Moshe*

---

[481] Exodus 34:1 וַיֹּאמֶר ה׳ אֶל מֹשֶׁה פְּסָל לְךָ שְׁנֵי לֻחֹת אֲבָנִים כָּרִאשֹׁנִים וְכָתַבְתִּי עַל הַלֻּחֹת אֶת הַדְּבָרִים אֲשֶׁר הָיוּ עַל הַלֻּחֹת הָרִאשֹׁנִים אֲשֶׁר שִׁבַּרְתָּ.

[482] *Yalkut Shimoni* on Song of Songs 5, paragraph 991 "וְהַלֻּחֹת מַעֲשֵׂה אֱ-לֹהִים" (שמות ל״ב, ט״ז)... רבי מנחמא בשם רבי אבין אמר: וחצובין מגלגל חמה.

[483] *Midrash Tanchuma, Parashath Kee Tisa* 30 כל ימים שהיה הכתב על הלוחות לא היה משה מרגיש בהם. כיוון שפרח הכתב, נמצאו כבדים על ידיו והשליכם ונשתברו.

Rabbeinu's tent.[484] This symbolized a lower level of faith. Sapphire does not give off its own light. It only sparkles when it reflects light from another source. The faith the Jews had after they repented was a mere reflection of the faith-sense (חוּשׁ הָאֱמוּנָה) that permitted them to perceive how *Hashem* permeates the universe yet remains separate from it and never changes.[485]

❧ I Will Be that which I Will Be

When *Moshe Rabbeinu* asked what he should tell the Jewish slaves when they asked who sent him, *Hashem* replied, "I will be that which I will be; and He said [to Moses]: So shall you say to the Children of Israel, 'I will be' sent me to you."[486]

At first glance, *Hashem's* statement seems neither responsive to *Moshe Rabbeinu's* question nor informative in any other way because it appears to make the obvious statement that "I am whatever I am."

What was the real meaning of this response?

Avodath Hakodesh states that the Ten Commandments are surrounded by the Divine Name "I will be" (אֶהְיֶה) because they begin with *Alef* (א) and end with *Kaf* (ך) which together have a numeric value of twenty-one, the same numeric value as "I will be" (אֶהְיֶה).[487]

Tikunei Zohar compares the two Tablets of the Ten Commandments to an upper eyelid and a lower eyelid with the Divine Presence between them, corresponding to a pupil. These

---

[484] *Pirkei D'Rabbi Eliezer* 45 כשאמר הקב״ה למשה, "פְּסָל לְךָ שְׁנֵי לֻחֹת אֲבָנִים" (שמות ל״ד, א'), מחצב סנפרינון נברא לו למשה בתוך אוהלו וחצבן.

[485] See *S'fath Emeth, Parashath Ekev* 5651 והעניין הוא כי אחר החטא ניתנו הלוחות מלמטה תחת השמיים והוא בדרך הכ״ח עתים שתחת השמש. אבל לוחות הראשונות היו למעלה מן השמש ולא היו בזמן ובמקום ידוע.

[486] Exod. 3:14 וַיֹּאמֶר אֱ-לֹהִים אֶל מֹשֶׁה אֶ-הְיֶה אֲשֶׁר אֶ-הְיֶה וַיֹּאמֶר כֹּה תֹאמַר לִבְנֵי יִשְׂרָאֵל אֶהְיֶה שְׁלָחַנִי אֲלֵיכֶם

[487] *Avodath Hakodesh*, 4:34 ולזה באו הדברות חתומים בשם אהי״ה שהרי תחילתן אל״ף וסופן ך' /

three together correspond to the three Hebrew words which form the phrase "I will be that which I will be" (אֶ-הְיֶה אֲשֶׁר אֶ-הְיֶה) and to the *Halachic* principle of "general rule, specification, general rule" (כְּלָל וּפְרָט וּכְלָל)[488] which works as follows:

Whenever the *Torah* declares a general rule, follows it with a specification, and then restates the general rule, the general rule is limited to things resembling the specification (כְּלָל וּפְרָט וּכְלָל, אִי אַתָּה דָן אֶלָּא כְּעֵין הַפְּרָט).

Here is an example:

The *Torah* states, "You shall make a *Menorah* of pure gold; the *Menorah* shall be made as a complete piece."[489] Rabbi Yehudah Hanassi uses the following reasoning to explain why the *Menorah* could be made from any metal, but not from clay, wood, stone, or other materials. The *Torah* first states, "You shall make a *Menorah*," a general statement which implies that it may be made from any material. The *Torah* then specifies, "of pure gold." Next, the *Torah* goes back and makes a general statement: "the *Menorah* shall be made as a complete piece," again implying that any material may be used. When there is a general rule followed by a specification and then the general rule is repeated, the general rule is limited to things which resemble the specification (כְּלָל וּפְרָט וּכְלָל, אִי אַתָּה דָן אֶלָּא כְּעֵין הַפְּרָט). Accordingly, the *Menorah* may be

---

[488] *Tikunei Zohar* 145B תְּרֵי כַנְפֵי עֵינָא תְּרֵי לוּחֵי, וַעֲלַיְיהוּ אִתְּמַר, "תָּמִיד עֵינֵי ה' אֱ-לֹהֶיךָ בָּהּ מֵרֵאשִׁית הַשָּׁנָה" (דברים י"א, י"ב). וּמַאי "בָּהּ"? בְּבַת עַיִן, דְּאִיהִי שְׁכִינְתָּא. וְכַנְפֵי עֵינָא עֲלַיְיהוּ אִתְּמַר, "פִּתְחוּ לִי שַׁעֲרֵי צֶדֶק" (תהלים קי"ח, י"ט). תְּלַת גַּוְונִין – כְּלָל וּפְרָט וּכְלָל, דְּאִינוּן "אֶ-הְיֶה אֲשֶׁר אֶ-הְיֶה". וְאִינוּן "אֶ-הְיֶה אֲשֶׁר אֶ-הְיֶה", דְּאִינוּן כְּלָל בְּכָל אוֹרַיְיתָא – "אֶהְיֶה" כְּלָל, "אֲשֶׁר" פְּרָט, "אֶהְיֶה" כְּלָל.

[489] Exodus 25:31 וְעָשִׂיתָ מְנֹרַת זָהָב טָהוֹר מִקְשָׁה תֵּיעָשֶׂה הַמְּנוֹרָה יְרֵכָהּ וְקָנָהּ גְּבִיעֶיהָ כַּפְתֹּרֶיהָ וּפְרָחֶיהָ מִמֶּנָּה יִהְיוּ. *Rashi* ad. loc. explains that the expression "as a complete piece" (מִקְשָׁה) means that the parts of the *Menorah* could not be fashioned separately and then joined together. Rather, it had to be carved or hammered out from a single lump of material.

fashioned from any material which resembles gold, i.e., any metal, but not from non-metals.[490]

How does this principle apply to the Divine appellation, "I will be that which I will be" (אֶ-הְיֶה אֲשֶׁר אֶ-הְיֶה), which represents the two Tablets of the Ten Commandments surrounding the Divine Presence?

Orchoth Tzaddikim explains that the expression "I will be that which I will be" (אֶ-הְיֶה אֲשֶׁר אֶ-הְיֶה) alludes to the Divine Attribute of Truth (אֱמֶת) because this phrase suggests multiplying the numeric value of "I will be" (אֶהְיֶה), which is twenty-one, by itself, and twenty-one times twenty-one equals 441, the numeric value of "truth" (אֱמֶת).[491]

In addition, the *Torah* states that the Tablets were written by the "finger of God" (אֶצְבַּע אֱ-לֹהִים).[492] The sages explain that this metaphor refers to the stamp, or seal, *Hashem* used to fashion Creation.[493] Since *Hashem's* stamp, or seal, is truth,[494] the implication is that He used the Divine Attribute of Truth to create Heaven and Earth and to inscribe the Tablets of the Ten Commandments.[495]

---

[490] B.T. *Sukkah* 50B כלל. "זָהָב טָהוֹר", כלל. "מִקְשָׁה תֵּיעָשֶׂה הַמְּנוֹרָה", חזר וכלל. "וְעָשִׂיתָ מְנֹרַת", פרט. "מִקְשָׁה תֵּיעָשֶׂה הַמְּנוֹרָה", ופרט וכלל, אי אתה דן אלא כעין הפרט. מה הפרט מפורש של מתכת, אף כל של מתכת.

[491] *Orchoth Tzaddikim*, Gate 23, *Sha'ar Ha'emeth* שהקדוש ברוך הוא א-להים אמת, כי תמצא כ"א פעמים אהי"ה שהוא בגימטריא אמ"ת, וגם כן אהי"ה בגימטריא כ"א.

[492] Exodus 31:18 וַיִּתֵּן אֶל מֹשֶׁה כְּכַלֹּתוֹ לְדַבֵּר אִתּוֹ בְּהַר סִינַי שְׁנֵי לֻחֹת הָעֵדֻת לֻחֹת אֶבֶן כְּתֻבִים בְּאֶצְבַּע אֱ-לֹהִים.

[493] *Megaleh Amukoth Al Hatorah, Parashath Vayeitzei* אצבע אלוקים שהוא גושפנקא דביה איתבריאו שמיא וארעא.

[494] B.T. *Shabbath* 55A דַּאֲמַר רַבִּי חֲנִינָא: חוֹתָמוֹ שֶׁל הַקָּדוֹשׁ בָּרוּךְ הוּא אֱמֶת

[495] The initial letters of "Heaven and Earth" (אֶת הַשָּׁמַיִם וְאֵת הָאָרֶץ) form the Divine Name א-ה-ו-ה. When these letters are spelled out (אל"ף ה"י וי"ו ה"י), they have a combined numeric value of 163, the same as "finger" (אֶצְבַּע). (*Megaleh Amukoth Al Hatorah, Parashath Vayeitzei* הרי סוד אצבע אלוקים שהוא גושפנקא דביה איתבריאו שמיא וארעא כדאיתא בזוהר על פסוק "אֶת הַשָּׁמַיִם וְאֵת הָאָרֶץ" (בראשית א', א'). התחלת שם של אהי"ה וסוף שם של הוי"ה, (שהוא במילוי אל"ף ה"י וי"ו ה"י, בגימטריא קס"ג בחשבון אצבע).

We may now understand the expression "I will be that which I will be" as follows:

Truth may be viewed as having three aspects. The first is reality as it actually exists. For example, if a person owns a sweater, then all the characteristics of the sweater are true. If the sweater is a certain shade of blue, made of one hundred percent lamb's wool, and cut to a certain size, then those attributes are all part of reality and constitute truth.

There is also a second type of truth. If the sweater is blue, then it is not orange, or red, or yellow, or purple, and so on. Although these attributes are false because they do not match reality, they are true when stated conditionally. In other words, statements of realistic possibilities, such as, "Instead of being blue, this sweater could have been red," or, "Instead of having a V-neck, this sweater could have been made with a ring neck," are also true statements.

These two aspects of truth — what really exists and what people know could exist — are comprehensible to human beings, but there is a third aspect of truth which is not intelligible to people. There are possibilities which only *Hashem* Himself can conceive and create. As an example, although we know that it is possible for a woolen sweater to have a wide variety of colors, from our perspective it is impossible for a sweater to be at one and the same time both completely blue and also completely red. Likewise, a sweater cannot simultaneously be made of one hundred percent lamb's wool and also one hundred percent cotton.

The first "I will be" (אֶהְיֶה) is a general principle (כְּלָל). It represents the all-encompassing creative force *Hashem* used to produce the universe including all three aspects of truth: a) reality as it exists; b) possibilities people can understand because they are consistent with commonly observed phenomena; and c) possibilities which defy human logic but which are possible for God because He can do anything.

The term "which" (אֲשֶׁר) in Hebrew can also mean to "certify" or "verify" and therefore refers to truth. The *Torah* states, "*Hashem* told Moses, 'Carve for yourself two stone tablets like the first ones, and I will write on the tablets the words which were on the first tablets which you broke." [496] The sages interpret the phrase "which you broke" (אֲשֶׁר שִׁבַּרְתָּ) as meaning that *Hashem* verified that what *Moshe Rabbeinu* did was proper (יִישָׁר כֹּחֲךָ שֶׁשִּׁבַּרְתָּ). [497]

The term "which" (אֲשֶׁר) in the phrase "which you broke" (אֲשֶׁר שִׁבַּרְתָּ) alludes to truth in the limited sense of Creation as it actually exists without considering any other possibilities. The Jews fashioned the golden calf because, according to their calculations, *Moshe Rabbeinu* was late returning from Mount Sinai. The possibility that they had miscalculated or that some other reasonable explanation existed either did not occur to them or, if it did, they refused to accept it. They could accept only actual reality as true and were unwilling to recognize any other conceivable possibility.

The term "which" (אֲשֶׁר) in the phrase "I will be that which I will be" (אֶ-הְיֶה אֲ-שֶׁר אֶהְיֶה) bears the same implication — reality limited to what actually exists.

The repetition of the term "I will be" again refers to truth from *Hashem's* perspective — a truth which includes matters which are impossible from a human point of view. According to

---

[496] Exodus 34:1 וַיֹּאמֶר ה׳ אֶל מֹשֶׁה פְּסָל לְךָ שְׁנֵי לֻחֹת אֲבָנִים כָּרִאשֹׁנִים וְכָתַבְתִּי עַל הַלֻּחֹת אֶת הַדְּבָרִים אֲשֶׁר הָיוּ עַל הַלֻּחֹת הָרִאשֹׁנִים אֲשֶׁר שִׁבַּרְתָּ.

[497] B.T. *Shabbath* 87A וּמְנָלָן דְּהִסְכִּים הַקָּדוֹשׁ בָּרוּךְ הוּא עַל יָדוֹ? שֶׁנֶּאֱמַר, "אֲשֶׁר שִׁבַּרְתָּ", וְאָמַר רֵישׁ לָקִישׁ: יִישָׁר כֹּחֲךָ שֶׁשִּׁבַּרְתָּ.

the principle of "general rule, specification, general rule" (כְּלָל וּפְרָט וּכְלָל), truth must be limited to matters which resemble the specification. Accordingly, the ordinary operation of the universe is limited to either reality as it actually exists or realistic possibilities. It cannot include possibilities which make sense only to *Hashem* such as a sweater which is simultaneously both size ten and size twenty, or which is made completely of cotton and also completely of wool, or which functions both as a sweater and also as a jetliner, and so on.

The Tablets of the Ten Commandments were an exception to this rule. They included all three truths, meaning that they possessed attributes which are inconceivable and illogical to human beings. They were carved all the way through, but people could read the same thing on each side, or, in the alternative, people could read the first five commandments from one side and the second five from the other, and the centers of the carved out letters hung miraculously in midair — characteristics which are outside the realm of physical possibility as we know it.[498]

🙟🙜 The Finger of God (אֶצְבַּע אֱ-לֹהִים)

As mentioned above, the expression "finger of God" (אֶצְבַּע אֱ-לֹהִים) — the instrument used to form the inscription on the Tablets — refers to *Hashem's* seal, which is truth. The "finger of God" refers to the way in which *Hashem* inscribed the Tablets of the Ten Commandments with all three truths mentioned above.

---

[498] This explains how the Tablets simultaneously both existed and did not exist, because they rested inside the Holy Ark (אֲרוֹן הַקֹּדֶשׁ), which took up no space מְקוֹם אָרוֹן אֵינוֹ מִן הַמִּדָּה. תַּנְיָא נַמִי הָכֵי: אָרוֹן שֶׁעָשָׂה מֹשֶׁה, יֵשׁ לוֹ עֶשֶׂר אַמּוֹת לְכָל (B.T. *Megillah* 10B רוּחַ).

ഇരുണ The Plague of Lice

The *Torah* states that:

Aaron stretched forth his hand with his staff and struck the dirt of the land, and there were lice upon man and beast. All the dirt of the land became lice throughout the Land of Egypt. The sorcerers [tried] to do likewise with their spells to bring forth lice, but they could not, and the lice were upon man and beast. The sorcerers told Pharaoh, "This is the finger of God."[499]

The *Midrash* states that the *Torah's* use of the term "finger of God" (אֶצְבַּע אֱ-לֹהִים) suggests that the plague of lice and the writing on the Tablets of the Ten Commandments were connected.[500]

What possible connection can there be between the two?

Yalkut Shimoni states that God "struck the Egyptians with fourteen kinds of lice. The smallest was the size of a hen's egg, and the largest was the size of a goose egg."[501] This seems to contradict the view of Rabbi Eliezer who states in the *Gemara* that the lice were smaller than a grain of barley.[502] This is not necessarily a case of conflicting opinions, however. It may be that the lice were at one and the same time two different sizes!

The sorcerers could perform magic to produce something which can possibly exist, but not something which from a human perspective cannot exist. Since the "finger of God" (אֶצְבַּע אֱ-לֹהִים) consisted of all three truths described above, including *Hashem's*

[499] Exodus 8:13-15 (יג) וַיַּעֲשׂוּ כֵן וַיֵּט אַהֲרֹן אֶת יָדוֹ בְמַטֵּהוּ וַיַּךְ אֶת עֲפַר הָאָרֶץ וַתְּהִי הַכִּנָּם בָּאָדָם וּבַבְּהֵמָה כָּל עֲפַר הָאָרֶץ הָיָה כִנִּים בְּכָל אֶרֶץ מִצְרָיִם. (יד) וַיַּעֲשׂוּ כֵן הַחַרְטֻמִּים בְּלָטֵיהֶם לְהוֹצִיא אֶת הַכִּנִּים וְלֹא יָכֹלוּ וַתְּהִי הַכִּנָּם בָּאָדָם וּבַבְּהֵמָה. (טו) וַיֹּאמְרוּ הַחַרְטֻמִּם אֶל פַּרְעֹה אֶצְבַּע אֱ-לֹהִים הִוא וַיֶּחֱזַק לֵב פַּרְעֹה וְלֹא שָׁמַע אֲלֵהֶם כַּאֲשֶׁר דִּבֶּר ה'.

[500] *Yalkut Reuveni Al Hatorah, Parashath Yayera* "וַיַּעֲשׂוּ כֵן הַחַרְטֻמִּים בְּלָטֵיהֶם" ולא יכלו להוציא הכינים, אבל הודו בעל כרחם שזה אינו ממין הכשפות שלהם. אך אמרו "אֶצְבַּע אֱ-לֹהִים הִוא", רמז לסוד הלוחות שנאמר בהם, "כְּתֻבִים בְּאֶצְבַּע אֱ-לֹהִים", שגם הם ממין הנפלאות הא-לוהות.

[501] *Yalkut Shimoni, Shemoth 7*, paragraph 182 ארבע עשר מיני כינים הביא עליהם. הקטנה שבהן כביצה של תרנגולת והגדולה שבהן כביצה של אווז.

[502] B.T. *Sanhedrin* 67B אָמַר רַבִּי אֱלִיעֶזֶר: מִיכָּן שֶׁאֵין הַשֵּׁד יָכוֹל לִבְרֹאות בְּרִיָּה פְּחוֹת מִכַּשְׂעוֹרָה

ability to perform acts that are inconceivable to the human mind, it was capable of producing lice which were simultaneously both at least as large as a hen's egg yet smaller than a barleycorn![503]

ஐஐ Teth (ט), the Missing Letter

The letter *Teth* (ט), whose numeric value is nine, does not appear in the first set of the Ten Commandments listed in the Book of Exodus (שְׁמוֹת) but does appear in the second set found in the Book of Deuteronomy (דְּבָרִים).[504]

The Prophet Jeremiah declared that, "*Hashem* is a God of truth."[505] The *Midrash* explains that this is because He lives and endures eternally.[506] *Ye'aroth Devash* comments that the small number value of "truth" (אֱמֶת) is nine. (The full numeric value of "truth" is 441. The small number value is calculated by adding these digits together: 4 + 4 + 1 = 9.)

Nine has the unique property that the digits of its multiples always add up to nine. For example, $9 \times 2 = 18$, and $1 + 8 = 9$. Likewise, $9 \times 3 = 27$, and $2 + 7 = 9$. This pattern continues so that even much higher multiples of nine display this feature. For example, $9 \times 613 = 5517$. The sum of these digits is eighteen ($5 + 5 + 1 + 7 = 18$), and the sum of the digits of eighteen, $1 + 8$, is nine.

---

[503] The numeric value of lice (כִּנִּים) is 120, and the numeric value of "nature" (טֶבַע) is 81. The difference between 120 and 81 is thirty-nine, the same numeric value as "*Hashem* is one" (י-ה-ו-ה אֶחָד). This hints that the plague of lice could not occur naturally but only through direct Divine intervention.

[504] *Yalkut Reuveni, Parashath Ve'ethchanan* כל אל"ף בי"ת כתיב בעשרת הדברות האחרונים. טי"ת אין בתוכה בלוחות ראשונים.

[505] Jeremiah 10:10 וַה' אֱ-לֹהִים אֱמֶת

[506] *Vayikra Rabbah* 26:1 למה הוא אמת? אמר רבי אבין: שהוא א-לוהים חיים ומלך עולם

The number nine therefore represents the truth of *Hashem's* eternal immutability.[507]

The letter *Teth* (ט), with a numeric value of nine, did not need to appear in the first set of Tablets because those were carved by *Hashem* Himself and whoever saw them immediately understood that they contained eternally unchanging truth, including all three aspects of truth described above. The second Tablets were fashioned by *Moshe Rabbeinu* after which *Hashem* inscribed the Ten Commandments on them. The *Teth* (ט) had to appear on those Tablets to clarify that they also included all three types of truth even though they were produced by *Moshe Rabbeinu.*

৪৩৪৩ The Potential Embedded in Creation

A slightly different interpretation of the term "which" (אֲשֶׁר) found in the phrase "I will be that which I will be" (אֶ-הְיֶה אֲשֶׁר אֶ-הְיֶה) is as follows.

"Which" (אֲשֶׁר) has a numeric value of 501, the same as the initial letters of the ten plagues *Hashem* inflicted upon Egypt (דצ"ך עד"ש באח"ב).

What is the significance of this set of abbreviations? Why do we make a point of mentioning them at the *Pesach Seder*, and why were they inscribed on *Moshe Rabbeinu's* staff?[508]

---

[507] *Ye'aroth Devash* 1:12 כבר נודע מה שכתוב במדרש... "למה אמת? שהוא חי וקיים", והוא כי אמת חי וקיים וקיים היותו במספר קטן תשעה, ותשעה חי וקיים, כי אם תכפילו בכל אופן שתרצה יישאר לעולם תשעה, ולכך חותמו אמת שהוא חי וקיים.

[508] The *Haggadah* states, "Rabbi Yehudah used to apply symbols to [the plagues]." The source for this is *Sifrei, Parashath Thavo* 5 (רבי יהודה היה נותן בהם סימנים: דצ"ך עד"ש באח"ב).

Shemoth Rabbah 5:6 states that the abbreviations were inscribed on *Moshe Rabbeinu's* staff (מהו "כָּל הַמֹּפְתִים אֲשֶׁר שַׂמְתִּי בְיָדֶךָ" (שמות ד', כ"א)? זה המטה שהיו כתובין עליו י' מכות – שהיה כתוב עליו נוטריקון דצ"ך עד"ש באח"ב).

To understand the answer requires first understanding the significance of abbreviations.

The *Torah* uses the initial letters of a set of words (נוֹטָרִיקוֹן) for homiletic purposes. For example, *Hashem* told Abraham, "Your name shall be no longer be Abram, but your name shall be Abraham because I have made you father of a multitude of nations,"[509] and Abraham (אַבְרָהָם) is a shorthand way of saying "father of a multitude" (אַב הֲמוֹן).[510]

What is the rationale behind this method of interpretation?

Whenever something comes first in a series, it includes the potential for everything which follows after it. For instance, the *Malbim* explains that the very first word of the *Torah* (בְּרֵאשִׁית) which starts the description of *Hashem's* act of Creation includes within it all of Creation.[511]

The first letter of a word therefore represents its potential — all the words that may be formed from it.[512] Since the initial letters of a group of words in the *Tanach* hold the latent potential to form many other words, they can be interpreted as hinting at different words or concepts besides those explicitly stated in the text.[513]

---

[509] וְלֹא יִקָּרֵא עוֹד אֶת שִׁמְךָ אַבְרָם וְהָיָה שִׁמְךָ אַבְרָהָם כִּי אַב הֲמוֹן גּוֹיִם נְתַתִּיךָ Genesis 17:5

[510] B.T. *Shabbath* 105A אָמַר רַב יוֹחָנָן מִשּׁוּם רַבִּי יוֹסֵי בֶן זִמְרָא: מִנַּיִן לִלְשׁוֹן נוֹטָרִיקוֹן מִן הַתּוֹרָה? שֶׁנֶּאֱמַר, "כִּי אַב הֲמוֹן גּוֹיִם נְתַתִּיךָ" (בראשית י"ז, ה').

The *Talmud* calls this method *Notarikon* (נוֹטָרִיקוֹן), a Greek word (νοταρικόν) which translates as "notetaking" or "shorthand."

[511] *Malbim* on Song of Songs 5:13, הדבור הכללי הנכלל במילת "בְּרֵאשִׁית", שבו נעשה הכל בכוח, כמי שזורע זרעים בבת אחת טרם יצמחו, וזה נעשה ביום הראשון שהוציא הכל יש מאין.

[512] *Ohr Hameir, Parashath Emor* כי הנה נתבאר לנו... עניין ראשי תיבות וסופי תיבות. והכוונה כלליות הארה ותענוגים של כללות אותיות, צירוף התיבה, המה מקובצים תחילה באות ראשונה. ולכן אות ב' דבראשית רברבא.

[513] The spiritual forces inherent in any particular word are also represented by the last letter of that word. For example, the rabbis base several teachings on the fact that the initial letters of the words "Let the Heavens rejoice and the

The term "which" (אֲשֶׁר) alludes to this idea because its function is to indicate that more information will follow about a noun or phrase. For example, in the sentence, "The horse has a long tail which it uses to swat flies," the term "which" indicates that more information will follow about the horse's long tail, namely, that it uses it to swat flies. Since "which" (אֲשֶׁר) is an indicator that more information will follow but offers no hint about what that information will be, it symbolizes the power of initial letters to signify alternate meanings and interpretations.

Hashem formed the universe by creating and then blending spiritual forces in a manner corresponding to speech, words, and letters. The initial letter of a word represents a raw, undeveloped spiritual force, so the initial letter of each plague sent against the Egyptians could just as easily stand for something beneficial as it could for something harmful. For example, the *Beth* (ב) which begins "hail" (בָּרָד) could just as easily begin "blessing" (בְּרָכָה), the *Tzadi* (צ) which begins "frog" (צְפַרְדֵּעַ) could just as easily begin "charity" (צְדָקָה), and so on. The initial letters of the ten plagues were carved on *Moshe Rabbeinu's* staff to hint that the plagues did not have to happen. Those letters symbolized spiritual potentials which could manifest themselves as punishments or as rewards according to the choices made by the Egyptians.

The Tablets of the Ten Commandments may be viewed as slabs of stone that had "which" (אֲשֶׁר) inserted between them. The malleable potential of initial letters gave the letters on the Tablets their miraculous quality.

Earth celebrate" (יִשְׂמְחוּ הַשָּׁמַיִם וְתָגֵל הָאָרֶץ) (Psalms 96:11) spell *Hashem's* Ineffable Name (י-ה-ו-ה) while the final letters spell "in His image" (צַלְמוֹ). (See, e.g., *Tziyuni, Parashath Shelach Lecha*).

THE RELATIONSHIP BETWEEN THE SPIRITUAL AND THE PHYSICAL

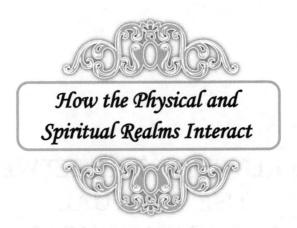

How the Physical and Spiritual Realms Interact

It is not possible for human beings to fully grasp how something non-physical can affect something physical. Nevertheless, a partial explanation of how this happens is as follows.

For two things to interact with one another, they must have some contact point. For objects in the physical realm, which are bound by space and time, such a connecting point must be both spatial and temporal. For example, two rooms cannot connect to one another unless they are situated in such a way that they have a common doorway, hallway, or other connecting space between them. They also must exist at the same time. If one room existed many years ago but has since been destroyed or if it will exist in the future and has not yet been built, then no connection between the two is currently possible.[514]

---

[514] The author has ignored the theory of quantum mechanics in accordance with the view of Rabbi Moshe Feinstein who states that Jewish law and philosophy only consider phenomena which are visible to the unaided eye and ignore observations made with microscopes or other specialized equipment (*Iggroth Moshe, Even Ha'ezer* III:33).

Since the dimensions of time and space do not exist in the higher spiritual realms, it seems impossible for those realms to be connected to the lower realms which exist within those confines.

For the physical realm, which is bound by time and space, to connect to the spiritual realm, which is not, the two realms must have something in common. It follows that the physical realm must have some non-spatial, non-temporal aspects.

Time consists of past, present, and future. The present is the instant when the past disappears and the future comes into being. That instant is imperceptible to human beings, and they cannot quantify it. In this sense, although the present is a feature of time, it also transcends time.

Rabbi Yitzchak Isaac Chaver explains that this is why the destruction of Egypt's firstborn occurred precisely at midnight. Midnight is the midpoint of the night, with the first half before it and the second half after it. Like the moment called "present," this midpoint cannot be precisely determined by human beings. Although it is part of time, it also stands beyond time and therefore beyond nature. That is why a supernatural miracle could happen then.[515]

The same concept applies to three-dimensional space. Every physical object has three dimensions — length, width, and height. Each of these, in turn, consists of two opposite directions, for a total of six — right and left, front and back, top and bottom.

There is also a seventh defining aspect of every three-dimensional object — the point which lies at its center. According

---

[515] *Biurei Aggadoth (Afikei Yam), Moed Daf Katan* 3A. וזה עניין ב׳ הנהגות – הטבע והניסיי. שהטבע הוא כולו בשבע המזלות שהוא תלוי בזמן, אבל הניסים הם בעולם הנבדל שאינו תלוי בזמן והוא למעלה מן הזמן... ונמצא שממש רגע חצות לילה מה שבין חצות הראשון לחצות השני (*החצי הראשון לחצי האחרון*) שאין לו מציאות נרגש בעוה״ז שהרי הרגעים תכופים ומחוברים זה לזה העבר עם העתיד, מכל מקום ישנו במציאות נבדל ובו היה הנס.

to Euclidean geometry, a point is infinitely small and has no length, width, or height. Since the centerpoint of an object has no materiality and cannot be defined as having opposite directions as the other aspects of three-dimensional objects do, it may be viewed as transcending spatial limitations.[516]

It thus emerges that every object in the physical universe has within it a characteristic of transcending time and space because it exists in the present and has a centerpoint. Since physical objects include these qualities, they are not totally detached from those spiritual realms which transcend time and space.

ॐ The Relationship between the Realms where Time Exists and those where It Does Not

Rabbi Nachman of Breslov points out that when people sleep and dream, their intellect is temporarily elevated, and they may visualize the passage of seventy years merely to awaken and discover that only a short time has passed.[517]

This is not just a matter of perception. Rather, time itself changes according to intellect. It is shorter when a strong intellect is involved and longer when a weak intellect is involved.

A simple example illustrates this idea. Most adults can add twenty-four and thirty-seven in their heads within a matter of seconds. By contrast, to get a very young child to do so requires preparation. First, the child needs to understand the concept of numbers and learn which symbols are used to represent

---

[516] *Biurei Aggadoth (Afikei Yam), Moed Daf Katan* 3A כמו כן הוא במקום שהמקום גם כן מתחלק לשניים והיינו שבכל גשם שהוא תחת המקום יש בו ג׳ קוטרים (*ממדים*) שהם האורך והרוחב והגובה, ובכל א׳ יש ב׳ קצוות שהאורך מתחלק לשניים — למזרח ומערב, והרוחב מתחלק לב׳ — צפון ודרום, והגובה מתחלק למעלה ומטה. נמצא שכל א׳ מורכב מב׳ דברים, מה שאין כן האמצע אינו מתחלק לא למזרח ומערב ולא לדרום וצפון ולא למעלה ומטה כי הוא נקודה המרכזית באמצע ממש.

[517] *Likutei Moharan, Mahadura Bathra* 61 כָּל מַה שֶׁהַשֵּׂכֶל גָּדוֹל בְּיוֹתֵר, הַזְּמַן נִקְטָן וְנִתְבַּטֵּל בְּיוֹתֵר, כִּי בַּחֲלוֹם, שֶׁאָז הַשֵּׂכֶל נִסְתַּלֵּק וְאֵין לוֹ רַק פֹּח הַמְדַמֶּה, אֲזַי בְּרֶבַע שָׁעָה יְכוֹלִים לַעֲבֹר כָּל הַשִּׁבְעִים שָׁנָה.

each one. The child then needs to learn how to do addition. This takes some time, especially with numbers above ten, because the child needs to learn about tens units and how to carry over to the tens column. In short, what an adult can accomplish in several seconds might require weeks or even months for a very young child.

The supernal worlds are configured in a way which matches human traits. The first three spheres in each world are called Wisdom (חָכְמָה), Understanding (בִּינָה), and Knowledge (דַּעַת). Just as human intellect involves a process through which people identify facts, analyze them, and reach a conclusion, these upper spheres process *Hashem's* Divine light so that it can be transmitted to the lower spiritual realms.

The three spheres of Wisdom (חָכְמָה), Understanding (בִּינָה), and Knowledge (דַּעַת) of even the lowest spiritual world comprise an intellect far greater than any human intellect. Just as an adult can process a simple mathematical problem much faster than a young child can, the processing speed of even the lowest spiritual world is much faster than that of any human being. Accordingly, what people view as seventy years is a matter of minutes in the lowest spiritual world. Likewise, what equates to seventy years in the lowest spiritual realm is a far shorter time in the spiritual realm immediately above it. The same is true when comparing that spiritual realm to the one immediately above it, and this pattern continues until the very highest spiritual worlds where time disappears.[518]

---

[518] *Likutei Moharan, Mahadura Bathra 62* וּבֶאֱמֶת בְּהַשֵּׂכֶל הַגָּבוֹהַ לְמַעְלָה מִשֵּׂכְלֵנוּ גַּם מַה שֶּׁנֶּחֱשָׁב אֶצְלֵנוּ לְשִׁבְעִים שָׁנָה מַמָּשׁ הוּא גַם כֵּן רַק רֶבַע שָׁעָה אוֹ פָּחוֹת... וְכֵן לְמַעְלָה מַעְלָה שֶׁבַּשֵּׂכֶל שֶׁהוּא גָּבוֹהַ עוֹד יוֹתֵר לְמַעְלָה, גַּם אוֹתוֹ הַזְּמַן שֶׁבַּשֵּׂכֶל שֶׁבַּגָּבוֹהַ מִשֵּׂכְלֵנוּ אֵינוֹ נֶחֱשָׁב שָׁם בַּשֵּׂכֶל הַגָּבוֹהַ עוֹד יוֹתֵר, רַק לְזְמַן מְעַט וּפָחוּת מְאֹד. וְכֵן לְמַעְלָה מַעְלָה עַד אֲשֶׁר יֵשׁ שֵׂכֶל גָּבוֹהַ כָּל כָּךְ שֶׁשָּׁם כָּל הַזְּמַן כֻּלּוֹ אֵינוֹ נֶחֱשָׁב כְּלָל, כִּי מֵחֲמַת גֹּדֶל הַשֵּׂכֶל מְאֹד כָּל הַזְּמַן אַיִן וָאֶפֶס לְגַמְרֵי...עַד שֶׁהַזְּמַן נִתְבַּטֵּל לְגַמְרֵי.

The highest spiritual realms in which time no longer exists correspond to faith (אֱמוּנָה) because faith involves recognizing that something is true without engaging in any intellectual process. Wisdom (חָכְמָה), Understanding (בִּינָה), and Knowledge (דַּעַת) merge at that level and time ceases to exist.

୧୦୫୦ How the Spies Altered Time

Ten of the spies who scouted out the Land of Israel discouraged the Jews from entering it on the grounds that they could never defeat the powerful Canaanites.[519] The remaining two, Caleb and Joshua, tried to counteract the report of the others, saying, "If *Hashem* is pleased with us, He will bring us to this land and give it to us."[520]

When the rest of the Jewish men[521] accepted the view that conquering the Land was impossible, *Hashem* sought to destroy the nation, but *Moshe Rabbeinu* intervened on their behalf, "And *Hashem* said, 'I forgive [them] because of your words.'"[522] Nevertheless, *Hashem* required the Jews to wander through the Sinai Desert for forty years corresponding to the forty days the spies had explored the Land.[523]

If *Hashem* forgave Israel, then why did they need to wander through the Sinai Desert for forty years?

When *Hashem* commanded the Jews to enter the Land of Israel and drive out the Canaanites, they should have had faith

---

[519] Numbers 13:31 וְהָאֲנָשִׁים אֲשֶׁר עָלוּ עִמּוֹ אָמְרוּ לֹא נוּכַל לַעֲלוֹת אֶל הָעָם כִּי חָזָק הוּא מִמֶּנּוּ

[520] Numbers 14:8 אִם חָפֵץ בָּנוּ ה' וְהֵבִיא אֹתָנוּ אֶל הָאָרֶץ הַזֹּאת וּנְתָנָהּ לָנוּ אֶרֶץ אֲשֶׁר הִוא זָבַת חָלָב וּדְבָשׁ

[521] The women did not adopt this view (*Tanchuma, Parashath Pinchas* 7 והנשים לא נשתתפו במעשה העגל וכן במרגלים).

[522] Numbers 14:20 וַיֹּאמֶר ה' סָלַחְתִּי כִּדְבָרֶךָ according to *Rashi*.

[523] Numbers 14:34 בְּמִסְפַּר הַיָּמִים אֲשֶׁר תַּרְתֶּם אֶת הָאָרֶץ אַרְבָּעִים יוֹם יוֹם לַשָּׁנָה יוֹם לַשָּׁנָה תִּשְׂאוּ אֶת עֲוֹנֹתֵיכֶם אַרְבָּעִים שָׁנָה וִידַעְתֶּם אֶת תְּנוּאָתִי.

that they would succeed. There was no need for any intellectual process — no need to analyze how they would do so. Had the Jews had faith in *Hashem* and obeyed Him without sending out spies, they would have entered the Land immediately.[524]

Instead, the Jewish men insisted on conducting a forty-day investigation into the matter.[525] They thereby lowered their spiritual stature. Just as time is shorter in each higher spiritual realm than it is in the one below it, Israel's lower spiritual level changed the amount of time needed to prepare for the conquest of the Land from zero to forty years.

---

[524] *Klee Yakar* on Deuteronomy 1:37 ואילו לא חטאו המרגלים היו נכנסים לארץ מיד
[525] *Rashi* on Numbers 26:64 states that the Jewish women did not participate in this sin because had faith in *Hashem's* promise that the nation would succeed in conquering the Land (אבל על הנשים לא נגזרה גזרת המרגלים לפי שהן היו מחבבות את הארץ).

The Mouth of the Earth: The Equilibrium among the Spiritual, Physical, and Impure Realms

৪০ How the Earth Swallowed Korah

One of the ten things *Hashem* created at twilight on the first *Shabbath* eve was the mouth of the Earth — the opening which swallowed Korah and his followers.[526]

This seems to contradict a statement *Moshe Rabbeinu* made which implies that the opening was created in his time: "If *Hashem* produces a new creation, and the Earth opens its mouth and swallows them and all that is theirs, and they descend alive into hell, [then] you will know that these men quarreled with *Hashem*."[527]

---

[526] *Pirkei Avoth* 5:6 ... עֲשָׂרָה דְבָרִים נִבְרְאוּ בְעֶרֶב שַׁבָּת בֵּין הַשְּׁמָשׁוֹת, וְאֵלּוּ הֵן: פִּי הָאָרֶץ
[527] Numbers 16:30 וְאִם בְּרִיאָה יִבְרָא ה' וּפָצְתָה הָאֲדָמָה אֶת פִּיהָ וּבָלְעָה אֹתָם וְאֶת כָּל אֲשֶׁר לָהֶם וְיָרְדוּ חַיִּים שְׁאֹלָה וִידַעְתֶּם כִּי נִאֲצוּ הָאֲנָשִׁים הָאֵלֶּה אֶת ה'.

The *Gemara* resolves this apparent contradiction by explaining that an opening between the physical world and *Gehinnom* existed from the time of Creation and that *Hashem* created nothing new in *Moshe Rabbeinu's* time. Instead, *Hashem* moved the entrance of *Gehinnom* to Korah and his followers, and they fell in.[528]

A *Midrash* elaborates on what is meant by bringing the entrance of *Gehinnom* to the rebels:

> Rabbi Yehudah said: At that time, many mouths opened in the Earth [to swallow the rebels wherever they were], as it says, "in the midst of all Israel," [implying that the Earth opened wherever they were].
>
> Rabbi Nechemiah said: But observe how it is written, "The Earth opened its mouth" [in the singular, implying that there was but one mouth].
>
> [Rabbi Yehudah] argued: And how do you explain "in the midst of all Israel?"
>
> [Rabbi Nechemiah] responded: The ground became funnel-like so that wherever one of them was, he rolled down and came [to the mouth]. You can thus properly explain both "in the midst of Israel" and "the Earth opened its mouth."[529]

---

[528] B.T. *Sanhedrin* 110A-B "דָּרַשׁ רַבָּא: מַאי דִּכְתִיב, "וְאִם בְּרִיאָה יִבְרָא ה' וּפָצְתָה הָאֲדָמָה אֶת פִּיהָ (במדבר ט"ז, ל')? אָמַר מֹשֶׁה לִפְנֵי הַקָּדוֹשׁ בָּרוּךְ הוּא: "אִם בְּרִיאָה גֵּיהִנָּם מוּטָב, וְאִם לָאו, יִבְרָא ה'". לְמַאי? אִילֵימָא לְמִיבְרֵי מַמָּשׁ, וְהָא, "וְאֵין כָּל חָדָשׁ תַּחַת הַשָּׁמֶשׁ" (קהלת א', ט'), אֶלָּא לְקָרוֹבֵי פִּתְחָא.

[529] *Bamidbar Rabbah* 18:13 "אמר רבי יהודה: באותה שעה נפתחו לארץ פיפיות הרבה שנאמר, "אֲשֶׁר פָּצְתָה הָאָרֶץ אֶת פִּיהָ וַתִּבְלָעֵם וְאֶת בָּתֵּיהֶם וְאֵת אָהֳלֵיהֶם וְאֵת כָּל הַיְקוּם אֲשֶׁר בְּרַגְלֵיהֶם) בְּקֶרֶב כָּל יִשְׂרָאֵל" (דברים י"א, ו'). אמר רבי נחמיה: והרי כתיב, "וַתִּפְתַּח הָאָרֶץ אֶת פִּיהָ" (במדבר ט"ז, ל"ב). אמר לו: והיאך את מקיים, "בְּקֶרֶב כָּל יִשְׂרָאֵל"? אלא שנעשית הארץ כמשפך וכל היכן שהיה אחד מהם היה מתגלגל ויורד ובא עמו. נמצאת מקיים, "בְּקֶרֶב כָּל יִשְׂרָאֵל", ומקיים, "וַתִּפְתַּח הָאָרֶץ אֶת פִּיהָ".

The *Netziv* comments that Korah and his co-conspirators were drawn to the opening of *Gehinnom* by an attractive force which resembled gravity.[530]

The *Malbim* states that gravity exists throughout the universe and affects all physical objects.[531] Everything in the physical realm has a parallel in the spiritual realm, so there is a kind of gravity, or attractive force, which exists in the spiritual realm.

৵৵৵ How Spiritual Gravity Functions

The *Tanach* states that *Hashem* "suspends the Earth in a void (בְּלִימָה)."[532] In addition to its plain meaning that the Earth is situated in the vacuum of space, the verse implies that the physical realm is suspended between the realm of holiness and the realm of impurity.

The term "void" (בְּלִימָה) in the above verse refers to *Tohu* (תּוֹהוּ) — the primordial substance which *Hashem* created ex nihilo (יֵשׁ מֵאַיִן) and from which He then fashioned the rest of Creation.[533] It is a pristine simple substance in the realm of holiness, a

---

[530] *Hemek Davar* on Numbers 16:32 אותו הפה החל לבלוע בכוח המשיכה אחד אחד מי שהיה ראוי להיבלע.

[531] *Malbim* on Psalms 8:2 ועתה הנה סיבוב הכוכבים כולמו בנוי על חוק אחד טבעי – הוא כוח המשיכה המשותף לכל החומריים. וחוק הזה בעצמו אשר בו ועל ידו תמשוך הארץ אליה את הגופים הקטנים אשר סביבה, ואשר על ידו יפול האבן הנזרק למעלה לארץ, הוא עצמו ימשוך את הגופים הגדולים זה לזה, ועל פי חוקי התנועה והמאכאניק המשותפים לכל הגשמים באו החוקרים האחרונים כל מלאכת השמים וסיבוב הכוכבים כנודע בספריהם, עד שנאמר כי חכמה אחת והמצאה אחת אשר שם היוצר בטבע החומריים כולנה.

[532] Job 26:7 נֹטֶה צָפוֹן עַל תֹּהוּ תֹּלֶה אֶרֶץ עַל בְּלִימָה

[533] *Perush Haram Botril Lesefer Yetzirah* 1 והחומר הזה שקראוהו היוונים 'היולי' נקרא בלשון הקודש 'תוהו' והמילה נגזרת מלשון רז"ל 'תוהה על הָרִאשׁוֹנוֹת' מפני שאם בא אדם לגזור לו שם תוהה נמלך לקראו בשם אחר כי לא לבש צורה שייתפס בו השם כלל.

Shelah Hakadosh, Parashath Breishith, בָּרָא הַקָּדוֹשׁ בָּרוּךְ הוּא מֵאֲפִיסָה מֻחְלֶטֶת מַחְלֶטֶת 'נְקֻדָּה', וְנִקְרֵאת בִּלְשׁוֹן הַקֹּדֶשׁ 'תֹּהוּ', וּבִלְשׁוֹן חֲכָמִים 'אֶבֶן שְׁתִיָּה', וּבִלְשׁוֹן יְוָנִי 'היוּלִי'.

The verse itself implies this because it begins, "He lays out the Earth on *Tohu*." (See commentary of *Metzudoth David* on Job 26:7). *Perush Haram Botril Lesefer Yetzirah* 1 בלימה על שם הפסוק, "תֹלֶה אֶרֶץ עַל בְּלִימָה", רוצה לומר על תוהו

complex substance in the physical realm, and the refuse of these two realms makes up the impure realm.[534]

ಶಲಾಜಲಾ The Three Manifestations of Primordial Matter

Pardes Rimonim explains that the Hebrew for "void" (בְּלִימָה) has three meanings, all of which express the same idea. It means "without substance," "to bridle," as in bridling one's mouth, and "to stop up." All three suggest that the ten supernal spheres, which consist of highly concentrated *Tohu* (תּוֹהוּ), are incomprehensible to human beings who must bridle and stop up their mouths from attempting to describe them.

Although the spiritual worlds are called Kindness (חֶסֶד), Judgment (גְּבוּרָה), and so on, these descriptions are only based on human perception of them. In reality, the supernal spheres are unbounded and not limited to any description. This is why the spheres can serve as the medium through which the Infinite One and His finite Creation are connected.[535]

As humans see things, the realm of holiness — the realm of the supernal spheres — resembles the Infinite One more closely than the physical realm because it is less confined than

---

[534] *Kehillath Yaakov, Erech Daleth.* ד' קליפות שורשן תוהו, בהו, חשך, רוח המוזכר בפרשת בראשית. תוהו הוא הפסולת שיצא מטיפת אמא אחר הבירור הטוב.

ומן האפשר הגמור עשה תוהו, שהוא החומר הראשון הנקרא היולי. וזה התוהו *Get Hashemoth* הוא ראשית שני החומרים, השמים שהוא פשוט, וחומר הארץ שהוא מורכב.

[535] *Pardes Rimonim* 3:4 וזה פירושה "עֶשֶׂר סְפִירוֹת בְּלִי מָה" (ספר יצירה א', ב') פירוש המילה הזאת נחלקת לשתים שרוצה לומר "בלי מה" ופירוש "מה" היינו "מהות". והכוונה שעשר ספירות הם בלי מהות לפי שאין מהותם מושג אלינו. ואף אם נאמר זו דין וזו רחמים וכיוצא בזה, הכל מושג אלינו מתוך פעולתם אבל מתוך עצמותם הם בלימה. עוד הוא מלשון "בלום" כדכתיב, "עֶדְיוֹ לִבְלוֹם" (תהלים ל"ב, ט'), שראוי לאדם לבלום פיו ואל ירבה דבריו במהותם ובעניינם מפני קוצר המשיג ועומק המושג. או יהיה מלשון הסתר והעלם כמו "עֶדְיוֹ לִבְלוֹם" והיינו כסוי העדי והסתרו. והנה הספירות נקראו "בלימה", רוצה לומר ספירות ההעלם שהן נעלמות. וג' פירושים אלה עולים אל מקום אחד שהכוונה להורות על העלמם וקוצר השגה ושאין ראוי להאריך בהן הדבור מפני העלמן. ואמר מידתן עשר ומפני שמזה יומשך היות להן גבול חס ושלום, לזה אמר שאין להם סוף. ועם היות שהוא דבר והפכו שאנו נותנים בו גבול ואחר כך נאמר שאין להם גבול, כבר פירשתי בפרקים הקודמים כי בערך שיש להן בחינתם אל המאציל אין להם גבול, אבל בערך בחינתם ופעולתם הנמשכות אלינו יש להם גבול אל פעולתם כפי קבלתנו שאנו בעלי גבול וזה כוח גדולתו של יוצרינו מבלי גבול יגבילהו ויצמצמהו לתועלת התחתונים בעלי גבול ותכלית.

the physical realm. The realm of impurity least resembles the Infinite One because it is even more restricted and limited than the physical realm.[536] The realm of holiness is therefore called "close" to *Hashem* whereas the realm of impurity is called "distant" from Him.

Ironically, excessive restriction creates a superficial appearance of the opposite. If a person tries to pour two liters of water into a one-liter bottle, the excess water will overflow onto the outside the bottle. In a similar way, the excessive restriction of the realm of impurity makes it impossible for it to fully contain *Hashem's* Divine light. The Divine light therefore overflows and surrounds the impure worlds. The impure worlds are identified with falsehood and deception because Divine light, with its quality of limitlessness, shines outside them, but their insides are impure, constricted, and evil.[537]

As Rabbi Chaim Vital explains, "layers of primordial matter (תּוֹהוּ) lie above *Gehinnom*."[538] It is surrounded by an overflow of this substance, also called "void" (בְּלִימָה), which it cannot properly assimilate or contain.

The Prophet Isaiah stated that, "[*Hashem*] did not create [the Earth] for the sake of formlessness [i.e., primordial matter] (תּוֹהוּ), but for habitation He created it."[539] *Hashem* wants people to inhabit the world and serve Him. When people fail to do so,

---

[536] *Kelach Pithchei Chochmah* 30 מה שאין כן הסטרא אחרא, שכוחה מוגבל באמת, שאין לה אלא מה שיש בה, ואי אפשר לה לצאת מגבולה כרצונה כלל.

Likutei Amarim Tanya, Iggereth Hakodesh 26 (*הדומה ל'אסיר'*) וזהו לשון 'אסור' שהקליפה שורה עליו ואינו יכול לעלות למעלה כדבר המותר.

[537] *Five Hundred Fifteen Tefilloth, Tefillah* 370 שהרי מדריגות הטומאה, אף על גב שאור מקיף עליהם שהוא לבונה זכה, הרי בקרבו ישים ארבו, ושם עומד כל טומאה שלא נראה לחוץ כדי לרמות בני אדם.

[538] *Perush Haramaz Al Zohar Shemoth* 792 citing Rabbi Chaim Vital שגם על גיהנם יש רקיעי (*דובדי*) תוהו.

[539] Isaiah 45:18 לֹא תֹהוּ בְרָאָהּ לָשֶׁבֶת יְצָרָהּ

they are drawn into *Gehinnom*, which lies in the realm of impurity surrounded by raw primordial matter (תּוֹהוּ).

❧❧❧ How the Realms of Holiness, Physicality, and Impurity Remain in Equilibrium

For purposes of illustration, let the reader consider three objects with equal magnetic or gravitational fields resting at equal distances from one another. If these objects exert equal attractive forces on one another, they will remain perfectly balanced at the same distance from one another.[540]

This is how the realm of holiness, the physical realm, and the realm of impurity interact with one another, as illustrated below.[541]

---

[540] The *Gemara* records a similar case. King Jeroboam placed magnets inside a golden calf in such a way that it floated in midair, giving people the impression that it possessed supernatural power. The king thereby duped onlookers into practicing idolatry (B.T. *Sotah* 47A אִיכָּא דְּאָמְרֵי: אֶבֶן שׁוֹאֶבֶת תָּלָה לָהּ לְחַטַּאת יָרָבְעָם וְהֶעֱמִידוֹ בֵּין שָׁמַיִם לָאָרֶץ).

[541] *Perush Haramaz Al Hazohar, Shemoth* 792 כללו של דבר ששלוש הנקודות הנזכרות כאן הן העולם הזה וגיהנם וגן עדן התחתונים באופן זה: גיהנם לצד צפון של העולם הזה ואחר כך העולם הזה שהוא באמצע ואחר כך גן עדן. אבל צריך שתדע שאל כללות כל השלש קורא בשם עולם שהוא כולל כל מה שעשה השם יתברך למטה...והן ממש בניקוד שלש נקודות הנקראים קבוץ.

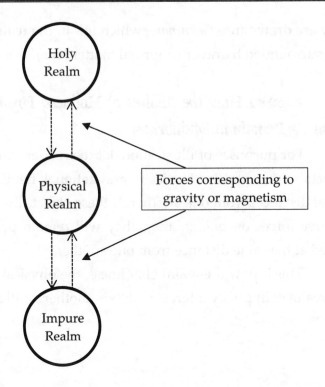

Parenthetically, the comparisons the sages make between physical phenomena and spiritual ones are metaphorical. The spiritual realms do not have any spatial relationships, and any explanations or illustrations showing such relationships are merely allegorical.

ಐಐಐಐ Korah and His Followers Upset the Equilibrium of the Three Realms

Ordinarily, a precise balance exists among the three realms. When people sin, however, they move themselves closer to the realm of impurity. If enough sins accumulate, or if a sin is severe enough, they come so close to the realm of impurity that they upset the equilibrium, and the attraction between themselves and the impure realm causes them to be drawn into

Gehinnom. People do not usually detect this happening. The novelty, or "creation," that took place with Korah was that this process was openly revealed. Everyone could see Korah and his followers being drawn into *Gehinnom*.

ೞೞೞೞ Why Korah's Rebellion Caused this Novel Revelation

The term for "void" (בְּלִימָה) in the verse, "[*Hashem*] suspends the Earth in a void"[542] also means "stopped up." The sages teach that, "The world does not remain in existence except for the sake of one who stops up (בּוֹלֵם) his mouth during a quarrel."[543]

Moshe Rabbeinu and Aaron repeatedly humbled themselves during quarrels. For example, when the Jews complained that they lacked food during their sojourn in the Sinai Desert, *Moshe Rabbeinu* answered, "What are we that you complain against us?"[544]

When people live in unity and harmony, they imitate the unity and harmony which exist in the supernal worlds. This causes the physical realm to maintain enough similarity to the realm of holiness to keep it from being drawn towards the realm of impurity and being destroyed.

Moshe Rabbeinu attempted to placate Korah and his followers, as the *Torah* states, "Moses arose and went to Dathan and Abiram, [Korah's main supporters], and the elders of Israel

---

[542] Job 26:7 נֹטֶה צָפוֹן עַל תֹּהוּ תֹּלֶה אֶרֶץ עַל בְּלִימָה

[543] B.T. *Chullin* 89A וְאָמַר רָבָא וְאִיתֵימָא רַבִּי יוֹחָנָן: אֵין הָעוֹלָם מִתְקַיֵּים אֶלָּא בִּשְׁבִיל מֹשֶׁה וְאַהֲרֹן. כְּתִיב הָכָא, "וְנַחְנוּ מָה" (שמות ט"ז, ז, ח'), וּכְתִיב הָתָם, "תֹּלֶה אֶרֶץ עַל בְּלִימָה" (איוב כ"ו, ז). אָמַר רַבִּי אִילְעָא: אֵין הָעוֹלָם מִתְקַיֵּם אֶלָּא בִּשְׁבִיל מִי שֶׁבּוֹלֵם אֶת עַצְמוֹ בִּשְׁעַת מְרִיבָה שֶׁנֶּאֱמַר, "תֹּלֶה אֶרֶץ עַל בְּלִימָה" (איוב כ"ו, ז).

[544] Exodus 16:7 וּבֹקֶר וּרְאִיתֶם אֶת כְּבוֹד ה' בְּשָׁמְעוֹ אֶת תְּלֻנֹּתֵיכֶם עַל ה' וְנַחְנוּ מָה כִּי תַלִּונוּ [תַלִּינוּ קרי] עָלֵינוּ

followed after him."[545] By restraining themselves in the face of the rebellion and trying to reconcile with the rebels, *Moshe Rabbeinu* and Aaron maintained the unity of the Jewish people that upholds the equilibrium among the realms of holiness, physicality, and impurity. This prevented the people as a whole from falling into *Gehinnom.*

By contrast, Korah and his supporters rejected the attempts of *Moshe Rabbeinu* and Aaron to reconcile and persisted in fomenting discord.[546] Their actions destroyed the equilibrium among the three realms. They distanced themselves so much from the realm of holiness that they were drawn into *Gehinnom.*

ॐ Balaam Attempted to Cause the Earth to Swallow Israel

Later, when the Jews were preparing to enter the Land of Israel, Balaam tried to create an opening between the physical realm and the impure realm with the hope of causing the nation to fall through it.

How did Balaam seek to do this?

The numeric value of "intent" (כַּוָונָה) is the same as "void" (בְּלִימָה) — primordial matter. When people speak with strong enough intent (כַּוָונָה), their speech fashions the primordial matter (בְּלִימָה) into a creation. Thus, when people pray with intent (כַּוָונָה), their prayers produce spiritual forces from raw primordial matter (בְּלִימָה).[547] Similarly, when *Tzaddikim* give blessings, their good

---

[545] Numbers 16:25 וַיָּקָם מֹשֶׁה וַיֵּלֶךְ אֶל דָּתָן וַאֲבִירָם וַיֵּלְכוּ אַחֲרָיו זִקְנֵי יִשְׂרָאֵל as explained in B.T. *Sanhedrin* 110A אָמַר רֵישׁ לָקִישׁ: מִכָּאן שֶׁאֵין מַחֲזִיקִין בְּמַחֲלֹקֶת

[546] Numbers 16:12-13 (יב) וַיִּשְׁלַח מֹשֶׁה לִקְרֹא לְדָתָן וְלַאֲבִירָם בְּנֵי אֱלִיאָב, וַיֹּאמְרוּ, לֹא נַעֲלֶה. (יג) הַמְעַט כִּי הֶעֱלִיתָנוּ מֵאֶרֶץ זָבַת חָלָב וּדְבַשׁ לַהֲמִיתֵנוּ בַּמִּדְבָּר כִּי תִשְׂתָּרֵר עָלֵינוּ גַּם הִשְׂתָּרֵר.

[547] *Ma'or Vashamesh, Parashath Yithro* וזהו ידוע שהמלאך שנברא מדברי אדם הוא כפי שכלו שאדם מניח בזה הדיבור כך גדול כוח המלאך.

intent (כַּוָּנָה) forms primordial matter (בְּלִימָה) into spiritual forces which benefit the recipients of their blessings.

৵৵৵ The Power of a Curse

The Ten Commandments include admonitions against idolatry, adultery, and murder — the three prohibitions Jews must not violate even when failing to do so will result in death.[548] Nevertheless, there is only one commandment concerning which the sages state that the Earth trembled when it was given — the prohibition against uttering a false or vain oath using *Hashem's* Name.[549]

Why did the Earth shake only then?

An oath administered in a Jewish court is an extremely solemn event. One who makes such an oath must do so using *Hashem's* Name while holding a *Torah* scroll.[550] In addition, the *Halachah* requires the judges to discourage people from making oaths. They must warn litigants in very graphic terms of the dire consequences of uttering a false or pointless oath.[551] If a litigant nevertheless insists on making an oath, those present recite the language *Moshe Rabbeinu* used just before the Earth swallowed Korah and his followers — "Depart from around the tents of

---

[548] B.T. *Sanhedrin* 74A אָמַר רַבִּי יוֹחָנָן מִשּׁוּם רַבִּי שִׁמְעוֹן בֶּן יְהוֹצָדָק: נִימְנוּ וְנָמְרוּ בַּעֲלִיַּת בֵּית נִתְזָה בְּלוּד: כָּל עֲבֵירוֹת שֶׁבַּתּוֹרָה אִם אוֹמְרִין לְאָדָם, "עֲבֹר וְאַל תֵּיהָרֵג", יַעֲבֹר וְאַל יֵיהָרֵג, חוּץ מֵעֲבוֹדַת זָרָה וְגִילּוּי עֲרָיוֹת וּשְׁפִיכוּת דָּמִים.

[549] B.T. *Shavuoth* 39A שֶׁכָּל הָעוֹלָם כֻּלּוֹ נִזְדַּעֲזַע בְּשָׁעָה שֶׁאָמַר הַקָּדוֹשׁ בָּרוּךְ הוּא בְּסִינַי, "לֹא תִשָּׂא אֶת שֵׁם ה' אֱ-לֹהֶיךָ לַשָּׁוְא" (שמות כ', ז).

[550] *Shulchan Aruch, Choshen Mishpat* 87:17 הנשבע אוחז ספר תורה בזרועו ועומד ונשבע בשם או בכינוי.

[551] *Shulchan Aruch, Choshen Mishpat* 87:20 משביעין אותו בכל לשון שהוא מבין. ויאיימו עליו...קודם שישביעוהו ואומרים לו: הוי יודע שכל העולם נזדעזע בשעה שאמר הקב"ה "לא תשא אֶת שֵׁם ה' אֱ-לֹהֶיךָ לַשָּׁוְא כִּי לֹא יְנַקֶּה ה' אֶת אֲשֶׁר יִשָּׂא אֶת שְׁמוֹ לַשָּׁוְא) (שמות כ', ז)...

these wicked men, and do not touch anything that is theirs lest you be killed through their sin."[552]

Under such conditions, one who takes an oath obviously has his mind focused on what he is saying. This intent (כַּוָּנָה) gives the oath the power to fashion spiritual forces from primordial matter (בְּלִימָה). Those who utter a vain or false oath produce impure spiritual forces that cause an extreme disturbance in the equilibrium among the three realms, and the physical realm is drawn towards the realm of impurity. Such people therefore risk a fate similar to that of Korah and his supporters. The world shook when *Hashem* said, "Do not take the Name of *Hashem*, your God, in vain,"[553] foreshadowing the instability among the three realms that occurs when a person utters a false or useless oath.

Moshe Rabbeinu knew how to use speech to cause primordial matter to affect the physical realm in a destructive way. As the sages teach, he killed an Egyptian who was attacking a Jew by pronouncing one of *Hashem's* Names.[554] However, *Moshe Rabbeinu* only used this power as a last resort and only when he was absolutely certain that a wrongdoer deserved it. When the *Torah* states that *Moshe Rabbeinu* "looked this way and that, and saw that no man was present,"[555] it means that he first checked to see whether anything worthwhile might emerge from that Egyptian or any of his descendants. He only proceeded after he determined that it would not.[556]

---

[552] *Shulchan Aruch, Choshen Mishpat* 87:20 אם אמר: "הריני נשבע", וחבירו תובע, העומדים שם אומרים זה לזה, "סורו נָא מֵעַל אָהֳלֵי הָאֲנָשִׁים הָרְשָׁעִים הָאֵלֶּה" (במדבר ט״ז, כ״ו).

[553] B.T. *Shavuoth* 39A שֶׁכָּל הָעוֹלָם כֻּלּוֹ נִזְדַּעֲזַע בְּשָׁעָה שֶׁאָמַר הַקָּדוֹשׁ בָּרוּךְ הוּא בְּסִינַי, "לֹא תִשָּׂא אֶת שֵׁם ה' אֱ-לֹהֶיךָ לַשָּׁוְא" (שמות כ', ז).

[554] *Shemoth Rabbah* 1:29 "וַיַּךְ אֶת הַמִּצְרִי" (שמות ב', י״ב). במה הרגו? ...רבנן אמרי: הזכיר עליו את השם והרגו שנאמר, "הַלְהָרְגֵנִי אַתָּה אֹמֵר (כַּאֲשֶׁר הָרַגְתָּ אֶת הַמִּצְרִי)" (שמות י״ב, י״ד).

[555] Exodus 2:12 וַיִּפֶן כֹּה וָכֹה וַיַּרְא כִּי אֵין אִישׁ וַיַּךְ אֶת הַמִּצְרִי וַיִּטְמְנֵהוּ בַּחוֹל

[556] *Vayikra Rabbah* 32:4 ורבנן אמרין: ראה שאין תוחלת עתידה לעמוד ממנו ולא מבניו ולא מבני בניו עד סוף כל הדורות. מיד, "וַיַּךְ אֶת הַמִּצְרִי" (שמות ב:יב).

Balaam was *Moshe Rabbeinu's* evil counterpart.[557] Through his prophetic powers he became aware of how Korah and his followers were destroyed by being sucked into the realm of impurity. He then tried to do the same thing to the Jewish nation.[558]

The *Torah* hints at this when it states concerning Korah and his followers that, "The Earth opened its mouth and swallowed them."[559] The sages employ a homiletic method called *Notarikon* (נוֹטָרִיקוֹן) whereby a group of words can be interpreted as an acrostic.[560] The phrase "swallowed them" (וַתִּבְלַע אֹתָם) may therefore be understood as hinting at Balaam, whose name (בִּלְעָם) may be read to mean "he swallowed a nation" (בָּלַע עַם).[561]

Furthermore, *Tosafoth* explains that Balaam's plan was to utter the expression "destroy them" (כַּלֵם) to exterminate the Jews during God's daily moment of rage.[562] When *Hashem* was about to punish Korah and his followers, He told *Moshe Rabbeinu* and Aaron, "Separate yourselves from this congregation, for I

---

[557] *Bamidbar Rabbah* 14:19 "וְלֹא קָם נָבִיא עוֹד בְּיִשְׂרָאֵל כְּמשֶׁה" (דברים ל"ד, י') – בישראל לא קם, אבל באומות העולם קם כדי שלא יהא פתחון פה לאומות העולם לומר: "אילו היה לנו נביא כמשה היינו עובדים להקב"ה". ואיזה נביא היה להם כמשה? זה בלעם בן בעור.

[558] According to *Ohr Hameir* on *Parashath Korach*, both Korah and Balaam derived from the impurity of Cain. הסטרא אחרא הולכת כקוף בפני אדם דקדושה, ונתפלגה גם כן מבחינת כלליות, לבחינת פרטיות. מה שהיו כלולים תחילה בקין בסוד אחדות, מתגלגלים ונתהפכים מדור לדור בפירוד הגופים מכלליות לפרטיות, ועשו ובלעם ובלק וקרח כולם המה מאותו הגלגול של קין.

[559] Numbers 16:32 וַתִּפְתַּח הָאָרֶץ אֶת פִּיהָ וַתִּבְלַע אֹתָם וְאֶת בָּתֵּיהֶם וְאֵת כָּל הָאָדָם אֲשֶׁר לְקֹרַח וְאֵת כָּל הָרְכוּשׁ.

[560] See note 510 above.

[561] The Romm Vilna edition of B.T. *Sanhedrin* 105A interprets Balaam's name as "without a nation" (בִּלְעָם – בְּלֹא עַם), but the *Aruch* has a version of the text which reads "swallowed a nation" (בִּלְעָם – בָּלַע עַם).

[562] B.T. *Berachoth* 7A רֶגַע זַעְמוֹ? וְכַמָּה זַעְמוֹ? רֶגַע (תהלים ז:יב). "וְאֵ-ל זֹעֵם בְּכָל יוֹם". *Tosafoth* on B.T. *Berachoth* 7A sub verba *"She'ilmalei"* (שאלמלי) comments ואם תאמר מה היה יכול לומר בשעת רגע? יש לומר, "כַּלֵם".

shall destroy them momentarily"[563] (וַאֲכַלֶּה אֹתָם כְּרָגַע), a phrase which uses a slightly different form of the same word.

Balaam tried to combine his evil intent (כַּוָּנָה) with primordial matter (בְּלִימָה) to fashion an opening between the physical realm and the impure realm just as happened with Korah. It was Balaam's intent that Israel be sucked through that opening into *Gehinnom*. *Hashem* frustrated Balaam's efforts, as the *Torah* states, "*Hashem*, your God, did not want to listen to Balaam, and *Hashem*, your God, converted the curse into a blessing, for *Hashem*, your God, loves you."[564] Since the actual words Balaam was forced to utter were blessings, his intent was overcome and his efforts to destroy Israel failed.

---

[563] Numbers 16:21 הִבָּדְלוּ מִתּוֹךְ הָעֵדָה הַזֹּאת וַאֲכַלֶּה אֹתָם כְּרָגַע

[564] Deuteronomy 23:6, וְלֹא אָבָה ה' אֱ-לֹהֶיךָ לִשְׁמֹעַ אֶל בִּלְעָם, וַיַּהֲפֹךְ ה' אֱ-לֹהֶיךָ לְךָ אֶת הַקְּלָלָה לִבְרָכָה, כִּי אֲהֵבְךָ ה' אֱ-לֹהֶיךָ.

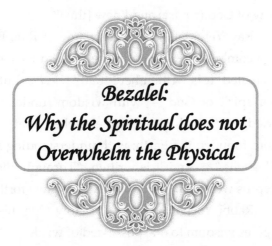

Bezalel: Why the Spiritual does not Overwhelm the Physical

❧ Bezalel's Name

Rabbi Sh'muel bar Nachmani said in the name of Rabbi Yochanan: Bezalel (בְּצַלְאֵל) was so called on account of his wisdom. When the Holy One, Blessed be He, said to Moshe, "Go tell Bezalel, 'Make for Me a Tabernacle, ark, and utensils,'" Moshe altered the sequence and said, "Make an ark, utensils, and a Tabernacle."

Bezalel told him, "*Moshe Rabbeinu*, the custom of the world is for a person to build a house and afterwards bring inside utensils, yet you tell me, 'Make an ark, utensils, and a Tabernacle.' Inside what will I put the utensils that I make?

Perhaps the Holy One, Blessed be He, told you, 'Make a Tabernacle, ark, and utensils.'"

Moshe Rabbeinu answered, "Perhaps you were in the shadow of God (בְּצֵל אֵ-ל) and knew [this]!"

Rav Yehudah said in the name of Rav: Bezalel knew how to combine the letters through which Heaven and Earth were created. It is written here that, "[*Hashem*] filled [Bezalel] with a spirit of God — with wisdom, understanding, and knowledge."[565] And it is written elsewhere that, "*Hashem* with wisdom founded the Earth; with understanding He prepared the Heavens."[566] And it is written, "Through His knowledge the depths were split, [and the Heavens gave forth dew]."[567]

Rabbi Yochanan said: The Holy One, Blessed be He, only gives wisdom to one possessed of wisdom.[568]

This passage seems strange. *Hashem* showed *Moshe Rabbeinu* how the Tabernacle and its utensils were to be fashioned and how they were to look when completed.[569] How could he have erred about the order in which they should be made? In addition, since *Moshe Rabbeinu* had seen models of these items, why he did not make them himself? Why was it necessary to delegate the work to Bezalel?

To make matters even more puzzling, the *Torah* itself records both sequences. It starts off by stating, "Like all that I show you — the design of the Tabernacle and the design of its utensils

---

[565] Exodus 35:31 וַיְמַלֵּא אֹתוֹ רוּחַ אֱ-לֹהִים בְּחָכְמָה בִּתְבוּנָה וּבְדַעַת וּבְכָל מְלָאכָה

[566] Proverbs 3:19 ה' בְּחָכְמָה יָסַד אֶרֶץ כּוֹנֵן שָׁמַיִם בִּתְבוּנָה

[567] Proverbs 3:20 בְּדַעְתּוֹ תְּהוֹמוֹת נִבְקָעוּ וּשְׁחָקִים יִרְעֲפוּ טָל

[568] B.T. *Berachoth* 55A. See Appendix G for the full Hebrew text.

[569] Exodus 25:9 כְּכֹל אֲשֶׁר אֲנִי מַרְאֶה אוֹתְךָ אֵת תַּבְנִית הַמִּשְׁכָּן וְאֵת תַּבְנִית כָּל כֵּלָיו וְכֵן תַּעֲשׂוּ

Bamidbar Rabbah 12:8, רבי יהושע דסכנין בשם רבי לוי אמר: בשעה שאמר הקב"ה למשה
"עשו לי משכן", היה לו להעמיד ארבע קונטיסים ולמתוח את המשכן עליהם, אלא מלמד שהראה הקב"ה למשה
למעלן אש אדומה, אש ירוקה, אש שחורה, אש לבנה. אמר לו: "כתבנית אשר אתה מראה בהר".

— so shall you do,"[570] implying that the correct order is to start with the Tabernacle. In the verses which follow, however, the *Torah* first describes how to make the Ark and other utensils and then how to make the Tabernacle. Why, then, did *Moshe Rabbeinu* agree that the order suggested by Bezalel was the correct one?

Gaon Yaakov explains that *Moshe Rabbeinu* was more attuned to spirituality than Bezalel was. He perceived primarily the spirituality of the ark and the other utensils and secondarily their physical aspects. That which is spiritual has no boundaries and therefore no need to be enclosed inside anything. Accordingly, *Moshe Rabbeinu* was not bothered by Bezalel's question, "Inside what will I put the utensils that I make?"

Bezalel, on the other hand, was assigned the task of fashioning the physical Tabernacle and its contents. He focused primarily on their material qualities and only secondarily on their spiritual qualities. *Moshe Rabbeinu* never said that he himself was wrong. He simply agreed that from Bezalel's perspective the question of how to contain the utensils was valid.[571]

ഽ൚ The Power to Create and Destroy Worlds Lies Hidden in the Torah

Toldoth Yaakov Yosef offers a different explanation. *Hashem* used the *Torah* as the blueprint for creating the world,[572] but

---

[570] Exodus 25:9 כְּכֹל אֲשֶׁר אֲנִי מַרְאֶה אוֹתְךָ אֵת תַּבְנִית הַמִּשְׁכָּן וְאֵת תַּבְנִית כָּל כֵּלָיו וְכֵן תַּעֲשׂוּ

[571] *Gaon Yaakov* cited in *Chiddushei Geonim* on B.T. *Berachoth* 55A, citing למראה עין משה היו הכלים רוחניים (ת)אין מקום לשאלת בצלאל, "כלים כו' להיכן אכניסם?" כי הדבר הרוחני אין צריך למקום להגבילו כי אינו בעל הקצוות כדרך המגושם. אבל בצלאל שנבחר להיות פועל אומן על הכלים במלאכת חורש וחושב והוא בגשמיות ורוחניות והוא בהרגשה יותר להמגושם מתחילה ואחר כך להרוחניות אשר בקרבו בהיות הוא בעולם המגושם שאל כהוגן... והשיב לו משה, "בצל א-ל היית", רוצה לומר יפה דיברת כי לא היית במדור שלי אשר הוא מקום רוחני והרגשתי הרוחניות מתחילה, אבל אתה בעולם הגשמי שהוא צל של העולם העליון.

[572] *Zohar* I:134B and II:161A דְּכַד בָּרָא קוּדְשָׁא בְּרִיךְ הוּא עָלְמָא, אִסְתַּכַּל בָּהּ בְּאוֹרַיְיתָא וּבָרָא עָלְמָא

revealed its text to us out of chronological order.[573] If the text were revealed in the correct order, those who study it would have the potentially dangerous ability to create and destroy worlds. Although *Hashem* told *Moshe Rabbeinu* to make the "Tabernacle, ark, and utensils," He did not command him to follow this sequence, and *Moshe Rabbeinu* repeated it out of order because of the aforesaid concern.

Bezalel pointed out that he already knew how to combine the letters which God used to create the universe and therefore knew how to create and destroy worlds. Accordingly, there was no reason for *Moshe Rabbeinu* to switch around the order when conveying it to him. Moreover, the building of the Tabernacle and its contents was tantamount to the creation of the world because Creation was incomplete without it. For this reason, it was crucial to know the correct order for constructing it even if *Hashem* did not command *Moshe Rabbeinu* to follow that order.[574]

❧ The Order of Fashioning the Tabernacle and its Contents is Connected to Faith (אֱמוּנָה)

Some pose the above questions differently. The sages state that Bezalel was only thirteen years old when *Hashem* put him in charge of constructing the Tabernacle and its utensils.[575] When deciding which order of construction to follow, why did

---

[573] B.T. *Pesachim* 6B and B.T. *Sanhedrim* 49B אֵין מוּקְדָם וּמְאוּחָר בַּתּוֹרָה

[574] *Toldoth Yaakov Yosef* on *Parashath Pekudei* 5 דידוע מה שכתבו המקובלים דלכך אין מוקדם ומאוחר בתורה (מסכת פסחים ו', ב'), דאילו נכתבה כסדר, היו יכולין לברוא שמים וארץ ולהחריבן. נמצא יש לומר דמשה ודאי היה יודע סדרה דבכל ביתו נאמן הוא (במדבר י"ב, ז'), אלא שנכתבה שלא כסדר לכוונה הנזכר לעיל שלא ישתמשו בה לבנות עולם ולהחריבו. ובזה יובן דמשה היפך סדר התורה, שנאמרה לו פרשת המשכן תחילה ואחר כך פרשת ארון וכלים, ומשה היפך לכוונה שעשה בכל התורה שנכתבה ונאמרה לישראל שלא כסדר שלא לברוא עולמות וכו', ואמר לו בצלאל, "ארון שאעשה להיכן אכניסו?"... "וכי תימא דבכוונה היפך הסדר שלא לברוא עולמות, לכך אמר הא בלאו הכי יודע היה בצלאל לצרף אותיות שנברא בהם שמים וארץ, דעשיית המשכן היינו ממש בריאת עולם, שהיה העולם תוסס עד הקמת המשכן, ועל כן היה צריך לידע סדר הצירוף כמו בבריאת שמים וארץ וקיימא לן.

[575] B.T. *Sanhedrin* 69B וְכִי עָבַד בְּצַלְאֵל מִשְׁכָּן בַּר כַּמָּה הֲוֵי? בַּר תְּלֵיסַר.

the mature intellect of *Moshe Rabbeinu* not lead him to the same conclusion as that of a mere boy?

The *Kedushath Levi* identifies two types of faith: (a) A basic faith that there is a God who created the universe. Such faith does not require a well-developed intellect. (b) An enhanced faith which comes from developing the intellect by studying and observing the *Mitzvoth*.

The Tabernacle symbolized the basic form of faith which is overarching and all-inclusive just as a building includes all its contents. The ark and other utensils inside the Tabernacle represented detailed, well-developed intellectual faith.

Moshe Rabbeinu had a mature intellect and a highly developed faith. He assumed that the rest of the nation had a similar type of faith and therefore wanted to start with the utensils. Bezalel realized that Israel had not yet achieved this level of faith, so he wanted to commence with the Tabernacle which represented the more basic all-encompassing faith, something even a youngster can manage if he or she is serious about it.[576]

✲ The Type of Wisdom Needed to Construct the Tabernacle and its Contents

In the *Talmudic* passage quoted above, Rabbi Yochanan stated that God only grants wisdom to those already possessed of wisdom. How did this apply to Bezalel, who was only thirteen years old? Even if he was a child prodigy, the spiritual source of

---

[576] *Kedushath Levi, Parashath Pekudei* המשכן הוא מרמז על אמונת הבורא יתברך כאשר בארנו שאמונת הבורא יתברך הוא השראת השכינה. והכלים של המשכן הם המצות הבורא יתברך. והנה השם יתברך ציווה למשה להורות לישראל תחילת המשכן, דהיינו להאמין תחילה סתם שיש בורא ברוך הוא ואחר כך הכלים להורות להם המצות ועל ידי המצות ישיגו את האמונה השכליות. אך משה, שהיה לו שכל גדול ולא היה צריך כלל לבחינת הא', רק על ידי המצות השיג אמונת השכליות. והיה משה סבור שכל ישראל הם בבחינתו, וציווה תחילה על הכלים לעשות המצות ואחר כך המשכן האמונה השכליות אשר הוא השראת שכינה. ובצלאל עשה בבחינת ישראל – תחילה המשכן כנ"ל ואחר כך הכלים.

Moshe Rabbeinu's soul was the supernal world of Knowledge (דַּעַת),[577] and the Generation of the Desert was called the "Generation of Knowledge" (דּוֹר דֵּעָה).[578] Surely Bezalel's intellect did not match that of his elders, much less exceed it.

The *Shelah Hakadosh* explains that true wisdom consists of realizing that it is impossible to understand *Hashem*.[579] This is something that even a young person can achieve if he possesses sufficient humility.

Although Bezalel was only thirteen years old, he merited building the Tabernacle and its contents because of his grandfather, Hur.[580] Hur's outstanding trait was the realization that one cannot grasp *Hashem*. The name Hur (חוּר) means "hole" — something empty. Hur recognized how empty he was — how he could not hope to grasp the true nature of God. By contrast, those who fancied themselves wise enough to know all about *Hashem* decided that the best way to relate to Him was by constructing a golden calf. When Hur protested, the rebels murdered him.[581]

Hur's trait of realizing that one cannot understand *Hashem* was passed down to his grandson, Bezalel. It was this understanding that made Bezalel worthy of knowing how to use the letters through which Heaven and Earth were created.

The *Gemara* teaches:

---

[577] *Beth Olamim* 132B ידוע שמשה רבינו עליו השלום היה סוד הדעת

[578] *Baal Shem Tov Al Hatorah, Parashath Vayishlach* משה שהיה סוד הדעה לכן בני דורו היו גם כן דור דעה.

[579] *Shelah Hakadosh, Hagaoth Lesefer Bamidbar Devarim, Chukath* שֶׁאָמְרוּ חַכְמֵי הַמֶּחְקָר עַל הַבּוֹרֵא יִתְבָּרַךְ: "תַּכְלִית מַה שֶּׁנֵּדַע הוּא שֶׁלֹּא נֵדָעוּךְ". כְּלוֹמַר, שֶׁיְּרַדְנוּ כָּל כָּךְ בְּעֹמֶק הַהַשָּׂגָה, שֶׁהִשַּׂגְנוּ שֶׁלֹּא נוּכַל לְהַשִּׂיגָךְ.

[580] *Chatham Sofer* on Exodus 31:2 כל גדולתו של בצלאל בהיותו בן י"ג שנה...להיות יודע לצרף אותיות שנבראו בו שמים וארץ היה הכל לכבוד זקנו חור שנהרג על קדושת השם יתברך בעגל.

[581] *Midrash Tanchuma, Parashath Titzaveh* 10 בשעה שביקשו ישראל לעשות אותו מעשה אמרו לאהרן, "קוּם עֲשֵׂה לָנוּ אֱ-לֹהִים" (שמות ל"ב, א'). עמד חור בן כלב וגער בהן. מיד עמדו עליו והרגוהו.

Rava said: If the righteous want, they can create worlds...

Rava [himself] created a human-like creature which he sent before Rabbi Zera. [The latter] spoke with it, but it did not respond [because it was not a real person]. He said, "You must be from the rabbis! Return to your dust!"

Rabbi Chanina and Rabbi Hoshaya used to sit together on every Sabbath eve, delve into the *Book of Formation* (סֵפֶר יְצִירָה), and create for themselves a choice calf.[582]

Rashi comments that when the *Gemara* states that, "Bezalel knew how to combine the letters through which Heaven and Earth were created," it means that he was familiar with the methods outlined in the *Book of Formation* (סֵפֶר יְצִירָה).[583] Bezalel did not merely take materials such as gold, silver, wool, or linen and fashion them into the Tabernacle and its utensils. Instead, he applied the methods outlined in the *Book of Formation* (סֵפֶר יְצִירָה) to those materials to create whatever was needed.

This fits in with the purpose of the Tabernacle which was to serve as a bridge between the physical and spiritual realms. Bezalel accomplished this by taking physical materials and accessing the spirituality inherent in them.

This also clarifies the importance of Bezalel's age. Having just turned thirteen, he was at the juncture between childhood and adulthood. This gave him the power to create a connection between physicality and spirituality in the Tabernacle.

How so?

---

[582] B.T. *Sanhedrin* 65B. אָמַר רָבָא: אִי בָּעוּ צַדִּיקֵי, בָּרוּ עָלְמָא... רָבָא בָּרָא גַּבְרָא. שַׁדְרֵיהּ לְקַמֵּיהּ דְּרַבִּי זֵירָא. הֲוָה קָא מִשְׁתָּעֵי בַּהֲדֵיהּ וְלָא הֲוָה קָא מְהַדֵּר לֵיהּ. אָמַר לֵיהּ: "מִן חַבְרַיָּא אַתְּ! הֲדַר לַעֲפָרֵיךְ!" רַבִּי חֲנִינָא וְרַבִּי הוֹשַׁעְיָא הֲווּ יַתְבֵי כָּל מַעֲלֵי שַׁבְּתָא וְעָסְקֵי בְּסֵפֶר יְצִירָה וּמִיבְּרוּ לְהוּ עִיגְלָא תִּילְתָּא.
[583] *Rashi* on B.T. *Berachoth* 55A "אוֹתִיּוֹת שֶׁנִּבְרְאוּ בָּהֶן שָׁמַיִם וָאָרֶץ" – על ידי צירופן. ובספר יצירה תני להו.

The sages teach that the *Torah* learning of children is not tainted by sin[584] because, being minors, their sins do not count. On the other hand, such learning has a downside because the *Torah* exempts children from all *Mitzvoth*, including *Torah* learning, and the *Mitzvoth* of one who is not commanded have less value than the *Mitzvoth* of those who are commanded.[585]

The spiritual realm may be compared to a child. It is pristine, pure, and close to *Hashem*. On the other hand, like a child, the spiritual realm is also immature, undeveloped, and incomplete because *Hashem* wants to have a dwelling place in the physical realm[586] — a Tabernacle.

A boy who has just turned thirteen still has the purity of a child because he has not yet had the opportunity to sin. At the same time, he is now obligated in *Mitzvoth*. This resembles the ideal combination of spirituality and physicality which *Hashem* desires — an ideal which was realized in the Tabernacle. Bezalel's young age therefore made him the ideal person to oversee its construction.

ജ്ഞ The Connection between Moshe Rabbeinu and Bezalel

Many of the expressions the *Torah* uses when setting out the requirements for constructing the Tabernacle and its contents are formulated in the second person singular implying that these

---

[584] B.T. *Shabbath* 119B אָמַר רֵישׁ לָקִישׁ מִשּׁוּם רַבִּי יְהוּדָה נְשִׂיאָה: אֵין הָעוֹלָם מִתְקַיֵּים אֶלָּא בִּשְׁבִיל הֶבֶל תִּינוֹקוֹת שֶׁל בֵּית רַבָּן. אָמַר לֵיהּ רַב פַּפָּא לְאַבַּיֵי: "דִּידִי וְדִידָךְ מַאי?" אָמַר לֵיהּ: "אֵינוֹ דוֹמֶה הֶבֶל שֶׁיֵּשׁ בּוֹ חֵטְא לְהֶבֶל שֶׁאֵין בּוֹ חֵטְא."

[585] As Rabbi Chanina explained, "One who is commanded and performs [a *Mitzvah*] is greater than one who is not commanded and performs [a *Mitzvah*]" (B.T. *Kiddushin* 31A גָּדוֹל מְצֻוֶּה וְעוֹשֶׂה מִמִּי שֶׁאֵינוֹ מְצֻוֶּה וְעוֹשֶׂה).

[586] *Midrash Tanchuma, Parashath Nasso* 16 נתאווה שיהא לו דירה בתחתונים כמו שיש בעליונים

commandments were directed to *Moshe Rabbeinu* personally. Indeed, during the seven-day inauguration of the Tabernacle, *Moshe Rabbeinu* personally set up and dismantled the Tabernacle twice each day.[587]

Nevertheless, *Hashem* commanded *Moshe Rabbeinu* to have Bezalel supervise the construction of the Tabernacle and its contents.[588] This suggests that *Moshe Rabbeinu* could not have completed the task on his own and that Bezalel possessed some special trait needed for the successful construction of the Tabernacle.

What was that trait?

The *Midrash* clarifies that *Moshe Rabbeinu* represented the theoretical, spiritual aspect of the Tabernacle whereas Bezalel represented its practical, physical aspect.[589] The purpose of the Tabernacle was for the Divine Presence to manifest itself in the physical world. *Moshe Rabbeinu* was too spiritual to accomplish this. He needed Bezalel to form the bridge between spirituality and physicality that allowed the Divine Presence to rest in the Tabernacle. As the *Zohar* comments, "*Moshe* and Bezalel were like one — *Moshe* was above, and Bezalel was below."[590]

---

[587] *Bamidbar Rabbah* 12:9 אמר רב חייא בר יוסף: כל שבעת ימי המילואים היה משה מעמיד המשכן ומפרקו בכל יום ב' פעמים. ואם תאמר שהיה אחד משבטו של לוי נותן לו יד, לאו, אלא אמרו חכמים [ש]היה קובעו ומפרקו ולא סייעו ולא אחד מישראל.

[588] Numbers 31:2 et. seq.

[589] *Shemoth Rabbah* 35:3 "וְעָשִׂיתָ אֶת הַקְּרָשִׁים" (שמות כ"ו, ט"ו) – מה כתיב למעלה מן העניין? "וּרְאֵה וַעֲשֵׂה" (שמות כ"ה, מ'). וכי משה עשה את המשכן? והלא כתיב, "וְעָשָׂה בְצַלְאֵל וְאָהֳלִיאָב וְכֹל אִישׁ חֲכַם לֵב" (שמות ל"ו, א')? אלא משה לתלמוד ובצלאל למעשה. מכאן אמרו רבותינו: ליתן שכר למעשה כעושה, שכן מצינו במשה שעשה בצלאל למלאכת המשכן והעלה עליו הקב"ה כאלו הוא עשאו, שנאמר, "וּמִשְׁכַּן ה' אֲשֶׁר עָשָׂה מֹשֶׁה בַּמִּדְבָּר" (דברי הימים"א כ"א, כ"ט).

[590] *Zohar* II:224B מֹשֶׁה וּבְצַלְאֵל כַּחֲדָא הֲווֹ – מֹשֶׁה לְעֵילָא, בְּצַלְאֵל תְּחוֹתֵיה

ೞೕೞ How the Divine Presence Revealed Itself in the Tabernacle

On a deeper level, the *Midrash* teaches that the Holy One, Blessed be He, told *Moshe Rabbeinu*:

> If you make that which is above below, [i.e., if you fashion the earthly Tabernacle to resemble the one I showed you in Heaven, then] I will leave My Heavenly Council, and I will descend and shrink My Divine Presence [so that it will dwell] among [the Jews] below.[591]

In a manner of speaking, God shrank Himself and created a vacuum — an area where He is not present — so that Creation could exist. This phenomenon is called *Tzimtzum* (צִמְצוּם), meaning "contraction." According to the most widely accepted opinion, this doctrine is not meant literally. Rather, *Hashem* hid Himself so that He appears to be withdrawn from the physical realm.[592]

The passage of the *Gemara* quoted earlier stated that Bezalel's name hints that he dwelled "in the shadow of God" (בְּצֵל אֵ-ל).

---

[591] *Bamidbar Rabbah* 12:8 אמר הקב"ה למשה: "אם את עושה מה שלמעלה למטה, אני מניח סנקליטון (הוועד) שלי של מעלה וארד ואצמצם שכינתי ביניהם למטה".

[592] *Likutei Amarim Tanya, Sha'ar Hayichud Veha'emunah*, chap. 7 והנה מכאן יש להבין שגגת מקצת חכמים בעיניהם, ה' יכפר בעדם, ששגו וטעו בעיונם בכתבי האריז"ל והבינו עניין הצמצום המוזכר שם כפשוטו, שהקב"ה סילק עצמו ומהותו ח"ו מעולם הזה, רק שמשגיח מלמעלה בהשגחה פרטית על כל היצורים כולם אשר בשמים ממעל ועל הארץ מתחת. והנה מלבד שאי אפשר כלל לומר עניין הצמצום כפשוטו שהוא ממקרי הגוף על הקב"ה הנבדל מהם ריבוא רבבות הבדלות עד אין קץ, אף גם זאת לא בדעת ידברו מאחר שהם מאמינים בני מאמינים שהקב"ה יודע כל היצורים שבעולם הזה השפל ומשגיח עליהם ועל כן אין ידיעתו אותם מוסיפה בו ריבוי וחידוש מפני שיודע הכל בידיעת עצמו – הרי כביכול מהותו ועצמותו ודעתו הכל א' וזהו שכתוב בתיקונים (בספר תיקוני זהר), תיקון נ"ז, דלית אתר פנוי מיניה לא בעילאין ולא בתתאין. For a full discussion of this topic, see *Understanding Emunah*, Rabbi Yehuda Cahn (2016, Ohr Nissan Talmud Center, Inc., Baltimore), pp. 21-31.

Shadow alludes to *Tzimtzum* (צִמְצוּם).[593] Almost nothing of an object's true appearance can be detected from its shadow. One cannot determine what materials the object consists of nor its texture, color, or thickness. In a similar way, *Hashem's* true nature is hidden from humans, and they can only grasp the sketchiest ideas about Him.

Bezalel was keenly aware of the limitations of his understanding of God and spirituality. Measure for measure, God granted him the ability to detect to some degree how He appears to limit Himself to allow Creation to exist — how *Tzimtzum* (צִמְצוּם) works. This revelation included showing Bezalel the spiritual sources of physical objects.

Every object in Creation has two opposite aspects. On the one hand, it is limited by its physical characteristics such as its length, width, height, shape, color, location, and the time when it exists. On the other hand, it also has an aspect of limitlessness which derives from its spiritual source and, ultimately, from God Himself.

Ohev Yisrael explains that Bezalel's special wisdom consisted of the ability to combine the two opposing characteristics of limitation and limitlessness inherent in every object in Creation. This is hinted at by the verse which describes how the Jews donated the materials used for the Tabernacle and its contents: "The [materials needed for] the work were sufficient for performing all the work, and there was excess."[594] The materials "were sufficient" — a limit had been reached, yet at the same

---

[593] *Likutei Halachoth, Orach Chaim, Hilchoth Sukkah* 3 הַצִּמְצוּם...בְּחִינַת צֵל
[594] Exodus 36:7 וְהַמְּלָאכָה הָיְתָה דַיָּם לְכָל הַמְּלָאכָה לַעֲשׂוֹת אֹתָהּ וְהוֹתֵר

time, "there was excess" — the materials transcended limitations.[595]

Moshe Rabbeinu was highly familiar with the concept of the "shadow of God" (צֵל אֵ-ל). When he asked to see *Hashem's* glory, *Hashem* had him stand in a cave that had been hollowed out of a rock and told him, "I will remove My hand, and you will see My back, but My face cannot be seen."[596]

The *Malbim* explains:

> [*Hashem*] informed him about how Creation and existence emerged from the Infinite One… "My face" is the Infinite One Himself who is incomprehensible…[whereas] "My back," is the entire Creation that was made by His command, and which is something one can grasp. However, the channel through which Creation passed from the Infinite One, who is utterly unbounded, to that which has is bounded and limited…concerning which [*Moshe Rabbeinu*] requested, "Please show me Your glory"…requires examining the doctrine of *Tzimtzum* (צִמְצוּם), meaning how He contracted Himself and made a void and vacant space in which all the worlds stand. Here, He referred to this void where all Creation exists as a "hollow of the rock"…because [the term] "rock" (צוּר) [alludes to] "creation" (יְצוּר)…
>
> [*Hashem*] explained to him that to grasp…the channel itself — how there was transition from infinite to finite and from the unlimited to the limited — as well as the concept of *Tzimtzum* (צִמְצוּם) itself, [which is] the "hollow of the rock"…is

---

[595] *Ohev Yisrael, Likutim Chadashim, Parashath Pekudei* העיקר הוא מְנדבת הלב והרצון וכסופא (*תשוקה*) של כל אחד. נמצא שהיה מעשה בגשמיות לצמצום וגם מחשבה ורצון ברוחניות להתפשטות אין סוף ב״ה. וזהו חכמתו של בצלאל במה שצירף המחשבה אל המעשה ועשה קומה שלימה. וזהו, ״וְלַחְשֹׁב מַחֲשָׁבֹת לַעֲשֹׂת בַּזָּהָב וּבַכֶּסֶף וּבַנְחֹשֶׁת״ (שמות ל״ה, ל״ב), היינו שפעל במחשבה וגם בעשייה. וזהו אמרה, ״הָיְתָה דַיָּם...וְהוֹתֵר״, היינו שהיו ב׳ בחינות – בגשמיות היה צמצום כביכול וזהו בחינת דיים ובבחינת הרצון והרעותא היה התפשטות אין סוף ב״ה וזהו והותר.

[596] Exodus 33:23 וַהֲסִרֹתִי אֶת כַּפִּי וְרָאִיתָ אֶת אֲחֹרָי וּפָנַי לֹא יֵרָאוּ

covered with darkness and obscurity... Concerning this [*Hashem*] said, "I will cover My hand over you while I pass by," for the concept of this transition — how I passed from the infinite to the finite worlds — I will cover from you with My hand.[597]

Moshe Rabbeinu ascended to a higher level of comprehension of *Hashem* than Bezalel did. The *Torah* therefore calls him a "man of God" (אִישׁ הָאֱ-לֹהִים),[598] reports that he spoke to God "mouth to mouth," and that he, so to speak, "saw an image of *Hashem*."[599]

By contrast, Bezalel's comprehension of *Hashem* was only at the level of a "shadow of God" (צֵל אֵ-ל). It was specifically this lower spiritual level which gave Bezalel the ability to fashion a physical Tabernacle that could, as it were, contain God's Presence. *Moshe Rabbeinu* was on too lofty a spiritual level to accomplish this.

ೞೞೞೞ The Shadow of God (צֵל אֵ-ל) ೞೞೞೞ

The reader should not suppose, however, that Bezalel was on a low spiritual level, for the "shadow of God" (צֵל אֵ-ל) represents a highly abstract idea. Although not even *Moshe Rabbeinu* can fully understand how the Infinite One, in a manner of speaking, contracts Himself to create an "empty space" for Creation, it

---

[597] *Malbim* on Exodus 33:22 הודיעו...אֵיךְ יָצָא הַיְצוּר וְהַמְּצִיאוּת מִן הָאֵין סוֹף... הִנֵּה צַד אֶחָד שֶׁנִּקְרָא "פָּנַי", שֶׁהוּא מַהוּת הָאֵין סוֹף בְּעַצְמוֹ, הוּא נִמְנַע הַהַשָּׂגָה. וְהַצַּד שֶׁנִּקְרָא "אֲחֹרָי", שֶׁהִיא הַבְּרִיאָה כֻּלָּהּ שֶׁנַּעֲשָׂה בִּפְקוּדָתוֹ, זֶה דָבָר שֶׁיָּכוֹל לְהַשִּׂיג. אָמְנָם הַמַּעֲבָר שֶׁעָבְרָה הַבְּרִיאָה מִן הָאֵין סוֹף וְהַבִּלְתִּי בַּעַל תַּכְלִית אֶל הַגְּבוּל וְהַסּוֹף...שֶׁבִּיקֵּשׁ עָלֶיהָ, "הַרְאֵנִי נָא אֶת כְּבֹדֶךְ"...שֶׁבָּזֶה תָעָיַן בְּעִנְיַן הַצִּמְצוּם – אֵיךְ צִמְצֵם אֶת עַצְמוֹ וְנַעֲשָׂה חָלָל פְּנוּי וּמָקוֹם שֶׁבּוֹ יַעַמְדוּ כָּל הָעוֹלָמוֹת וְחָלָל זֶה קוֹרָא פֹּה "נְקֶרֶת הַצּוּר"...וְעַל שֵׁם זֶה זֶה קָרָא חָלָל זֶה שֶׁבּוֹ עוֹמֵד כָּל הַיְצוּר "נְקֶרֶת הַצּוּר", שֶׁצּוּר הוּא הַיְצוּר...בֵּיאֵר לוֹ שֶׁלְּהַשִּׂיג אֶת...הַמַּעֲבָר עַצְמוֹ אֵיךְ עָבַר מִן הָאֵין סוֹף אֶל הַסּוֹף, וּמִן הַבִּלְתִּי בַּעַל תַּכְלִית אֶל הַצִּמְצוּם וְעִנְיַן הַצִּמְצוּם וּנְקֶרֶת הַצּוּר עַצְמוֹ...זֶה יְכוּסֶה בֶּעָנָן וְהָעֶלֶם...שֶׁעַל זֶה אָמַר, "וְשַׂכֹּתִי כַפִּי עָלֶיךָ עַד עָבְרִי", שֶׁעִנְיַן הַהַעֲבָרָה אֵיךְ עָבַרְתִּי מִן הָאֵין סוֹף אֶל עוֹלָמוֹת בַּעֲלֵי גְּבוּל אֶסוֹכֵךְ עָלֶיךָ אֶת כַּפִּי.

[598] Deuteronomy 33:1 וְזֹאת הַבְּרָכָה אֲשֶׁר בֵּרַךְ מֹשֶׁה אִישׁ הָאֱ-לֹהִים אֶת בְּנֵי יִשְׂרָאֵל לִפְנֵי מוֹתוֹ

[599] Numbers 12:8 פֶּה אֶל פֶּה אֲדַבֶּר בּוֹ וּמַרְאֶה וְלֹא בְחִידֹת וּתְמֻנַת ה' יַבִּיט וּמַדּוּעַ לֹא יְרֵאתֶם לְדַבֵּר בְּעַבְדִּי בְמֹשֶׁה.

is possible to get a vague notion of how this works by carefully observing the behavior of a shadow.

A light source shining on a given object produces an umbra surrounded by a penumbra, as illustrated below.

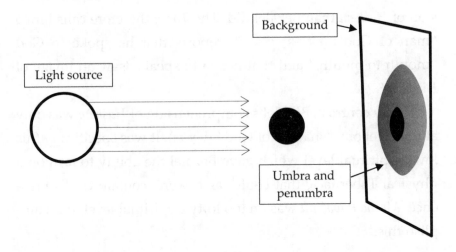

The larger the light source, the smaller the umbra produced by the object blocking the light and the fainter the penumbra. If the light source would be infinite, then no umbra or penumbra would exist behind the object blocking the light. Rather, their existence would be merely theoretical.

By way of analogy, *Hashem*, so to speak, shines His Divine light on combinations of letters — spiritual configurations — to create a physical world, and the physical world resembles a shadow formed by those letters. However, because the Divine light is infinite, from a certain perspective, the physical realm has no existence at all — there really is no shadow, and the physical realm exists only theoretically.

How does this work? How can there be any Creation at all if its existence is only theoretical?

The distinction between the theoretical and the practical — between thought and action — does not exist with respect to *Hashem*. Rather, *Hashem's* thought of Creation and His act of Creation are one and the same, as the *Zohar* explains:

> When it arose in thought before the Holy One, Blessed be He, to create His world, all the worlds arose in thought at once, and with this thought they were all created. This is [the meaning of] that which is written, "You made all of them with wisdom."[600] With this thought, which [the verse calls] "wisdom," [both] this world and the world above were created.[601]

Hashem's thought and the act of Creation are identical, but this is not readily apparent to His creatures except in the highest of all the spiritual realms called the World of Emanation (אֲצִילוּת). As Rabbi Chaim Vital explains:

> The parable for this is that when a person wishes to walk to a given place, he need not speak to his legs and command them to go there. Rather, when the matter occurs to him, his legs immediately walk of their own accord, and so it is with other [routine] activities.
>
> If we expand upon this idea further, we can say that we find that thought and action happen simultaneously [when a person performs routine tasks], for when a person eats, he need not think first how he will chew the food, how he will move his

---

[600] Psalms 104:24 מָה רַבּוּ מַעֲשֶׂיךָ ה' כֻּלָּם בְּחָכְמָה עָשִׂיתָ מָלְאָה הָאָרֶץ קִנְיָנֶךָ

[601] *Zohar* II:20A בְּשָׁעָה שֶׁעָלָה בְּמַחֲשָׁבָה לִפְנֵי הַקָּדוֹשׁ בָּרוּךְ הוּא לִבְרוֹא עוֹלָמוֹ, כָּל הָעוֹלָמוֹת עָלוּ בְּמַחֲשָׁבָה אַחַת וּבְמַחֲשָׁבָה זוּ נִבְרְאוּ כּוּלָּם. הֲדָא הוּא דְכְתִיב, "כֻּלָּם בְּחָכְמָה עָשִׂיתָ" (תהלים ק"ד, כ"ד). וּבְמַחֲשָׁבָה זוּ שֶׁהִיא הַחָכְמָה נִבְרָא הָעוֹלָם הַזֶּה וְהָעוֹלָם שֶׁל מַעְלָה.

teeth, how he will swallow the food, and then afterwards eat the food. Rather, the thought extends itself into the limbs through which he eats with the result that the eating and the thought occur together simultaneously.

In this same way, the World of Emanation (אֲצִילוּת) is called the "world of thought"…because the Infinite One, when He invests Himself in supernal wisdom, which is called thought, literally extends Himself through [all] the levels of [the World of] Emanation (אֲצִילוּת) such that thought and deed in [the World of] Emanation (אֲצִילוּת) are all one thing.[602]

The purpose of the Tabernacle was to reveal the same unity of thought and action in the physical realm as exists in the spiritual world of Emanation (אֲצִילוּת).[603]

Rabbi Chaim Vital's analogy between God's thought and the thought processes of people offers a rough idea of how God manifests Himself in the highest spiritual realm, and Bezalel's thought processes resembled those of found in the world of Emanation (אֲצִילוּת), as Rabbi Pinchas of Koritz explains:

Every [ordinary] person has knowledge only in his mind so that when he does something [complicated such as

---

[602] *Kithvei Ha'arizal, Shaar Hahakdamoth* 87B-88A המשל בזה כאשר ירצה האדם ללכת אל איזה מקום, איננו צריך לדבר אל רגליו ולצוותם שילכו שם. אמנם בַּעֲלוֹת הדבר במחשבתו, תכף רגליו הולכות מאליהם. ועל דרך זה בשאר פעולות הדברים. ונרחיב העניין בזה יותר ונאמר כי הנה מצאנו שהמחשבה עם הפעולה באות כאחד [כאשר האדם עושה פעולות בלתי-מורכבות], כי הנה כאשר האדם אוכל לא יצ[ט]רך לחשוב בתחילה איך ילעוס המאכל ואיך ינוע שיניו ואיך יבלע המאכל ואחר כך יאכל המאכל ההוא. אמנם המחשבה מתפשטת בתוך האיברים שבהם אוכל ונמצא המאכל [מעשה האכילה] והמחשבה נגמרים ובאים כאחד ביחד. על דרך זה עולם האצילות נקרא עולם המחשבה... כי הנה האין סוף בהיותו מתלבש בחכמה עליונה הנקראת 'מחשבה' מתפשט בתוך מדרגות האצילות ממש ואז מחשבה ומעשה שבאצילות הכל הם דבר אחד.

[603] *Beth Olamim* 129B שצורת המשכן והמקדש הוא תבנית כל האצילות; *Tzeror Hamor* on Numbers 7:88 כי תכלית המשכן ואלו הקורבנות לא היה אלא להוריד השכינה לתחתונים

The letter *Alef* (א) represents God because it has a numeric value of one, and God is one. When *Alef* (א) is added to "shadow" (צֵל), it forms the word *Etzel* (אֵצֶל), which means "near" or "next to" and which is the root of "emanation" (אֲצִילוּת), the spiritual realm nearest to *Hashem*.

constructing the Tabernacle and its contents], he needs to think about the thing he does. This was not the case with Bezalel, who was filled with the spirit [of God, as the verse states, "I will fill [Bezalel] with a spirit of God...to think thoughts..."],[604] for all of his limbs thought thoughts, and his hands themselves did what was necessary because they themselves had knowledge.[605]

Bezalel fashioned the Tabernacle and its contents in a manner somewhat similar to the way in which *Hashem* created the universe with simultaneous thought and action.

೫೦೫೦೫೦೫೦೫೦ Martyrdom

The purpose of Creation is for human beings to draw *Hashem's* presence into the physical realm. They accomplish this by striving to resemble Him, and those who give up their lives for *Hashem* achieve the highest level of such resemblance.

To quote a passage cited earlier:

Rav Yehudah said in the name of Rav: At the time when *Moshe Rabbeinu* ascended on high, he found the Holy One,

---

[604] Exodus 31:3-4 וָאֲמַלֵּא אֹתוֹ רוּחַ אֱ-לֹהִים בְּחָכְמָה וּבִתְבוּנָה וּבְדַעַת וּבְכָל מְלָאכָה. לַחְשֹׁב מַחֲשָׁבֹת לַעֲשׂוֹת בַּזָּהָב וּבַכֶּסֶף וּבַנְּחֹשֶׁת.

[605] *Imrei Finchas* 1:92, כל אדם יש לו דעת רק במוח וכשעושה דבר צריך המוח לחשוב אותו דבר שעושה, מה שאין כן בצלאל, שהיה מלא רוח וכו', שגם כל אבריו היו חושבין מחשבות והיידיים בעצמם עושים מה שנצרך שהיה בהם דעת בפני עצמם.

He cites as a basis for this the commentary of Rabbi Moshe Alshich on Exodus 35:30-33: והנה היה אפשר יהי כן בחכמת לב בצלאל, אך בפועל כפיו לא יהיה בו רוחניות א-לוהי רק טבעי, כי אין היידיים כלי לחול בו רוח א-להין קדישין אלהן (אלא דק) במוח ולב. על כן, "וַיְמַלֵּא אֹתוֹ רוּחַ אֱ-לֹהִים" (שמות ל"ה, ל"א), והוא כי אחת מבחינות הנפש ליוצרה היא שממלאה את הגוף, אך לא בשווה. כי הכוח אשר בעין שנותן בו ראות, או אשר בשכל שנותן בו השכלה, או בלב שנותן בו מחשבה, אינו ככוח אשר ביידיים ודומיהם שלא יוכנו רק לקבל כוח מישוש. אמר כי בבצלאל הייתה גדולה זו, כי רוח א-לוהים בקרבו הממלא את כל הגוף היה ממלאו בשכל הכולל חכמה ותבונה ודעת וגם ביידיים אשר בם כל מלאכה.

Blessed be He, sitting and affixing crowns to letters [of the alphabet].[606]

Moshe Rabbeinu inquired, "Why must You have these [crowns]?"

"There is one person," answered God, "who will live after several generations, and Akiva ben Yosef is his name. In the future, he will derive from each and every strand [of these crowns] piles upon piles of *Halachoth*."

"Master of the Universe, show him to me."

"Turn behind you."

[*Moshe Rabbeinu*] went and sat behind eight rows [of Rabbi Akiva's disciples], but he did not comprehend what they were saying, [and] his strength failed him.

When they reached a certain topic, [Rabbi Akiva's disciples] asked him, "Rabbi, from where do you know this?"

He replied, "It is a law given to Moshe at Sinai."

[*Moshe Rabbeinu's*] mind was set at ease.

He went back before the Holy One, Blessed be He and said, "Master of the Universe, You have a person like this, yet you give the *Torah* through me?"

"Be silent," answered God, "for so it arose in thought before Me."

"Master of the Universe, You showed me his *Torah*. Show me his reward."

"Turn behind you."

[*Moshe Rabbeinu*] turned around and saw [how the Romans brutally tortured Rabbi Akiva to death and] weighed his

---

[606] When written in *Torah* scrolls, *Tefillin*, and *Mezuzoth*, some letters have flourishes that resemble crowns — שֵׁעַטְנֵ֨ז גֵּץ (B.T. *Menachoth* 29B אמר רבא: שבעה אותיות צריכות שלושה זיונין, ואלו הן: שעטנ"ז ג"ץ). It is also customary to add one or two flourishes to other letters (*Shulchan Aruch, Orach Chaim* 36:3 צריך לתייג שעטנ"ז ג"ץ, והסופרים נהגו לתייג אותיות אחרות, ואם לא תייג אפילו שעטנ"ז ג"ץ, לא פסל).

flesh in the market. He declared, "Master of the Universe, is this the *Torah*, and is this its reward!?!"

God answered, "Be silent, for so it arose in thought before Me."[607]

Moshe Rabbeinu wondered how the spiritual forces represented by the Hebrew letters could create a universe considering that God's infinite Divine light overwhelms them. *Hashem* explained that there are people who connect thought with action parallel to the way in which *Hashem's* thought and action are both identical and simultaneous, as hinted at by the expression "so it arose in thought before Me." Such people provide the spiritual force which keeps the universe in existence.

Rabbi Akiva was a brilliant scholar, but his wisdom was not confined to theory. Rather, he put his knowledge into practice by sacrificing his life for the *Torah*, as the sages relate:

> When they took out Rabbi Akiva for execution, it was the time for reciting *Shema*. They were combing his flesh with iron combs while he was accepting upon himself the yoke of Heaven.
>
> His disciples asked, "Master, does [your devotion] extend this far?"
>
> He explained, "Throughout my life I was troubled over the verse, 'with all your soul,'[608] [which means] even if He takes your soul. I said to myself, 'When will the opportunity arrive that I may fulfill this?' Now that the opportunity has arrived, shall I not fulfill it?"

---

[607] B.T. *Menachoth* 29B. See Appendix H for full text.

[608] Deuteronomy 6:5 וְאָהַבְתָּ אֵת ה' אֱ-לֹהֶיךָ בְּכָל לְבָבְךָ וּבְכָל נַפְשְׁךָ וּבְכָל מְאֹדֶךָ

He stretched out [the recitation of the word] "one" [in the first verse of *Shema*] until his soul departed [while he was saying] it.

A Heavenly voice emerged and declared, "Fortunate are you, Rabbi Akiva, that your soul departed [while reciting] 'one.'"[609]

The *Mishnah B'rurah* states that, "When one reads *Shema*, he should accept upon himself the yoke of Heaven to be martyred for the sanctification of the Unique Name."[610] Of course, Rabbi Akiva fulfilled this *Halachah*, but he was concerned throughout his life that his theoretical devotion to *Hashem* — his thought — had never been combined with action. After all, it is one thing to declare one's willingness to die for *Hashem* and quite another thing to do so. Rabbi Akiva died at the moment he uttered the word "one" because he had succeeded in uniting his thought and action in a way which paralleled the unity of thought and action by which *Hashem* created and sustains the universe.[611]

Without *Tzaddikim* who unite thought with action as Rabbi Akiva did, the universe would cease to exist. This is the meaning of the verse, "Precious in the eyes of *Hashem* is the death of His pious ones."[612]

---

[609] B.T. *Berachoth* 61B בְּשָׁעָה שֶׁהוֹצִיאוּ אֶת רַבִּי עֲקִיבָא לַהֲרִיגָה, זְמַן קְרִיאַת שְׁמַע הָיָה. וְהָיוּ סוֹרְקִים אֶת בְּשָׂרוֹ בְּמַסְרְקוֹת שֶׁל בַּרְזֶל, וְהָיָה מְקַבֵּל עָלָיו עוֹל מַלְכוּת שָׁמַיִם. אָמְרוּ לוֹ תַּלְמִידָיו: "רַבֵּנוּ, עַד כָּאן?" אָמַר לָהֶם: "כָּל יָמַי הָיִיתִי מִצְטַעֵר עַל פָּסוּק זֶה, 'בְּכָל נַפְשְׁךָ' – אֲפִלּוּ הוּא נוֹטֵל אֶת נִשְׁמָתְךָ, 'מָתַי יָבוֹא לְיָדִי וַאֲקַיְּמֶנּוּ?' וְעַכְשָׁיו שֶׁבָּא לְיָדִי לֹא אֲקַיְּמֶנּוּ?" הָיָה מַאֲרִיךְ בְּ"אֶחָד" עַד שֶׁיָּצְאָה נִשְׁמָתוֹ בְּ"אֶחָד". יָצְתָה בַּת קוֹל וְאָמְרָה: "אַשְׁרֶיךָ רַבִּי עֲקִיבָא שֶׁיָּצְאָה נִשְׁמָתְךָ בְּ"אֶחָד"".

[610] *Mishnah B'rurah* on *Shulchan Aruch, Orach Chaim* 61:1, note 3 שיכוין בשעה שהוא קורא את שמע לקבל עליו עול מלכות שמים להיות נהרג על קידוש השם המיוחד.

[611] This explains why *Zohar* III:33A states that Jews should confess their sins and recite *Shema* when they are about to die וְכַד וְקֹדֶם דְּתִפּוּק נִשְׁמָתֵיהּ מִתְוַודֶּה בְּכַמָּה וִדּוּיִין. נָפִיק נִשְׁמָתֵיהּ הוּא הֲוָה מִתְכַּוֵּון לְגִמּוֹר אֶת הַשֵּׁם – שְׁמַע יִשְׂרָאֵל וּבָרוּךְ שֵׁם.

[612] Psalms 16:15 יָקָר בְּעֵינֵי ה' הַמָּוְתָה לַחֲסִידָיו

Hashem created the universe by, so to speak, negating Himself — by seemingly contracting His Presence to allow a place for Creation to exist. People who sacrifice their lives for the unity of God's Name imitate this self-negation and thereby achieve the highest possible level of unity between *Hashem* and Creation. Without people dying for the sake of *Hashem*, thought would separate from action, and the universe would separate from Him and cease to exist. This is one of the reasons why martyrs must exist in every generation until the final redemption.[613]

Bezalel's grandfather, Hur, accomplished the same thing as Rabbi Akiva when he gave up his life while protesting against the sin of the golden calf. In his merit, Bezalel had the power to use the spiritual forces represented by the Hebrew letters to fashion a Tabernacle capable of containing the Divine Presence — a structure with the power to resolve the contradiction between God's overwhelming Presence and a seemingly independent physical realm.

The design of the Tabernacle mirrored the act of Creation.[614] *Hashem* therefore told *Moshe Rabbeinu*, "I will fill [Bezalel] with a spirit of God, with wisdom, understanding, and knowledge, and every skill, to think thoughts to make [objects] with gold, silver, and copper."[615] The expression "think thoughts to make" (לַחְשֹׁב מַחֲשָׁבֹת לַעֲשׂוֹת) suggests that Bezalel made the components of the Tabernacle by using thought in a manner

---

[613] *Yalkut Reuveni, Shich'chath Haleket, Erech Ashiruth Ve'Aniyuth* והוכרחו לתועלת העניין הזה י' הרוגי מלכות וניצוצותיהם המתפשטים בכל דור ודור למסור נפשם על קדושת השם העולה עד המחשבה הגנוזה בקודש קדשים.

[614] *Yalkut Shimoni* on Numbers 8, continuation of paragraph 719 אמר רבי יהודה ברבי שלום: מצינו שהיה המשכן שקול כנגד מעשה בראשית.

[615] Exodus 31:3-4 וָאֲמַלֵּא אֹתוֹ רוּחַ אֱ-לֹהִים בְּחָכְמָה וּבִתְבוּנָה וּבְדַעַת וּבְכָל מְלָאכָה. לַחְשֹׁב מַחֲשָׁבֹת לַעֲשׂוֹת בַּזָּהָב וּבַכֶּסֶף וּבַנְּחֹשֶׁת.

analogous to the way in which *Hashem* created the universe with thought.

Moshe Rabbeinu never experienced martyrdom and was too divorced from physicality to understand how *Hashem's* thought and action can be unified in this way. For this reason, he could not understand Rabbi Akiva's lesson and wondered why *Hashem* did not give the *Torah* through Rabbi Akiva instead of through him.

ಶುಶುಶುಶುಶು Tɧe Ten Commandments

When *Hashem* uttered the Ten Commandments, He revealed to the entire Jewish nation how He created the universe using simultaneous thought and action.

All the other nations had insisted on understanding the *Torah* and knowing what it commanded before deciding whether to commit themselves to it. This is indeed the way that everyone behaves with respect to worldly matters. People do not marry without thoroughly investigating a proposed spouse. They do not buy a home without first making a thorough inspection.

Unlike the gentile nations, Israel recognized that because *Hashem* transcends the physical universe, the usual rules do not apply to Him. They therefore said, "We will do, and we will understand,"[616] reversing the usual order and accepting the *Torah* without knowing its contents.[617]

Hashem transcends time, so His thought and action occur simultaneously. Human beings, who are bound by time, cannot

---

[616] Exodus 24:7 וַיִּקַּח סֵפֶר הַבְּרִית וַיִּקְרָא בְּאָזְנֵי הָעָם וַיֹּאמְרוּ כֹּל אֲשֶׁר דִּבֶּר ה' נַעֲשֶׂה וְנִשְׁמָע

[617] B.T. *Shabbath* 88A-B הַהוּא צְדוּקִי דְּחַזְיֵיה לְרָבָא דְּקָא מְעַיֵּין בִּשְׁמַעֲתָּא וְיָתְבָא אֶצְבְּעָתָא דְּיָדֵיה תּוּתֵי כַּרְעֵייה וְקָא מָיֵיץ בְּהוּ וְקָא מַבְּעָן אֶצְבְּעָתֵיה דָּמָא. אָמַר לֵיהּ: "עַמָּא פְּזִיזָא דְּקַדְמִיתוּ פּוּמַייְכוּ לְאוּדְנַייְכוּ! אַכַּתִּי בְּפַחֲזוּתַייְכוּ קָיְמִיתוּ. בְּרֵישָׁא אִיבַּעְיָא לְכוּ לְמִשְׁמַע. אִי מָצִיתוּ, קַבְּלִיתוּ. וְאִי לָא, לָא קַבְּלִיתוּ". אָמַר לֵיהּ: "אֲנַן דְּסָגֵינָן בִּשְׁלֵמוּתָא, כְּתִיב בַּן, 'תֻּמַּת יְשָׁרִים תַּנְחֵם' (משלי י"א, ג'). הַנַּךְ אִינָּשֵׁי דְּסָגָן בַּעֲלִילוּתָא, כְּתִיב בְּהוּ, 'וְסֶלֶף בּוֹגְדִים וְשַׁדֵּם [וְיִשָּׁדֵּם קרי]' (שם שם).

do this. The closest they can approach to such a concept is to reverse the usual order and place action before thought. This is what the Jews accomplished at the Giving of the *Torah*.

Because Israel imitated *Hashem* in this way, He revealed to them how He created the universe with thought and action occurring simultaneously. This is why, "He who spoke and the world came into being expressed all of the Ten Commandments in a single utterance."[618] *Hashem* gave the Ten Commandments, which include the totality of the *Torah*,[619] in a single utterance to give the Jews an inkling of how He created the universe with a single combination of thought and action.

This also explains why all the Jews died when *Hashem* uttered the first two of the Ten Commandments and were then revived.[620] They underwent the same experience as those martyrs who die for the sanctification of God's Name.

❦❦❦❦❦ Shabbath

The first time the *Torah* records the Ten Commandments, it states, "Remember (זָכוֹר) the Sabbath day,"[621] whereas the second time it states, "Observe (שָׁמוֹר) the Sabbath day."[622] The sages comment that *Hashem* uttered both "Remember" (זָכוֹר) and "Observe" (שָׁמוֹר) simultaneously — something that no human mouth can do and that no human ear can distinctly make out.[623]

---

[618] *Yalkut Shimoni* on Exodus 15, paragraph 250 מי שאמר והיה העולם אמר י׳ דברות בדבור אחד, מה שאי אפשר לבשר ודם לומר כן.

[619] *Rabbeinu Bachye* on Exodus 20:14 כשבאו ישראל, נתן להם עשרת הדברות שהן כוללות תרי״ג מצוות.

[620] B.T. *Shabbath* 38B וְאָמַר רַבִּי יְהוֹשֻׁעַ בֶּן לֵוִי: כָּל דִּיבּוּר וְדִיבּוּר שֶׁיָּצָא מִפִּי הַקָּדוֹשׁ בָּרוּךְ הוּא יָצְתָה נִשְׁמָתָן שֶׁל יִשְׂרָאֵל.

[621] Exodus 20:8 זָכוֹר אֶת יוֹם הַשַּׁבָּת לְקַדְּשׁוֹ

[622] Deuteronomy 5:12 שָׁמוֹר אֶת יוֹם הַשַּׁבָּת לְקַדְּשׁוֹ כַּאֲשֶׁר צִוְּךָ ה׳ אֱ-לֹהֶיךָ

[623] B.T. *Rosh Hashannah* 27A וְהָתַנְיָא: זָכוֹר וְשָׁמוֹר בְּדִיבּוּר אֶחָד נֶאֶמְרוּ, מַה שֶׁאֵין הַפֶּה יְכוֹלָה לְדַבֵּר וְאֵין הָאוֹזֶן יְכוֹלָה לִשְׁמֹעַ.

"Remember" (זָכוֹר) is the concept of thought, and "Observe" (שָׁמוֹר) is the concept of doing.[624] At first glance, it seems inconsistent to use a term which denotes doing with respect to *Shabbath* because the essence of its observance is refraining from certain activities. However, one of the purposes of this inactivity is for Jews to recognize that *Hashem* created the universe without doing anything. His thought (זָכוֹר) and action (שָׁמוֹר) occurred simultaneously.

As the *Midrash* teaches:

"Six days you shall labor and do all your work."[625] Is it possible for a person to complete all his work in six days? Rather, [the verse means that you should] rest as if your work is finished. Another interpretation is: Rest from thinking about work.[626]

This is reminiscent of *Hashem* "resting" after the act of Creation. Just as *Hashem's* thought of Creation was itself the act of Creation, so Jews should neither do work nor even think about work on *Shabbath*.

---

[624] *Shem Mishmuel, Parashath Metzora* 5670, שזכור ושמור הם נגד קדושת המחשבה והמעשה, דזכור הוא קדושת המחשבה, ושמור, שהוא שלא לעשות מלאכה, הוא קדושת המעשה.

[625] Exodus 20:9 שֵׁשֶׁת יָמִים תַּעֲבֹד וְעָשִׂיתָ כָּל מְלַאכְתֶּךָ

[626] *Yalkut Shimoni* on Exodus 20, Paragraph 296 "שֵׁשֶׁת יָמִים תַּעֲבֹד וְעָשִׂיתָ כָּל מְלַאכְתֶּךָ" (שמות כ', ט'). וכי אפשר לאדם לעשות כל מלאכתו בשישה ימים? אלא שבות כאילו מלאכתך עשויה. דבר אחר: שבות ממחשבת עבודה.

Shulchan Aruch, Orach Chaim 306:9 rules, "Thinking about one's [weekday] activities is permissible. Nevertheless, because of [the principle of] delighting in the Sabbath, it is a *Mitzvah* not to think about them at all, and it should be viewed in one's eyes as if his work is completed." ,הרהור בעסקיו מותר ומכל מקום משום עונג שבת מצוה שלא יחשוב בהם כלל ויהא בעיניו כאילו כל מלאכתו עשויה.

This clarifies why those activities forbidden on *Shabbath* are the same as those which were used in the construction of the Tabernacle.[627]

---

[627] B.T. *Shabbath* 49B הָא דִּתְנַן, "אֲבוֹת מְלָאכוֹת אַרְבָּעִים חָסֵר אָחָת", כְּנֶגֶד מִי? אָמַר לְהוּ רַבִּי חֲנִינָא בַּר חָמָא: כְּנֶגֶד עֲבוֹדוֹת הַמִּשְׁכָּן... תַּנְיָא כְּמַאן דַּאֲמַר כְּנֶגֶד עֲבוֹדוֹת הַמִּשְׁכָּן דְּתַנְיָא: אֵין חַיָּיבִין אֶלָּא עַל מְלָאכָה שֶׁכַּיּוֹצֵא בָה הַיְתָה בַּמִּשְׁכָּן.

Miriam's Wellspring

ಜಿ General Description

After the Jews departed Egypt, they journeyed to Rephidim where they complained that they had no water. *Hashem* instructed *Moshe Rabbeinu* to strike a rock with his staff, causing water to flow from it.[628] This wellspring followed Israel through the desert in the merit of Miriam and departed when she died.[629] The wellspring later returned through the merit of *Moshe Rabbeinu* and Aaron.[630]

The *Mishnah* lists the mouth of Miriam's wellspring among ten things created at twilight on the very first Sabbath

---

[628] Exodus 17:1-6 וַיִּסְעוּ כָּל עֲדַת בְּנֵי יִשְׂרָאֵל מִמִּדְבַּר סִין לְמַסְעֵיהֶם עַל פִּי ה׳ וַיַּחֲנוּ בִּרְפִידִים וְאֵין מַיִם לִשְׁתֹּת הָעָם. (ב) וַיָּרֶב הָעָם עִם מֹשֶׁה וַיֹּאמְרוּ תְּנוּ לָנוּ מַיִם וְנִשְׁתֶּה וַיֹּאמֶר לָהֶם מֹשֶׁה מַה תְּרִיבוּן עִמָּדִי מַה תְּנַסּוּן אֶת ה׳... (ה) וַיֹּאמֶר ה׳ אֶל מֹשֶׁה עֲבֹר לִפְנֵי הָעָם וְקַח אִתְּךָ מִזִּקְנֵי יִשְׂרָאֵל וּמַטְּךָ אֲשֶׁר הִכִּיתָ בּוֹ אֶת הַיְאֹר קַח בְּיָדְךָ וְהָלָכְתָּ. (ו) הִנְנִי עֹמֵד לְפָנֶיךָ שָׁם עַל הַצּוּר בְּחֹרֵב וְהִכִּיתָ בַצּוּר וְיָצְאוּ מִמֶּנּוּ מַיִם וְשָׁתָה הָעָם וַיַּעַשׂ כֵּן מֹשֶׁה לְעֵינֵי זִקְנֵי יִשְׂרָאֵל.
[629] B.T. *Ta'anith* 9A בְּאֵר וְעָנָן וּמָן. בְּאֵר בִּזְכוּת מִרְיָם... מֵתָה מִרְיָם נִסְתַּלֵּק הַבְּאֵר.
[630] *Shir Hashirim Rabbah* 4:14 on Song of Songs 7:4 מתה מרים ופסקה הבאר... וחזרה בזכות משה ואהרן.

eve.[631] The *Maharal* notes that the *Mishnah* does not say that the wellspring itself was created then, only its opening. He therefore takes the view that the wellspring itself did not travel through the desert. Rather, its opening miraculously followed the Jews and provided them with water.[632]

Rabbi Chiya states that the wellspring looked like a kind of round sieve.[633] The *Midrash* adds that it resembled a round beehive which rolled along as Israel journeyed through the Sinai Desert. Whenever they camped, it came to rest in the courtyard of the Tent of Meeting (אֹהֶל מוֹעֵד). The leaders of the Tribes came, stood next to it, and declared, "Arise well!" The water would then rise.[634]

The *Torah* tells how Sarah's servant, Hagar, fled to the desert where an angel appeared to her next to a spring.[635] Hagar recognized *Hashem* speaking through the angel as "the God who sees me," so the spring came to be known as *Lachai Ro'ee* (לַחַי רֹאִי) meaning, "the Living One sees me."[636] This was the same wellspring.[637]

---

[631] *Pirkei Avoth* 5:6 עֲשָׂרָה דְבָרִים נִבְרְאוּ בְּעֶרֶב שַׁבָּת בֵּין הַשְּׁמָשׁוֹת, וְאֵלוּ הֵן... וּפִי הַבְּאֵר

[632] *Derech Chaim* 5:6 ולא אמר רק 'פי הבאר'. אבל נראה לומר כי בכל מקום שהיו הולכים הבאר עולה ונובע מים ונברא אל הבאר הזה פה שיצאו המים בכל מקום שהולכין, ולכך קאמר 'פי הבאר'.

[633] B.T. *Shabbath* 35A אָמַר רַבִּי חִיָּיא: הָרוֹצֶה לִרְאוֹת בְּאֵרָהּ שֶׁל מִרְיָם יַעֲלֶה לְרֹאשׁ הַכַּרְמֶל וְיִצְפֶּה וְיִרְאֶה כְּמִין כְּבָרָה בַּיָּם וְזוֹ הִיא בְּאֵרָהּ שֶׁל מִרְיָם.

[634] *Bamidbar Rabbah* 1:2 והיאך הייתה הבאר עשויה? סלע כמין כוורת הייתה ומתגלגלת ובאת עמהם במסעות. וכיוון שהיו הדגלים חונים והמשכן עומד, היה אותו הסלע בא ויושב לו בחצר אהל מועד, והנשיאים באים ועומדים על גביו ואומרים, "עֲלִי בְאֵר" (במדבר כ"א, י"ז), והייתה עולה.

[635] Genesis 16:6-7 (ו) וַיֹּאמֶר אַבְרָם אֶל שָׂרַי הִנֵּה שִׁפְחָתֵךְ בְּיָדֵךְ עֲשִׂי לָהּ הַטּוֹב בְּעֵינָיִךְ וַתְּעַנֶּהָ שָׂרַי וַתִּבְרַח מִפָּנֶיהָ. (ז) וַיִּמְצָאָהּ מַלְאַךְ ה' עַל עֵין הַמַּיִם בַּמִּדְבָּר עַל הָעַיִן בְּדֶרֶךְ שׁוּר.

[636] Genesis 16:13-14 (יג) וַתִּקְרָא שֵׁם ה' הַדֹּבֵר אֵלֶיהָ אַתָּה אֵ-ל רֳאִי כִּי אָמְרָה הֲגַם הֲלֹם רָאִיתִי אַחֲרֵי רֹאִי. (יד) עַל כֵּן קָרָא לַבְּאֵר בְּאֵר לַחַי רֹאִי הִנֵּה בֵין קָדֵשׁ וּבֵין בָּרֶד.

Yalkut Simoni, Breishith 109 "!רְאֵה בעלבוני" שישבה על הבאר ואמרה לחי עולמים

In the alternative, לַחַי רֹאִי refers to the angel who appeared there (Onkelos ad. loc. (על כן קרא לבארא בארא דמלאך קימא אתחזי.

[637] *Imrei Emeth, Parashath Vayera* ואותה הבאר הנקראת "בְּאֵר לַחַי רֹאִי" הלכה עם ישראל במדבר מ' שנה.

Later, Abraham gave Hagar and Ishmael supplies and sent them away. When their water ran out, the *Torah* states that, "God opened [*Hagar's*] eyes, and she saw a spring of water and went and filled the skin bottle with water and gave drink to the lad."[638] This was also the same wellspring.[639]

When Jacob journeyed to Padan Aram to seek a wife, he found a wellspring covered by a huge stone which the local shepherds could only roll away when all were present working together. When Jacob saw Rachel, however, he rolled the stone away all by himself.[640] That, too, was Miriam's wellspring.[641]

✺ Why Miriam Merited the Wellspring

The *Midrash* states that Miriam merited the wellspring because of the song she led at the Reed Sea,[642] but the *Zohar* asserts that it was her willingness to wait to see what would befall *Moshe Rabbeinu* when his mother set him adrift in the Nile River that caused her to merit the wellspring.[643] A third opinion is that

---

[638] Genesis 21:19 וַיִּפְקַח אֱלֹהִים אֶת עֵינֶיהָ וַתֵּרֶא בְּאֵר מָיִם וַתֵּלֶךְ וַתְּמַלֵּא אֶת הַחֵמֶת מַיִם וַתַּשְׁקְ אֶת הַנָּעַר

[639] *Ramban* on Numbers 20: 8 שהיה מעולם באר נסי מקור מים נובע בכל מקום שיהיה שם הרצון עליו. העלה אותו לישמעאל במדבר באר שבע ונבקע בחורב מן הצור ההוא שהיה שם.

[640] Genesis 29:8 and 10 (ח) וַיֹּאמְרוּ לֹא נוּכַל עַד אֲשֶׁר יֵאָסְפוּ כָּל הָעֲדָרִים וְגָלְלוּ אֶת הָאֶבֶן מֵעַל פִּי הַבְּאֵר וְהִשְׁקִינוּ הַצֹּאן. (י) וַיְהִי כַּאֲשֶׁר רָאָה יַעֲקֹב אֶת רָחֵל בַּת לָבָן אֲחִי אִמּוֹ וְאֶת צֹאן לָבָן אֲחִי אִמּוֹ וַיִּגַּשׁ יַעֲקֹב וַיָּגֶל אֶת הָאֶבֶן מֵעַל פִּי הַבְּאֵר וַיַּשְׁקְ אֶת צֹאן לָבָן אֲחִי אִמּוֹ.

[641] *Yalkut Shimoni* on Genesis 29, paragraph 123 (בראשית כ"ט, ב') "וַיַּרְא וְהִנֵּה בְאֵר בַּשָּׂדֶה" – זה הבאר

Brith Avraham comments on *Yalkut Shimoni* והיה והוא סלע שזבין ממנו מים מתגלגל והולך עם ישראל במדבר.

מַאן בְּאֵר ? דָּא הוּא דִכְתִּיב, "בְּאֵר חֲפָרוּהָ שָׂרִים כָּרוּהָ נְדִיבֵי הָעָם" (במדבר כ"א, *Zohar* III:62A י"ח).

[642] *Bamidbar Rabbah* 1:2 והבאר בזכות מרים שאמרה שירה על המים

[643] *Zohar* III:103A בְּאֵר בְּזְכוּת מִרְיָם, דְּהָא הִיא וַדַּאי בְּאֵר אִתְקְרֵי. וּבְסִפְרָא דְּאַגַּדְתָּא, (שמות ב') וַתְּתַצַּב אֲחוֹתוֹ מֵרָחוֹק לְדֵעָה וְגוֹ'" (שמות ב', ד'). דָּא הוּא בְּאֵר מַיִם חַיִּים, וְכֹלָּא קְשׁוּרָא חַד.

Abraham's trait of bestowing kindness caused Miriam to merit the wellspring.[644]

According to the *Ramban*, the wellspring originally flowed like a river. After Miriam died, it only held water like a well one digs in the ground.[645] *Etz Hada'ath Tov* adds that it flowed only for Israel, but not for the mixed multitude.[646]

৪৩ The Source of Moshe Rabbeinu's Prophetic Ability

The term "Adam" (אָדָם) includes both genders, as the *Torah* states: "Male and female He created them, and He blessed them and called their name 'Adam' (אָדָם) on the day He created them."[647] According to Rabbi Sh'muel bar Nachman, Adam and Chavah were created together as one unit, and *Hashem* then separated them.[648] Being created directly by *Hashem*, they possessed natural prophetic powers which they lost after they sinned.[649] To restore this prophetic power required a reunification of male and

---

[644] *Megaleh Amukoth, Parashath Devarim* אברהם בעל גמילות חסדים שבזכות זה הייתה מרים מפרנסת הדור במדבר – באר של מרים. לכן ראשי תיבות מ"י י"תן ר"אשי מ"ים – ראשי תיבות "מרים" שבזכותה היו ישראל יונקים מבאר מים חיים ומידת אברהם נמשלה למים.

[645] *Ramban* on Exodus 17:5 ואף על פי שהיה הכל באר של מרים, כקבלת רבותינו (במדבר י"ט, כ"ה), יתכן שהיה בפעם הראשון וכל הארבעים שנה מושך מים כנהרות שוטפות, ובפעם השנית מפני העונש אשר היה שם נעשה כמו באר חפורה מלאה מים חיים.

[646] *Kithvei Ha'arizal, Etz Hada'ath Tov, Parashath Chukath* ועתה במות מרים חזרה הבאר גם הוא בזכות משה ולכן נתמעט קצת כוחו במיתת מרים ולא נתחזק כבראשונה ולא יצא רק להשקות את ישראל הנקראים עדה ולא את הערב רב.

See, however, *Pardes Yosef* on Exodus 17:6 who states that Miriam's merit was not as great as *Moshe Rabbeinu's* (ומרים לא היה זכותה גדול כל כך כמשה, ולא היה בכוח דבור בעלמא... אבל אחר כך כשחזר בזכות משה היה יכול לפעול אף בדבור, אבל משה רבינו שהיה עניו לא רצה לדבר ולהראות שזכותו גדול ממרים ולזה הכה).

[647] Genesis 5:2 זָכָר וּנְקֵבָה בְּרָאָם וַיְבָרֶךְ אֹתָם וַיִּקְרָא אֶת שְׁמָם אָדָם בְּיוֹם הִבָּרְאָם

[648] *Breishith Rabbah* 8:1 אמר רב שמואל בר נחמן: בשעה שברא הקב"ה את אדם הראשון דיו-פרצופים בראו ונסרו.

[649] *Tifereth Yehonathan* on Genesis 2:25 כן היו אז קודם החטא אדם וחווה במדרגת נבואה

Shoshan Sodoth 13 צריך אתה לדעת כי אדם וחווה כשנבראו בקומתם ובצביונם ובדעתם נבאו, כי לא הייתה סיבה אחר סיבה כשאר בני אדם כי מכוח עליון נבראו.

female.[650] Accordingly, the prophetically inspired song at the Reed Sea had to include both males and females, with *Moshe Rabbeinu* leading the men and Miriam leading the women.[651]

৪৩৪৩ Extra Understanding (בִּינָה יְתֵירָה)

The rabbis state that, "The Holy One, Blessed be He, gave extra understanding to women beyond [what He gave to] men."[652]

"Understanding" (בִּינָה) means deriving one thing from another, that is to say, figuring out implications.[653] "Extra understanding" (בִּינָה יְתֵירָה) therefore suggests an enhanced ability to foresee the outcome of a given course of action — how one thing leads to another.

People fall prey to the enticement of the evil inclination when they fail to fully appreciate the consequences of their actions. *Hashem* created Chavah in the hope that she would shield Adam from the evil inclination by using her extra understanding (בִּינָה יְתֵירָה) to call his attention to those consequences. That is why *Hashem* said, "I will fashion a helper against him" (עֵזֶר כְּנֶגְדּוֹ),[654] rather than "a helper for him" (עֵזֶר לוֹ). The expression "against him" indicates that sometimes a wife helps her husband by opposing him and pointing out the flaws in a course of action he plans to take. Although Chavah failed in this regard, righteous women who lived after her had this ability.

---

[650] *Beth Elokim, Sha'ar Hayesodoth* 56 שאין שום נביא מתנבא כי אם בהיותו כבר נשוי שהוא אדם שלם, כדכתיב, "זָכָר וּנְקֵבָה בְּרָאָם...וַיִּקְרָא אֶת שְׁמָם אָדָם" (בראשית ה׳, ב׳). כי אז נפשו שלימה עם נפש האישה הנאצלת מנפשו בזיווג ראשון.

[651] *Sifthei Kohen* on Exodus 15:20 מן הראוי שלא יקלסו אלא אנשים עם נשים... וכן מצינו שרה כשאמר הקב״ה, "כֹּל אֲשֶׁר תֹּאמַר אֵלֶיךָ שָׂרָה שְׁמַע בְּקֹלָהּ", שאמרו ז״ל (שמות רבה א׳, א׳) שאברהם היה טפל לשרה בנבואה כדי שתהיה נבואתו שלימה בהיות הנבואה מזכר ונקבה.

[652] B.T. *Niddah* 45B שֶׁנָּתַן הַקָּדוֹשׁ בָּרוּךְ הוּא בִּינָה יְתֵירָה בָּאִשָּׁה יוֹתֵר מִבָּאִישׁ

[653] B.T. *Chagigah* 14A וְנָבוֹן זֶה הַמֵּבִין דָּבָר מִתּוֹךְ דָּבָר

[654] Genesis 2:18 וַיֹּאמֶר ה׳ אֱ-לֹהִים לֹא טוֹב הֱיוֹת הָאָדָם לְבַדּוֹ אֶעֱשֶׂה לּוֹ עֵזֶר כְּנֶגְדּוֹ

This is why the *Torah* records that, "*Hashem* said to Jacob, 'Return to the land of your fathers and to your birthplace, and I will be with you,'"[655] and then describes how Jacob first consulted Rachel and Leah before leaving Laban.

Once God ordered Jacob to do something, one would expect him to obey without hesitation. Why did he first consult his wives?

With the exception of *Moshe Rabbeinu*, who served as a mouthpiece for the Divine Presence,[656] prophets experience their prophecies in ways each can personally understand, perceiving their prophetic visions in the context of their individual backgrounds and personalities.[657] Knowing this, Jacob was concerned that perhaps he had misinterpreted what God had revealed to him. He therefore consulted Rachel and Leah and only proceeded when they said, "Whatever God has told you, do,"[658] agreeing that he had correctly understood matters.

Likewise, Rabbi Elazar ben Azariah consulted his wife before accepting the position of head of the *Sanhedrin*. The fact that he was offered such a position shows that he possessed superior intellect. Nevertheless, because he knew that a man might sometimes overlook something a woman sees, he refused to accept the appointment without first consulting his wife.[659]

---

[655] Genesis 31:3 וַיֹּאמֶר ה' אֶל יַעֲקֹב שׁוּב אֶל אֶרֶץ אֲבוֹתֶיךָ וּלְמוֹלַדְתֶּךָ וְאֶהְיֶה עִמָּךְ

[656] *Malbim* on Exodus 3:2 שהייתה שכינה מדברת מתוך גרונו של משה

[657] For example, King Josiah consulted the Prophet Huldah rather than Jeremiah because "women are merciful," and the king reasoned that Huldah's prophecy would be influenced by her merciful nature (B.T. *Megillah* 14B וְיֹאשִׁיָּה (גּוּפֵיהּ הֵיכִי שָׁבִיק יִרְמְיָה וּמְשַׁדַּר לְגַבָּהּ? אַמְרֵי דְּבֵי רַבִּי שִׁילָא: מִפְּנֵי שֶׁהַנָּשִׁים רַחֲמָנִיּוֹת הֵן).

[658] Genesis 31:16 כִּי כָל הָעֹשֶׁר אֲשֶׁר הִצִּיל אֱ-לֹהִים מֵאָבִינוּ לָנוּ הוּא וּלְבָנֵינוּ וְעַתָּה כֹּל אֲשֶׁר אָמַר אֱ-לֹהִים אֵלֶיךָ עֲשֵׂה.

[659] B.T. *Berachoth* 27B. אָמַר לְהוּ: אֵיזִיל וְאִימְלִיךְ בְּאִינְשֵׁי בֵּיתִי. אָזַל וְאִמְלִיךְ בִּדְבֵיתְהוּ.

৪৩৪৩৪৩ Miriam Enabled Moshe Rabbeinu to Achieve a Level of Prophecy no other Prophet can ever Match

No other prophet can ever rival *Moshe Rabbeinu*, whose prophecy was unique in that the Divine Presence spoke with him just as one person speaks to another.[660] Although the entire Jewish nation had direct contact with the Divine Presence at the Giving of the *Torah*, that was only a brief exceptional occurrence.[661] By contrast, *Moshe Rabbeinu* experienced this level of prophecy on an ongoing basis.

What enabled *Moshe Rabbeinu* to achieve this high spiritual level?

The *Gemara* states:

> Amram was the leader of the generation [of Jews who lived in Egypt, and everyone listened to him]. When the wicked Pharaoh decreed, "Every son who is born you shall cast into the river,"[662] [Amram] declared, "For naught we toil [to have children]," [so] he arose and divorced his wife. [All the other men followed his lead,] arose, and divorced their wives.
>
> His daughter [Miriam] admonished him, "Father, your decree is worse than Pharaoh's, for Pharaoh decreed only against the males, but you decreed against [both] the males and the females. Pharaoh did not decree except for this world, but you decreed [both] for this world and the world to come.[663]

---

[660] Exodus 33:11 וְדִבֶּר ה' אֶל מֹשֶׁה פָּנִים אֶל פָּנִים כַּאֲשֶׁר יְדַבֵּר אִישׁ אֶל רֵעֵהוּ וְשָׁב אֶל הַמַּחֲנֶה וּמְשָׁרְתוֹ יְהוֹשֻׁעַ בִּן נוּן נַעַר לֹא יָמִישׁ מִתּוֹךְ הָאֹהֶל.

Deuteronomy 34:10 וְלֹא קָם נָבִיא עוֹד בְּיִשְׂרָאֵל כְּמֹשֶׁה אֲשֶׁר יְדָעוֹ ה' פָּנִים אֶל פָּנִים

[661] Deuteronomy 5:4 פָּנִים בְּפָנִים דִּבֶּר ה' עִמָּכֶם בָּהָר מִתּוֹךְ הָאֵשׁ

[662] Exodus 1:22 וַיְצַו פַּרְעֹה לְכָל עַמּוֹ לֵאמֹר כָּל הַבֵּן הַיִּלּוֹד הַיְאֹרָה תַּשְׁלִיכֻהוּ וְכָל הַבַּת תְּחַיּוּן

[663] *Rashi* explains that if a child is never born, it cannot enjoy the world to come, but if it is born, then even if it dies prematurely, it has a share in the world to come (*Rashi* on B.T. *Sotah* 12A, sub verba *"Ella Ba'olam Hazeh"* (אלא בעולם הזה):
(אתה גזרת בעולם הזה ובעולם הבא שכיוון שאינם נולדים, אינן באין לעולם הבא.

Pharaoh is wicked, [so] it is doubtful whether his decree will be fulfilled. You are righteous, [so] surely your decree will be fulfilled."

[Upon hearing this, Amram] arose and remarried his wife, [leading to the birth of *Moshe Rabbeinu*].[664]

Most adults are reluctant to accept the advice of a child over their own thinking. Moreover, Amram was a highly intelligent, learned man and the leader of his generation. Nonetheless, Amram was aware that women, who have extra understanding (בִּינָה יְתֵירָה), sometimes possess insight into a situation which men lack. He therefore carefully reconsidered his position and realized that Miriam was right.

ಞಞಞ Miriam's Extra Understanding and Faith

Understanding how things may work out differently than anticipated is the key to faith in God.[665] People constantly observe that the righteous suffer but the wicked prosper. Nevertheless, loyal Jews recognize that they are not seeing everything there is to see and that what appears to be unjust is really for the best.

In the alternative, *Hashem* rewards those who perform *Mitzvoth* regardless of any outcome. Accordingly, Jews are rewarded for having children notwithstanding what happens to them after they are born. (See B.T. *Berachoth*

"וַיָּבוֹא אֵלָיו יְשַׁעְיָהוּ בֶן אָמוֹץ הַנָּבִיא, וַיֹּאמֶר אֵלָיו, כֹּה אָמַר ה' צְבָאוֹת, צַו לְבֵיתֶךָ כִּי מֵת אַתָּה וְלֹא תִחְיֶה 10A וְגוֹ'" (ישעיה כ:א, ל"ח, א'). מַאי "כִּי מֵת אַתָּה וְלֹא תִחְיֶה"? "מֵת אַתָּה" בָּעוֹלָם הַזֶּה, וְ"לֹא תִחְיֶה" לָעוֹלָם הַבָּא. אָמַר לֵיהּ: "מַאי כּוּלֵי הַאי?" אָמַר לֵיהּ: "מִשּׁוּם דְּלָא עָסַקְתְּ בִּפְרָיָה וּרְבִיָּה". אָמַר לֵיהּ: "מִשּׁוּם דְּחַזַּאי לִי בְּרוּחַ הַקֹּדֶשׁ דְּנַפְקֵי מִנָּאי בְּנִין דְּלָא מַעֲלוּ". אָמַר לֵיהּ: "בַּהֲדֵי כַּבְשֵׁי דְּרַחֲמָנָא לָמָּה לָךְ? מַאי דְּמִפְקַדְתְּ אִיבָּעֵי לָךְ לְמֶעֱבַד, (וּמַה דְּנִיחָא קַמֵּיהּ קוּדְשָׁא בְּרִיךְ הוּא, לַעֲבֵיד".

[664] B.T. *Sotah* 12A תָּנָא: עַמְרָם גְּדוֹל הַדּוֹר הָיָה. כֵּיוָן (שֶׁרָאָה שֶׁאָמַר) [שֶׁגָּזַר] פַּרְעֹה הָרָשָׁע, "כָּל הַבֵּן הַיִּלּוֹד הַיְאֹרָה תַּשְׁלִיכֻהוּ" (שמות א', כ"ב), אָמַר: "לַשָּׁוְא אָנוּ עֲמֵלִין". עָמַד וְגֵירַשׁ אֶת אִשְׁתּוֹ. עָמְדוּ כּוּלָּן וְגֵירְשׁוּ נְשׁוֹתֵיהֶן. אָמְרָה לוֹ בִּתּוֹ: "אַבָּא, קָשָׁה גְּזֵירָתְךָ יוֹתֵר מִשֶּׁל פַּרְעֹה, שֶׁפַּרְעֹה לֹא גָּזַר אֶלָּא עַל הַזְּכָרִים וְאַתָּה גָּזַרְתָּ עַל הַזְּכָרִים וְעַל הַנְּקֵבוֹת. פַּרְעֹה לֹא גָּזַר אֶלָּא בָּעוֹלָם הַזֶּה, וְאַתָּה גָּזַרְתָּ בָּעוֹלָם הַזֶּה וְלָעוֹלָם הַבָּא. פַּרְעֹה רָשָׁע, סָפֵק מִתְקַיֶּימֶת גְּזֵרָתוֹ, סָפֵק אֵינָהּ מִתְקַיֶּימֶת. אַתָּה צַדִּיק, בְּוַדַּאי שֶׁגְּזֵירָתְךָ מִתְקַיֶּימֶת... עָמַד וְהֶחֱזִיר אֶת אִשְׁתּוֹ.

[665] *Tikunei Zohar* 2A וְהָאֱמוּנָה דְּאִיהִי בִּינָה; *Kehillath Yaakov, Erech Emunah* בינה נקרא אמונה

Miriam's ability to foresee how things might work out differently from the way her father anticipated reflected an extremely high level of extra understanding (בִּינָה יְתֵירָה). The rabbis therefore identify Miriam with the loftiest level of the spiritual world of Understanding (בִּינָה).[666]

Moshe Rabbeinu's birth was the direct result of Miriam's superior understanding and faith.

When *Moshe Rabbeinu* was three months old, his mother hid him in a basket among the reeds at the edge of the Nile River to evade the Egyptian soldiers who sought him.[667] Amram tapped Miriam on the head and said, "My daughter, what became of your prophecy?" Nevertheless, Miriam faithfully waited at the riverbank to see how her prophecy would be fulfilled.[668]

Hashem controls royal decision-making, as the *Tanach* states, "The heart of a king is [like] a stream of water in the hand of *Hashem*. He directs it wherever He desires."[669] Miriam therefore reasoned that Pharaoh would not have issued a decree to throw all baby boys into the Nile River unless *Hashem* wanted it. At the same time, she knew that *Hashem* can cause matters to develop in unexpected ways. The literal wording of the decree was, "Every son who is born you shall cast into the river."[670] Since Pharaoh mentioned nothing about drowning, Miriam realized that once her mother placed the basket with her baby brother into the river, the decree had been fulfilled and salvation was at hand. Thus, the very first salvation *Moshe Rabbeinu* experienced

---

[666] *Dan Yadin* 13 סוד 'בינה דכתר שבכתר' היא סוד מרים הנביאה

[667] Exodus 2:2-3 (ב) וַתַּהַר הָאִשָּׁה וַתֵּלֶד בֵּן וַתֵּרֶא אֹתוֹ כִּי טוֹב הוּא וַתִּצְפְּנֵהוּ שְׁלֹשָׁה יְרָחִים. (ג) וְלֹא יָכְלָה עוֹד הַצְּפִינוֹ וַתִּקַּח לוֹ תֵּבַת גֹּמֶא וַתַּחְמְרָה בַחֵמָר וּבַזָּפֶת וַתָּשֶׂם בָּהּ אֶת הַיֶּלֶד וַתָּשֶׂם בַּסּוּף עַל שְׂפַת הַיְאֹר.

[668] B.T. *Sotah* 13A וְכֵיוָן שֶׁהִטִּילוֹהוּ לַיְאוֹר, עָמַד אָבִיהָ וּטְפָחָהּ עַל רֹאשָׁהּ. אָמַר לָהּ: "בִּתִּי הֵיכָן נְבוּאָתֵךְ?" וְהַיְינוּ דִּכְתִיב, "וַתֵּתַצַּב אֲחֹתוֹ מֵרָחֹק לְדֵעָה מַה יֵּעָשֶׂה לוֹ" (שמות ב', ד') — מַה יְּהֵא בְּסוֹף נְבוּאָתָהּ.

[669] Proverbs 21:1 פַּלְגֵי מַיִם לֶב מֶלֶךְ בְּיַד ה' עַל כָּל אֲשֶׁר יַחְפֹּץ יַטֶּנּוּ

[670] Exodus 1:22 וַיְצַו פַּרְעֹה לְכָל עַמּוֹ לֵאמֹר כָּל הַבֵּן הַיִּלּוֹד הַיְאֹרָה תַּשְׁלִיכֻהוּ וְכָל הַבַּת תְּחַיּוּן

was based on Miriam's exceptional faith and understanding, and it too laid the foundation for his ability to achieve an unparalleled level of prophecy.

❧❧❧❧ Faith (אֱמוּנָה) is a Prerequisite for Prophecy

Miriam's name (מִרְיָם) means "bitterness,"[671] but if the vowels are changed, it means to "elevate" (מֵרִים).[672] Miriam had a special ability to see the good in any situation and thereby elevate bitterness and convert it into sweetness. Her high level of faith gave her a unique merit which converted the unpalatable bitter waters at Rephidim into sweet, drinkable water.[673] As *Arvei Nachal* explains, Miriam's superior understanding was so powerful that she attached a physical rock to its spiritual source so that water flowed from it.[674]

No human being can achieve prophecy without intense faith in *Hashem* because prophecy entails a relationship with *Hashem* which surpasses any relationship available through intellect — a perception rather than a mere logical inference. Since *Moshe Rabbeinu's* birth and subsequent rescue from the Nile River were intertwined with Miriam's intense faith, he gained the potential to experience a unique form of prophecy.

The letters of Miriam's name (מִרְיָם) can be rearranged to mean the "head, or source, of waters" (ר' מַיִם). The sages teach that the *Torah* is compared to water,[675] and they call faith "a

---

[671] *Yalkut Shimoni* on Exodus 1, paragraph 162 מרים שנקראת על שם המרור

[672] See, for example, Exodus 35:24 כָּל מֵרִים תְּרוּמַת כֶּסֶף וּנְחֹשֶׁת הֵבִיאוּ אֵת תְּרוּמַת ה' וְכֹל אֲשֶׁר נִמְצָא אִתּוֹ עֲצֵי שִׁטִּים לְכָל מְלֶאכֶת הָעֲבֹדָה הֵבִיאוּ.

[673] *Rabbeinu Bachye* on Exodus 17:6 הצור הזה שברפידים הוא הסלע שבקדש – הכל אחד, והוא היה בארה של מרים.

[674] *Arvei Nachal, Parashath Chukath* שמרים במדרגתה הגדולה ורוח מבינתה וקדשה פתחה המקור והשורש העליון של הסלע, (ככל נמצא שיש לו שורש בגבהי מרומים וגבוה מעל גבוה), והיה השורש ההוא שופע על אותו הסלע יום ולילה.

[675] B.T. *Baba Kama* 17A וְאֵין מַיִם אֶלָּא תוֹרָה

wellspring which is the source of living waters."[676] Miriam's exceptionally powerful faith was the wellspring, or source, of *Moshe Rabbeinu's* ability to receive the *Torah* and transmit it to Israel.[677]

When the Jews rejoiced with song after crossing the Reed Sea, the *Torah* records how Miriam and the women sang with drums, whereas the men did not. *Rashi* explains that the women had greater faith than the men. They foresaw that *Hashem* would perform miracles for them which would warrant song, so they brought drums with them when they left Egypt.[678]

Moshe Rabbeinu led the men in prophetic song at their level while Miriam led the women at their higher level. Both songs were essential elements of the Divine revelation which occurred at the Reed Sea.[679]

---

[676] *Zohar* III:266A. בְּאֵר מְקוֹר מַיִם חַיִּים – דָּא רְשׁוּתָא קַדִּישָׁא, מְהֵימְנוּתָא קַדִּישָׁא.

[677] See *Zohar* I:141B בֵּירָא דְּמַיִּין נָבְעִין הַאי אִיהוּ רָזָא עִלָּאָה בְּגוֹ רָזָא דִּמְהֵימְנוּתָא. בֵּירָא דְּאִית בֵּיהּ מוֹצָא מַיִם, וְאִיהוּ בֵּירָא דְּאִתְמַלְּיָא מֵהַהוּא מוֹצָא מַיִם, וְאִינּוּן תְּרֵין דַּרְגִּין דְּאִינּוּן חַד, דְּכַר וְנוּקְבָּא כְּחֲדָא כְּדְקָא יָאוּת.

[678] *Rashi* on Exodus 15:20 "בְּתֻפִּים וּבִמְחֹלֹת" – מובטחות היו צדקניות שבדור שהקדוש ברוך הוא עושה להם נסים והוציאו תופים ממצרים.

[679] Rabbi Moshe Feinstein notes that although the *Torah* excuses women from a number of *Mitzvoth* that are incumbent upon men, when it comes to prophecy the same rules apply to both genders (*Iggroth Moshe, Orach Chayim* 4, Responsa 49 והרבה מהנשים שהיו נביאות ויש להן כל דיני נביא שבאנשים, ובהרבה דברים נשתבחו בין בקראי (בין בדברי חז"ל עוד יותר מלאנשים.).

Rabbeinu Bachye on Exodus 15:20 מרים הנביאה מקלסת לשכינה וכל הנשים אחריה ואומרת השירה הזו בעצמה כמשה ובני ישראל. ועוד תמצא עיקרים גדולים שבתורה מפורשים על ידי נשים כעניין העולם הבא הנקרא "צְרוֹר הַחַיִּים" על ידי אביגיל, ועניין תחיית המתים וסדרי תחינה על ידי חנה, ועניין הגלגול על ידי התקועית.

৪০৪০৪০৪০ The Song at the Reed Sea on a Deeper Level

The sounds, shapes, and numeric values of the letters of the Hebrew alphabet correspond to the spiritual worlds.[680] Songs and music also have a relationship to those worlds.[681]

Ordinary speech consists of emitting sounds within a limited range of frequencies, or pitches. Song, however, entails matching syllables of speech to a wider range of pitches in special patterns according to a rhythm. Sound travels in a wave-like pattern of concentric spheres emanating from a given source. This resembles the spiritual worlds which are likened to concentric spheres.[682]

At the Reed Sea, the Jews experienced a revelation of spirituality in which they perceived the supernal spheres. They were inspired to sing because song parallels the process of arranging and rearranging *Hashem's* Divine light in patterns which resemble concentric spheres, a process which is the source of Creation.[683]

---

[680] *Sefer Yetzirah* 1:1 ובּרא את עולמו בשלשה ספרים – בּספר וספר ספור

[681] *Chatham Sofer* on Leviticus 25:8 (א ,ק"נ תהלים) "הַלְלוּ אֶ-ל בְּקָדְשׁוֹ" כי במזמור תראה הנה נאמר עשרה מיני שיר שהם נגד עשר [ספירות].

[682] See *Sefer Hapliah* sub verba "*Gam Amar Li*" (לי אמר גם):
שאמרו רבותינו ז"ל: "כל השירים קודש, ושיר השירים קודש קדשים" – רוצה לומר הוא ספירות קודש.

Parenthetically, *Sefer Hapliah* and others seem to have had a version of the *Mishnah* in *Yadayim* 3:5 which differed slightly from the Romm Vilna edition which quotes Rabbi Akiva as saying: שֶׁכָּל הַכְּתוּבִים קֹדֶשׁ, וְשִׁיר הַשִּׁירִים קֹדֶשׁ קֳדָשִׁים

[683] *Likutei Halachoth, Even Ha'ezer, Hilchoth Pirya Verivyah Ve'ishuth* 3 בַּעֲשָׂרָה"
מַאֲמָרוֹת נִבְרָא הָעוֹלָם וְכוּ'", כְּמוֹ שֶׁכָּתוּב, "בִּדְבַר ה' שָׁמַיִם נַעֲשׂוּ וּבְרוּחַ פִּיו כָּל צְבָאָם", 'דְּבַר ה'', וְ'רוּחַ פִּיו', זֶה בְּחִינַת קוֹלוֹת וְדִבּוּרִים שֶׁכְּלוּלִים בַּעֲשָׂרָה מִינֵי נְגִינָה שֶׁבָּהֶם נִבְרְאוּ כָּל הָעוֹלָמוֹת.

෨෨෨෨෨ Moshe Rabbeinu's Gravesite

According to some opinions, *Moshe Rabbeinu's* gravesite was among the items created at twilight on the first Sabbath eve.[684]

What supernatural characteristic did the gravesite possess?

The *Torah* states:

> Moses, the servant of *Hashem*, died there in the Land of Moab by the mouth of *Hashem*. [God] buried him in the valley in the Land of Moab opposite Beth Pe'or, and no man knows the site of his grave until this day.[685]

This passage contains an obvious contradiction. It identifies the location of *Moshe Rabbeinu's* gravesite but then states that no one knows where it is!

A story in the *Gemara* compounds this mystery:

> The Evil Empire [of Rome] sent [an order] to the governor of Beth Pe'or [commanding], "Find out where *Moshe* is buried!"
>
> [When the governor's men] stood above [the gravesite], it appeared to be below them. [When they stood] below, it appeared to be above them.
>
> They divided into two units, [with one going above and the other going below]. For those who stood above, it appeared to be below. For those below, it appeared to be above, [so as] to fulfill that which is written, "And no man knows the site of his grave."

---

[684] *Pirkei Avoth* 5:6   וְיֵשׁ אוֹמְרִים: אַף הַמַּזִּיקִין וּקְבוּרָתוֹ שֶׁל מֹשֶׁה

[685] Deuteronomy 34:5-6   (ה) וַיָּמָת שָׁם מֹשֶׁה עֶבֶד ה' בְּאֶרֶץ מוֹאָב עַל פִּי ה'. (ו) וַיִּקְבֹּר אֹתוֹ בַגַּי בְּאֶרֶץ מוֹאָב מוּל בֵּית פְּעוֹר וְלֹא יָדַע אִישׁ אֶת קְבֻרָתוֹ עַד הַיּוֹם הַזֶּה.

Rabbi Chama, son of Rabbi Chanina, added: Even *Moshe Rabbeinu* does not know where he is buried![686]

To understand all this requires analyzing another *Talmudic* passage:

Both Rav and Sh'muel agree: Fifty gates of understanding were created in the world, and all of them were given to Moshe except one, as it says, "You made him a bit less than God."[687] [688]

Why do Rav and Sh'muel use the roundabout expression, "Fifty gates of understanding were created in the world, and all of them were given to *Moshe* except one"? Why not simply say that forty-nine gates of understanding were given to *Moshe Rabbeinu*?

The answer is that *Moshe Rabbeinu* partially grasped the fiftieth gate of understanding. That fiftieth gate is called "except one" or "lacking one" (חָסֵר אָחָת) because it consists of recognizing our lack of ability to grasp *Hashem*.[689]

---

[686] B.T. *Sotah* 13B-14A "שָׁלְחָה מַלְכוּת הָרְשָׁעָה אֵצֶל גַּסְטְרָא שֶׁל בֵּית פְּעוֹר: "הַרְאֵנוּ הֵיכָן מֹשֶׁה קָבוּר!" עָמְדוּ לְמַעְלָה, נִדְמָה לָהֶם לְמַטָּה. לְמַטָּה, נִדְמָה לָהֶם לְמַעְלָה. נֶחְלְקוּ לִשְׁתֵּי כִּיתוֹת. אוֹתָן שֶׁעוֹמְדִים לְמַעְלָה, נִדְמָה לָהֶן לְמַטָּה. לְמַטָּה, נִדְמָה לָהֶן לְמַעְלָה. לְקַיֵּים מַה שֶׁנֶּאֱמַר, "וְלֹא יָדַע אִישׁ אֶת קְבֻרָתוֹ" (דברים ל"ד, ו'). רַבִּי חָמָא בְּרַבִּי חֲנִינָא אָמַר: אַף מֹשֶׁה רַבֵּנוּ אֵינוֹ יוֹדֵעַ הֵיכָן קָבוּר!

The *Torah* itself hints at this bizarre phenomenon when it states that *Moshe Rabbeinu* was buried in a valley that, ironically, was situated at the top of a mountain. (See *Rabbeinu Bachye* on Deuteronomy 3:39 "וַיֵּשֶׁב בַּגַּיְא מוּל בֵּית פְּעוֹר" וכבר ישבנו בגיא הזה שהוא ראש הפסגה –.)

[687] Psalms 8:6 וַתְּחַסְּרֵהוּ מְּעַט מֵאֱ-לֹהִים וְכָבוֹד וְהָדָר תְּעַטְּרֵהוּ

[688] B.T. *Nedarim* 38A רַב וּשְׁמוּאֵל דְּאָמְרֵי תַּרְוַיְיהוּ: חֲמִשִּׁים שַׁעֲרֵי בִינָה נִבְרְאוּ בָּעוֹלָם, וְכוּלָּם נִתְּנוּ לְמֹשֶׁה חָסֵר אָחָת, שֶׁנֶּאֱמַר, "וַתְּחַסְּרֵהוּ מְּעַט מֵאֱ-לֹהִים" (תהלים ח', ו').

[689] Compare *Panim Yafoth* on Exodus 34:29 "וּמשֶׁה לֹא יָדַע כִּי קָרַן עוֹר פָּנָיו וגו'" (שמות ל"ד, כ"ט). במדרש איתא: "מאין היה לו עור פניו? משיורי דיו שבקולמוס" (ילקוט שמעוני, פרשת כי תשא, רמז ת"ז). יש להבין המשל הזה כאדם הרוצה לכתוב וממלא הקולמוס דיו ומשתייר בו. והנה אמרו חז"ל: "וַתְּחַסְּרֵהוּ מְּעַט מֵאֱ-לֹהִים" (תהלים ח:ו) חמישים שערי בינה נמסרו למשה חסר אחד" (מסכת ראש השנה כ"א, ע"ב)... מכל מקום קיבל משער החמישים והוא קרן עור פניו משיורי האור.

Likutei Halachoth, Orach Chayim, Birkath Harayach Ubirkath Hoda'ah 3 בְּשָׁעָה שֶׁהָאָדָם נִתְבַּטֵּל אֲפִלּוּ הוּא עַצְמוֹ אֵינוֹ יוֹדֵעַ

This fiftieth gate is detached from the lower levels of understanding and contrary to them because those lower levels are marked by an increasing intellectual grasp of *Hashem* whereas the fiftieth level is marked by a non-intellectual relationship to Him — a realization of human inability to fully comprehend Him. Understood this way, the fiftieth gate corresponds to faith — an understanding that extends beyond the intellect.

The *Torah* states that, "Isaac arrived after coming from the wellspring of *Lachai Ro'ee* (לַחַי רֹאִי),"[690] which was also Miriam's well. *Avodath Yisrael* notes that the phrase "after coming" (מִבּוֹא) has a numeric value of forty-nine, alluding to the forty-nine gates of understanding.[691]

Miriam's well symbolized the same concept as *Moshe Rabbeinu's* gravesite because other water sources are connected to the ground whereas it was detached from the ground and traveled with the Jews through the desert. This detachment correlated to the detachment of the fiftieth gate of understanding from the lower forty-nine gates of understanding.

ಝಝಝಝ Two Levels of Faith

There are two levels of faith — a lower, inferior level of faith (מְהֵימְנוּתָא תַּתָּאָה) and a higher, superior level (מְהֵימְנוּתָא עִלָּאָה).[692]

---

[690] Genesis 24:62 וְיִצְחָק בָּא מִבּוֹא בְּאֵר לַחַי רֹאִי וְהוּא יוֹשֵׁב בְּאֶרֶץ הַנֶּגֶב

[691] *Avodath Yisrael, Parashath Chayei Sarah* ויצחק בא "מבוא" (ככתיב) מלא גימטריא מ"ט שערי בינה.

[692] The expression "superior faith" (מְהֵימְנוּתָא עִלָּאָה) appears frequently in the *Zohar*. See, for example, Zohar I:38A.

The lower level of faith involves understanding the most one can and, on that basis, believing and accepting what one cannot understand.[693]

The higher level of faith, however, refers to directly perceiving spirituality as implied by the grammatical root of "faith" (אֱמוּנָה), which is *Amen* (אָמֵן), meaning to verify or confirm.[694] Such faith is a form of prophecy. It transcends the intellect not because it contradicts logic or because one makes a "leap of faith," but because it is more reliable than intellect and surpasses it.

One need not engage in sophisticated reasoning to conclude that ice is cold or that a candle gives off light because such phenomena are readily observable. In the same way, *Moshe Rabbeinu* and the Jews who stood at Mount Sinai did not need to engage in profound philosophical reflection to determine that God is real and that a spiritual realm exists because they observed them.[695]

Moshe Rabbeinu experienced this higher level of faith on an ongoing basis. Accordingly, he did not believe in God despite an inability to rationally understand Him — the lower level of faith. Instead, *Moshe Rabbeinu* knew that God exists because he interacted with Him.[696] Ironically, however, it was precisely this direct perception which gave him an acute realization that no one can fully comprehend God — the fiftieth gate of understanding.

---

[693] See *Pri Ha'aretz, Parashath Lech L'cha* (בראשית "וַיַּחְשְׁבֶהָ לּוֹ צְדָקָה" בַּה' "וְהֶאֱמִן", וזהו שאמר ט"ו, ר'), שכל האמונה שהשיג אחר כל העיונים והשכלים לא חשב לשום השגה כי אם למדריגה התחתונה שהוא "אמונה צדקה" שהרי כל ההשגות בטלים כנגדו יתברך.

[694] *Shefa Tal, Hakdamah Ben Meah Shanah* "אמת" פירושו "אמן"

[695] *Hayad Hachazakah, Hilchoth Yesodei Hatorah* 8:3 ...שנבואת משה רבינו אינה על פי האותות אלא בעינינו ראינוה ובאזנינו שמענוה כמו ששמע הוא.

[696] *Zohar* I:76A וְלָא הֲוָה כְּמֹשֶׁה שַׁמָּשׁ מְהֵימָן בְּכָלְהוּ דַּרְגִּין וְלָא סָטָא לְבֵיהּ בְּתִיאוּבְתָּא דְּחַד מִנַּיְיהוּ. אֶלָּא קָאִים בִּמְהֵימְנוּתָא עִלָּאָה כַּדְקָא יָאוּת.

For this reason the sages teach that, "Whereas all the other prophets saw [the Divine Presence] through non-transparent glass, *Moshe Rabbeinu* saw [the Divine Presence] through transparent glass."[697] *Rashi* explains that other prophets thought they saw *Hashem* clearly but did not, whereas *Moshe Rabbeinu* saw clearly yet realized that he was not seeing *Hashem's* "face" — His true nature.[698]

The fact that the *Torah* identifies *Moshe Rabbeinu's* burial site and yet no one knows where he is buried corresponds to this idea that people know in a general way that there is an inscrutable Creator but cannot grasp *Moshe Rabbeinu's* level of realization of how unknowable He is. As Rabbi Chama, son of Rabbi Chanina, explained, even *Moshe Rabbeinu* does not know where he is buried. Even *Moshe Rabbeinu* himself cannot rationally understand his prophetic level because it includes direct observation of the incomprehensibility of *Hashem*.[699]

The *Zohar* refers to this superior level of faith as a wellspring and teaches that its source is the harmonious unity of male and female[700] — an allusion to Miriam's wellspring and the song at the Reed Sea.

---

[697] B.T. *Yevamoth* 49B כָּל הַנְּבִיאִים נִסְתַּכְּלוּ בְּאַסְפַּקְלַרְיָא שֶׁאֵינָהּ מְאִירָה. מֹשֶׁה רַבֵּנוּ נִסְתַּכֵּל בְּאַסְפַּקְלַרְיָא הַמְּאִירָה.

[698] *Rashi* ad. loc., sub verba "*Nistachlu*" (נסתכלו): וכסבורים לראות ולא ראו. ומשה נסתכל באספקלריא המאירה וידע שלא ראהו בפניו.

[699] See *Likutei Moharan, Mahadura Kama* 65 "מֵרֹאשׁ אֲמָנָה" (שִׁיר הַשִּׁירִים ד', ח') דַּיְקָא, הַיְנוּ בְּחִינַת אֱמוּנָה עֶלְיוֹנָה זוֹ הַנַּ"ל, שֶׁהוּא רֹאשׁ לְכָל הָאֱמוּנוֹת... וְלִבְחִינַת זֶמֶר שֶׁל אֱמוּנָה הָעֶלְיוֹנָה הַזֹּאת, אֵין מִי שֶׁיִזְכֶּה, כִּי אִם צַדִּיק הַדּוֹר, שֶׁהוּא בְּחִינַת מֹשֶׁה, שֶׁהוּא בְּמַדְרֵגַת אֱמוּנָה זוֹ, שֶׁהוּא בְּחִינַת שְׁתִיקָה... הַיְנוּ שֶׁהִיא עֲדַיִן לְמַעְלָה מֵהַדִּבּוּר כַּנַּ"ל. כִּי מֹשֶׁה הוּא בְּחִינוֹת שְׁתִיקָה.

[700] *Zohar* I:141B תָּא חֲזֵי: בֵּירָא דְּמַיִן נָבְעִין, הַאי אִיהוּ רָזָא עִלָּאָה בְּגוֹ רָזָא דִּמְהֵימְנוּתָא. בֵּירָא דְּאִית בֵּיהּ מוֹצָא מַיִם, וְאִיהוּ בֵּירָא דְּאִתְמַלְּיָא מֵהַהוּא מוֹצָא מַיִם, וְאִינּוּן תְּרֵין דַּרְגִּין דְּאִינּוּן חַד, דְּכַר וְנוּקְבָּא כַּחֲדָא כְּדְקָא יָאוֹת.

✽ Miriam was Stricken with Tzara'ath (צָרַעַת)

The *Torah* describes how Miriam criticized *Moshe Rabbeinu* for separating from his wife. She asked her brother Aaron, "Did *Hashem* speak exclusively with Moses? Did He not also speak with us?"[701] As a result, she was stricken with a disease called *Tzara'ath* (צָרַעַת) until *Moshe Rabbeinu* prayed for her recovery.

The level of prophecy at the Reed Sea was far lower than the prophecy at Mount Sinai and did not require the men and women to live separately from one another.

By contrast, prior to the Giving of the *Torah* at Mount Sinai *Moshe Rabbeinu* told the men, "Be prepared for three days. Do not approach your wives."[702] This separation was only temporary for the rest of the nation, but for the remainder of his life *Moshe Rabbeinu* retained this level of prophecy and stayed apart from his wife.

✽✽ The Difference between the Revelation at the Reed Sea and the Revelation at Mount Sinai

"Male" represents the concept of giving, whereas "female" represents the concept of receiving.[703] *Hashem* is only a Giver because He is completely independent from Creation and receives nothing from it. In this sense He is, so to speak, the only true "male," as the sages teach, "There is no 'man' other than the Holy One, Blessed be He."[704] By contrast, even the highest spiritual world has both a masculine and a feminine aspect. It is

---

[701] Numbers 12:2 וַיֹּאמְרוּ הֲרַק אַךְ בְּמֹשֶׁה דִּבֶּר ה' הֲלֹא גַּם בָּנוּ דִבֵּר וַיִּשְׁמַע ה'

[702] Exodus 19:15 וַיֹּאמֶר אֶל הָעָם הֱיוּ נְכֹנִים לִשְׁלֹשֶׁת יָמִים אַל תִּגְּשׁוּ אֶל אִשָּׁה

[703] *Torah Temimah* on Genesis 1:27, note 63 שכל נברא שבעולם יש במינו כוח המשפיע וכוח המקבל, ומכוונה כוח המשפיע בשם זכר והמקבל בשם נקבה.

[704] B.T. *Sotah* 42B וְאֵין "אִישׁ" אֶלָּא הַקָּדוֹשׁ בָּרוּךְ הוּא, שֶׁנֶּאֱמַר, "ה' אִישׁ מִלְחָמָה" (שמות ט"ו, ג').

feminine because it receives the Divine light and also masculine because it transmits that light to the world below it.[705]

At Mount Sinai, *Hashem* revealed that He is the only true Giver,[706] and in relation to Him, all creatures are receivers.[707] The separation of men and women at the time of the Giving of the *Torah* helped enable the Jews to grasp this.

Ma'or Vashamesh explains that when Miriam led the women in song at the Reed Sea, she drew down a level of supernal light from a spiritual source above the concepts of male and female.[708] This does not mean that the distinction between masculine and feminine does not exist at all at very high spiritual levels. Rather, male and female are so closely united that it is as if they are one unit in the same way that Adam and Chavah were initially created as one unit. For this reason, although they sang *Hashem's* praises separately, husbands and wives could live together in the same way as they usually do.

Although no one can ever be as great a prophet as *Moshe Rabbeinu*, the sages teach that, "The one who causes another to do [a *Mitzvah*] is greater than the one who performs it."[709] From

---

[705] *Klee Yakar* on Genesis 1:31 כיצד? הרי הקב"ה המשפיע הראשון הנותן אמרי שפע אל העולם העליון, אבל הוא יתברך אינו מושפע מזולתו. והעולם העליון חוזר ומשפיע אל העולם האמצעי. נמצא שהעולם העליון יש בו דמיון הזכר והנקבה כאחד שהרי הוא מושפע כנקבה מן (ה/)סיבה ראשונה יתברך ומשפיע כזכר אל העולם האמצעי. וכן העולם התיכון מקבל השפע מן העולם העליון וחוזר ומשפיע אל העולם התחתון. אם כן, גם העולם האמצעי נקרא זכר ונקבה כאחד משפיע ומושפע... עד אשר בכולם שייך לומר שהוא מושפע ומשפיע כאחד בלתי לה' לבדו יש לייחס תואר האיש לבד — משפיע ואינו מושפע. זהו שאמרו רז"ל בכמה מדרשים, אין איש אלא הקב"ה, שנאמר, "ה' אִישׁ מִלְחָמָה" (שמות ט"ו, ג') (מסכת סוטה מ"ב, ע"ב). רוצה לומר, אין לייחס תואר האיש המורה על המשפיע ובלתי מקבל בלתי לה' לבדו כי כולם צריכין אליו יתברך והוא יתברך אינו צריך לשום אחד מהם. ומה שמצינו לשון 'אִישׁ' אצל הבריות, אינו בעצם כי אם בהשאלה בצירוף האישה, אבל שם העצם של איש אין לייחס כי אם אליו יתברך.

[706] *Megaleh Amukoth Al Hatorah, Parashath Vayikra* והנה בשעת מתן תורה קיבל משה תר"ך אותיות של דברות שאז זכה לעלמא דדכורא.

[707] However, like the supernal worlds, in relation to one another all men and women are in some ways both givers and receivers.

[708] *Ma'or Vashamesh, Parashath Beshalach* שעשתה עמהם הקפה כמחול הכרם בסוד נקבה תסובב גבר ובזה המשיכה אור עליון אשר אין שם בחינת דכר ונוקבא.

[709] B.T. *Baba Bathra* 9A. אָמַר רַבִּי אֶלְעָזָר: גָּדוֹל הַמְעַשֶּׂה יוֹתֵר מִן הָעוֹשֶׂה.

this perspective, Miriam's spiritual level exceeded *Moshe Rabbeinu's* because her faith and understanding were the source of his prophetic ability.[710] Considering her exalted spiritual level, Miriam should have understood that *Moshe Rabbeinu* needed to separate from his wife to retain the spiritual level achieved at the Giving of the *Torah*.

ఌఌఌ The Origin of Creation

The second verse of the *Torah* begins, "The Earth was *Tohu* (תהו) and *Bohu* (בהו),"[711] often translated as "emptiness and nothingness." The *Gemara* explains that, "*Tohu* (תהו) is a line the color of *Yarok* (יָרוֹק) which surrounds all the world… *Bohu* (בהו) consists of smooth stones sunk into the depths from which water emerges."[712]

What was this "line the color of *Yarok* (קַו יָרוֹק)" which preceded the rest of Creation?

As stated above, *Hashem* is only a Giver, not a receiver. Prior to Creation, when only *Hashem* existed, there was no concept of receiving. *Hashem* therefore had to create the potential for receiving prior to the rest of Creation. The "line the color of *Yarok* (קַו יָרוֹק) which surrounds all the world," refers to that potential.

Although Rabbi Elazar said this regarding giving to *Tzedakah*, the same principle applies generally. (See, for example, *Bamidbar Rabbah* 14:9 למה נקראת התורה אור? שהיא מאירה את האדם מה יעשה. ולפי שהתורה מלמדת את האדם כיצד יעשה רצון המקום, (לפיכך שכר התלמוד גדול, וגדול הַמָּעֲשֶׂה יותר מן העושה).

[710] This would explain why some say that the wellspring did not regain all of its functions when *Moshe Rabbeinu's* merit caused it to be restored after Miriam's death. (*Ramban* on Exodus 17:5 ואף על פי שהיה הכל בארה של מרים, כקבלת רבותינו (במדבר י״ט, כ״ה), יתכן שהיה בפעם הראשון וכל הארבעים שנה מושך מים כנהרות שוטפות, ובפעם השנית (מפני העונש אשר היה שם נעשה כמו באר חפורה מלאה מים חיים).

[711] Genesis 1:2 וְהָאָרֶץ הָיְתָה תֹהוּ וָבֹהוּ וְחֹשֶׁךְ עַל פְּנֵי תְהוֹם וְרוּחַ אֱ-לֹהִים מְרַחֶפֶת עַל פְּנֵי הַמָּיִם

[712] B.T. *Chagigah* 12A "תהו" קַו יָרוֹק שֶׁמַּקִּיף אֶת כָּל הָעוֹלָם כּוּלוֹ… "בהו" אֵלוּ אֲבָנִים הַמְפוּלָמוֹת הַמְשׁוּקָעוֹת בְּתְהוֹם שֶׁמֵּהֶן יוֹצְאִין מַיִם.

❦❦❦❦ How Yarok (יָרוֹק) Reflects the Primordial Power of Receiving

Although *Yarok* (יָרוֹק) means "green" in modern Hebrew, its original meaning included both "green" and "yellow."[713] These two colors have an unusual relationship to one another. When green light and red light are blended, they yield yellow light, but when blue paint and yellow paint are blended, they yield green paint. *Yarok* (יָרוֹק) therefore refers to both a primary color of light (green) and a blended color of light (yellow) as well as a primary pigment (yellow) and a blended pigment (green). It thus represents at one and the same time both primary unmixed color and secondary blended color.

This quality of *Yarok* (יָרוֹק) mirrors the way in which *Hashem's* Divine light descends through the chain of spiritual worlds with its role switching back and forth. The light enters a spiritual world as a "masculine" (primary) influence, takes on a "feminine" (secondary) form in the world which receives it, and then resumes a "masculine" (primary) form as it descends to the next world.

Tohu (תֹּהוּ), also called Divine light, is the primordial substance from which all Creation derives.[714] At the highest spiritual level, *Tohu* (תֹּהוּ) is the initial stage of Creation, the prototype for the system of masculine/feminine transformation which follows. The sages state that its color is *Yarok* (יָרוֹק) to allude to this

---

[713] See, for example, *Tosafoth* on B.T. *Niddah* 19B sub verba *"Hayarok"* (הירוק): "ירוק ככרתי" – מכלל דסתם ירוק לאו הכי הוא.

[714] *Perush Haram Botril Lesefer Yetzirah* 1 והחומר הזה שקראוהו היוונים 'היולי' נקרא בלשון הקודש 'תוהו', והמילה נגזרת מלשון רז"ל 'תוהה על הראשונות' מפני שאם בא אדם לגזור לו שם תוהה – נמלך לקראו בשם (מ)אחר כי לא לבש צורה שייתפס בו השם כלל.

Shelah Hakadosh, Parashath Breishith בָּרָא הַקָּדוֹשׁ בָּרוּךְ הוּא מֵאֲפִיסָה מֻחְלֶטֶת 'נָקֻדָּה', וְנִקְרֵאת בִּלְשׁוֹן הַקֹּדֶשׁ 'תֹּהוּ', וּבִלְשׁוֹן חֲכָמִים 'אֶבֶן שְׁתִיָּה', וּבִלְשׁוֹן יְוָנִי 'הִיּוּלִי'.

primordial potential to switch back and forth between transmitter and recipient.

ೞೞೞೞೞ The Rama's Explanation of Yarok (יָרוֹק)

Rabbi Moshe Isserles (the *Rama*) elaborates upon the nature of *Tohu* (תֹהוּ) as the predecessor to the rest of Creation.

Hashem created the universe using spiritual forces which correspond to the letters of the Hebrew alphabet. Points and lines represent the earliest amorphous stage of Creation because they are the elements from which letters are formed. The letter *Yud* (י) is a point, and the letter *Vav* (ו) is a line, so the *Yud* (י) and *Vav* (ו) in *Yarok* (יָרוֹק) allude to points and lines. Its remaining letters spell "*Reek*" (רק), meaning "empty," and correspond to a two-dimensional plane — the empty space that exists before any three-dimensional physical object is created.[715]

ೞೞೞೞೞೞ Women and Yarok (יָרוֹק)

Rabbeinu Bachye explains that the "line the color of *Yarok* (קַו יָרוֹק)" corresponds to understanding (בִּינָה),[716] i.e., deriving one

---

[715] *Torath Ha'olah L'rama* 3:73 שאי אפשר לאותיות והוא הקו והנקודה, שאי אפשר לצייר שום אות בלא קו ונקודה. והנה אות הו' הוא כדמות קו, ואות הי' כדמות נקודה, ואי אפשר להשכיל קו או נקודה אלא באלו שני אותיות. ואף כי עיקר הקו והנקודה הוא דבר שאין בו ממש ושום גשמות, והוא אמרם בקו ירוק שמקיף העולם ומתאר הבריות, וזהו האמת כי דבר זה מקיף העולם, כי הנקודה סוף הקו, והקו הוא סוף השטח, והשטח סוף הגשם *(הצורה הבסיסית שממנה בנויה כל החפצים הגשמיים)*. אם כן, זהו מקיף העולם וכל אשר נמצא בעולם... והוא תוהו כי אין לו ממש במציאות, וקראו "קו ירוק" מצד שני דברים: האחד מצד שיתוף השם, להיות כי תיבת ''ירוק'' הוא *(כולל אותיות)* י''ו ר''ק – י''ו הוא הנקודה והקו ור''ק הוא הריקות *(ריקנות)* שאין בה ממש בעודן נקודה וקו מחשבית *(היינו שהן עדיין בצורתן הקדמונית טרם נברא מהן שום דבר)*. ואף כי ר''ק הוא מורה לנו השטח בעולם שהוא מרחק מוגבל בלא גשם, והנה גילה לנו במילות *(כמילה)* ''ירוק'' על כל שלושה.

This explains why Hebrew words are sometimes fully spelled out, with *Vavs* and *Yuds* to show how to pronounce them (כְּתִיב מָלֵא), and sometimes not (כְּתִיב חָסֵר). Whereas other letters symbolize the more developed spiritual forces which underlie the physical universe, these two letters symbolize the less well-defined state which pre-existed those forces.

[716] *Rabbeinu Bachye* on Genesis 1:2 תוהו הוא הבינה שהוא קו ירוק שהוא מקיף את כל העולם

concept from another.[717] This parallels the act of creation which involves a similar process of passing primordial *Tohu* (תהו) through a series of spiritual worlds to derive one thing from another until the physical world is produced.

Women, who have "extra understanding" (בִּינָה יְתֵירָה), have a special relationship to the very first step in the act of Creation which entailed creating the potential for receiving. Female prophets therefore had a close connection to this concept. For this reason, the sages state that Queen Esther had a greenish or yellowish tinge (יְרַקְרוֹקֶת).[718]

The prophet with the keenest recognition of this concept was Miriam. The *Rama* explains that *Bohu* (בהו), the substance which follows from *Tohu* (תהו) and which the *Gemara* calls "smooth stones" (אֲבָנִים הַמְפוּלָמוֹת), refers to the letters of the Hebrew alphabet from which the first physical substance emerged. That substance was water, as stated at the end of the verse: "The Earth was *Tohu* (תהו) and *Bohu* (בהו), and darkness was on the surface of the depths, and God's spirit hovered over the surface of the water."[719] [720] The *Ben Ish Chai* states that the expression "smooth stones" (אֲבָנִים הַמְפוּלָמוֹת) refers to "perforated stones."[721] This corresponds to Miriam's wellspring which the sages describe as being a perforated stone from which water flowed.[722]

---

[717] B.T. *Chagigah* 14A וְנָבוֹן זֶה הַמֵּבִין דָּבָר מִתּוֹךְ דָּבָר

[718] B.T. *Megillah* 13A רַבִּי יְהוֹשֻׁעַ בֶּן קָרְחָה אוֹמֵר: אֶסְתֵּר יְרַקְרוֹקֶת הָיְתָה

[719] Genesis 1:2 וְהָאָרֶץ הָיְתָה תֹהוּ וָבֹהוּ וְחֹשֶׁךְ עַל פְּנֵי תְהוֹם וְרוּחַ אֱ-לֹהִים מְרַחֶפֶת עַל פְּנֵי הַמָּיִם

[720] *Torath Ha'olah L'rama* 3:73 ונראה שהם עניין האותיות שהם האבנים מפולמות, והוא מלשון "פְּלֹנִי אַלְמֹנִי" (שמואל-א כ"א, ג), כמו שכתב הרלב"ג ריש בראשית. אי נמי שהוא לשון "לַחֹות", כמו שכתבו החכמים בזה מלשון "דָּגִים מְפוּלָמוֹת" (מסכת ביצה כ"ד, ב'), ונקראו "אבנים מפולמות" להיות כי מתוכן יצאות) הליחות שהוא המים, שנאמר, "וְרוּחַ אֱ-לֹהִים מְרַחֶפֶת עַל פְּנֵי הַמָּיִם" (בראשית א',ב), שהם היו תחילת הברואים.

[721] *Benayahu Ben Yehoyada* on B.T. *Chagigah* 12A "אֲבָנִים הַמְפוּלָמוֹת" – פירש רש"י לשון 'לחלוח', ובפירוש המילות של הזוהר פירש 'בריאות וחזקות', ועוד פירש 'מנוקבות', וזה הפירוש של מנוקבות יבוא נכון יותר, שממה יוצאים) המים.

[722] B.T. *Shabbath* 35A אָמַר רַבִּי חִיָּיא: הָרוֹצֶה לִרְאוֹת בְּאֵרָהּ שֶׁל מִרְיָם יַעֲלֶה לְרֹאשׁ הַכַּרְמֶל וְיִצְפֶּה וְיִרְאֶה כְּמִין כְּבָרָה בַּיָּם וְזוֹ הִיא בְּאֵרָהּ שֶׁל מִרְיָם.

ೞೞೞೞೞೞ Miriam's Seclusion

After curing Miriam, "*Hashem* said to Moses, 'If her father would spit before her, would she not be ashamed for seven days? Let her be isolated for seven days outside the camp and then be returned.'"[723]

The expression the *Torah* uses for "spit" (יָרֹק יָרַק) alludes to the color *Yarok* (יָרוֹק). Indeed, the repetition of this verb (יָרֹק יָרַק) hints at the two colors which *Yarok* (יָרוֹק) denotes (green and yellow) and the concepts of transmitting and receiving — the transfer of Divine light from a higher world to a lower one, also corresponding to the concepts of male and female.[724] This system only came into being after the creation of the feminine concept of receiving.

Prophets can only rise to a level of prophecy commensurate with the spiritual source of their souls.[725] For this reason, like all other prophets, Miriam did not experience the level of prophecy of *Moshe Rabbeinu*. Nevertheless, like the concept represented by *Yarok* (יָרוֹק), which is the embryonic source from which all Creation came into being, her faith and understanding were the source of *Moshe Rabbeinu's* prophetic ability. Accordingly, she should have realized that *Moshe Rabbeinu's* prophecy stood above the level where the system of give and take — male and

---

[723] Numbers 12:14 וַיֹּאמֶר ה' אֶל מֹשֶׁה וְאָבִיהָ יָרֹק יָרַק בְּפָנֶיהָ הֲלֹא תִכָּלֵם שִׁבְעַת יָמִים תִּסָּגֵר שִׁבְעַת יָמִים מִחוּץ לַמַּחֲנֶה וְאַחַר תֵּאָסֵף.

[724] The rabbis disagree about whether the *Torah's* use of this type of repetition hints at anything. According to some, the *Torah* employs the same idioms people do, so a doubled expression merely connotes emphasis (B.T. *Sanhedrin* 90B דִּבְּרָה תּוֹרָה כִּלְשׁוֹן בְּנֵי אָדָם). For example, the phrase בֹּא יָבֹא found in Psalms 126:6 means "he will certainly come." Others, including Rabbi Akiva, maintain that such expressions should be interpreted homiletically (B.T. *Sanhedrin* 90B).

[725] *Kithvei Ha'arizal, Sha'arei Kedushah* 3:6 מחשבת הנביא מתפשטת ועולה ממדרגה למדרגה ממטה למעלה עד הגיעו למקום אחיזת שורש נשמתו.

female — begins,[726] and that is why he had to separate from his wife.

Moshe Rabbeinu's prophetic ability derived from this highest spiritual level, a level where masculine and feminine do not exist because *Hashem* is revealed there as the sole unique and ultimate Giver.[727] The verse, "If her father would spit (יָרֹק יָרַק) before her, would she not be ashamed for seven days?"[728] may therefore be taken to mean, "If her Father in Heaven revealed the concept of *Yarok* (יָרֹק) to her, yet she spoke as she did, should she not be ashamed for seven days?"

---

[726] The numeric value of the expression "spit" יָרֹק יָרַק is 620, the same as crown (כֶּתֶר), hinting that Miriam's understanding reached the very highest spiritual level.

[727] Zohar III:261B "וְאַתָּה פֹּה עֲמֹד עִמָּדִי" (דברים ה׳, כ״ח). מֶהָכָא, אִתְפְּרַשׁ מִכֹּל וָכֹל מָאִתְּתֵיהּ וְאִתְדַּבָּק וְאִסְתַּלָּק בַּאֲתָר אַחֲרָא דִּדְכוּרָא וְלָא בְּנוּקְבָּא.

[728] Numbers 12:14 וַיֹּאמֶר ה׳ אֶל מֹשֶׁה וְאָבִיהָ יָרֹק יָרַק בְּפָנֶיהָ הֲלֹא תִכָּלֵם שִׁבְעַת יָמִים תִּסָּגֵר שִׁבְעַת יָמִים מִחוּץ לַמַּחֲנֶה וְאַחַר תֵּאָסֵף.

RESURRECTION

תחיית המתים

Aaron's Ability to Revive the Dead

೫ Aaron's Staff

The *Mishnah* lists *Moshe Rabbeinu's* staff among ten things created at twilight on the first Sabbath eve.[729] According to some authorities, the same staff is also sometimes identified as belonging to Aaron.[730] According to others, Aaron had a different staff that was created at the same time as *Moshe Rabbeinu's*.[731]

In any event, Aaron had the ability to make the staff come alive, as the *Torah* states:

---

[729] *Pirkei Avoth* 5:6   עֲשָׂרָה דְבָרִים נִבְרְאוּ בְעֶרֶב שַׁבָּת בֵּין הַשְּׁמָשׁוֹת, וְאֵלוּ הֵן...וְהַמַּטֶּה הֵן.

[730] Rabbi Avraham ibn Ezra on Exodus 4:20   ומטה הא-להים הוא מטה משה והוא מטה אהרן.

     Beth Elokim, Shaar Hayesodoth 23   בביאור עניין המטה ומה תועלתו שנברא בין השמשות, ומה טעם נתייחס פעמים למשה פעמים לאהרן.

[731] *Sifthei Kohen* on Exodus 2:1   ועל זה המטה נאמר לו למשה, "וְהַמַּטֶּה אֲשֶׁר נֶהְפַּךְ לְנָחָשׁ תִּקַּח בְּיָדֶךָ" (שמות ז', ט"ו), ואינו מטה של משה כי מטה היה של משה היה נקרא "מַטֵּה הָאֱ-לֹהִים" (שמות ד', כ') וזה המטה היה של אהרן.

Hashem spoke to Moses and Aaron, saying, "When you speak with Pharaoh, and he tells you to produce a sign [to prove that I sent you], you shall tell Aaron, 'Take your staff and cast it before Pharaoh,' and it will become a serpent."

Moses and Aaron came to Pharaoh and did so, just as *Hashem* had commanded. Aaron cast down his staff before Pharaoh and before his servants, and it became a serpent. Pharaoh called his wisemen and magicians, and the sorcerers of Egypt also did the same with their enchantments. Each man cast down his staff, and they became serpents, but Aaron's staff swallowed their staves.[732]

The sages comment that this was a "miracle within a miracle" because Aaron's staff swallowed the staves of the sorcerers after it had already turned back into wood.[733] In other words, the staff remained alive even then.

Aaron displayed the same ability to bring an inanimate object to life after the Earth swallowed Korah and his followers. *Moshe Rabbeinu* took Aaron's staff and placed it together with the staves of the leaders of the other Tribes. The following morning, the other staves remained as they were, but Aaron's staff blossomed and produced almonds.[734]

---

[732] Exodus 7:8-12 (ח) וַיֹּאמֶר ה' אֶל מֹשֶׁה וְאֶל אַהֲרֹן לֵאמֹר. (ט) כִּי יְדַבֵּר אֲלֵכֶם פַּרְעֹה לֵאמֹר תְּנוּ לָכֶם מוֹפֵת וְאָמַרְתָּ אֶל אַהֲרֹן קַח אֶת מַטְּךָ וְהַשְׁלֵךְ לִפְנֵי פַרְעֹה יְהִי לְתַנִּין. (י) וַיָּבֹא מֹשֶׁה וְאַהֲרֹן אֶל פַּרְעֹה וַיַּעֲשׂוּ כֵן כַּאֲשֶׁר צִוָּה ה' וַיַּשְׁלֵךְ אַהֲרֹן אֶת מַטֵּהוּ לִפְנֵי פַרְעֹה וְלִפְנֵי עֲבָדָיו וַיְהִי לְתַנִּין. (יא) וַיִּקְרָא גַּם פַּרְעֹה לַחֲכָמִים וְלַמְכַשְּׁפִים וַיַּעֲשׂוּ גַם הֵם חַרְטֻמֵּי מִצְרַיִם בְּלַהֲטֵיהֶם כֵּן. (יב) וַיַּשְׁלִיכוּ אִישׁ מַטֵּהוּ וַיִּהְיוּ לְתַנִּינִם וַיִּבְלַע מַטֵּה אַהֲרֹן אֶת מַטֹּתָם.
[733] Shemoth Rabbah 9:7 ...אמר רבי אלעזר: נס בתוך נס. מלמד שחזר המטה מטה כברייתו ובלע אותן אמר רבי יוסי בר רבי חנינא: נס גדול נעשה במטה שאע"פ שבלע כל אותן המטות שהשליכו שהיו רבים לעשות מהן י' עומרים ולא הועבה, וכל מי שרואה אותו אומר: זה מטה אהרן
[734] Numbers 17:17-23 (יז) דַּבֵּר אֶל בְּנֵי יִשְׂרָאֵל וְקַח מֵאִתָּם מַטֶּה מַטֶּה לְבֵית אָב מֵאֵת כָּל נְשִׂיאֵהֶם לְבֵית אֲבֹתָם שְׁנֵים עָשָׂר מַטּוֹת אִישׁ אֶת שְׁמוֹ תִּכְתֹּב עַל מַטֵּהוּ. (יח) וְאֵת שֵׁם אַהֲרֹן תִּכְתֹּב עַל מַטֵּה לֵוִי כִּי מַטֶּה אֶחָד לְרֹאשׁ בֵּית אֲבוֹתָם. (יט) וְהִנַּחְתָּם בְּאֹהֶל מוֹעֵד לִפְנֵי הָעֵדוּת אֲשֶׁר אִוָּעֵד לָכֶם שָׁמָּה. (כ) וְהָיָה הָאִישׁ אֲשֶׁר אֶבְחַר בּוֹ מַטֵּהוּ יִפְרָח וַהֲשִׁכֹּתִי מֵעָלַי אֶת תְּלֻנּוֹת בְּנֵי יִשְׂרָאֵל אֲשֶׁר הֵם מַלִּינִם עֲלֵיכֶם. (כא) וַיְדַבֵּר מֹשֶׁה אֶל בְּנֵי יִשְׂרָאֵל וַיִּתְּנוּ אֵלָיו כָּל נְשִׂיאֵיהֶם מַטֶּה לְנָשִׂיא אֶחָד מַטֶּה לְנָשִׂיא אֶחָד לְבֵית אֲבֹתָם שְׁנֵים עָשָׂר מַטּוֹת וּמַטֵּה אַהֲרֹן בְּתוֹךְ מַטּוֹתָם. (כב) וַיַּנַּח מֹשֶׁה אֶת הַמַּטֹּת לִפְנֵי ה' בְּאֹהֶל הָעֵדֻת. (כג) וַיְהִי מִמָּחֳרָת וַיָּבֹא מֹשֶׁה אֶל אֹהֶל הָעֵדוּת וְהִנֵּה פָּרַח מַטֵּה אַהֲרֹן לְבֵית לֵוִי וַיֹּצֵא פֶרַח וַיָּצֵץ צִיץ וַיִּגְמֹל שְׁקֵדִים.

ಸಾ Aaron's Ability to Resurrect the Dead

In addition to bringing inanimate objects to life, Aaron had the ability to counteract death.

After the Earth swallowed Korah and his supporters, the Jews complained to *Moshe Rabbeinu* and Aaron, "Why did you kill *Hashem's* people?" *Hashem* then punished the nation with a plague, after which the *Torah* states:

> Aaron took [the incense] as Moses had instructed and ran into the midst of the assembly and behold the plague had started among the people. He put the incense [there] and atoned for the people. He stood between the dead and the living, and the plague was stopped.[735]

The *Midrash* elaborates on this incident:

> [Aaron] found the Angel [of Death] standing and destroying. Aaron stood up to him and did not permit him to destroy [further]. Rather, [Aaron] stood among the dead, [blocking the angel].
>
> The Angel of Death told Aaron, "Leave me to perform my mission!"
>
> "Moshe sent me," replied Aaron, "and the Holy One, Blessed be He, sent you. Behold, the Holy One, Blessed be He,

---

It is unclear whether this was the same staff Aaron used in front of Pharaoh. The *Midrash* suggests that it may have been Judah's staff, or *Moshe Rabbeinu's* staff, or a new staff *Moshe Rabbeinu* cut from a block of wood specifically for this occasion (*Bamidbar Rabbah* 18:23 ומטה אהרן יש אומרים הוא המטה שהיה ביד יהודה... ויש אומרים הוא המטה שהיה ביד משה ומעצמו פרח... ואית דאמרי נטל משה קורה אחת וחתכה לשנים עשר נסרים ואומר להם: "כולכם מָקורה אחת טלו מקלכם!").

[735] Numbers 17:12-13 (יב) וַיִּקַּח אַהֲרֹן כַּאֲשֶׁר דִּבֶּר מֹשֶׁה וַיָּרָץ אֶל תּוֹךְ הַקָּהָל וְהִנֵּה הֵחֵל הַנֶּגֶף בָּעָם וַיִּתֵּן אֶת הַקְּטֹרֶת וַיְכַפֵּר עַל הָעָם. (יג) וַיַּעֲמֹד בֵּין הַמֵּתִים וּבֵין הַחַיִּים וַתֵּעָצַר הַמַּגֵּפָה.

and Moshe are in the Tent of Meeting (אֹהֶל מוֹעֵד). Let us go to them [to decide who is right]."

The angel paid him no mind until Aaron seized him by the waist and forced him to go.[736]

Aaron's ability to conquer the Angel of Death was so great that even when it came time for him to depart this world, the Angel of Death could not overcome him. Instead, the sages teach that Aaron died by a "kiss" from *Hashem*.[737] He did not die as everyone else does but is hidden away at his burial site.[738]

The blossom which grew from Aaron's staff after this incident hints at his ability to neutralize death. The numeric value of "blossom" (פֶּרַח) is two hundred eighty-eight, the same numeric value as "good" (טוֹב) and "evil" (רַע),[739] alluding to the Tree of Knowledge of Good and Evil. Aaron's tremendous righteousness, particularly his zeal for pursuing peace, gave him the power to overcome death which came into the world as a result of Adam and Chavah eating the fruit of the Tree of Knowledge.[740]

---

[736] *Midrash Tanchuma, Parashath Titzaveh* 15 מצא למלאך עומד ומחבל. עמד אהרן כנגדו ולא היה מניחו לחבל, אלא "וַיַּעֲמֹד בֵּין הַמֵּתִים". אמר לו לאהרן: "הניחני ואעשה שליחותי!" אמר לו אהרן: "משה שלחני והקב"ה שלחך, והרי הקב"ה ומשה באוהל מועד. נלך אצלם". לא השגיח המלאך עד שעצרו אהרן במתניו והוליכו.

[737] B.T. *Baba Bathra* 17A תָּנוּ רַבָּנָן: שִׁשָּׁה לֹא שָׁלַט בָּהֶן מַלְאַךְ הַמָּוֶת וְאֵלּוּ הֵן: אַבְרָהָם יִצְחָק וְיַעֲקֹב מֹשֶׁה אַהֲרֹן וּמִרְיָם.

     Rashi comments on this אלא מתו בנשיקה על פי שכינה. *Malbim* explains this "kiss" as meaning that the soul departs from the body due to its tremendous yearning to join *Hashem* (*Malbim* on Numbers 20:24 רק על ידי לא על ידי ממית מבחוץ. התפשטות נפשו מגופו ברוב חשק הנפש לצאת מן מאסר הגוייה ולהדבק בצרור החיים את ה' א-להיה).

[738] *Likutei Halachoth, Hilchoth Choshen Mishpat, Hilchoth Sheluchin* 5 שֶׁבְּוַדַּאי הָאֱמֶת כֵּן הוּא שֶׁאַהֲרֹן לֹא מֵת וְהוּא חַי וְקַיָּם וּמֻטָּל בְּמִטָּתוֹ בִּמְנוּחָתוֹ בְּשָׁלוֹם.

[739] *Panim Yafoth* on Genesis 31:24 ידוע כי הניצוצות שנפלו הם רפ"ח והוא מספר טוב ורע עם (הכולל המחברם).

[740] The word "blossom" appears twice in Numbers 17:23 (וַיְהִי מִמָּחֳרָת וַיָּבֹא מֹשֶׁה אֶל אֹהֶל הָעֵדוּת וְהִנֵּה פָּרַח מַטֵּה אַהֲרֹן לְבֵית לֵוִי וַיֹּצֵא פֶרַח וַיָּצֵץ צִיץ וַיִּגְמֹל שְׁקֵדִים), alluding to this ability.

ಜಜ Nadab and Abihu

The *Torah* relates:

Nadab and Abihu, the sons of Aaron, each took an incense pan, put fire in it, placed incense on [the fire], and offered it before *Hashem* — an unauthorized fire which He had not commanded them. Fire came forth from before *Hashem* and consumed them, and they died before *Hashem*. Moses said to Aaron, "This is what *Hashem* spoke [about], saying, 'With those who are close to Me shall I be sanctified. Before all the nation will I be honored.'" And Aaron was silent.[741]

The *Midrash* teaches that Nadab and Abihu died because Aaron participated in the sin of the golden calf[742] and that their deaths atoned for that sin,[743] but this seems to contradict the *Torah's* statement that they died because they presented an unauthorized offering. Accordingly, it must be that their actions alone did not justify their deaths. Rather, Aaron's involvement with the golden calf combined with their actions to cause their deaths.

This still seems odd, however, because the *Torah* promises that *Hashem* will not punish adult children for the sins of their

---

Two times 288 equals 576, the same numeric value as "and revives the dead" (ומחייה המתים) found in the second blessing of the *Amidah* prayer if one is added for each word.

[741] Leviticus 10:1-3   (א) וַיִּקְחוּ בְנֵי אַהֲרֹן נָדָב וַאֲבִיהוּא אִישׁ מַחְתָּתוֹ וַיִּתְּנוּ בָהֵן אֵשׁ וַיָּשִׂימוּ עָלֶיהָ קְטֹרֶת וַיַּקְרִיבוּ לִפְנֵי ה' אֵשׁ זָרָה אֲשֶׁר לֹא צִוָּה אֹתָם. (ב) וַתֵּצֵא אֵשׁ מִלִּפְנֵי ה' וַתֹּאכַל אוֹתָם וַיָּמֻתוּ לִפְנֵי ה'. (ג) וַיֹּאמֶר מֹשֶׁה אֶל אַהֲרֹן הוּא אֲשֶׁר דִּבֶּר ה' לֵאמֹר בִּקְרֹבַי אֶקָּדֵשׁ וְעַל פְּנֵי כָל הָעָם אֶכָּבֵד וַיִּדֹּם אַהֲרֹן.

[742] *Vayikra Rabbah* 10:5 [דברים] "וּבְאַהֲרֹן הִתְאַנַּף ה' מְאֹד לְהַשְׁמִידוֹ וָאֶתְפַּלֵּל גַּם בְּעַד אַהֲרֹן בָּעֵת הַהִוא" ט', כ'). אמר רבי יהושע דסכנין בשם רבי לוי: אין השמדה אלא כילוי בנים... כיון שהתפלל משה עליו נמנעה ממנו חצי הגזירה — מתו שניים ונשתיירו שניים.

[743] *Meshech Chochmah* on Numbers 9:10   במיתת נדב ואביהוא, אשר מיתתן היה כפרה על מעשה העגל.

parents unless they repeat their parents' offences.[744] This principle should have applied to Nadab and Abihu whose unauthorized incense offering seems unrelated to the golden calf. How were these two matters connected?

ೞೞೞ Aaron and the Golden Calf

Aaron used his ability to give life to inanimate objects to fashion the golden calf, as the *Midrash* explains:

> Aaron found among the [gold] rings [presented by those who demanded that he fashion a golden calf] one gold sheet which had the Holy Name written on it and a sort of image of a calf carved into it. That alone he cast into the furnace, and the calf emerged, lowing.[745]

Those who wanted to make the golden calf demanded that Aaron fashion it because only he had the power to bring inanimate gold to life just as he had converted his staff into a snake. Although he tried to evade them, eventually he relented.

When Nadab and Abihu died, the *Torah* states that "Aaron was silent." The verb the *Torah* uses for "was silent" (וַיִּדֹּם) has the connotation of remaining still and refraining from action, as in, "The sun stood still" (וַיִּדֹּם הַשֶּׁמֶשׁ).[746] This suggests that Aaron did not merely refrain from speaking, but also from taking an

---

[744] B.T. *Berachoth* 7A וְהָא כְּתִיב, "פֹּקֵד עֲוֹן אָבֹת עַל בָּנִים" (שמות כ', ה'), וּכְתִיב, "וּבָנִים לֹא יוּמְתוּ עַל אָבוֹת" (דברים כ"ד, ט"ז). וּרְמִינָן קְרָאֵי אַהֲדָדֵי וּמְשַׁנִּינָן, לָא קַשְׁיָא – הָא כְּשֶׁאוֹחֲזִין מַעֲשֵׂה אֲבוֹתֵיהֶם בִּידֵיהֶם, הָא כְּשֶׁאֵין אוֹחֲזִין מַעֲשֵׂה אֲבוֹתֵיהֶם בִּידֵיהֶם.
       Rashi on Deuteronomy 24:16 "אִישׁ בְּחֶטְאוֹ יוּמָתוּ" (דברים כ"ד, ט"ז) – אבל מי שאינו איש מת בעוון אביו והקטנים מתים בעוון אבותם בידי שמים.
[745] *Pirkei D'Rabbi Eliezer* 44 ומצא אהרן בין הנזמים ציץ של זהב אחד כתוב עליו שם הקודש וחרות עליו כצורת עגל. ואותו לבד השליך לכור של אש... ויצא העגל הזה גועה.
[746] Joshua 10:13 וַיִּדֹּם הַשֶּׁמֶשׁ וְיָרֵחַ עָמָד עַד יִקֹּם גּוֹי אֹיְבָיו הֲלֹא הִיא כְתוּבָה עַל סֵפֶר הַיָּשָׁר וַיַּעֲמֹד הַשֶּׁמֶשׁ בַּחֲצִי הַשָּׁמַיִם וְלֹא אָץ לָבוֹא כְּיוֹם תָּמִים.

action he could have taken. Aaron could have revived his sons, but *Moshe Rabbeinu* convinced him to accept God's judgment.

The rabbis teach that a true penitent is one who overcomes his impulse to sin when placed in a situation identical to the one in which he originally stumbled.[747] Aaron misused his ability to give life to inanimate objects and revive the dead when he gave life to the golden calf. He corrected that misdeed by accepting God's judgment and not reviving Nadab and Abihu.

༄ Nadab and Abihu's Error

Moshe Rabbeinu told Aaron that *Hashem* said, "With those who are close to Me shall I be sanctified. Before all the nation I will be honored."[748] *Midrash Tanchuma* elaborates:

> Thus said Moshe, "At the time when [*Hashem*] told me, 'Through those who are close to Me shall I be sanctified,' I thought He would strike me or you. Now I know that [Nadab and Abihu] are greater than me or you."[749]

Nadab and Abihu were *Tzaddikim* who committed a minor indiscretion. When *Hashem* punishes the righteous, His Name becomes revered because onlookers reason, "If this is how it is with them, how much more so with the wicked!"[750]

---

[747] B.T. *Yoma* 86B הֵיכִי דָמֵי בַּעַל תְּשׁוּבָה? אָמַר רַב יְהוּדָה: כְּגוֹן שֶׁבָּאת לְיָדוֹ דְּבַר עֲבֵירָה פַּעַם רִאשׁוֹנָה וּשְׁנִיָּה וְנִיצַּל הֵימֶנָּה. מַחְוֵי רַב יְהוּדָה: בְּאוֹתָהּ אִשָּׁה בְּאוֹתוֹ פֶּרֶק בְּאוֹתוֹ מָקוֹם.

[748] Leviticus 10:3 וַיֹּאמֶר מֹשֶׁה אֶל אַהֲרֹן הוּא אֲשֶׁר דִּבֶּר ה' לֵאמֹר בִּקְרֹבַי אֶקָּדֵשׁ וְעַל פְּנֵי כָל הָעָם אֶכָּבֵד וַיִּדֹּם אַהֲרֹן.

[749] *Midrash Tanchuma, Parashath Shemini* 1 וכן אמר משה לאהרן: "העת שאמר לי, 'בִּקְרֹבַי אֶקָּדֵשׁ' (ויקרא י', ג'), חשבתי כי בי או בך יפגע ועכשיו אני יודע כי הם גדולים ממני וממך.

[750] *Rashi* on Leviticus 10:3 citing B.T. *Zevachim* 115B וְעַל פְּנֵי כָל הָעָם אֶכָּבֵד – כשהקב"ה עושה דין בצדיקים, מתיירא ומתעלה ומתקלס. אם כן באלו (אז) כל שכן ברשעים.

What was the error in judgment that led to Nadab and Abihu's death?

❧❧❧❧❧ How Hashem Used Faith (אֱמוּנָה) to Create the Universe

The Book of Psalms states, "For upright is the word of *Hashem*. All of His deeds are [accomplished] with faith."[751]

How does *Hashem* use faith to accomplish His deeds?

The *Rambam* explains that whereas a person and the information he knows are distinct from one another, *Hashem* and His knowledge are coextensive.[752]

Hashem created all existence by, so to speak, contracting and withdrawing Himself to form a place where Creation could exist, a phenomenon called *Tzimtzum* (צָמְצוּם).[753] Since *Hashem* and His knowledge are identical, this means that He, as it were, reduced or contracted His knowledge.

Faith consists of recognizing that something is true absent a full logical understanding of the matter. One of God's first acts of Creation was to create faith. He contracted Himself, which is also His knowledge, to make room for Creation. What remained

---

[751] Psalms 33:4 כִּי יָשָׁר דְּבַר ה' וְכָל מַעֲשֵׂהוּ בֶּאֱמוּנָה

[752] *Hayad Hachazakah, Hilchoth Yesodei Hatorah* 2:10 ואינו יודע בדעה שהיא חוץ ממנו כמו שאנו יודעין שאין אנו ודעתנו אחד. אבל הבורא יתברך הוא ודעתו וחייו אחד מכל צד ומכל פינה ובכל דרך ייחוד.

[753] The rabbis have a difference of opinion about whether this is meant literally or is only a metaphor for the way in which *Hashem* hides His presence. For a full discussion of this topic, see *Understanding Emunah*, Rabbi Yehuda Cahn (2016, Ohr Nissan Talmud Center, Inc., Baltimore), pp. 21-31.

was faith.[754] *Hashem* then introduced His will (also called His light) into this vacuum to produce Creation.[755]

The universe cannot exist without this act of seeming withdrawal because otherwise Creation would not appear to be separate from the Creator. Parallel to this, human beings rely on faith that *Hashem* exists rather than complete knowledge, for if they would fully comprehend Him, they would no longer be separate from Him and would cease to exist.[756]

Even so, some knowledge of *Hashem* can develop from faith. This may be compared to a student who learns a new idea. When the teacher introduces such an idea, the student must first accept its validity. Then the teacher can proceed to elaborate on the details necessary for the student to grasp it. A student who refuses to believe in the truth of the new idea from the start will be unreceptive to any further explanation and will never understand it. Similarly, once a person has a basic belief in *Hashem*, then some knowledge of Him becomes possible.[757]

Even after a person gains some knowledge of *Hashem* and His ways, he must continue to rely upon faith because each

---

[754] *Likutei Halachoth, Hilchoth Yoreh Deah, Hilchoth Niddah* 2:3 וְהַכְּלָל שֶׁאֱמוּנָה הִיא יְסוֹד כָּל הָעוֹלָמוֹת כֻּלָּם וִיסוֹד כָּל הַתּוֹרָה כֻּלָּהּ, כִּי ה' יִתְבָּרַךְ, כִּבְיָכוֹל, לֹא הָיָה יָכֹל לְהַתְחִיל לִבְרֹא שׁוּם עוֹלָם עַד שֶׁבָּרָא תְּחִלָּה אֶת מִדַּת הָאֱמוּנָה, דְּהַיְנוּ שֶׁיִּהְיֶה כֹּחַ בְּהַשֵּׂכֶל לְהַאֲמִין בְּהָאֱמֶת, אַף עַל פִּי שֶׁאֵינוֹ מְבִינוֹ כְּלָל. וְזֶה עִקַּר בְּחִינַת תְּחִלַּת הַצִּמְצוּם שֶׁנִּשְׁאַר הֶחָלָל הַפָּנוּי, דְּהַיְנוּ שֶׁצִּמְצֵם אֱלֹקוּתוֹ, כִּבְיָכוֹל, שֶׁהוּא הַשֵּׂכֶל, כִּי ה' יִתְבָּרַךְ הוּא עֶצֶם הַחָכְמָה, כִּבְיָכוֹל, כַּיָּדוּעַ. וּכְשֶׁפָּנָה הַשֵּׂכֶל מִשָּׁם נִשְׁאַר הַמָּקוֹם פָּנוּי בְּלִי שֵׂכֶל וְלֹא נִשְׁאָר שָׁם כִּי אִם בְּחִינַת אֱמוּנָה.

[755] *Kithvei Ha'arizal, Etz Chaim* 1:2 והנה אחר הצמצום הנ"ל אשר אז נשאר מקום החלל ואויר פנוי וריקני באמצע אור האין סוף ממש כנ"ל, הנה כבר היה מקום שיוכלו להיות שם הנאצלים והנבראים ויצורים והנעשים. ואז המשיך מן אור אין סוף קו א' ישר מן האור העגול שלו מלמעלה למטה ומשתלשל ויורד תוך החלל ההוא.

[756] *Likutei Amarim Tanya*, ch. 21 וככה ממש דרך משל מיוחדות דיבורו ומחשבתו של הקב"ה בתכלית היחוד במהותו ועצמותו יתברך גם אחר שיצא דיבורו יתברך אל הפועל בבריאות העולמות כמו שהיה מיוחד עמו קודם בריאת העולמות ואין שום שינוי כלל לפניו יתברך, אלא אל הבבראים המקבלים חיותם מבחינת דיבורו יתברך בבחינת יציאתו כבר אל הפועל בבריאת העולמות שמתלבש בהם להחיותם על ידי השתלשלות מעילה לעלול וירידת המדרגות בצמצומים רבים ושונים עד שיוכלו הברואים לקבל חיותם והתהוותם ממנו ולא יתבטלו במציאות.

[757] See *Likutei Halachoth, Hilchoth Yoreh Deah, Hilchoth Niddah* 2:3 בְּתְחִלָּה אִי אֶפְשָׁר לְהָאָדָם שֶׁיָּבִין שׁוּם דָּבָר וְשׁוּם הַשָּׂגָה, כִּי הַכֹּל אֶצְלוֹ בִּבְחִינַת אֵין סוֹף. וְצָרִיךְ שֶׁיִּהְיֶה לוֹ בִּתְחִלָּה אֱמוּנָה שְׁלֵמָה בְּלִי שׁוּם שֵׂכֶל וְזֶהוּ בְּחִינַת הַצִּמְצוּם כַּנַּ"ל. וְאָז כְּשֶׁהוּא חָזָק בֶּאֱמוּנָתוֹ, אָז ה' יִתְבָּרַךְ מֵאִיר עֵינָיו וּמֵבִין אַחַר כָּךְ הַדָּבָר בְּשִׂכְלוֹ, שֶׁזֶּהוּ בְּחִינַת הַמְשָׁכַת הָאוֹרוֹת וְהַמִּדּוֹת לְתוֹךְ הֶחָלָל הַפָּנוּי, לְתוֹךְ הַצִּמְצוּם שֶׁהִיא בְּחִינַת הָאֱמוּנָה.

higher level of knowledge requires the same process of first having faith and then developing knowledge. For this reason, it is imperative that people proceed slowly and not try to reach a level of knowledge for which they are not yet prepared.[758]

❧❧❧❧❧❧ Adam and Chavah's Error

Adam and Chavah did not want to follow this process. Instead, they ate from the fruit of the Tree of Knowledge because they wanted to increase their knowledge of *Hashem* without first developing their faith,[759] and that sin brought death into the world.

This explains the statement of the sages that, "Adam was a heretic."[760]

How could someone created by God and who directly interacted with Him deny His existence?

The sages mean that Adam and Chavah's attempt to acquire greater knowledge of *Hashem* without the prerequisite faith yielded an opposite result — a more defective knowledge of *Hashem*. For people on their spiritual level, this counted as heresy.

In addition, Adam and Chavah's sin contradicted the order *Hashem* followed when He created the universe — first creating faith by withdrawing Himself and then filling the void thus created. For people on their spiritual level, this was equivalent to a declaration that God did not create the universe.

---

[758] *Likutei Halachoth, Hilchoth Yoreh Deah, Hilchoth Niddah* 2:3 וְגַם אֲפִלוּ אַחַר כָּךְ כְּשֶׁזוֹכִין שֶׁיִּהְיֶה נִמְשָׁךְ אֵיזֶה דַּעַת וְהַשָּׂגָה אִי אֶפְשָׁר לְקַבֵּל הַדַּעַת כִּי אִם דֶּרֶךְ הָאֱמוּנָה הַקְּדוֹשָׁה, כִּי אָסוּר לִסְמֹךְ עַל הַשֵּׂכֶל לְבַד וְאֵין קִיּוּם לְהַשֵּׂכֶל בְּלֹא הָאֱמוּנָה... כִּי אִי אֶפְשָׁר לְקַבֵּל הַשֵּׂכֶל כִּי אִם דֶּרֶךְ כַּמָּה צִמְצוּמִים, וְכָל הַצִּמְצוּמִים הֵם עַל יְדֵי הָאֱמוּנָה שֶׁהוּא שֹׁרֶשׁ כָּל הַצִּמְצוּמִים כַּנַּ"ל. וְעַל כֵּן אָסוּר לַחֲקֹר לְמַעֲלָה מִמַּדְרֵגָתוֹ.

[759] *Likutei Halachoth, Hilchoth Yoreh Deah, Hilchoth Niddah* 2:4 וְזֶה בְּחִינַת חֵטְא אָדָם הָרִאשׁוֹן שֶׁאָכַל מֵעֵץ הַדַּעַת טוֹב וָרָע... כִּי הָיָה צָרִיךְ לְהִתְחַזֵּק בֶּאֱמוּנָה שְׁלֵמָה וְהוּא רָצָה לֵידַע בְּדַעְתּוֹ דַּיְקָא... כִּי הָעֵץ הַדַּעַת הָיָה לוֹ כֹּחַ הַזֶּה שֶׁמִּי שֶׁיֹּאכַל מִמֶּנּוּ נִכְנָס בּוֹ יֵצֶר הָרָע וְיִתְאַוֶּה לִרְדֹּף לָדַעַת וּלְהִסְתַּכֵּל בַּמֶּה שֶׁאֵין לוֹ רְשׁוּת, שֶׁעַל יְדֵי זֶה גּוֹרְמִין בְּחִינַת שְׁבִירַת כֵּלִים, חַס וְשָׁלוֹם, דְּהַיְנוּ שֶׁנִּשְׁבָּר כְּלִי הָאֱמוּנָה מֵאַחַר שֶׁאֵינוּ רוֹצֶה לִסְמֹךְ עַל אֱמוּנָה לְבַד וְרוֹצֶה לָדַעַת וּלְהָבִין דַּיְקָא בְּלִי אֱמוּנָה.

[760] B.T. *Sanhedrin* 38B וְאָמַר רַב יְהוּדָה אָמַר רַב: אָדָם הָרִאשׁוֹן מִין הָיָה, שֶׁנֶּאֱמַר, "וַיִּקְרָא ה' אֱ-לֹהִים אֶל הָאָדָם וַיֹּאמֶר לוֹ אַיֶּכָּה ?" (בראשית ג', ט') – אָן נָטָה לִבְּךָ ?

ೞೞೞೞ The Rectification of Adam and Chavah's Sin

The only commandment *Hashem* gave Adam and Chavah was not to eat the fruit of the Tree of Knowledge — to have faith in Him before trying to understand Him intellectually. When a person has unwavering faith in *Hashem*, knowledge follows automatically. Likewise, the level of faith Adam and Chavah originally possessed enabled them to know intuitively how *Hashem* wanted them to behave. As the *Imrei Emeth* explains, there was no need for any other commandment because Adam and Chavah were on such a lofty spiritual level that their limbs could sense what was right and what was wrong.[761]

At the time of the Giving of the *Torah*, Israel declared, "We will do [first], and [afterwards] we will understand" (נַעֲשֶׂה וְנִשְׁמָע).[762] Since they placed faith before understanding, they regained the sensitivity of Adam and Chavah before the sin, and their limbs had the ability to automatically discern God's will.[763]

Rabbeinu Bachye states that, "Adam's sin and Israel's sin in the desert resemble one another."[764]

The sin of the golden calf was not idolatry. Instead, the Jews were impatient for greater knowledge of *Hashem*, and they fashioned the golden calf as an intermediary for that purpose. An ox or calf represents knowing God, as the Prophet Isaiah

---

[761] *Imrei Emeth, Parashath Pinchas* קודם החטא של אדם הראשון כתיב, "וַיַּנִּחֵהוּ בְּגַן עֵדֶן לְעָבְדָהּ וּלְשָׁמְרָהּ" (בראשית ב', ט"ו), היינו מצות עשה ומצות לא תעשה, שהאיברים עצמן הרגישו רצון השם יתברך.

[762] Exodus 24:7 וַיִּקַּח סֵפֶר הַבְּרִית וַיִּקְרָא בְּאָזְנֵי הָעָם וַיֹּאמְרוּ כֹּל אֲשֶׁר דִּבֶּר ה' נַעֲשֶׂה וְנִשְׁמָע

[763] *Imrei Emeth, Parashath Pinchas* בני ישראל זכו למדרגה זו במתן תורה שהקדימו 'נעשה' ל'נשמע' גם כן בלא ציווי.

[764] *Rabbeinu Bachye* on Leviticus 4:14 חטאו של אדם הראשון וחטא ישראל במדבר דומין זה לזה

states, "The ox knows its master and a donkey the trough of its owner, [yet] Israel does not know [Me]."[765]

The Jews should have remained steadfast, strengthened their faith, and waited for *Moshe Rabbeinu* to descend from Mount Sinai with the *Torah*. Such enhanced faith would have enabled them to achieve an even higher level of knowledge of God than they already possessed as a result of hearing the first two of the Ten Commandments. Instead, the Jews sought to gain this knowledge without first intensifying their faith.

After Aaron produced the golden calf, the mixed multitude declared, "This is your leader Israel."[766] The phrase "this is your leader" (אֵלֶּה אֱלֹהֶיךָ) has the same numeric value as "faith" (אֱמוּנָה). Moreover, "faith" (אֱמוּנָה) has the same numeric value as "calf" (עֵגֶל) if one is added for the word itself. The Jews tried to use the golden calf as a substitute for the faith necessary to proceed to a higher level of knowledge of *Hashem*. This misguided approach led to the opposite. The Jews lost the exalted level they had achieved and reverted to the level from which they started.

Nadab and Abihu tried to reinstate the nation's lofty spiritual level by offering incense that had not been commanded. Their superior faith in *Hashem* permitted them to know what He wanted without the need for any commandment just as Adam and Chavah originally had the ability to sense what *Hashem* wanted of them. However, to restore Israel to its earlier status required action either by the entire nation or by its representative. Their offering was consistent with *Hashem's* will but

---

[765] Isaiah 1:3 יָדַע שׁוֹר קֹנֵהוּ וַחֲמוֹר אֵבוּס בְּעָלָיו יִשְׂרָאֵל לֹא יָדַע עַמִּי לֹא הִתְבּוֹנָן

[766] Exodus 32:4 וַיִּקַּח מִיָּדָם וַיָּצַר אֹתוֹ בַּחֶרֶט וַיַּעֲשֵׂהוּ עֵגֶל מַסֵּכָה וַיֹּאמְרוּ אֵלֶּה אֱלֹהֶיךָ יִשְׂרָאֵל אֲשֶׁר הֶעֱלוּךָ מֵאֶרֶץ מִצְרָיִם.

unauthorized because they did not represent the entire nation, as the sages teach:

> *Moshe Rabbeinu* and Aaron were walking along, with Nadab and Abihu behind them, [followed by] all Israel behind them.
>
> Nadab said to Abihu, "When will these two old men die so that you and I can lead the generation?"
>
> Said the Holy One, Blessed be He, "We will see who buries who!"[767]

Nadab and Abihu were great *Tzaddikim* who did not seek to lead the nation merely to enjoy power and prestige. Rather, they wished to replace *Moshe Rabbeinu* and Aaron so that as leaders of the nation they could rectify the sin of the golden calf. Their impatience caused them to try to do so before they achieved that status, and that is why they failed.[768]

By contrast, when Aaron saw what happened to Nadab and Abihu, he could have used his power over death to revive them. Instead, he restrained himself and trusted *Hashem's* judgment. In as much as the sin of the golden calf resulted from a lack of faith, Aaron's display of faith upon the death of Nadab and Abihu atoned for his role in it.

✣ The Mechanism by which Aaron Revived the Dead ✣✣ Self-Control Causes the Revival of the Dead

---

[767] B.T. *Sanhedrin* 52A וּכְבָר הָיוּ מֹשֶׁה וְאַהֲרֹן מְהַלְּכִים בַּדֶּרֶךְ, וְנָדָב וַאֲבִיהוּא מְהַלְּכִין אַחֲרֵיהֶם, וְכָל יִשְׂרָאֵל אַחֲרֵיהֶן. אָמַר לוֹ נָדָב לַאֲבִיהוּא: "אֵימָתַי יָמוּתוּ שְׁנֵי זְקֵנִים הַלָּלוּ וַאֲנִי וְאַתָּה נַנְהִיג אֶת הַדּוֹר?" אָמַר לָהֶן הַקָּדוֹשׁ בָּרוּךְ הוּא: "הַנִּרְאֶה מִי קוֹבֵר אֶת מִי!"

[768] *Imrei Emeth, Parashath Acharei Moth* נדב ואביהוא רצו לתקן חטא אדם הראשון. הם רצו לבטל את להט החרב המתהפכת, אך הם דחקו את השעה שעדיין לא היה הזמן מוכשר לזה.

Ironically, it was Aaron's suppression of his impulse to revive his sons that reflected his ability to do so.

The second blessing of the *Amidah* prayer states, "You are eternally mighty *Hashem*, reviving the dead."[769] The term "mighty" (גָּבּוֹר) connotes self-restraint, as the *Mishnah* states, "Who is mighty (גָּבּוֹר)? One who conquers his evil inclination."[770]

This concept of self-restraint or self-limitation applies to the Creator who, as it were, limited Himself to create the universe.[771]

A similar concept of self-restraint applies to resurrecting the dead. The rabbis teach that the soul is "literally a piece of God."[772] It has a trait of infinitude and is incompatible with a finite body, yet in an act of extreme self-control and self-limitation *Hashem* unites the soul with the body. Resurrection involves reuniting the soul with the body — the same act of might (גְּבוּרָה) and self-restraint.

Aaron, who exercised self-control and refrained from reviving his sons, imitated *Hashem* and therefore had the ability to revive the dead even though he did not use it in this instance.[773]

---

[769] אַתָּה גִּבּוֹר לְעוֹלָם אֲ-דֹנָי מְחַיֶּה מֵתִים אַתָּה רַב לְהוֹשִׁיעַ

[770] *Pirkei Avoth* 4:1 אֵיזֶהוּ גִבּוֹר? הַכּוֹבֵשׁ אֶת יִצְרוֹ

[771] The *Gemara* states: Daniel came along and said, "Foreigners enslave His children! Where is His might?" [The Men of the Great Assembly] came along and responded, "To the contrary! This is the very greatness of His might — that He conquers His impulse [to avenge Israel] and acts with patience towards the wicked." (B.T. *Yoma* 69B אָתָא דָנִיּאֵל, אָמַר: "נָכְרִים מִשְׁתַּעְבְּדִים בְּבָנָיו! אַיֵּה גְבוּרוֹתָיו?"... אָתוּ אִינְּהוּ (וְאָמְרוּ: "אַדְרַבָּה! זוֹ הִיא גְּבוּרַת גְּבוּרָתוֹ שֶׁכּוֹבֵשׁ אֶת יִצְרוֹ שֶׁנּוֹתֵן אֶרֶךְ אַפַּיִם לָרְשָׁעִים".

[772] *Panim Yafoth* on Exodus 20:3 נשמת כל ישראל הוא ממש חלק א-לוה ממעל

[773] Some of Aaron's descendants inherited his ability to enliven inanimate objects and revive the dead. For example, Aaron's son, Elazar, assisted Joshua in conducting the lottery used to determine which shares of the Land of Israel went to each Tribe. When Joshua drew a lot, it became animate and announced, "I am the lot of such and such a tribe, and I have been assigned to such and such a location." (*Bamidbar Rabbah* 21:9 ומעשה נסים היה בגורל. אלעזר בן אהרן

❧ Aaron was Connected to the Spiritual Level that Preceded Creation

Miriam was punished for speaking *Lashon Hara* about *Moshe Rabbeinu* because she initiated the conversation in which she and Aaron criticized *Moshe Rabbeinu*, but Aaron also participated, as the *Torah* states, "They said, 'Was it only with Moses that *Hashem* spoke? Did He not also speak with us?'"[774]

Hashem is absolutely one and indivisible. For Creation to be possible He had to first create the potential for division. Once division became possible, death became possible because death entails the separation of the soul from the body and the body's disintegration. Conversely, peace involves overcoming and eliminating division and separation. Peace is therefore the opposite of death,[775] and because Aaron pursued peace,[776] he could forestall and even reverse death.

Aaron was on a spiritual level similar to Miriam's and had access to the realm of *Yarok* (יָרֹק) — the primordial,

---

מלובש אורים ותומים וקלפי הגורל לפני יהושע... ועד שלא יעלה הגורל אלעזר אומר ברוח הקודש, "גורל שבט פלוני עולה שיטול ממקום פלוני". ויהושע פושט ידו ועולה... וזו הייתה יתירה שהיה הגורל צווח בשעת עלייתו, ("אני גורל פלוני השבט ! עליתי לו במקום פלוני !")

Likewise, Elazar's son, Phinehas, who was identical to Elijah, revived the dead and never died. (*Kedushath Levi, Parashath Pinchas* פנחס זה אליהו, והוא חי וקיים)

[774] Numbers 12:2 וַיֹּאמְרוּ הֲרַק אַךְ בְּמֹשֶׁה דִּבֶּר ה' הֲלֹא גַּם בָּנוּ דִבֵּר וַיִּשְׁמַע ה'

[775] As the *Kaddish* prayer states, "May there be great peace from Heaven and life upon us and all Israel" (יְהֵא שְׁלָמָא רַבָּא מִן שְׁמַיָּא וְחַיִּים עָלֵינוּ וְעַל כָּל יִשְׂרָאֵל). Moreover, *Hashem* referred to His blessing that Phinehas, who was the same as Elijah, would never die as "a covenant of peace" (*Rabbeinu Bachye* on Numbers 25:12 "הִנְנִי נֹתֵן לוֹ אֶת בְּרִיתִי שָׁלוֹם"...ומכאן היה ראוי שיחיה לעולם, ולכן כתוב, "בְּרִיתִי הָיְתָה אִתּוֹ הַחַיִּים וְהַשָּׁלוֹם" (מלאכי ב', ה'), כי החיים מכוח הרחמים, וזהו שאמר, "אֲשֶׁר קִנֵּא לֵא-לֹהָיו" (במדבר כ"ה, י"ג), כלשון "צֶדֶק וְשָׁלוֹם נָשָׁקוּ" (תהלים פ"ה, י"א), שהוא החיבור העליון שהעולם מתקיים בו.

[776] *Pirkei Avoth* 1:12 הִלֵּל אוֹמֵר: הֱוֵי מִתַּלְמִידָיו שֶׁל אַהֲרֹן – אוֹהֵב שָׁלוֹם וְרוֹדֵף שָׁלוֹם, אוֹהֵב אֶת הַבְּרִיּוֹת וּמְקָרְבָן לַתּוֹרָה.

amorphous forces described above which *Hashem* created prior to the rest of Creation, including the transitional stage between *Hashem's* absolute indivisible oneness and divisibility. Aaron's commitment to peace permitted him to access this pre-Creation state and thereby counteract death.

ಐಐಐಐ The Seeming Randomness of Death

If one rearranges the letters of *Yarok* (יָרֹק), they form "haphazard" (קֶרִי), as in the verses, "If you act haphazardly with Me, and do not wish to listen to Me…then I will also act haphazardly with you."[777]

As noted earlier, if only one outcome is possible, then a random result is not possible.[778] Only when two or more outcomes are possible, can a result be random. The embryonic, formless state of *Yarok* (יָרֹק) is the realm where these two opposites meet — the absolute indivisible oneness of *Hashem* which precludes chance happenings and divisible Creation in which seemingly random happenings are possible.

King Solomon wrote, "For everyone the same randomness applies, whether righteous or wicked [because everyone dies]."[779] The phrase "the same randomness" (מִקְרֶה אֶחָד) accurately describes the dual nature of death. To the extent that, for now, death is inevitable for every human being, and there are no

---

[777] Leviticus 26:21-24 וְאִם תֵּלְכוּ עִמִּי קֶרִי וְלֹא תֹאבוּ לִשְׁמֹעַ לִי...וְהָלַכְתִּי אַף אֲנִי עִמָּכֶם בְּקֶרִי

[778] *Kedushath Levi, Kedushah Rishonah, Purim* רק אם גורל, והנה אם אין רק דבר אחד אינו שייך יש שני דברים דומים זה לזה (ת)מי שבורר לו דבר אחד שייך גורל. שגורל אינו רק הבורר אחד משני דברים הדומים זה לזה. לכן, בעולם הזה אשר מלכותו והנהגותו מכוסה שייך גורל אחד לה' וכו'... אבל למעלה ששם אחדותו נראה ואין רואין רק מלכותו יתברך שמו (*אינו שייך מושג ההגרלה*).

[779] Ecclesiastes 9:2 הַכֹּל כַּאֲשֶׁר לַכֹּל מִקְרֶה אֶחָד לַצַּדִּיק וְלָרָשָׁע לַטּוֹב וְלַטָּהוֹר וְלַטָּמֵא וְלַזֹּבֵחַ וְלַאֲשֶׁר אֵינֶנּוּ זֹבֵחַ כַּטּוֹב כַּחֹטֶא הַנִּשְׁבָּע כַּאֲשֶׁר שְׁבוּעָה יָרֵא.

other alternatives, it is not random.[780] On the other hand, the circumstances in which death occurs vary greatly. From this perspective, death always appears to occur randomly.[781]

Since death has elements of both inevitability and randomness, it corresponds to the realm of *Yarok* (יָרֹק) where these concepts coexist. Accessing that spiritual level enabled Aaron to counteract death.

---

[780] Even for people such as the Prophet Elijah life in this world comes to an end. The difference is merely that Elijah and a few others entered *Gan Eden* without dying.

[781] The phrase "the same randomness" (מִקְרֶה אֶחָד), which can also be translated as "the same event," has the same numeric value as "serpent" (נָחָשׁ), alluding to the way in which the primordial serpent, who is identical to the Angel of Death, presents death as a random occurrence even though it never happens unless *Hashem* wills it.

Elijah and Elisha Revive the Dead

❧ Elijah Resurrects a Child

The *Tanach* describes how a severe drought struck the Land of Israel:

> Elijah arose and went to Zarephath and came to the entrance of the city. Here there was a widow gathering wood. He called to her and said, "Take a bit of water for me in a container, and I will drink." She went to get it, and he called to her, saying, "Take a slice of bread for me in your hand."
>
> She replied, "By the existence of *Hashem*, your God, [I swear that] I have [not even] a loaf [of bread], but only a handful of flour in a jug and a smidgen of oil in a flask. I am gathering two [logs of] wood to go and make [bread] for myself and my son, and we will die [after we eat it because we have no more food]."

Elijah told her, "Fear not. Come and do as you say, but first make for me a small loaf from it and bring it out to me, and for yourself and your son make afterwards."

...She went and did according to the words of Elijah, and the two of them as well as [the members of] her household ate from [what she baked] for a year.

...It was after these matters that the son of the mistress of the house grew ill, and his illness was so severe that his soul did not remain within him. She said to Elijah, "What [quarrel] exists between me and you, man of God, [that] you came to me to recall my sin and to kill my son?"

[Elijah] answered her, "Give me your son." He took him from her lap and brought him up to the attic where [Elijah] dwelled and lay him down on his bed. He called out to *Hashem*, saying, "*Hashem*, my God, indeed do no evil to the widow with whom I dwell to kill her son."[782] He stretched himself over the child three times, and called to *Hashem*, saying, "*Hashem*, my God, restore the soul of this child to his innards."

Hashem listened to the voice of Elijah and restored the soul of the child to his innards, and he revived.[783]

This child grew up to be the Prophet Jonah.[784]

ಶ Elijah's Disciple, Elisha, also Resurrected a Child

A similar episode happened with Elisha when he traveled to Shunem where a barren woman and her husband hosted him.

---

[782] The translation of this verse follows *Targum Yonathan* וצלי קדם ה' ואמר, ה' א-להי ברם על ארמלתא די אנא דר עמה לא יתבאש לה ולא ימות ברה.

[783] I Kings 17:10-22. See Appendix I for the full text.

[784] *Yalkut Shimoni* on I Kings 17, paragraph 209: רבי שמעון אומר: מכוח הצדקה המתים עתידין להחיות. מנין אנו למידין? מאליהו ז"ל שקבלתו אלמנה בכבוד גדול. ואמו של יונה הייתה.

[The prophet] told [her], "At precisely the time [when a woman who becomes pregnant now is due to give birth], you will give birth, and you will hug a son."[785]

She replied, "Do not disappoint your maidservant, man of God."

The lady became pregnant and bore a son at precisely the time Elisha had told her.

The child grew, and a day came when he went out to [watch] his father [supervise] the harvesters. [Suddenly,] he called to his father, "My head! My head!"

[His father] told a helper, "Carry him to his mother."

[The helper] carried him and brought him to his mother, and [the boy] sat on her knees until noontime and died. She went up [to Elisha's guest quarters in the attic of her home], lay him on the bed of the man of God, closed [the door] on him, and left.

She called to her husband and said, "Send me one of the helpers and one of the donkeys, and I will run over to the man of God and come back."

"Why are you going to him today?" he asked. "It is not the [first of the] month or the Sabbath [when one typically pays such a visit]."

"All is well," she answered.

…She came to the man of God, to the mountain, threw herself at his feet…and said, "Did I ask for a son from my lord? Did I not say, 'Do not mislead me'?"

[Elisha] told Gehazi, [his assistant], "Hurry, take my staff in your hand, and go. If you happen upon a person, do not greet him, and if anyone greets you, do not answer him. Place my staff on the face of the youth."

---

[785] The translation of this verse follows *Metzudoth David* לזמן הבא כעת הראויה להיות חיה, רוצה לומר יולדת, והיא ככלות תשעה חודשים, שהם ימי הריון.

The mother of the youth said, "As God exists, and by the life of your soul, I will not leave you unless you rise [and return with me]."

[So] he followed after her.

Gehazi went ahead of them and placed the staff on the youth's face, but there was no murmur and no sound. He went back towards [Elisha] and reported to him, saying, "The youth did not awaken."

Elisha came to the house, and there lay the youth, dead upon [Elisha's] bed. He entered and closed the door on the two of them and prayed to *Hashem*. [Then] he went up and lay over the child and placed his mouth on [the child's] mouth, his eyes on his eyes, his hands on his hands, stretched out on him, and the child's flesh warmed.

[Elisha] went off [the bed] and paced back and forth in the house, went up [again on the bed], and stretched himself on [the child]. The lad sneezed seven times, [and then] the lad opened his eyes.[786]

This boy grew up to be the Prophet Habakkuk.[787]

৪০ How Elijah and Elisha Accomplished These Miracles

The *Mishnah* states that, "A [type of prophecy called a] spirit of holiness (רוּחַ הַקֹּדֶשׁ) leads to the resurrection of the dead, and the resurrection of the dead comes through Elijah, who is remembered for good, Amen!"[788] *Tosafoth Yom Tov* comments that in the end of days *Hashem* will invest the dead with this spirit of holiness (רוּחַ הַקֹּדֶשׁ) to revive them.

---

[786] II Kings 4:17-35. See Appendix J for the full text.

[787] *Zohar* I:7B "ה' שָׁמַעְתִּי שִׁמְעֲךָ יָרֵאתִי" (חבקוק ג', ב'). הַאי קְרָא חֲבַקּוּק אָמַר (אמרו) בְּשַׁעֲתָא דְּחֲמָא מִיתָתֵיהּ וְאִתְקָיַּים עַל יְדָא דֶאֱלִישָׁע.

[788] *Sotah* 9:15 וְרוּחַ הַקֹּדֶשׁ מְבִיאָה לִידֵי תְחִיַּת הַמֵּתִים וּתְחִיַּת הַמֵּתִים בָּאָה עַל יְדֵי אֵלִיָּהוּ זָכוּר לַטּוֹב, אָמֵן

The *Midrash* teaches that, "Whoever occupies himself with the dew of the *Torah*, the dew of the *Torah* revives him."[789] Rabbi Tzadok Hakohen of Lublin clarifies that this dew is the same prophetic spirit of holiness (רוּחַ הַקֹּדֶשׁ) mentioned in the *Mishnah*.

The Ineffable Name (י-ה-ו-ה) is the manifestation of *Torah* in actual practice which *Moshe Rabbeinu* revealed to Israel. The letters of the alphabet which follow those of the Ineffable Name (כוז"ו)[790] have a numeric value of thirty-nine, the same as "dew" (טַל). These letters represent the hidden aspect of the *Torah*. Although this aspect of the *Torah* was not revealed, its spiritual influence continually flows into the world. When people's faith motivates them to act completely for the sake of Heaven, they become fit to receive this hidden aspect of the *Torah*. It permeates their limbs and enables them to be resurrected. The merit of those great individuals who act completely for the sake of Heaven spreads to all members of the Jewish people so that in the end of days, the dew of the *Torah* will be fully revealed and revive all the dead of Israel.

Individuals such as Elijah and Elisha, who acted strictly out of the purest motives, achieve this spiritual level and have the ability to resuscitate the dead even now.[791]

---

[789] *Yalkut Shimoni* on Isaiah 26, paragraph 431 כל המשתמש בטל תורה טל תורה מחייהו

[790] It is customary to write these letters on the back of the *Mezuzah* parchment opposite two places where the Tetragrammaton (י-ה-ו-ה) appears on the front (*Rama, Shulchan Aruch, Yoreh Deah* 288:15 עוד נוהגין לכתוב מבחוץ: כוז"ו במוכס"ז כוז"ו נגד (ה' א-להינו ה').

[791] *Yisrael Kedoshim* 6 ורוח הקודש הוא הטל תורה היורד מלמעלה על הנפשות דבני ישראל כידוע, דאותיות שאחרי שם הוי"ה הם בגימטריא 'טל'. כי שם הוי"ה הוא התגלות הדברי תורה בפועל והוא התורה שהוריד לנו משה רבינו ע"ה ומסרה לבני ישראל בפומבי. והטל הוא האחוריים והנעלם ממנה והוא שופע תמיד ולא מיעצר. רק כאשר יהיה כלי מוכן וראוי לקבל אותו הטל דברכה אז הוא נקלט בכל רמ"ח איבריו הרוחניים המחיים להגופניים ונקשר בהם עד שאין נפרד גם לאחר מיתה והסתלקות הנפש הוא נשאר תוך ההבלא דגרמי שבעצם הלוז שאין נרקב וכלה לעולם כדברי חז"ל (בראשית רבה כ"ח, ג'). ודבר זה הוא על ידי הקדושה הגמורה שבזרע יעקב שגם כל עניני הגופניים הם כולם לה' לבדו. דעל כן אמרו (חז"ל) יעקב אבינו ע"ה לא מת (מסכת

This explains why the children Elijah and Elisha revived grew up to be prophets themselves — Jonah and Habakkuk. They retained some of the prophetic spirit of holiness (רוּחַ הַקֹּדֶשׁ) which revived them.[792]

℘℘ Faith (אֱמוּנָה) Enabled Elijah and Elisha to Achieve this Level of Prophecy

Ma'or Vashamesh explains how the prophecy of *Moshe Rabbeinu* differed from that of other prophets:

The sages state that, "Whereas all the other prophets saw [the Divine Presence] through a non-transparent glass, *Moshe Rabbeinu* saw [the Divine Presence] through a transparent glass."[793]

When a sheet of glass is transparent, one sees completely through it and perceives what is on the other side with almost no distortion. *Moshe Rabbeinu* perceived the Divine Presence to the highest degree that any human being can, as if he were gazing through a clear pane of glass.

When glass has a backing, such as silver, it reflects the image of the person looking at it. Other prophets saw an image of the Divine Presence that was mixed with their own personalities. The degree to which these prophets could make out the Divine

---

תענית ה', ע"ב) כי מי שכל ענייניו הגופניים בקדושה כיעקב לא שייך ביה מיתה כלל...וגם כל זרעו אף העמי הארצות נקראים בשם 'יעקב' כמו שאמרו בבבא מציעא (ל"ג, ב') שיש בהם גם כן קדושה זו, אלא שהוא בעולם הזה בהעלם עצום... כי בהשגת רוח הקודש הוא זוכה ממילא גם כן לקדושה זו העליונה קדושת יעקב אבינו ע"ה שכל מעשיו לשם שמים ואז זוכה לתחיית המתים מצד עצמו ולא מצד דיבוקו לתלמיד חכם כשאר עם הארץ כי כבר יצא מכלל עם הארץ אחר שזכה לרוח הקודש... אף אם איזה יחידים זכו לזה, הרי לא זכו לזה עדיין כל הכנסת ישראל וכולם קומה אחת ואי אפשר לתקן אבר ממנה ולהפרידו מכלל הקומה שזהו פירוד משורשו.

792 *Beth Elokim, Shaar Hayesodoth* 60 כיונה וחבקוק שחיו על ידי אליהו ואלישע הנביאים ונזרקה בם קצת נבואתם.

793 B.T. *Yevamoth* 49B כִּדְתַנְיָא: כָּל הַנְּבִיאִים נִסְתַּכְּלוּ בְּאַסְפַּקְלַרְיָא שָׁאֵינָהּ מְאִירָה. מֹשֶׁה רַבֵּנוּ נִסְתַּכֵּל בְּאַסְפַּקְלַרְיָא הַמְּאִירָה.

Presence depended upon the strength of their faith because faith enables people to look beyond themselves and perceive God.[794]

The greater a prophet's faith, the more clearly he or she could perceive the Divine Presence. Prophets whose faith was exceptionally strong had a high degree of attachment to the light of the Divine Presence, which is the Source of Life (מְקוֹר הַחַיִּים),[795] and gained the power to revive the dead.

The root of the verb the *Tanach* uses to describe Elijah stretching himself over Jonah (וַיִּתְמֹדֵד) literally means "to measure oneself," from the Hebrew root *Middah* (מִדָּה).[796] The same word also means "attribute," so the Hebrew וַיִּתְמֹדֵד can be read to mean "to gain an attribute." "Attribute" (מִדָּה) bears the connotation of "resemblance" because things which share a certain attribute resemble one another. For example, all red objects share the common attribute of reflecting red light. The Hebrew for "attribute" (מִדָּה) hints at this because one can transpose its letters to spell "resemble" (דִּמָּה). The word which describes Elijah as stretching himself (וַיִּתְמֹדֵד) therefore implies that he used his tremendous faith to make himself resemble the Divine Presence and resurrect Jonah.

The same principle applied to Elisha. *Ma'or Vashamesh* explains that Elisha's staff represented faith, which supports a person just as a staff does. Although Gehazi studied under Elisha, he lacked faith. To the contrary, Gehazi mockingly told whoever

---

[794] *Ma'or Vashamesh, Shir Hashirim* והנה כל נביא ונביא השיג כפי מדריגתו באמונתו כן נתפשט אליו דמיון ה(כ.)בואה דכתיב, "וּבְיָד הַנְּבִיאִים אֲדַמֶּה" (הושע י"ב, י"א), לשון דמיון לכל אחד לפי מדריגתו, לבד (חרץ מ)משה שהיה באספקלריא המאירה, לא בדמיון...כדרך משל מראה הזכוכית שמתראה בה כל הצוורות והדמיונות מפני שיש בה זה דבר שמסתיר מעבר השני ואינו מאיר מעבר לעבר. אבל אם לא היה מסתיר ומסך מעבר השני לא היה נראה הדמיון של הרואה אלא היה מסתכל מעבר לעבר ומביט מה שהוא האמת. ולכן הנביאים שקיבלו נבואתם במראה דמיון כדרך הרואה במראה נתראה אליו צרותו ודמיונו של עצמו כן הנביאים כפי התקשרותו והראותו במראה שכינה, כן ראה בחינת דמיון שורשו של עצמו.

[795] *Arvei Nachal, Parashath Toldoth* אור השכינה שהוא מקור החיים

[796] *Rashi* on I Kings 17:21 וַיִּתְמֹדֵד – מלשון 'מדה', נשתטח עליו.

he met on his way to Shunem, "Do you believe that this staff can revive the dead?"[797] For this reason, Gehazi's efforts to revive Habakkuk failed.[798]

By contrast, Habakkuk's mother had complete faith in *Hashem* and His prophet. When her son died, her perfect faith allowed her to maintain her composure, and she did not reveal what had happened to anyone else. Her faith combined with that of Elisha to permit the prophet to resuscitate her son.

This explains why the Prophet Habakkuk later said, "The righteous lives by his faith."[799] With a slight change in pronunciation, this verse can be read to mean, "The righteous resurrects with his faith" (וְצַדִּיק בֶּאֱמוּנָתוֹ יְחַיֶּה).[800]

✌ The Talmudic Sages also Revived the Dead

The *Gemara* records many instances where the sages revived the dead. In fact, this practice was so widespread that the Roman Emperor Antoninus declared, "I know that the least among you can resurrect the dead."[801]

A well-known principle of the Jewish religion is that people who lived in former times were greater than those who lived later on. Elijah and Elisha lived hundreds of years prior to the *Talmudic* period. Why, then, did they seem to have far more difficulty reviving the dead than the rabbis of the *Talmud*, and why

---

[797] *Pirkei D'Rabbi Eliezer* 32 "התאמין: אומר היה שהיה פוגע אדם וכל בעיניו כשוחק הדבר היה שהמטה הזה מחיה את המת?" לפיכך לא עלתה בידו.

[798] *Ma'or Vashamesh, Shir Hashirim* שאלישע שלחו להחיות את המת ואמר לו שאף שידעת וקיבלת ולמדת ממני עניין זה, מכל מקום העיקר היא המשענת שעליה נשען הכל שהיא האמונה שאם תיקח האמונה כאשר היא אצלי בחזוק תוכל להחיות המת... ואמנם גיחזי אף שלקח המשענת לא הועיל כי לא לקח בשלימות כאשר צריכה להיות.

[799] Habakkuk 2:4 הִנֵּה עֻפְּלָה לֹא יָשְׁרָה נַפְשׁוֹ בּוֹ, וְצַדִּיק בֶּאֱמוּנָתוֹ יְחַיֶּה

[800] *Zohar* I:7B אַמַּאי אִקְרֵי חֲבַקּוּק? בְּגִין דִּכְתִיב, "לַמּוֹעֵד הַזֶּה כָּעֵת חַיָּה אַתְּ חוֹבֶקֶת בֵּן" (מלכים-ב, ד', ט"ז). וְדָא בְּרֵיהּ (ברה) דְּשׁוּנַמִּית הֲוָה.

[801] B.T. *Avodah Zarah* 10B יָדַעְנָא דְּזוּטֵי דְּאִית בְּכוּ מְחַיֶּה

was their feat considered such an unusual miracle whereas reviving the dead was commonplace in *Talmudic* times?[802]

✽✽✽ How Moshe Rabbeinu Killed an Egyptian who Attacked a Jew

The *Torah* records that:

It was in those days that Moses grew up and went out to his brothers and observed their travails. He saw an Egyptian man beating a Hebrew man from [among] his brothers. He looked this way and that, saw that there was no man, struck the Egyptian [dead], and hid him in the sand.[803]

The sages explain that the expression "saw that there was no man" means that, "[*Moshe Rabbeinu*] foresaw that there was no hope that righteous people would emerge from [this Egyptian] or any of his descendants to the end of all generations."[804]

When *Moshe Rabbeinu* saw that neither that Egyptian nor any of his descendants would succeed in rectifying some aspect of the spiritual realm, he uttered one of *Hashem's* Divine Names and thereby killed him.[805]

How did uttering a Divine Name accomplish this?

All existence comes from combinations and permutations of God's Divine Names. By pronouncing one of these Names, *Moshe Rabbeinu* connected the Egyptian to the spiritual source

---

[802] *Sha'arei Haleshem* 2:11, *Bayith Sheni* raises this issue: הנה מצאנו לכמה תנאים ואמוראים שעשו נסים נפלאים בנקל מאוד, מה שנעשו בדורות הראשונים רק על ידי הנביאים המצוינים והיו להם כל זה לאות ולמופת.

[803] Exodus 2:11-12 (יא) וַיְהִי בַּיָּמִים הָהֵם וַיִּגְדַּל מֹשֶׁה וַיֵּצֵא אֶל אֶחָיו וַיַּרְא בְּסִבְלֹתָם וַיַּרְא אִישׁ מִצְרִי מַכֶּה אִישׁ עִבְרִי מֵאֶחָיו. (יב) וַיִּפֶן כֹּה וָכֹה וַיַּרְא כִּי אֵין אִישׁ וַיַּךְ אֶת הַמִּצְרִי וַיִּטְמְנֵהוּ בַּחוֹל.

[804] *Shemoth Rabbah* 1:29 ורבנן אמרי: ראה שאין תוחלת של צדיקים עומדות הימנו ולא מזרעו עד סוף כל הדורות.

[805] *Shemoth Rabbah* 1:29 רבנן אמרי: הזכיר עליו את השם והרגו

from whence he came. Since this Egyptian served no further purpose in Creation, once he was attached to his spiritual source, he died.

❧❧❧ Elijah and Elisha Implemented this Process in Reverse

Since Jonah and Habakkuk died as young children, they must have completed their missions on Earth. Furthermore, because they died too young to have any children of their own, they were not destined to have any descendants who would rectify any aspect of the spiritual realm. In other words, they died because their lives served no further purpose in the scheme of Creation. Accordingly, Elijah and Elisha could only revive Jonah and Habakkuk by altering their preordained missions and the course of history.

When the *Tanach* states that Elisha "placed his mouth on [the child's] mouth, his eyes on his eyes, his hands on his hands," it means that he accessed corresponding aspects of the spiritual realm. In doing so, Elisha infused Habakkuk with a new life mission. As the sages explain, that mission was to teach the centrality of faith to the Jewish religion.[806]

Elijah followed the same procedure to revive Jonah. Jonah's new mission in life was to demonstrate the power of repentance as he did when he convinced the Gentiles of Nineveh to give up their evil ways. Jonah's name (יוֹנָה) has a numeric value of seventy-one corresponding to the seventy nations of the world plus Israel, because repentance can help anyone, including non-Jews.

---

[806] B.T. *Makkoth* 24A (חבקוק ב', ד') שֶׁנֶּאֱמַר, "וְצַדִּיק בֶּאֱמוּנָתוֹ יִחְיֶה" – שֶׁנֶּאֱמַר עַל אַחַת בָּא חֲבַקוּק וְהֶעֱמִידָן

ഇഇഇ The Rabbis of the Talmud did not Alter History

The life missions of people who lived in earlier generations were far more vital to the course of history than were the life missions of those who came later. As Rabbi Moshe Chaim Luzzatto explains:

> The main branches of the tree of our father Abraham, may peace by upon him, were 600,000, who were those who emerged from Egypt... And all who followed after them are considered details of the offshoots of those main branches.[807]

Jonah and Habakkuk possessed lofty souls typical of people who lived in their times. Once they finished their missions in life, Elijah and Elisha needed to go to great lengths to acquire new missions for them so that they could be revived, with the result that Jonah and Habakkuk became prophets whose prophecies have lasting significance for all generations.

Although people who lived in *Talmudic* times were much greater than those living today, they were on a far lower spiritual level than those who lived in the times of the prophets. Their souls were details of the offshoots of the souls of earlier generations. The *Talmudic* rabbis had no need alter the course of history and assign a momentous new mission to a corpse in order to revive it. Accordingly, the sages succeeded in reviving the dead more easily and more frequently than Elijah and Elisha did, and this feat was not considered to be of any great consequence.

May we all merit to fulfill our missions in life and to witness the ultimate redemption very soon!

---

[807] *Derech Hashem* 2:4:5, ענפי אילנו של אברהם אבינו עליו השלום, הכוללים, הנה הם עד ששים ריבוא, שהם אותם שיצאו ממצרים... וכל הבאים אחריהם, נחשבים פרטים לתולדות הכוללים האלה.

APPENDICES

APPENDIX A

B.T. *Bechoroth* 8B-9A

אָמַר לוֹ קֵיסָר לְרַבִּי יְהוֹשֻׁעַ בֶּן חֲנַנְיָה: "נָחָשׁ לְכַמָּה מִיעַבֵּר וּמוֹלִיד?" אָמַר לֵיהּ: "לְשֵׁב שָׁנֵי". וְהָא סָבֵי דְבֵי אַתּוּנָא אַרְבְּעִינְהוּ וְאוֹלִיד לִתְלָת". "הַנֵּהוּ מִיעַבְּרֵי הֲווֹ מֵעִיקָּרָא אַרְבַּע שְׁנִין"..."וְהָא חַכִּימֵי אִינּוּן". "אֲנַן חַכִּימִינַן מִנַּיְיהוּ". "אִי חֲכִימַת זִיל זַכִּינְהוּ וְאַיְיתִינְהוּ לִי". אָמַר לֵיהּ: "כַּמָּה הֲווּ?" "שִׁיתִין גַּבְרֵי". אֲמַר לֵיהּ: "עֲבִיד לִי סְפִינָתָא דְּאִית בָּהּ שִׁיתִין בָּתֵי וְכָל בֵּיתָא אִית בָּהּ שִׁיתִין בִּסְתַּרְקֵי". עֲבִיד לֵיהּ. כִּי מָטָא לְהָתָם (עַל) לְבֵי טַבָחָא. אַשְׁכָּחֵיהּ לְהַהוּא גַּבְרָא דְּקָא פָּשִׁיט חַיּוּתָא. אָמַר לֵיהּ: "רֵישָׁךְ לְזָבּוּנֵי?" אֲמַר לֵיהּ: "אִין". אָמַר לֵיהּ: "בְּכַמָּה?" אָמַר לֵיהּ: "בְּפַלְגָא דְזוּזָא". יְהַב לֵיהּ. לְסוֹף אָמַר לֵיהּ: "אֲנָא רֵישָׁא דְחַיּוּתָא אֲמַרִי לָךְ". אָמַר לֵיהּ: "אִי בָעֵית דְּאִישְׁבְּקָךְ סַגִּי אַחֲוֵי לִי פִּיתְחָא דְבֵי אַתּוּנָא". אָמַר לֵיהּ: "מִסְתְּפִינָא דְּכָל דְּמֶחֲוֵי קַטְלֵי לֵיהּ". אָמַר לֵיהּ: "דָּרֵי כְּרִיכָא דְקַנְיָא וְכִי מָטִית לְהָתָם זַקְפֵהּ כְּמַאן דְּקָא מִתְּפַּח". אֲזַל אַשְׁכַּח דָּרְבָּנֵי מִגַּוַּאי וְדָרְבָּנֵי מִבָּרָאֵי דְּאִי חֲזוּ כַּרְעָא דְעָיְילָא קַטְלֵי לְהוּ לְבָרָאֵי וּדְנַפְקָא קַטְלֵי לְהוּ לְגַוָּאֵי. אַפְכָהּ לְסַנְדְּלֵיהּ קַטְלֵי לְהוּ לְגַוַּאי אַפְכָהּ לְסַנְדְּלֵיהּ קַטְלִינְהוּ לְכוּלְּהוּ. (אֲזַל) אַשְׁכַּח יְנוּקֵי מִלְּעֵיל סָבֵי מִלְּתַחַת. אָמַר: "אִי יָהֵיבְנָא שְׁלָמָא לְהָנֵי קַטְלֵי לִי הַנֵי. סָבְרִי אֲנַן עֲדִיפָנַן דְּאֲנַן קַשִׁינַן טְפֵי וְאִינְהוּ דַרְדְּקֵי". אָמַר: "שְׁלָמָא לְכוּ". אָמְרוּ לֵיהּ: "מַאי עֲבִידְתִּיךְ?" אָמַר לְהוּ: "חַכִּימָא דִיהוּדָאֵי אֲנָא. בָּעֵינָא לְמִיגְמַר חָכְמְתָא מִינַּיְיכוּ". "אִי הָכִי נִיבְעֵי לָךְ". אָמַר לְהוּ: "לְחַיֵּי. אִי זְכִיתָא (לִי) כָּל דְּבָעִיתוּ עֲבִידוּ בֵּי וְאִי זָכֵינָא בְּכוּ אִיכְלוּ גַּבַּאי בְּסַפִּינָתָא". אֲמַרִי לֵיהּ: "הַהוּא גַבְרָא דְאָזִיל וְאָזֵיל וּבָעֵי אִתְּתָא וְלָא יַהֲבוּ לֵיהּ מַאי חֲזִי לֵיהּ דְּאָזֵיל הֵיכָא דְּמַדְלוּ מִינֵּיהּ?" שָׁקֵל סִיכְתָּא דָּצָהּ לְתַתַּאי לָא עָאל לְעֵילָאִי עָאל. אָמַר: "הַאי נָמֵי מִתְרְמֵי בַת מַזְלֵיהּ". "גַּבְרָא דְאוֹזֵיף וְטָרִיף, מֵי חֲזָא דְּהָדַר אוֹזֵיף?" אָמַר לְהוּ: "גַּבְרָא אֲזַל לְאַגְמָא, קְטַל קַמָּא טוּנָא, וְלָא מַצֵּי בֵּיהּ, קָטִיל וּמַנַּח עִילָוֵיהּ עַד דְּאִיתְרְמֵי אִינָשׁ מַדְלֵי לֵיהּ". אֲמְרוּ לֵיהּ: "אֵימָא לָן מִילֵּי דְּבַדָּאֵי". אָמַר לְהוּ: "הֲוָה לָן כּוּדְנְיָיתָא דִּילִידָא וְהַוָה תָּלֵי לֵיהּ פִּיתְקָא וְכָתֵיב בֵּיהּ דְּמַסִּיק בְּבֵי אַבָּא מְאָה אַלְפָּא זוּזֵי". אָמְרוּ לֵיהּ: "וְכוּדְנְיָיתָא מִי יָלְדָה?!" אָמְרוּ לְהוּ: "הֵי נִיהוּ מִילֵּי דְּבַדָּאֵי". "מִילְחָא כִּי סָרְיָא בַּמַּאי מַלְחֵי לָהּ?" אָמַר לְהוּ: "בְּסִילְתָּא דְּכוּדַנְיָתָא". "וּמִי אִיכָּא סִילְתָּא לְכוּדַנְיָתָא?! "וּמִילְחָא מִי סָרֵי?" "בְּנֵי לָן בֵּיתָא בַּאֲוִירָא דְעָלְמָא". אֲמַר שֵׁם תַּלָּא בֵּין רְקִיעָא לְאַרְעָא. אָמַר לְהוּ: "אַסֵּיקוּ לִי לִיבְנֵי וְטִינָא!" "מִצֵּיעוּתֵיהּ דְּעָלְמָא הֵיכָא?" זָקְפָהּ לְאֶצְבַּעָתֵיהּ אָמַר לְהוּ: "הָכָא". אָמְרוּ לֵיהּ: "מִי יֵימַר?" "אַיְיתוּ אֲשֵׁלֵי וּמַשְׁחוּ". "אִית לָן בֵּירָא בְדַבְרָא". עַיְיְלֵיהּ לְמָתָא! אָמַר לְהוּ: "אִיפְשִׁילוּ לִי חַבְלֵי מִפָּארֵי וְאֵיעַיְילֵי"...אַיְיתוּ לֵיהּ תְּרֵי בֵיעֵי. אָמְרוּ לֵיהּ: "הֵי דְּזָגָתָא אוּכְמְתֵי וְהֵי דְזָגָתָא חִיוַּורְתִּי?" אַיְיתִי לְהוּ אִיהוּ תְּרֵי גְבִינֵי. אָמַר לְהוּ: "הֵי דְּעִיזָא אוּכַּמְתֵי וְהֵי דְּעִיזָא חִיוַּורְתִי?"...אַיְיתִינְהוּ. כָּל חַד וְחַד כִּי חֲזִי שִׁיתִין בִּסְתַּרְקֵי אָמַר: "כּוּלְּהוּ חַבְרָאֵי לְהָכָא אַתּוּ"...אָמַר לֵיהּ לְסַפּוּנָא: "שָׁרֵי סְפִינְתָּךְ!" ...כִּי מָטֵי לְבֵי בְּלִיעִי מְלָא כּוּזָא דְמַיָּא מִבֵּי בְּלִיעִי...אָמַר לֵיהּ: "כָּל דְּבָעֵית עֲבִיד בְּהוּ". אַיְיתִינְהוּ מַיָּא דְּאֵייתֵי מִבֵּי בְּלִיעֵי. שָׁדִינְהוּ בְּתִיגְדָּא. אָמַר לְהוּ: "מַלְיוּהּ לְהוּ וְאִיזִילוּ לְכוּ". מְלָא שָׁדוּ בֵּיהּ קַמָּאֵי קַמָּאֵי וּבָלַע לְהוּ. מְלוּ עַד דְּשָׁמִיט כְּתַפַּיְיהוּ וּבְלוּ וַאֲזוּל.

APPENDIX B

B.T. *Avodah Zarah* 3A-3B

[כָּךְ] אוֹמְרִים [הָעוֹבְדֵי כּוֹכָבִים] לִפְנֵי [הַקָּדוֹשׁ בָּרוּךְ הוּא], "רִבּוֹנוֹ שֶׁל עוֹלָם, יִשְׂרָאֵל שֶׁקִּיבְּלוּהָ הֵיכָן קִיְּמוּהָ?" אָמַר לָהֶם הַקָּדוֹשׁ בָּרוּךְ הוּא, "אֲנִי מֵעִיד בָּהֶם שֶׁקִּיְּמוּ אֶת הַתּוֹרָה [כּוּלָּהּ]". ...אָמְרוּ לְפָנָיו, "רִבּוֹנוֹ שֶׁל עוֹלָם, תְּנָה לָנוּ מֵרֹאשׁ וְנַעֲשֶׂנָה". אָמַר לָהֶן הַקָּדוֹשׁ בָּרוּךְ הוּא,

"שׁוֹטִים שֶׁבָּעוֹלָם! מִי שֶׁטָּרַח בְּעֶרֶב שַׁבָּת יֹאכַל בְּשַׁבָּת. מִי שֶׁלֹּא טָרַח בְּעֶרֶב שַׁבָּת מֵהֵיכָן יֹאכַל בְּשַׁבָּת? אֶלָּא אַף עַל פִּי כֵן, מִצְוָה קַלָּה יֵשׁ לִי וְסוּכָּה שְׁמָהּ. לְכוּ וַעֲשׂוּ אוֹתָהּ"... שֶׁאֵין הַקָּדוֹשׁ בָּרוּךְ הוּא בָּא בִּטְרוּנְיָא עִם בְּרִיּוֹתָיו... מִיָּד כָּל אֶחָד [וְאֶחָד] נוֹטֵל וְהוֹלֵךְ וְעוֹשֶׂה סוּכָּה בְּרֹאשׁ גַּגּוֹ. וְהַקָּדוֹשׁ בָּרוּךְ הוּא מַקְדִּיר הוּא עֲלֵיהֶם חַמָּה בִּתְקוּפַת תַּמּוּז, וְכָל אֶחָד וְאֶחָד מְבַעֵט בְּסוּכָּתוֹ וְיוֹצֵא... וְהָא אָמַרְתָּ, "אֵין הַקָּדוֹשׁ בָּרוּךְ הוּא בָּא בִּטְרוּנְיָא עִם בְּרִיּוֹתָיו?" מִשּׁוּם דְּיִשְׂרָאֵל נַמֵּי זִמְנֵי דְּמַשְׁכָא לְהוּ תְּקוּפַת תַּמּוּז עַד חַגָּא, וְהַרֵי לְהוּ צַעֲרָא. וְהָאָמַר רָבָא: מִצְטַעֵר פָּטוּר מִן הַסּוּכָּה? נְהִי דְּפָטוּר, בְּעוּטֵי מִי מַבְעִיטֵי? מִיָּד הַקָּדוֹשׁ בָּרוּךְ הוּא יוֹשֵׁב וּמְשַׂחֵק עֲלֵיהֶן... אָמַר רַבִּי יִצְחָק: אֵין שְׂחוֹק לִפְנֵי הַקָּדוֹשׁ בָּרוּךְ הוּא אֶלָּא אוֹתוֹ הַיּוֹם בִּלְבָד. אִיכָּא דְּמַתְנֵי לְהָא דְּרַבִּי יִצְחָק אַהָא דְּתַנְיָא... [שֶׁבְּעָתִיד יִהְיוּ עוֹבְדֵי כּוֹכָבִים] שֶׁנַּעֲשׂוּ גֵּרִים גְּרוּרִים וּמַנִּיחִין תְּפִילִין בְּרָאשֵׁיהֶם, תְּפִלִּין בִּזְרוֹעוֹתֵיהֶם, צִיצִית בְּבִגְדֵיהֶם, מְזוּזָה בְּפִתְחֵיהֶם. כֵּיוָן שֶׁרוֹאִין מִלְחֶמֶת גּוֹג וּמָגוֹג, אוֹמֵר לָהֶן, "עַל מַה בָּאתֶם?" אוֹמְרִים לוֹ, "עַל ה' וְעַל מְשִׁיחוֹ"!... וְכָל אֶחָד מְנַתֵּק מִצְוָתוֹ וְהוֹלֵךְ... וְהַקָּדוֹשׁ בָּרוּךְ הוּא יוֹשֵׁב וּמְשַׂחֵק... אָמַר רַבִּי יִצְחָק: אֵין לוֹ לְהַקָּדוֹשׁ בָּרוּךְ הוּא שְׂחוֹק אֶלָּא אוֹתוֹ הַיּוֹם בִּלְבָד.

APPENDIX C

The *Kabbalists* refer to twelve diagonal relationships among the supernal spheres. These resemble the way light reflects back and forth between concave mirrors, as illustrated below.

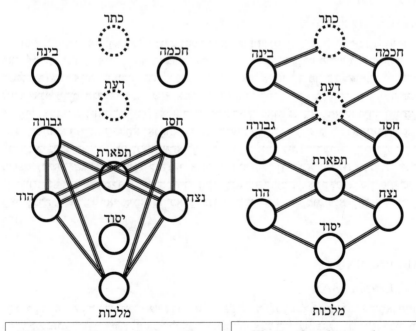

| The twelve diagonals according to Rabbi Moshe Cordovero | The twelve diagonals according to the *Vilna Gaon* |

APPENDIX D

B.T. *Shabbath* 156B

דִּשְׁמוּאֵל וְאַבְלֵט הֲווּ יָתְבִי, וַהֲווּ קָאָזְלֵי הָנַךְ אֵינָשֵׁי לְאַגְמָא. אֲמַר לֵיהּ אַבְלֵט לִשְׁמוּאֵל: "הַאי גַּבְרָא אָזֵיל וְלָא אָתֵי. טָרֵיק לֵיהּ חִיוְיָא וּמָיֵית". אֲמַר לֵיהּ שְׁמוּאֵל: "אִי בַּר יִשְׂרָאֵל הוּא, אָזֵיל וְאָתֵי". אַדְּיָתְבִי, אָזֵיל וְאָתֵי. קָם אַבְלֵט. שְׁדֵי לְטוּנֵיהּ. אַשְׁכַּח בֵּיהּ חִיוְיָא דִּפְסִיק וּשְׁדֵי בִּתְרֵתֵּי גּוּבֵי. אֲמַר לֵיהּ שְׁמוּאֵל: "מַאי עֲבַדְתְּ?" אֲמַר לֵיהּ: "כָּל יוֹמָא הֲוָה מַרְמִינַן רִיפְתָּא בַּהֲדֵי הֲדָדֵי וְאָכְלִינַן. הָאִידְנָא הֲוָה אִיכָּא חַד מִינַן דְּלָא הֲוָה לֵיהּ רִיפְתָּא. הֲוָה קָא מִכְסָף. אֲמִינָא לְהוּ, 'אֲנָא קָאֵימְנָא וְאַרְמֵינָא'. כִּי מְטַאי לְגַבֵּיהּ, שָׁוֵאי נַפְשַׁאי כְּמַאן דְּשָׁקֵילִי מִינֵיהּ כִּי הֵיכִי דְּלָא לִיכְסִיף". אֲמַר לֵיהּ: "מִצְוָה עֲבַדְתְּ". נְפַק שְׁמוּאֵל וְדָרֵשׁ: "'וּצְדָקָה תַּצִּיל מִמָּוֶת' (משלי י׳, ב׳; י״א, ד׳) וְלֹא מִמִּיתָה מְשׁוּנָּה, אֶלָּא מִמִּיתָה עַצְמָהּ"... דְּרַבִּי עֲקִיבָא הֲוָיָא לֵיהּ בְּרַתָּא. אָמְרֵי לֵיהּ כַּלְדָּאֵי: "הַהוּא יוֹמָא דְּעָיְילָה לְבֵי גְּנָנָא טָרֵיק לָהּ חִיוְיָא וּמָיְתָא". הֲוָה דְּאִיגְּנָא אַמִּילְתָא טוּבָא. הַהוּא יוֹמָא, שְׁקַלְתָּהּ לְמַכְבַּנְתָּא, דַּצְתַהּ בְּגוּדָא. אִיתְרְמֵי אִיתֵּיב בְּעֵינֵיהּ דְּחִיוְיָא. לְצַפְרָא, כִּי קָא שָׁקְלָה לַהּ הֲוָה קָא סָרֵיךְ וְאָתֵי חִיוְיָא בַּתְרַהּ. אֲמַר לָהּ אֲבוּהַּ: "מַאי עֲבַדְתְּ?" אָמְרָה לֵיהּ: "בְּפַנְיָא, אֲתָא עַנְיָא, קְרָא אַבָּבָא, וַהֲווּ טְרִידֵי כּוּלֵי עָלְמָא בִּסְעוּדָתָא, וְלֵיכָּא דְּשַׁמְעֵיהּ. קָאֵימְנָא, שְׁקַלְתֵּי לְרִיסְתָּנַאי דִּיהַבְתְּ לִי, יְהַבְתֵּיהּ נִיהֲלֵיהּ". אֲמַר לָהּ: "מִצְוָה עֲבַדְתְּ". נְפַק רַבִּי עֲקִיבָא וְדָרֵשׁ: "'וּצְדָקָה תַּצִּיל מִמָּוֶת', וְלֹא מִמִּיתָה מְשׁוּנָּה, אֶלָּא מִמִּיתָה עַצְמָהּ".

APPENDIX E

B.T. *Chagigah* 4B-5A

רַב יוֹסֵף כִּי מָטֵי לְהַאי קְרָא בָּכֵי — "וְיֵשׁ נִסְפֶּה בְּלֹא מִשְׁפָּט" (משלי י״ג, כ״ג). אֲמַר: "מִי אִיכָּא דְּאָזֵיל בְּלָא זִמְנֵיהּ?" אִין, כִּי הָא דְּרַב בִּיבִי בַּר אַבַּיֵי הֲוָה שְׁכִיחַ גַּבֵּיהּ מַלְאַךְ הַמָּוֶת. אֲמַר לֵיהּ לִשְׁלוּחֵיהּ: "זִיל אַיְיתִי לִי מִרְיָם מְגַדְּלָא שֵׂיעַר נַשַׁיָּיא". אָזַל אַיְיתִי לֵיהּ מִרְיָם מְגַדְּלָא דַּרְדְּקֵי. אֲמַר לֵיהּ: "אֲנָא מִרְיָם מְגַדְּלָא שֵׂיעַר נַשַׁיָּיא אֲמַרִי לָךְ!" אֲמַר לֵיהּ: "אִי הָכִי אַהְדְּרַהּ". אֲמַר לֵיהּ: "הוֹאִיל וְאַיְיתֵיתַהּ לֶיהֱוֵי לְמִנְיָנָא, וְאֶלָּא הֵיכִי יָכְלַתְּ לָהּ?" הֲוַת נְקִיטָא מַתְאָרָא בִּידַהּ וְהַוָת קָא שָׁגְרָא וּמַחְרְיָא תַּנּוּרָא. שְׁקַלְתָּא וְאַנַּחְתָּא אַגַּבֵּא דְּכַרְעַהּ. קַדְחָה וְאִיתְּרַע מַזָּלַהּ וְאַיְיתֵיתַהּ". אֲמַר לֵיהּ רַב בִּיבִי בַּר אַבַּיֵי: "אִית לְכוּ רְשׁוּתָא לְמֶיעְבַּד הָכִי?" אֲמַר לֵיהּ: "וְהָכְתִיב, 'וְיֵשׁ נִסְפֶּה בְּלֹא מִשְׁפָּט' (משלי י״ג, כ״ג)?" אֲמַר לֵיהּ: "וְלֹא כְּתִיב, 'דּוֹר הֹלֵךְ וְדוֹר בָּא' (קהלת א׳, ד׳)?" אֲמַר: "דְּרָעֵינָא לְהוּ אֲנָא עַד דְּמָלוּ לְהוּ לְדָרָא וַהֲדַר מַשְׁלֵימְנָא לֵיהּ לִדוּמָה". אֲמַר לֵיהּ: "סוֹף סוֹף שְׁנֵיהּ מַאי עֲבַדְתְּ?" אֲמַר: "אִי אִיכָּא צוּרְבָּא מֵרַבָּנָן דְּמַעֲבִיר בְּמִילֵּיהּ מוּסְפֵינָא לְהוּ לֵיהּ וְהַוְיָא חֲלוּפֵיהּ".

APPENDIX F

B.T. *Eruvin* 13A

וְהָאָמַר רַב יְהוּדָה אָמַר שְׁמוּאֵל מִשּׁוּם רַבִּי מֵאִיר: כְּשֶׁהָיִיתִי לוֹמֵד תּוֹרָה אֵצֶל רַבִּי עֲקִיבָא, הָיִיתִי מַטִּיל קַנְקַנְתּוֹם לְתוֹךְ הַדְּיוֹ, וְלֹא אָמַר לִי דָּבָר. וּכְשֶׁבָּאתִי אֵצֶל רַבִּי יִשְׁמָעֵאל, אָמַר לִי: "בְּנִי, מַה מְּלַאכְתְּךָ?" אָמַרְתִּי לוֹ: "לַבְלָר אֲנִי". אָמַר לִי: "בְּנִי, הֱוֵי זָהִיר בִּמְלַאכְתְּךָ, שֶׁמְּלַאכְתְּךָ מְלֶאכֶת שָׁמַיִם הִיא. שֶׁמָּא אַתָּה מְחַסֵּר אוֹת אַחַת, אוֹ מְיַיתֵּר אוֹת אַחַת, נִמְצֵאתָ מַחֲרִיב אֶת כָּל הָעוֹלָם כּוּלּוֹ". אָמַרְתִּי לוֹ: "דָּבָר אֶחָד יֵשׁ לִי, וְקַנְקַנְתּוֹם שְׁמוֹ, שֶׁאֲנִי מֵטִיל לְתוֹךְ הַדְּיוֹ". אָמַר לִי: "וְכִי

מַטִּילִין קַנְקַנְתּוֹם לְתוֹךְ הַדְּיוֹ? וַהֲלֹא אָמְרָה תּוֹרָה, "וְכָתַב" "וּמָחָה" – כְּתָב שֶׁיָּכוֹל לִמְחוֹת". מַאי קָאָמַר לֵיהּ? וּמַאי קָא מְהַדַּר לֵיהּ? הָכִי קָאָמַר לֵיהּ: "לָא מִיבַּעְיָא בַּחֲסִירוֹת וִיתֵרוֹת, [דְּלָא טָעֵינָא] דְּבָקִי אֲנָא. אֶלָּא אֲפִילוּ מֵיחַשׁ לְזִבוּב נָמִי דִּלְמָא אָתֵי וְיָתֵיב אַתַּגֵּיהּ דְּדַלֵי"ת וּמַחֵיק לֵיהּ, וּמַשַּׁוֵי לֵיהּ רֵי"שׁ – דָּבָר אֶחָד יֵשׁ לִי וְקַנְקַנְתּוֹם שְׁמוֹ, שֶׁאֲנִי מַטִּיל לְתוֹךְ הַדְּיוֹ".

APPENDIX G

B.T. *Berachoth* 55A

אָמַר רַבִּי שְׁמוּאֵל בַּר נַחְמָנִי אָמַר רַבִּי יוֹנָתָן: בְּצַלְאֵל עַל שֵׁם חָכְמָתוֹ נִקְרָא. בְּשָׁעָה שֶׁאָמַר לוֹ הַקָּדוֹשׁ בָּרוּךְ הוּא לְמֹשֶׁה: "לֵךְ אֱמוֹר לוֹ לִבְצַלְאֵל, 'עֲשֵׂה לִי מִשְׁכָּן אָרוֹן וְכֵלִים'", הָלַךְ מֹשֶׁה וְהָפַךְ וְאָמַר לוֹ: "עֲשֵׂה אָרוֹן וְכֵלִים וּמִשְׁכָּן". אָמַר לוֹ: "מֹשֶׁה רַבֵּנוּ, מִנְהָגוֹ שֶׁל עוֹלָם אָדָם בּוֹנֶה בַּיִת וְאַחַר כָּךְ מַכְנִיס לְתוֹכוֹ כֵּלִים, וְאַתָּה אוֹמֵר לִי, 'עֲשֵׂה אָרוֹן וְכֵלִים וּמִשְׁכָּן'? כֵּלִים שֶׁאֲנִי עוֹשֶׂה לְהֵיכָן אַכְנִיסֵם? שֶׁמָּא כָּךְ אָמַר לְךָ הַקָּדוֹשׁ בָּרוּךְ הוּא, 'עֲשֵׂה מִשְׁכָּן אָרוֹן וְכֵלִים'". אָמַר לוֹ: "שֶׁמָּא בְּצֵל אֵ-ל הָיִיתָ וְיָדַעְתָּ!" אָמַר רַב יְהוּדָה אָמַר רַב: יוֹדֵעַ הָיָה בְּצַלְאֵל לְצָרֵף אוֹתִיּוֹת שֶׁנִּבְרְאוּ בָּהֶן שָׁמַיִם וָאָרֶץ. כְּתִיב הָכָא, "וַיְמַלֵּא אֹתוֹ רוּחַ אֱ-לֹהִים בְּחָכְמָה בִּתְבוּנָה וּבְדַעַת" (שמות ל"ה, ל"א) וּכְתִיב הָתָם, "ה' בְּחָכְמָה יָסַד אָרֶץ כּוֹנֵן שָׁמַיִם בִּתְבוּנָה" (משלי ג', י"ט) וּכְתִיב, "בְּדַעְתּוֹ תְּהוֹמוֹת נִבְקָעוּ" (משלי ג', כ'). אָמַר רַבִּי יוֹחָנָן: אֵין הַקָּדוֹשׁ בָּרוּךְ הוּא נוֹתֵן חָכְמָה אֶלָּא לְמִי שֶׁיֵּשׁ בּוֹ חָכְמָה.

APPENDIX H

B.T. *Menachoth* 29B

אָמַר רַב יְהוּדָה אָמַר רַב: בְּשָׁעָה שֶׁעָלָה מֹשֶׁה לַמָּרוֹם מְצָאוֹ לְהַקָּדוֹשׁ בָּרוּךְ הוּא שֶׁיּוֹשֵׁב וְקוֹשֵׁר כְּתָרִים לָאוֹתִיּוֹת. אָמַר לְפָנָיו. אָמַר לְפָנָיו: "רִבּוֹנוֹ שֶׁל עוֹלָם, מִי מְעַכֵּב עַל יָדְךָ?" אָמַר לוֹ: "אָדָם אֶחָד יֵשׁ שֶׁעָתִיד לִהְיוֹת בְּסוֹף כַּמָּה דוֹרוֹת וַעֲקִיבָא בֶּן יוֹסֵף שְׁמוֹ שֶׁעָתִיד לִדְרוֹשׁ עַל כָּל קוֹץ וְקוֹץ תִּלִּין תִּלִּין שֶׁל הֲלָכוֹת". אָמַר לְפָנָיו: "רִבּוֹנוֹ שֶׁל עוֹלָם, הַרְאֵהוּ לִי". אָמַר לוֹ: "חֲזוֹר לַאֲחוֹרֶךָ". הָלַךְ וְיָשַׁב לְסוֹף שְׁמוֹנָה שׁוּרוֹת, וְלֹא הָיָה יוֹדֵעַ מָה הֵן אוֹמְרִים. תָּשַׁשׁ כֹּחוֹ. כֵּיוָן שֶׁהִגִּיעַ לְדָבָר אֶחָד, אָמְרוּ לוֹ תַּלְמִידָיו: "רַבִּי מִנַּיִן לְךָ?" אָמַר לָהֶן: "הֲלָכָה לְמֹשֶׁה מִסִּינַי". נִתְיַישְּׁבָה דַּעְתּוֹ. חָזַר וּבָא לִפְנֵי הַקָּדוֹשׁ בָּרוּךְ הוּא. אָמַר לְפָנָיו: "רִבּוֹנוֹ שֶׁל עוֹלָם, יֵשׁ לְךָ אָדָם כָּזֶה וְאַתָּה נוֹתֵן תּוֹרָה עַל יָדִי?" אָמַר לוֹ: "שְׁתוֹק! כָּךְ עָלָה בְּמַחֲשָׁבָה לְפָנַי". אָמַר לְפָנָיו: "רִבּוֹנוֹ שֶׁל עוֹלָם, הֶרְאִיתַנִי תּוֹרָתוֹ. הַרְאֵנִי שְׂכָרוֹ". אָמַר לוֹ: "חֲזוֹר [לַאֲחוֹרֶךָ]". חָזַר לַאֲחוֹרָיו. רָאָה שֶׁשּׁוֹקְלִין בְּשָׂרוֹ בְּמַקּוּלִין. אָמַר לְפָנָיו: "רִבּוֹנוֹ שֶׁל עוֹלָם, זוֹ תּוֹרָה וְזוֹ שְׂכָרָהּ?" אָמַר לוֹ: "שְׁתוֹק! כָּךְ עָלָה בְּמַחֲשָׁבָה לְפָנַי".

APPENDIX I

I Kings 17:10-22

וַיָּקָם וַיֵּלֶךְ צָרְפַתָה וַיָּבֹא אֶל פֶּתַח הָעִיר וְהִנֵּה שָׁם אִשָּׁה אַלְמָנָה מְקֹשֶׁשֶׁת עֵצִים וַיִּקְרָא אֵלֶיהָ וַיֹּאמַר קְחִי נָא לִי מְעַט מַיִם בַּכְּלִי וְאֶשְׁתֶּה. וַתֵּלֶךְ לָקַחַת וַיִּקְרָא אֵלֶיהָ וַיֹּאמַר לִקְחִי נָא לִי פַּת לֶחֶם בְּיָדֵךְ. וַתֹּאמֶר חַי ה' אֱ-לֹהֶיךָ אִם יֶשׁ לִי מָעוֹג כִּי אִם מְלֹא כַף קֶמַח בַּכַּד וּמְעַט שֶׁמֶן בַּצַּפָּחַת וְהִנְנִי מְקֹשֶׁשֶׁת שְׁנַיִם עֵצִים וּבָאתִי וַעֲשִׂיתִיהוּ לִי וְלִבְנִי וַאֲכַלְנֻהוּ וָמָתְנוּ. וַיֹּאמֶר אֵלֶיהָ אֵלִיָּהוּ אַל תִּירְאִי

כִּי אִם עֲשִׂי כִדְבָרֵךְ אַךְ עֲשִׂי לִי מִשָּׁם עֻגָה קְטַנָּה בָרִאשֹׁנָה וְהוֹצֵאת לִי וְלָךְ וְלִבְנֵךְ תַּעֲשִׂי בָּאַחֲרֹנָה. וַתֵּלֶךְ וַתַּעֲשֶׂה כִּדְבַר אֵלִיָּהוּ וַתֹּאכַל הוּא וָהִיא וּבֵיתָהּ יָמִים [הִיא וָהוּא קרי]... וַיְהִי אַחַר הַדְּבָרִים הָאֵלֶּה חָלָה בֶּן הָאִשָּׁה בַּעֲלַת הַבָּיִת וַיְהִי חָלְיוֹ חָזָק מְאֹד עַד אֲשֶׁר לֹא נוֹתְרָה בּוֹ נְשָׁמָה. וַתֹּאמֶר אֶל אֵלִיָּהוּ מַה לִּי וָלָךְ אִישׁ הָאֱ-לֹהִים בָּאתָ אֵלַי לְהַזְכִּיר אֶת עֲוֹנִי וּלְהָמִית אֶת בְּנִי. וַיֹּאמֶר אֵלֶיהָ תְּנִי לִי אֶת בְּנֵךְ וַיִּקָּחֵהוּ מֵחֵיקָהּ וַיַּעֲלֵהוּ אֶל הָעֲלִיָּה אֲשֶׁר הוּא יֹשֵׁב שָׁם וַיַּשְׁכִּבֵהוּ עַל מִטָּתוֹ. וַיִּקְרָא אֶל ה׳ וַיֹּאמַר ה׳ אֱ-לֹהָי הֲגַם עַל הָאַלְמָנָה אֲשֶׁר אֲנִי מִתְגּוֹרֵר עִמָּהּ הֲרֵעוֹתָ לְהָמִית אֶת בְּנָהּ. וַיִּתְמֹדֵד עַל הַיֶּלֶד שָׁלֹשׁ פְּעָמִים וַיִּקְרָא אֶל ה׳ וַיֹּאמַר ה׳ אֱ-לֹהָי תָּשָׁב נָא נֶפֶשׁ הַיֶּלֶד הַזֶּה עַל קִרְבּוֹ. וַיִּשְׁמַע ה׳ בְּקוֹל אֵלִיָּהוּ וַתָּשָׁב נֶפֶשׁ הַיֶּלֶד עַל קִרְבּוֹ וַיֶּחִי.

APPENDIX J

II Kings 4:17-35

וַתַּהַר הָאִשָּׁה וַתֵּלֶד בֵּן לַמּוֹעֵד הַזֶּה כָּעֵת חַיָּה אֲשֶׁר דִּבֶּר אֵלֶיהָ אֱלִישָׁע. וַיִּגְדַּל הַיֶּלֶד וַיְהִי הַיּוֹם וַיֵּצֵא אֶל אָבִיו אֶל הַקֹּצְרִים. וַיֹּאמֶר אֶל אָבִיו רֹאשִׁי רֹאשִׁי וַיֹּאמֶר אֶל הַנַּעַר שָׂאֵהוּ אֶל אִמּוֹ. וַיִּשָּׂאֵהוּ וַיְבִיאֵהוּ אֶל אִמּוֹ וַיֵּשֶׁב עַל בִּרְכֶּיהָ עַד הַצָּהֳרַיִם וַיָּמֹת. וַתַּעַל וַתַּשְׁכִּבֵהוּ עַל מִטַּת אִישׁ הָאֱ-לֹהִים וַתִּסְגֹּר בַּעֲדוֹ וַתֵּצֵא. וַתִּקְרָא אֶל אִישָׁהּ וַתֹּאמֶר שִׁלְחָה נָא לִי אֶחָד מִן הַנְּעָרִים וְאַחַת הָאֲתֹנוֹת וְאָרוּצָה עַד אִישׁ הָאֱ-לֹהִים וְאָשׁוּבָה. וַיֹּאמֶר מַדּוּעַ אַתִּי [אַתְּ קרי] הֹלֶכֶת [הֹלַכְתִּי קרי] אֵלָיו הַיּוֹם לֹא חֹדֶשׁ וְלֹא שַׁבָּת וַתֹּאמֶר שָׁלוֹם... וַתָּבֹא אֶל אִישׁ הָאֱ-לֹהִים אֶל הָהָר וַתַּחֲזֵק בְּרַגְלָיו... וַתֹּאמֶר הֲשָׁאַלְתִּי בֵן מֵאֵת אֲדֹנִי הֲלֹא אָמַרְתִּי לֹא תַשְׁלֶה אֹתִי. וַיֹּאמֶר לְגֵיחֲזִי חֲגֹר מָתְנֶיךָ וְקַח מִשְׁעַנְתִּי בְיָדְךָ וָלֵךְ כִּי תִמְצָא אִישׁ לֹא תְבָרְכֶנּוּ וְכִי יְבָרֶכְךָ אִישׁ לֹא תַעֲנֶנּוּ וְשַׂמְתָּ מִשְׁעַנְתִּי עַל פְּנֵי הַנָּעַר. וַתֹּאמֶר אֵם הַנַּעַר חַי ה׳ וְחֵי נַפְשְׁךָ אִם אֶעֶזְבֶךָּ וַיָּקָם וַיֵּלֶךְ אַחֲרֶיהָ. וְגֵחֲזִי עָבַר לִפְנֵיהֶם וַיָּשֶׂם אֶת הַמִּשְׁעֶנֶת עַל פְּנֵי הַנַּעַר וְאֵין קוֹל וְאֵין קָשֶׁב וַיָּשָׁב לִקְרָאתוֹ וַיַּגֶּד לוֹ לֵאמֹר לֹא הֵקִיץ הַנָּעַר. וַיָּבֹא אֱלִישָׁע הַבָּיְתָה וְהִנֵּה הַנַּעַר מֵת מֻשְׁכָּב עַל מִטָּתוֹ. וַיָּבֹא וַיִּסְגֹּר הַדֶּלֶת בְּעַד שְׁנֵיהֶם וַיִּתְפַּלֵּל אֶל ה׳. וַיַּעַל וַיִּשְׁכַּב עַל הַיֶּלֶד וַיָּשֶׂם פִּיו עַל פִּיו וְעֵינָיו עַל עֵינָיו וְכַפָּיו עַל כַּפָּו [כַּפָּיו קרי] וַיִּגְהַר עָלָיו וַיָּחָם בְּשַׂר הַיָּלֶד. וַיָּשָׁב וַיֵּלֶךְ בַּבַּיִת אַחַת הֵנָּה וְאַחַת הֵנָּה וַיַּעַל וַיִּגְהַר עָלָיו וַיְזוֹרֵר הַנַּעַר עַד שֶׁבַע פְּעָמִים וַיִּפְקַח הַנַּעַר אֶת עֵינָיו.

BIBLIOGRAPHY

AND

GLOSSARY

To the Reader:

Although the author has tried to make this bibliography as accurate as possible, certain limitations render complete accuracy impossible.

For one thing, when transliterating from Hebrew into English, a variety of spellings are possible. In addition, as a result of war and political conflict, the boundaries of various countries have frequently changed. For example, what is part of Poland today was once part of Germany. To complicate matters further, many rabbis were born in one locale, studied in a different one, and then went on to serve several different communities. Accordingly, it is not always possible to accurately match a scholar to a given place and because scholars were often identified by where they lived, different identities sometimes appear for the same person.

A famous example of some of these difficulties is Rabbi Nachman of Breslov who is also called Rabbi Nachman of Uman because he served both communities. Breslov is currently the capital of Slovakia and is called Bratislava in the Slovak language, but in German the same town is called Pressburg. At one time, this city was under the control of Poland and at another time under the control of Lithuania. Similarly, Uman is currently located in Ukraine but was at one time part of Poland.

Since records were not kept as systematically in prior times as they are today, it is sometimes difficult to pinpoint the exact dates of birth or death of a given individual. Adding to the confusion is the fact that many people had similar names. As an example, Rabbi Shabbethai Sheftel ben Akiva Halevi Horowitz, the nephew of the *Shelah Hakadosh* had almost the same name as the son of the *Shelah Hakadosh* — Shabbethai Sheftel ben Yishayah Halevi Horowitz because both the *Shelah Hakadosh*, whose name was Yishayah, and his brother, whose name was Akiva, named their sons after their father, Shabbethai Sheftel. In the past, this created some confusion about who authored *Shefa Tal*, one of the sources cited in the present work.

Abarbanel, Rabbi Yitzchak: Scholar who was born in Portugal and later moved to Spain, only to be forced to move to Italy in 1492 when all Jews were expelled from Spain (1437-1508). The rabbi's family name is sometimes written Abravanel.

Alshich: Rabbi Moshe Alshich was born in Adrianople, Turkey to a family which escaped the Spanish Inquisition. Later, he moved to the Land of Israel where he taught Rabbi Chaim Vital (1508-c.1593).

Amidah: A prayer Jews recite at least three times each day. During weekdays, the *Amidah* prayer consists of nineteen blessings. The word "*Amidah*" in Hebrew means "standing" because, if possible, one must stand while reciting it.

Arizal: Acronym meaning "the lion of blessed memory," an honorary title accorded to Rabbi Yitzchak Luria, the foremost *Kabbalist* of the late Middle Ages. Rabbi Luria was born in Poland in 1534 and died in the Land of Israel in 1572.

Aruch: A seminal work on Hebrew lexicography written by Rabbi Nathan ben Yechiel of Rome (1035-1110).

Aruch Lanair: Commentary on the Babylonian Talmud by Rabbi Yaakov Ettlinger (Germany, 1798-1871).

Arvei Nachal: Torah commentary by Rabbi David Shlomo Eibenschutz (Russia and Land of Israel, died 1816).

Avodath Hakodesh: Work by Rabbi Meir ben Yechezkel ibn Gabbai of Spain (1480-1540?).

Avodath Yisrael: *Chassidic* commentary on the *Torah* by Rabbi Yisrael, the Koznitzer Maggid (1737-1813). Rabbi Yisrael's disciples founded the famous *Gur* (*Gerrer*) and *Belz* branches of the *Chassidic* movement.

Avoth D'Rabbi Nathan: An expanded version of *Pirkei Avoth* written by Rabbi Nathan (Babylonia, 2nd century C.E.) and his disciples.

Ba'al Halachoth Gedoloth: Rabbi Shimon Kayyara of Babylonia authored a famous *Halachic* treatise called *Halachoth Gedoloth* during the eighth century and became known as the *Ba'al Halachoth Gedoloth* (Master of the Great Laws).

Ba'al Shem Tov: Founder of the *Chassidic* movement which stresses joy and enthusiasm in serving *Hashem*. His real name was Rabbi Yisrael ben Eliezer, but he came to be known as the "*Ba'al Shem Tov*," meaning "Master of the Good Name," because of his knowledge of the esoteric wisdom of the *Torah*. He lived in Poland from 1698 to 1760.

Bamidbar: Book of Numbers.

Batei Midrashoth: A compendium of *Midrashim* compiled from manuscripts by Rabbi Shlomo Aharon Wertheimer of Hungary (1866-1935) and later edited by his grandson, Rabbi Avraham Yosef Wertheimer.

Bath Ayin: Principal work of Rabbi Avraham Dov Auerbach (Ukraine and Land of Israel, 1760-1840).

Be'er Mayim Chayim: Commentary on the *Torah* by Rabbi Chaim Tirar of Chernowitz (1760-1817), a student of the *Maggid of Mezeritch* and Rabbi Yechiel Michel of Zlotchov. (Not to be confused with a commentary to *Sefer Chafetz Chaim* of the same name written by Rabbi Yisrael Meir Kagan, the *Chafetz Chaim*.)

Ben Ish Chai: *Halachic* work written by Rabbi Yosef Hayyim (Bagdad, 1832-1909). Although he wrote more than fifty books, this one was the most widely read, so the rabbi became known by its title.

Benayahu ben Yehoyada: Commentary on *Ein Yaakov* written by Rabbi Yosef Hayyim (Bagdad, 1832-1909).

Beth Elokim: Philosophical work by the *Mabit*, an acrostic for Rabbi Moshe ben Yosef of Tirani (Greece and Land of Israel, 1505-1585).

Beth Olamim: Work composed by Rabbi Yitzchak Isaac Chaver, a disciple of Rabbi Chaim of Volozhin. (Lithuania, early nineteenth century).

Biur Hagra: Commentary of the Vilna Gaon, the title of Rabbi Eliyahu Kramer (Lithuania, 1720-1797). *Gaon* means "genius." Rabbi Kramer was a child prodigy who wrote later extensively on just about every aspect of the *Torah*.

Biurei Aggadoth (Afikei Yam): Commentary on *Aggadoth* by Rabbi Yitzchak Isaac Chaver (Lithuania, early 1800's), one of the main disciples of Rabbi Chaim of Volozhin.

Book of Formation: A text composed in its basic form by the Patriarch Abraham called *Sefer Yetzirah* (סֵפֶר יְצִירָה) in Hebrew.

Braitha: Authoritative teaching of ancient scholars called *Tannaim* which was not incorporated into the *Mishnah*.

Breishith: Genesis.

Brith Avraham: Commentary on *Yalkut Shimoni* published in Livorno, Italy around 1650. The publisher identifies the commentary's author as Rabbi Avraham Gedaliah of Jerusalem and indicates that he was alive at that time.

Chassid (plural: *Chassidim*): The word *"Chassid"* literally means "pious" and traditionally denotes anyone who goes beyond the letter of the law.[1] At a certain point, the term came to denote followers of Rabbi Yisrael Ba'al Shem Tov and his disciples.

Chatham Sofer: Rabbi Moshe Schreiber (*Sofer* in Hebrew) (Germany and Austria-Hungary, 1762-1839).

Chessed L'Avraham: Work by Rabbi Avraham Azulai (1570-1643). A Moroccan scholar who moved to the Land of Israel in 1610, Rabbi Azulai's great great grandson was the renowned Rabbi Chaim Yosef David Azulai (the *Chida*).

Chiddushei Gaonim: A compendium of commentaries on *Ein Yaakov* compiled by the editors of the Romm Vilna edition.

Chiddushei Harim: *Torah* commentary of Rabbi Yitzchak Meir Rotenberg-Alter, first *Rebbe* of the *Gur (Gerrer) Chassidic* dynasty (Poland, 1799-1866).

Chomath Anach: *Torah* commentary by Rabbi Chaim Yosef David Azulai, popularly known as the *Chida* (Land of Israel and Italy, 1724-1806).

Chumash: Five Books of Moses (the Pentateuch).

Dan Yadin: Work by Rabbi Shimshon Ostropoler (Poland, died 1648).

Derech Hashem: Work by Rabbi Moshe Chaim Luzzatto who was born in Italy in 1707 and died in the Land of Israel in 1746.

---

[1] *Rambam* on *Pirkei Avoth* 6:1.

Devarim: Deuteronomy.

D'rashoth Haran: Discourses written by Rabbeinu Nissim (Spain, 1320-1376).

Ein Yaakov: A collection of *Aggadic* material compiled by Rabbi Yaakov ibn Chaviv who lived in Spain and Turkey from 1445-1516.

Emek Hamelech: *Torah* commentary and encyclopedia style compendium of *Torah* concepts in alphabetical order by Rabbi Naftali Hertz ben Yaakov Elchanan Bacharach (Germany, 17th century).

Emunah: Faith.

Feinstein, Rabbi Moshe: *Rosh Yeshivah* of *Mesivtha Tifereth Jerusalem* in New York, Rabbi Feinstein is considered by many to have been the foremost 20th century *Halachic* authority in North America (Russia and United States, 1895-1986).

Five Hundred Fifteen Tefilloth (תקט"ו תפילות): Work by Rabbi Moshe Chayim Luzzatto, the *Ramchal* (Italy, 1707-1746).

Gaon Yaakov: An anonymous commentary on *Ein Yaakov* which the editors of the Romm Vilna edition published from a manuscript.

Gehinnom: Hell.

Gemara: Section of the *Talmud* which elaborates upon the *Mishnah*.

Gevuroth Hashem: Philosophical treatise focusing on the enslavement and liberation of the Jewish nation in Egypt by the *Maharal* of Prague, Rabbi Yehudah Loewy (Prague, 1526-1609).

Gur Aryeh: Commentary on *Rashi's Torah* commentary by the *Maharal* of Prague, Rabbi Yehudah Loewy (Prague, 1526-1609).

Haggadah: Service performed in each Jewish home on the first night of Passover.

Hakethav Vehakabbalah: *Torah* commentary by Rabbi Yaakov Tzvi Mecklenberg (Germany, 1785-1865).

Halachah: Jewish law. Such laws may be ritual in nature, addressing the relationship between people and God, or civil in nature, addressing relationships among people. (Plural = *Halachoth*)

Hashem: God.

Hameiri: *Talmudic* commentary of Rabbi Menachem ben Shlomo Meiri (Spain, 1249-1306).

Hayad Hachazakah: A comprehensive codification of Jewish law written by the *Rambam* (Rabbi Moses Maimonides). He was born in 1135 in Spain but fled with his family to North Africa at a young age due to anti-Jewish persecution. He lived primarily in Egypt where he died in 1204.

Hemek Davar: *Torah* commentary of Rabbi Naftali Tzvi Yehudah Berlin, often referred to by the acronym *Netziv* (Belarus and Poland, 1816-1893).

Ibn Ezra, Rabbi Avraham: Biblical commentator (Spain, 1089-1167).

Iggra D'pirka: Collection of stories and insights from various Chassidic leaders written by Rabbi Tzvi Elimelech Spira of Dinov (Poland, 1783?-1841) who was a nephew of Rabbi Elimelech of Lizhensk and a disciple of the Seer of Lublin.

Imrei Emeth: The major work of Rabbi Avraham Mordechai Alter (1866-1948), third *Rebbe* of the *Gur Chassidic* dynasty of Poland. After escaping Nazi occupied Europe during World War II, he emigrated to the Land of Israel.

Imrei Finchas: *Chassidic* wrok by Rabbi Pinchas of Koritz (1728-1790), a close disciple of Rabbi Yisrael Baal Shem Tov, founder of the *Chassidic* movement.

Imrei Noam: *Torah* commentary by Rabbi Meir Horowitz of Dzikov, Poland (1819-1877).

J.T.: Jerusalem *Talmud*.

Kabbalah: Jewish mystical tradition. Although the general outlines of this tradition are available to the public at large, its details are known only to a few select students who have received them orally from their masters. Those who expound these traditions are called **Kabbalists**.

Kav Hayashar: Ethical treatise by Rabbi Aaron Shmuel Kaidanover (Vilna and Poland 1614-1676).

Kedushath Levi: *Torah* commentary by Rabbi Levi Yitzchak of Berdichev (Ukraine, 1740-1810). Rabbi Levi Yitzchak's daughter married the son of Rabbi Shneur Zalman of Liadi.

Kehillath Yaakov: Encyclopedia style work containing alphabetized explanations of Torah concepts by Rabbi Yaakov Tzvi Yalish (Yolles) of Dinov (Poland, 1778-1825), a disciple of the Seer of Lublin.

Kelach Pithchei Hachochmah: "One Hundred Thirty-Eight Inntroductions to Wisdom" — a work written by Rabbi Yitzchak Isaac Chaver (Lithuania, early 1800's), one of the main disciples of Rabbi Chaim of Volozhin.

Kisei David: Work of Rabbi Chaim Yosef David Azulai, popularly known as the *Chida* (Land of Israel and Italy, 1724-1806)

Kithvei Ha'arizal: Set of writings by Rabbi Chaim Vital based on the teachings of Rabbi Yitzchak Luria, the foremost *Kabbalist* of the late Middle Ages. Known by the title "the holy Lion," Rabbi Luria was born in Poland in 1534 and died in the Land of Israel in 1572.

Kithvei Hagaon M.M. Mi'Shklov: Writings of Rabbi Menachem Mendel of Shklov, a disciple of the Vilna Gaon (Lithuania and Land of Israel, 1750-1827). His writings include a commentary on *Mishnath Chassidim*, a Kabbalistic work by Rabbi Emanuel Chai Ricci (Italy and Land of Israel, 1688-1743).

Kithvei Harama Mifano: Writings Rabbi Menachem Azariah of Fano (Italy, 1548-1620).

Klee Yakar: Torah commentary by Rabbi Shlomo Ephraim Luntschitz (Poland and Prague, 1550-1619).

Kohen: A member of the clan who descended from *Moshe Rabbeinu's* brother, Aaron, who performed the Temple service. (Plural = *Kohanim*). The head of the clan was the *Kohen Gadol*, literally "great priest."

Kol Simchah: Written by Rabbi Simchah Bunim of Pershiska (spelled Przysucha in Polish) who was a disciple of the Seer of Lublin (Rabbi Yaakov Yitzchak Horowitz, 1745-1815) and the *Yehudi Hakadosh*, "the holy Jew" (Rabbi Yaakov Yitzchak of Pershiska, 1766-1813). Rabbi Simchah Bunim lived in Poland from 1765 to 1827.

Kosher: Acceptable according to Jewish law. Most commonly used to mean food prepared in compliance with Jewish dietary laws.

Lechah Dodi: A song welcoming the Sabbath which was composed by Rabbi Shlomo Halevi Alkabetz (see entry about him above).

Leshem Shevo Ve'achlamah: Work by Rabbi Shlomo Elyashiv, who was born in Lithuania and died in the Land of Israel (1841-1926).

Levite: A member of the Tribe of Levi which descended from Jacob's son, Levi. The Levites assisted the *Kohanim* in the Temple.

Likutei Amarim Tanya: The opus major of Rabbi Shneur Zalman of Liadi (1745-1813), a major disciple of the *Maggid of Mezeritch* and the first *Rebbe* of the Lubavitch *Chassidic* dynasty. Denounced to the Russian authorities by opponents, Rabbi Shneur Zalman spent a brief period of time in jail during which he composed the *Likutei Amarim Tanya*, more commonly simply called *"Tanya."*

Likutei Halachoth: *Chassidic* discourses written by Rabbi Nathan Sternhartz of Nemerov based on the teachings of his master, Rabbi Nachman of Breslov. Although the discourses are organized under headings such as "Laws of Reciting *Shema*," "Laws of Prayer," and so forth, the contents do not contain instructions on how to perform *Mitzvoth*. Rather, they offer deep spiritual insights into the *Mitzvoth*.

Likutei Moharan: Collected teachings of Rabbi Nachman of Breslov, also called Rabbi Nachman of Uman, a great grandson of the *Baal Shem Tov*, and a major Chassidic leader (Poland and Ukraine, 1772-1810).

Ma'arecheth Ha'elokuth: Work by Rabbi Peretz ben Yitzchak Hakohen of Gerondi (Spain, died c. 1380).

Maggid: A rabbi renowned for his preaching skills.

Maggid of Mezeritch: Rabbi Dov Ber, chief disciple of Rabbi Yisrael Baal Shem Tov, the founder of the *Chassidic* movement. He lived in Poland from 1704 to 1772.

Maharal: Acronym for Rabbi Yehudah Loewy (Prague, 1526-1609).

Maharsha: Acronym for **Moreinu Harav Sh'muel** Eliezer Eidels of Poland (1555-1632). A descendant of the *Maharal* of Prague (1526-1609), Rabbi Eidels acquired his last name from his wealthy mother-in-law, Rebbetzin Eidel Lifschitz, who generously provided support to him and his *Yeshivah*.

Malbim: Acronym for Rabbi Meir Laibush ben Yechiel Michael who published a highly popular commentary on the *Tanach* (Poland, 1809-1879).

Ma'or Einayim: Biblical commentary by Rabbi Menachem Nachum of Chernobyl, Ukraine who was a student of the *Ba'al Shem Tov* and the **Maggid of Mezeritch**. Rabbi Menachem Nachum (1730-1797) founded a long and distinguished line of *Chassidic* masters.

Ma'or Vashamesh: *Chassidic* commentary on the *Torah* by Rabbi Kalonymus Kalman Epstein of Krakow, Poland (died 1823).

Mashiach: Messiah. In Hebrew, *Mashiach* means "anointed," because in ancient times Jewish kings were anointed with special oil. The *Mashiach* is a king who will return the Jews to their homeland, rebuild the Temple, and restore the authority of Jewish law.

Mavoh Lechochmath Hakabbalah: An introductory *Kabbalistic* work written by Rabbi Sh'muel Toledano who lived in the Land of Israel during the 1900's.

Mechilta: *Midrashic* commentary on Exodus written by Rabbi Yishmael (Land of Israel, 2nd century C.E.) and his disciples.

Megaleh Amukoth: *Kabbalistic* work by Rabbi Nathan Nata ben Shlomo Spira, chief rabbi of Krakow (Poland, 1585-1633).

Meshech Chochmah: *Torah* commentary of Rabbi Meir Simchah Hakohen of Dvinsk, who is known as the *Ohr Sameach* after his commentary on the *Rambam's Mishnah Torah* (Lithuania and Latvia, 1843-1926).

Metzudoth: Two-part commentary on the *Tanach* by Rabbi David Altschuler (Poland, 18th century), parts of which were completed by his son, Rabbi Yechiel Hillel Altschuler.

Mezuzoth: Parchment scrolls containing the first two paragraphs of *Shema* which are affixed to doorposts.

Midrash: Homiletic interpretations of the *Tanach*. *Midrashic* works are often classified as either *Halachic Midrash*, which explains how religious law is derived from the text of the *Tanach*, or *Aggadic Midrash*, which discusses the philosophical, theological, and ethical aspects of the text.

Midrash Hane'elam: A section of the *Zohar*.

Midrash Tanchuma: *Midrashic* commentary on the *Torah* written by Rabbi Tanchuma bar Abba (Land of Israel, 4th century C.E.) and his disciples.

Mikveh: Ritual bath.

Mishlei: Book of Proverbs.

Mishnah: The Oral Law. A compilation of traditions passed down from generation to generation by word of mouth from the time of Moses until committed to writing during the third century C.E. (Plural = *Mishnayoth*).

Mishnah B'rurah: A commentary by Rabbi Yisrael Meir Kagan (Poland, 1838-1933 on the *Orach Chaim* section of the *Shulchan Aruch*. Rabbi Kagan is generally known as the "*Chafetz Chaim*" after his most popular and influential work.

Mitzvah: Religious commandment. (Plural = *Mitzvoth*)

Mogen Avoth L'Rashbatz: Philosophical work by Rabbi Shimon ben Tzemach Duran (Spain, 1361-1444).

Moreh Nevuchim: A wide-ranging philosophical treatise written by the *Rambam* (Rabbi Moses Maimonides).

Moshav Zekeinim: Commentary on the *Torah* compiled from the writings of the *Tosafists*, a group of Western European scholars who thrived from the twelfth to the fourteenth century and were most famous for their commentaries on the *Gemara*.

Mussaf: Prayer describing the additional sacrificial services performed on special occasions such as *Shabbath* and holidays in the Temple.

Nefesh Hachayim: Treatise on major tenets of the Jewish faith by Rabbi Chaim Volozhin, the main disciple of the *Vilna Gaon*.

Netzach Yisrael: A set of philosophical treatises concerning Israel's exile and ultimate redemption written by Rabbi Yehudah Loewy, the *Maharal* of Prague (1526-1609).

Ohev Yisrael: The principal work of Rabbi Avraham Yehoshua Heshel, a major Chassidic leader, also known as the Rebbe of Apt (Poland and Ukraine, 1748-1825).

Ohr Hameir: *Torah* commentary of Rabbi Ze'ev Wolf of Zhitomir who was a major disciple of the **Maggid of Mezeritch** (Poland, died 1800).

Onkelos: A nephew of the Roman Emperor Titus. Onkelos converted to Judaism and wrote an Aramaic translation of the *Torah*.[2] His translation is considered so authoritative that every printed edition of the *Chumash* includes it. (Land of Israel, 2nd century).

Orach Lechayim: Premier work of Rabbi Avraham Chaim of Zlotchov, a disciple of the Maggid of Mezeritch (Ukraine, c. 1726-1816).

Orchoth Tzaddikim: An anonymous ethical treatise written around the 14th century C.E. in western Europe.

Otzar Eden Hagnuz: Work by Rabbi Avraham Abulafia (1240-1291, Spain and Malta).

Otzar Hachayim: *Torah* commentary of Rabbi Yitzchak Isaac Eichenstein (Ukraine, 1740-1800), founder of the Komarna branch of Chassidism.

Ovadiah of Bartenura: Rabbi known for his commentary on the *Mishnah* and widespread travels (Italy, 1445-1515).

Panim Yafoth: *Torah* commentary of Rabbi Pinchas Halevi Horowitz, known as "the *Hafla'ah*" after his famous *Halachic* work of that name (Poland and Germany, 1731-1805).

Pardes Rimonim: Work written by Rabbi Cordovero (1522-1570). He lived in Safed in the Land of Israel where he studied under Rabbi Yosef Caro, author of the *Shulchan Aruch*.

Pardes Yosef: *Torah* commentary by Rabbi Yosef Patzanovski, also spelled Poznovsky (Poland, 1875-1942).

Perush Hagra Al Sefer Yetzirah: Commentary of the Vilna Gaon (Rabbi Eliyahu Kramer, Lithuania, 1720-1797) on *Sefer Yetzirah*.

Perush Haram Botril Lesefer Yetzirah: Commentary on *Sefer Yetzirah* written by Rabbi Moshe Botril in the early 1400's.

Perush Haramaz Al Zohar: Commentary of Rabbi Moshe Zacuto on the *Zohar* (Amsterdam, 1625-1698).

Perush Harekanati Al Hatorah: *Torah* commentary of Rabbi Menachem Recanati (Italy, 1250-1310).

Perush Ba'alei Hatosafoth: Collected commentary of *Tosafoth*, a group of approximately two hundred scholars who flourished in Western Europe during the twelfth and thirteenth centuries.

Pesach Seder: Service held on Passover night.

---

[2] B.T. *Gittin* 56B-57A and *Megillah* 3A.

Pesikta D'Rav Kahana: A collection of early *Midrashim*. The name *D'Rav Kahana* comes from the mention of Rav Kahana near the beginning of the work, a common way of naming texts.

Pesikta Rabbethai: A collection of *Midrashim* from the early Medieval period (probably 8th century C.E.).

Pirkei Avoth: "Ethics of the Fathers." A tractate of the *Mishnah*.

Pirkei D'Rabbi Eliezer: A *Midrash* composed by Rabbi Eliezer ben Hyrcanus (Land of Israel, 1st century C.E.) and his disciples.

Pithchei She'arim: "Entrances of the Gates" — a work written by Rabbi Yitzchak Isaac Chaver (Lithuania, early 1800's), one of the main disciples of Rabbi Chaim of Volozhin.

Pituchei Chotham: Work by Rabbi Yaakov Abuhatzeira (Morocco and Egypt, 1806-1800).

Pri Ha'aretz: Work by Rabbi Menachem Mendel of Vitebsk, also known as Menachem Mendel of Horodok, a disciple of the Maggid of Mezeritch (Belarus and Land of Israel, c. 1730-1788).

Pri Tzaddik: Work written by the highly prolific Rabbi Tzadok Hakohen of Lublin (Poland, 1823-1900). Rabbi Tzadok was renowned as a tremendous genius, having first completed study of the entire *Talmud* at the age of only seventeen.

Rabbeinu Bachye: There are two Medieval sages who bear this name. Rabbi Bachye ben Asher lived from 1263 until 1340 and wrote a famous Biblical commentary which appears in most major printed editions of the Hebrew Bible. Rabbeinu Bachye ben Yosef ibn Pakuda lived in the first half of the eleventh century and authored the ethical treatise *Chovoth Halevavoth* ("Duties of the Heart").

Radak: Acronym for **Rabbi David Kimchi**, author of a famous commentary on the Prophets and Writings. Rabbi Kimchi was born in Spain but fled with his family to France at a young age when a fanatical Islamic sect took power and tried to force Jews to convert (1160?-1235?).

Rama: Acronym for **Rabbi Moshe Isserles** who lived in Poland from 1530 to 1572. He is most famous for his glosses on the *Shulchan Aruch* and also authored the philosophical work *Torath Ha'olah*.

Rambam: An acrostic for "Rabbi Moshe Ben Maimon," known in English as Rabbi Moses Maimonides. He was born in Cordoba, Spain in 1135 and died in Egypt in 1204. A phenomenal *Halachic* scholar, he also formulated the clear and comprehensive statements of Jewish belief known as "The Thirteen Principles of Faith."

Ramban: An acrostic for "Rabbi Moshe Ben Nachman," known in English as Rabbi Moses Nachmanides. He lived in Spain but moved to the Land of Israel at the end of his life (1194-1270).

Ramchal: Acrostic or "Rabbi Moshe Chayim Luzzatto" (Italy, 1707-1746).

Rasha: wicked person

Rashbam: An acrostic for the name of **Rabbi Sh'muel Ben Meir** (France, 1080-1158), *Rashi's* grandson and one of his greatest disciples. His accomplishments include completing portions of *Rashi's Talmudic* commentary after *Rashi* died.

Rashi: An acrostic for the name of **Rabbi Shlomo Yitzchaki** who lived in France during the 11th century. His commentaries are considered so authoritative that they are included in every edition of the *Tanach* and *Talmud* which has ever been printed.

Rebbe: *Chassidic* master.

Romm Vilna: This famous publishing house in Europe was founded in 1789. Its editions of classic Jewish texts are considered highly authoritative because teams of scholars carefully reviewed and edited the texts based on earlier manuscripts and printings.

Rosh Hashanah: The Jewish New Year.

Satan: A spiritual force which tempts people to sin, and afterwards accuses them before the Heavenly Tribunal.

Sefer Gerushin L'Rabbi Moshe Cordovero: Work written by Rabbi Cordovero (1522-1570). He lived in Safed in the Land of Israel where he studied under Rabbi Yosef Caro, author of the *Shulchan Aruch*.

Sefer Habahir: A text attributed to Rabbi Nechuniah ben Hakana (Land of Israel, 1st century C.E.).

Sefer Habrith: Principal work of Rabbi Pinchus Eliyahu Hurwitz (Vilna, 1765-1821).

Sefer Ha'ikarim: Philosophical work by Rabbi Yosef Albo (Spain, 1380-1444).

Sefer Hapliah: Work by Rabbi Avigdor ben Yitzchak Karo (Prague, died 1439).

Sefer Yetzirah: A text composed in its basic form by the Patriarch Abraham.

S'fath Emeth: *Torah* and *Talmudic* commentaries of Rabbi Yehudah Aryeh Leib Alter, second *Rebbe* of the *Gur (Gerrer) Chassidic* dynasty (Poland, 1847-1905).

Sha'arei Haleshem: Work by Rabbi Shlomo Elyashiv, who was born in Lithuania and died in the Land of Israel (1841-1926).

Sha'arei Tzedek: Work by Rabbi Yosef ben Avraham Gikatilla (Spain, born 1284).

Shabbath: Sabbath.

Shefa Tal: Work by Rabbi Shabbethai Sheftel ben Akiva Halevi Horowitz, nephew of the *Shelah Hakadosh* (Prague, 1565-1619).

Shelah Hakadosh: *Shelah* is an acronym for *Shnei Luchoth Habrith* ("The Two Tablets of the Covenant"), the major work of Rabbi Yeshayah Horowitz, which gained such popularity that Rabbi Horowitz came to be known by its title. Born in Bohemia in 1560, Rabbi Horowitz later moved to the Land of Israel where he died in 1630.

Shem Mishmuel: Principal work of Rabbi Sh'muel Borenstein (1856-1926) who was the son of Rabbi Avraham of Sochotchev, Poland, author of the well-known *Halachic* work *Avnei Nezer*.

Shema: A prayer consisting of three paragraphs from the *Chumash* (Pentateuch) which Jews recite every morning and evening.

Shemoth: Exodus.

Shir Hashirim: The Song of Songs.

Shneur Zalman of Liadi, Rabbi: Author of numerous works including *Likutei Amarim Tanya*, a work which discusses a wide range of theological issues such as the nature of good and evil. In addition to possessing a profound grasp of *Kabbalah*, Rabbi Shneur Zalman was an expert in matters of *Halachah* and authored an edition of the *Shulchan Aruch* for use among *Chassidim*. Rabbi Shneur Zalman lived in Russia from 1745 to 1812 where he founded what later became the Lubavitch *Chassidic* dynasty.

Shofar: Ram's horn which Jews blow on the holiday of *Rosh Hashanah*.

Shomer Emunim Hakadmon: Principal writing of Rabbi Yosef ben Emmanuel Irgas (Italy, 1685-1730).

Shoshan Sodoth: Book of essays by a disciple of the *Ramban*.

Shulchan Aruch: A codification of Jewish law written by Rabbi Yosef Karo. Born in Spain in 1488, he and his family fled to Turkey to avoid the Inquisition. From there he moved to the Land of Israel in 1535 where he remained until his death in 1575.

The *Shulchan Aruch* is divided into four sections: *Orach Chaim* concerning everyday ritual practice; *Even Ha'ezer* concerning marital law; *Choshen Mishpat* concerning business and financial matters; and *Yoreh De'ah* concerning several topics that did not fit conveniently into the other categories, such as dietary laws and the agricultural laws which apply to the Land of Israel.

Siach Yitzchak: Collection of homiletic discourses by Rabbi Yitzchak Isaac Chaver, a disciple of Rabbi Chaim of Volozhin. (Lithuania, early nineteenth century).

Sifra: *Halachic Midrash* on Book of Leviticus. It is also called *Torath Kohanim* because much of the Book of Leviticus deals with the sacrificial service performed by the *Kohanim*.

Sifrei: *Halachic Midrash* on Books of Numbers and Deuteronomy.

Sifthei Kohen: Commentary on the *Torah* by Rabbi Mordechai Hakohen, a contemporary of the *Arizal*. (Safed, Land of Israel, 1523-1598).

Sukkah: A hut with three or four walls which Jews live in during the autumn festival of *Sukkoth* (Tabernacles).

Talmud: The *Mishnah* together with the commentary and additional material compiled during the sixth century C.E. by a group of sages known as *Amoraim*.

Tanach: An acrostic of the Jewish Bible consisting the $\underline{T}$orah (Pentateuch), $\underline{N}$eviim (Prophets) and $\underline{K}$ethuvim (Hagiographa, or Writings).

Tannaim: A group of scholars who lived roughly from 50 B.C.E. to 200 C.E. They compiled and edited the teachings of the Oral *Torah* to form the *Mishnah*.

Targum Yonathan: An Aramaic translation and commentary of the *Tanach* written by Rabbi Yonathan ben Uziel (Land of Israel, 1st century C.E.).

Tefillin: Leather boxes worn by adult Jewish males during weekday morning services which contain parchments upon which are written sections of the *Torah*.

Tehillim: Psalms.

Tifereth Sh'lomo: *Torah* commentary written by Rabbi Shlomo Hakohen of Radomsk (Radin), Poland (1803-1866) who was a disciple of Rabbi Meir of Apta.

Tifereth Yisrael: Commentary on the *Mishnah* by Rabbi Yisrael Lipschitz of Danzig (Germany, 1782-1860).

Tifereth Yehonathan: Torah commentary of Rabbi Yehonathan Eibschutz (Poland, Germany, Scandinavia, 1690-1764,).

Tikunei Zohar: *Kabbalistic* work attributed to Rabbi Shimon bar Yochai (Land of Israel, 2nd century C.E.) and his disciples.

Tisha B'Av: The ninth day of the month of *Av* when Jews fast and mourn the destruction of both Temples.

Toldoth Yaakov Yosef: The major work of Rabbi Yaakov Yosef of Polonoye (Ukraine, 1704-1794), a direct disciple of the *Ba'al Shem Tov*.

Toldoth Yitzchak: Commentary on the *Chumash* (Pentateuch) by Rabbi Yitzchak Karo (Spain, 1458-1535), who was the uncle of Rabbi Yosef Karo, author of the *Shulchan Aruch*.

Torah Temimah: Comprehensive *Torah* commentary by Rabbi Baruch Epstein (Belarus, 1860-1941) which cites and explains comments from classic *Talmudic* and *Midrashic* sources.

Torath Haminchah: Book including philosophical treatises by Rabbi Yaakov ben Chananel Scili (Spain, 14th century), a disciple of the *Rashba* (Rabbi Shlomo ben Aderet) and treatises from earlier rabbis.

Torath Ha'olah L'rama: Philosophical treatise by the **Rama**, **R**abbi **M**oshe Isserles (Poland, 1530-1572).

Tosafoth: A group of approximately two hundred scholars who flourished in Europe during the twelfth and thirteenth centuries. These scholars wrote and disseminated several versions of their commentaries on the *Talmud*.

Tosafoth Yom Tov: Commentary on the *Mishnah* by Rabbi Yom Tov Lipman Heller (Germany and Poland, 1579-1654), a disciple of the *Maharal* of Prague (1526-1609).

Tur Shulchan Aruch: Original version of the Code of Jewish law authored by Rabbi Yaakov, the son of *Rabbeinu Asher*. He lived in Spain from roughly 1275 to 1349.

Tzaddik: Righteous person (masculine); plural = *Tzaddikim*.

Tzedakah: charity.

Tzemach Tzaddik: Collection of the *Torah* thoughts of Rabbi Menachem Mendel Hager of Vizhnitz (Ukraine, 1830-1884).

Tzeror Hamor: Commentary of Rabbi Avraham Saba (Spain and Morocco, 1440-1508).

Tziyuni: *Torah* commentary by Rabbi Menachem Tziyuni ben Meir (Germany, 15th century).

Vayikra: Leviticus.

Vilna Gaon: Rabbi Eliyahu Kramer (Lithuania, 1720-1797). *Gaon* means "genius." Rabbi Kramer was a child prodigy who, as an adult, wrote extensively on just about every aspect of the *Torah*.

Vital, Rabbi Chaim: Chief disciple of the *Arizal*. Rabbi Vital authored the *Kithvei Ha'arizal*, a compendium of his master's teachings (Land of Israel, 1542-1620).

Volozhin, Rabbi Chaim: Principal disciple of the *Vilna Gaon*, he established a major *Yeshivah* in the town of Volozhin (Poland/Russia, 1749-1821).

Yalkut Reuveni: Anthology of *Midrashim* and other classical Jewish literature edited by Rabbi Avraham Reuven Sopher Katz (Prague, died 1673).

Yalkut Shimoni: Anthology of *Midrashim* on the *Tanach* edited by Rabbi Shimon Hadarshan (Frankfort, 13th century C.E.).

Ye'aroth Devash: Work by Rabbi Yehonathan Eibschutz (Poland, Germany, Scandinavia, 1690-1764).

Yeshivah: Academy of *Torah* study.

Yeshuoth Meshicho: An explanation of Jewish teachings about the *Mashiach* by Rabbi Yitzchak Abarbanel (sometimes called Abravanel) (Spain and Italy, 1437-1508).

Yesod Ha'avodah: Work by Rabbi Avraham Weinberg, first *Rebbe* of the *Slonimer Chassidic* dynasty (Belarus, 1804-1883).

Yismach Moshe: Principal work of Rabbi Moshe Teitelbaum (Hungary, 1759-1841).

Yisrael Kedoshim: Work written by the highly prolific Rabbi Tzadok Hakohen of Lublin (Poland, 1823-1900). Rabbi Tzadok was renowned as a tremendous genius, having first completed study of the entire *Talmud* at the age of only seventeen.

Yitav Lev: Chassidic *Torah* commentary by Rabbi Yekuthiel Yehudah Teitelbaum (Slovakia and Hungary, 1808-1883).

Yom Kippur: Day of Atonement.

Yonathan ben Uziel: A disciple of Hillel who produced an Aramaic translation of the Prophets (Land of Israel, first century C.E.).

Yosher Divrei Emeth: Work by Rabbi Meshulam Feivish of Zabriza (Poland, 1740-1795).

Zera Kodesh: Work of Rabbi Naftali Tzvi Horowitz, the Ropshitzer Rebbe (Poland, 1760-1827).

Zohar: *Kabbalistic* commentary on the *Torah* compiled by Rabbi Shimon bar Yochai (Land of Israel, 2nd century C.E.) and his disciples.

INDEX